Politics, Democracy,
and the
Supreme Court

Politics, Democracy, and the Supreme Court

Essays on the Frontier of Constitutional Theory

ARTHUR S. MILLER

Contributions in American Studies, Number 83

Greenwood Press
Westport, Connecticut • London, England

Library of Congress Cataloging in Publication Data

Miller, Arthur Selwyn, 1917-
  Politics, democracy, and the Supreme Court.

  (Contributions in American studies, ISSN 0084-9227 ;
no. 83)
  Bibliography: p.
  Includes index.
  1. Judicial review—United States. 2. Political
questions and judicial power. 3. United States.
Supreme Court. 4. United States—Constitutional law—
Interpretation and construction. I. Title. II. Series.
KF4575.M5 1985   347.73 ′12   85-5604
                         347.30712
ISBN 0-313-24831-1 (lib. bdg. : alk. paper)

Library of Congress Catalog Card Number: 85-5604
ISBN: 0-313-24831-1
ISSN: 0084-9227

First published in 1985

Greenwood Press
A division of Congressional Information Service, Inc.
88 Post Road West, Westport, Connecticut 06881

Printed in the United States of America

10 9 8 7 6 5 4 3 2 1

Contents

Preface

Except for Chapter 1, the articles reproduced here were published in ten different legal periodicals over a six-year period (1978-1984). They have been brought together, and introduced with a newly written 11th essay, to make them readily available in one handy volume. The central theme is that American constitutional theory, which for most commentators is concerned with judicial review, has come to a dead end. Theorists are more interested in the disputes of yesteryear—principally, the legitimacy of the role of the Supreme Court in government—than with the many new problems now confronting the American people. This mind-set is probably attributable to the fact that American constitutionalism is perceived as constitutional law, and thus the province of lawyers and judges, rather than the political theory that it really is.

Two centuries ago, the fifty-five men who drafted the Constitution were by no means clear about judicial review. One of the great silences of that document, therefore, is the power of the Supreme Court to review the validity of other acts of government. The silence began to be filled with the decision in *Marbury v. Madison* (1803). Since then, a running debate has been carried on over the propriety of an appointed group of judges with life tenure making ultimate public policy decisions—of being, that is, the voice of the Constitution.

I have long thought that the debate is unsatisfactory. Every student of the Constitution is fully aware of the arguments for and against judicial review, and many manage to publish them in a plethora of books and articles. Few minds are changed in the debate, which increasingly resembles medieval scholastics endlessly arguing over what Aristotle meant, all the while not noticing that their world was crumbling and disappearing outside.

So it is today. Mankind has, I believe, come to a major turning point in its relatively short (known) planetary existence. A new social order is emerging, bringing with it problems both unique and complex. Most constitutional scholars apparently are not aware of the paradigm shift that is occurring; or if they are, they choose to ignore it. They persist in arguing about yesterday's problems, when today's and tomorrow's press ever more insistently upon the human condition. With the rapid rate of social change, we are living in tomorrow's world today and still using yesterday's ideas. And most commentators assume, without question, that the Constitution, as written and as interpreted, is more than suitable to the resolution of the problems of tomorrow.

That simply is not accurate. As Americans count down to the 200th anniversary of their only constitutional convention, whether the Document of 1787 and the institutions it created are any longer up to the needs of the American people is a question that must be asked and answered by this generation, who must look not to the past for succor and revelation, but to the present and the emergent future. The men of 1787 did not write a perfect constitution. Its many silences and ambiguities meant that it was left to gather content from experience. Each generation of Americans writes its own constitution. The Document of 1787 is more a "do-it-yourself" instrument than a set of immutable truths.

The essays reproduced here are preliminary probes into a legal *terra incognita*. In them, I seek to establish a different, and more accurate, way of looking at the interrelations of the large concepts of "politics, democracy, and the Supreme Court." My main purpose is to take at least one small step away from the excessive concentration on judicial review, and to examine the concept of constitutionalism from different perspectives. The Constitution of the United States has always been relative to circumstances. The time, accordingly, has come to consider what it should be, both in the present day and in the emergent future.

Since the essays reproduced here were written at different times for different periodicals, there are some unavoidable—indeed, necessary— repetitions of some ideas. Given the nature of the printing process, this could not be helped. The repetitions are mentioned here only to indicate that I know about them and to say that, in my judgment, they do not detract from the overall flow of ideas. Rather, they permit each one to be read separately, without reference to the others.

Arthur S. Miller

Key West, Florida
January 1985

Politics, Democracy, and the Supreme Court

CHAPTER 1

Constitutional Myths— Constitutional Realities

I.

This chapter compares the *jurisprudence confidentielle* of the American constitutional order with the *jurisprudence publique*. It develops the idea that there is a wide and growing chasm between pretense and reality in the theory and practice of American constitutionalism and that a new theory is called for. The theme comes from an essay by Professor Sanford Levinson: "It is ironic that a culture which has experienced a centuries-long 'melancholy, long-withdrawing roar' from religious faith can believe so blithely in the continuing reality of citizens organized around a constitutional faith. The 'death of constitutionalism' may be the central event of our time just as the 'death of God' was that of the past century."[1]

The *jurisprudence confidentielle* is the operational code of the American political order—a private and largely unacknowledged set of rules that govern the behavior of governmental officers. The unwritten Constitution is a term that should not be confused with the more familiar notion of a "living" fundamental law, which refers to the evolution of the formal document through interpretations announced by courts, legislators, and executives. The living Constitution is an extension of the original text, but the operational code may and does differ, often quite widely, with that fundamental law. On the other hand, the *jurisprudence publique* is what is usually called constitutional law by lawyers, judges, and scholars. It is practiced *as if* it represented reality, which quite often it simply does not. Of the two, the *jurisprudence confidentielle* is the more important.

Lawyers have long asserted and largely succeeded in attaining a monopoly on the meaning to be given to the litigable clauses of the numinous document that is the Constitution. This is unfortunate, because the purblindness of the legal mind prevents accurate perceptions of the constitutional order. In what follows, principal attention will be accorded to constitutionalism rather than to constitutional law. The terms are not synonymous; they are complementary.

We begin with what will be called the *basic myth*, by which is meant the orthodox conception of constitutionalism as being limited government. The myth began early—not later than promulgation of the Bill of Rights in 1791. But it has never represented reality. The men who drafted the Constitution in 1787 were less interested in protecting human rights and liberties than in establishing a new structure of governmental power. They wanted to institutionalize power rather than to canalize or limit it. And they wanted a new form of government, with a separate executive, something quite different from the Articles of Confederation. The framers saw no need for a bill of rights, because, as Alexander Hamilton argued, the Constitution was itself a bill of rights—a specious and even disingenuous argument, rectified in the first Congress that assembled in 1789.

Under the orthodoxy, political power is to be tamed by depersonalizing it—by, that is, the "rule of law," with law being a body of external standards proscribing certain governmental actions.[2] One legacy of the Enlightenment is the idea that law is something apart from the state, a set of long-standing jural rules or of certain immutable principles, resting on God or "nature," that the state is supposed to enforce. The apposite label for this mind-set, this ideology, is legalism. Legalism is a traditional liberal tenet, similar to another legacy of the Enlightenment: the notion that the interests of all humans are basically common. Both beliefs have been so battered in this century that little credence can now be given to them. Like it or not, modern law is positive law, a set of authoritative pronouncements from the apparatus of the state: government. Any sociologist of law knows that the state and the legal system are closely entwined. We must therefore accept, as Holmes said in 1873, that law is Thrasymachusian—subject to the will of the stronger.[3] From this it follows, as Professor John Nowak has remarked, that there is "no demonstrably correct set of legal principles which will dictate the resolution of constitutional issues apart from the political philosophy and the exercise of political power by the [Supreme Court] Justices."[4] Those who argue, as does Professor Ronald Dworkin,[5] that the Constitution rests on a moral theory that people have certain rights against the state must confront the hard fact that those moral rights require validation at some time by the state. Constitutional adjudication thus is part of the political drama, and constitutional litigation is politics carried on under another name.

Americans, accordingly, must face up to the fact of the death of orthodox constitutionalism, but not, however, of constitutionalism as a way that political power is allocated and implemented. Properly seen, constitutionalism is concerned with the authoritative distribution of value in a nation-state such as the United States. Politics is antecedent to law, not vice versa. Law is much more a reflection of events and circumstances than a molder of them. The reality lurking behind the basic myth is that of power. No society has ever been able to dispense with political power.

Although not recognized because of the almost complete lack of litigation in the 19th century, the Constitution has always been one of powers rather than of limitations. This is to be seen, for example, in the way that the federal government followed Hamilton's influential *Report on Manufactures* in policies aimed at exploiting the resources of the continent.

The Bill of Rights and other apparent constitutional limitations have helped to perpetuate the orthodoxy about constitutionalism. That orthodoxy is in substantial part mythical, as the ensuing discussion will demonstrate. A myth, Rollo May observes, is "the unseen structure by which a people establishes and exists in a political community."[6] That definition can be varied somewhat for present purposes: The mythology of American constitutionalism is a group of beliefs that revolve around the perceived document of the formal Constitution plus the interpretative gloss on it that has accumulated since 1789. Reality is the "unseen structure" May mentions, a structure that is obscured by stubborn adherence to the *jurisprudence publique.*

Surrounding the basic myth is a cluster of other beliefs, which will be called submyths of American constitutionalism. The listing below is more illustrative than exhaustive. The submyths are not set forth in a special order of priority—all have equal importance.

II.

"*The* question of jurisprudence," Professor Dworkin has asserted, is "what, in general, is a good reason for decision by a court of law."[7] At best, this is dubious. It is based on the unwarranted assumption that the judiciary is the center of the legal universe, something that may never have been accurate in the United States and certainly is not true today. Reality is obscured by excessive attention paid in the law schools to what courts do. Our goal should be that of increasing understanding of the legal system and its role in society, rather than the much more limited one of trying to predict the course of judicial decision-making. Professor Lon L. Fuller once observed:

There may be said to exist two philosophies of science. The one sees the aim of science as *understanding*; the other as *prediction*. The first regards prediction as a by-product of understanding; we acquire the ability to predict events as our minds penetrate into the causes that underlie the happenings of nature. The adherents of the opposed theory see "understanding" as an illusory, metaphysical trapping superfluously tacked on the essential goal of acquiring predictive knowledge.[8]

Fuller opted for understanding. Surely he was correct. Legal education, essentially reductionist in nature, requires a holistic approach. Analysis of the myth structure of constitutionalism is a step in that direction.

1. The Myth of Representative Government. "The pefectionism of our constitution, if it has that quality," Professor Henry P. Monaghan argues, "inheres in its guarantee of an open and fairly structured political process. Perhaps that is enough. . . . In short, perhaps the constitutional guarantees only representative government, not perfect government."[9] That passage begs more questions than it answers. It comes at the end of an article in which Monaghan criticizes some commentators for being perfectionists—in his judgment, those who believe that the Constitution guarantees such liberal democratic values as equality and personal autonomy. His criticism may well be on the mark, but what can a "guarantee" of representative government mean? He seems to be asserting that ours is truly a representative government, a proposition that has not in the past, is not now, and shows no sign of being in the future a statement of fact—provided that representation refers to the people generally. Monaghan fails to address the questions of "representative of whom?" and "for what purposes?"

Any probe beneath the surface of the concept of representation quickly discloses a morass of complexity and ambiguity. Abstractly, it deals with the relationships between the citizenry supposedly being represented and the representatives supposedly acting on their behalf. Do, however, members of Congress represent the entire nation or only their particular constituencies? Do they have a "free" as compared with an "imperative" mandate? Do they, that is, seek to determine the best interests of the entire populace, and vote accordingly, or do they plumb the voters in their districts and states? Or is there a third alternative—that they represent neither the entire populace nor their constituencies but the interest groups of the nation? The latter seems to be the more likely.

The question deals with the very essence of democracy as that term is generally known in the United States. This brings up the notions of popular sovereignty and of the role of public opinion. No useful purpose is served by using any of the three terms in serious discourse. Democracy, whatever it means (there are more than 200 definitions of the word), is too nebulous. Calling governments democratic is usually a misleading piece of propaganda. Doctrine is confused with theory: We may desire the democratic element in government to be larger, but it is still only a segment of government. By no means were the men who wrote the Constitution interested in creating a democracy; the word does not appear in the Constitution they drafted. Democracy as such was abhorred early on—John Adams, for example, feared what he called a "democratical despotism"—and it is only in the 20th century that the word has been routinely used to "describe" American government. So, too, with popular sovereignty: Despite asseverations to the contrary, the people as such are not sovereign in the United States. Sovereignty rests in the state, which exercises authority through the three branches of the national government over the populace. The same may be said for public opinion; rather than being an identifiable entity, it is a congeries of opinions of a number of disparate groups. On most public issues, no uniform will or opinion of the people, or even of the majority of the people, exists. Several inconsistent opinions of different groups of people can be identified, along with a mass of largely uninterested or indifferent persons. With an ever-changing diversity of interests, demands, and opinions, it is difficult and perhaps impossible to give an accurate answer to the question of with which opinion the decisions of representatives have to be coordinated. The myth, of course, is to the contrary.

Any thoughtful analysis of representative government soon reveals that the common conceptions of representation are seriously faulty. National public policies are not made in accordance with the school-boy version of government found in high school civics texts. Dean Price has invited attention to "the notorious 'iron triangle' of government," by which he means a collusion among congressional committee leaders, the private interest groups affected, and the relevant administrative agencies in the development of policy.[10] These iron triangles—the so-called military-industrial complex is the most obvious—are the subgovernments of Washington, D.C. They make a mockery out of ideas of representation.

The triadic relationship of the iron triangles is the norm. This has long been known by knowledgeable observers, although the myth is otherwise. Political scientists, such as Professor Grant McConnell,[11] know that much of government has come "under the influence or control of narrowly based and largely autonomous elites." Since Arthur Bentley wrote in 1908,[12] the group basis of politics has been the accepted ideology of students of politics. Representation, accordingly, is of interest groups. Congress has few other functions than to put the decisions of iron triangles into formal law.

The myth of representative government and the reality of iron triangles are not secrets, but knowledge about the discrepancy between seeming and being does not appear in the standard books used in law schools. Legal scholars are content to study the *jurisprudence publique*, seen, for example, in the Supreme Court's one person/one vote decisions, as the *ne plus ultra* of representation.[13] They do not probe into the mysteries of the *jurisprudence confidentielle* of how public policies are formulated. Some go so far as to advocate a "representation-reinforcing" theory of judicial review, without examining the reality of representation. Constitutional theory, including the theory of judicial review, has as a consequence come either to a crossroads (as Professor Richard Parker suggests)[14] or to a dead end. The latter is the more probable. We will never get a full understanding of constitutionalism or of constitutional law until the professoriate recognizes, and acts upon the recognition, that "the law is a fraud,"[15] in that no obviously correct body of principles exists by which constitutional issues can be decided—in the sense that certain principles dictate certain results. Like it or not, the ultimate question is one of power and of the personal philosophies of those who judge.

2. The Myth of Separation of Powers. In *America's Unwritten Constitution*, Dean Price defines that Constitution as "the fixed political customs that have developed without formal constitutional amendment, but that have been authorized by statute or frozen, at least temporarily, in tradition."[16] That is a way of also describing the operational code of American constitutionalism. Price suggests that we should "quit talking about the constitutional separation of powers."[17] Indeed, we should, although the myth is otherwise.

In the myth, separation of powers is a doctrine, a term that connotes a carefully worked-out set of rules to govern the relationships between the three branches of government. But it is not a doctrine at all; rather, it is an unrealized and unrealizable political theory. In *The Federalist Papers*, Madison went to great lengths to show that the branches actually shared powers; and Hamilton maintained that the separation maxim really was "entirely compatible with a partial intermixture."[18] In 1908, Woodrow Wilson demonstrated that the norm between the branches was cooperation rather than conflict,[19] an idea developed by Professor Richard Neustadt in 1960 when he pointed out that the Constitution in fact established a system of *separated institutions sharing powers*.[20]

The branches are only seemingly independent—including the judiciary. Cooperation is essential, even though some notorious instances of inter-branch confrontation, such as Watergate, have occurred. A superpower in the modern age requires unified direction and purpose. By and large, this is the reality of "separation of powers." Within the three branches, to be sure, the presidency has slowly and steadily accreted power. The consequence is executive hegemony in government.

The judiciary seemingly differs: Judicial independence is one bright star in the diadem of American constitutional mythology. The reality is different: "The judiciary in any modern industrial society, however composed, under whatever economic system, is an essential part of the system of government and . . . its function may be described as underpinning the stability of that system and as protecting that system from attack by resisting attempts to change it."[21] Judges in the United States are invariably taken from the Establishment and are part of the governing coalition of the nation. Federal judges are seldom at odds with the other branches of government. "No regime is likely to allow significant political power to be wielded by an isolated judicial corps free of political restraints," asserts Professor Martin Shapiro.[22] When courts make law, as they routinely do, they are incorporated into the ruling elite. "The myth of judicial independence is designed to mollify the loser" in litigation.[23] Shapiro, again, asserts: "One of the most important aspects of the social control practiced by courts is that of wedding the populace to the regime, of strengthening the people's perception of the regime's legitimacy and their sense of loyalty to it."[24]

The Supreme Court of the United States is not immune from such an analysis. One is hard pressed to identify *any* Court decision upholding personal freedoms when *important* societal matters are at stake. The liberties of the Bill of Rights and the Civil War amendments are honored in American constitutionalism when their exercise makes little difference to the collectivity called the United States. Examples are easily located. In *Dennis v. United States* (1951),[25] the Supreme Court sustained criminal convictions of members of the Communist Party, not for what they did but for what they thought. A few years later, the Justices again upheld a form of thought control in *Barenblatt v. United States.*[26] And in 1968, the High Bench validated a savage sentence, over First Amendment objections, of a man for burning his draft card as a form of protest against the Vietnam "war."[27] These cases all came in times of peace—at least, not in times of congressionally declared war. During World War II, for instance, the pattern of suppression was even more clear: The Supreme Court became in effect a part of the "executive juggernaut."

3. The Myth of Governmental Accountability. If one believes in representative government and in judicial independence, it then follows inexorably that he must also believe that American government is *accountable*. But that, too, is a myth, however accountability may be defined.

Constitutionalism in the orthodoxy requires that political power be legitimate, which in turn means that power must in some way be accountable or responsible. Legitimacy refers to the right or title to rule. If a nation calls itself a democracy, that right or title is based ultimately on the consent of the people, either directly or through their representatives. Popular sovereignty is another myth, however. Americans, Dean Price tells us, have "lost their innocence about sovereignty—the kind of innocence that . . . made the parliamentary system possible by letting people know only the 'dignified' parts of the constitution while practical politicans in the Cabinet controlled the 'efficient' parts."[28] There is no way that the people can be privy to the facts of governance, even if they as individuals had the desire—which, emphatically, they do not. Moreover, their so-called representatives in Congress cannot, simply because of the demands of their office, be knowledgeable about more than a small number of the some 400 public laws enacted each year.

Despite the "We, the people . . ." phrase that begins the written Constitution, sovereignty lies in the state rather than the people. The state, as Chapter 2 adumbrates, is an indigenous form of corporatism—the syzygetic merger of the organs of public government with the entities of private government. Political power is conjoined with economic power to form a metaphysical entity, the state, which is a super-group-person. It is fundamental, nevertheless, to the basic myth of American constitutionalism that people believe that ultimate power rests in their hands. It does not—a proposition that became clear beyond peradventure of doubt when Lee laid down his sword at Appomattox. Popular sovereignty is a mere slogan, employed for propagandistic purposes to help pacify the people.

Difficult to define, accountability means at least this: Those who wield political power have to answer in another place and give reasons for decisions that are taken. Not mentioned in the formal Constitution and only inferential in *The Federalist Papers*, accountability meshes with the concept of responsibility to describe actions in which "the state imposes penalties on individual actions and in which officials and government are held accountable for policy and action.[29] To most lawyers, the courts are the principal means of effecting accountability. But that is really not so; law is neither omnicompetent nor omniscient. Accountability is really a political matter that is less dependent upon legalistic constitutional distinctions than on political adjustments and cooperation between those who govern. Dean Price says it well:

There is no center of political authority in existence with the capacity to put into effect a rational comprehensive policy. The United States government is not a single rational actor. The degree of independence of congressional committees and their staffs and the related independence of specialized executive bureaus and agencies make it impossible to carry out a coherent program. *There is no clear center of authority in either the Congress or the executive that the voters can hold responsible.* (Emphasis added)[30]

In other words, government is essentially nonaccountable, with the consequence that Americans drift from crisis to crisis in a dangerous and endangered world. A much more disciplined system is needed. (Chapter 6 discusses an aspect of this.) Political parties, not mentioned in the Constitution, have not filled the gap. As part of the operational code, it is readily perceivable that there is no real party discipline: Members of Congress look more to interest groups than to their parties for guidance. A part of the operational code is an attitude that refuses to concede that a disciplined party has the moral right to make compromises among competing interests or to force sacrifices upon any group strong enough to be a "veto group."

4. The Myth of a Sharp Division Between Public and Private. The Constitution, we are told, runs against governments only. But what is a government? Historically, the answer was that it included only the organs of *public* government (although it was not until 1948 that the Supreme Court conceded that the judiciary is a part of government). In legal parlance, the question is whether a given set of activities constitute "state action." An invention of the Supreme Court, the state action doctrine insulates purported private activities from the application of constitutional norms. But the line between public and private is basically arbitrary, and it is only by a transparent fiction that such allegedly private groups as the super-corporations, national trade unions, veterans, legions, farmers' leagues, and others are considered to be nongovernmental. The focus here is upon the supercorporation as the principal exemplar of private governance.

That corporations are governments has been known, or at least argued, for almost a century. The myth is otherwise—and the Supreme Court stoutly adheres to the notion that Exxon or IBM or any other supercorpora-tion is not different in the eyes of the law from a natural person. Whether a corporation is public or private is to be determined by its origins rather than its functions, as Chief Justice John Marshall held in 1819.[31] Americans, however, are governed as much by purportedly private organizations as they are by public government. The Supreme Court steadfastly adheres to a monistic theory of the state, considering people to be governed by one sovereign in a single community. That is manifestly absurd, as even the most casual view of the American political economy will quickly reveal.

Private groups, accordingly, are in a privileged position. Corporations by Supreme Court fiat are constitutional persons that have the protections of the Constitution, including the First Amendment, and have become a "black hole" in the protection of Americans' rights.[32] There is a need to confront and answer questions posed by Alexander Pekelis four decades ago:

Could it be that laws are so ready to assure equality before the government only because things which are really important are being taken care of by men who are smart enough to operate without the glamour of the public limelight? Is the Consti-tution a polished but empty political shell destined to screen and disguise the most arbitrary private governments, more dangerous than other tyrannies because totally anonymous, totally irresponsible, and refined to such a point as to deny their own existence? It has been said of the Devil that he played his neatest trick when he persuaded western man that the Devil does not exist. Is constitutionalism plus freedom of private association the latest and most refined trick of age-old enemies of justice and liberty who went underground and persuaded mankind that they cannot possibly be tyrants for the simple and conclusive reason that they are not governments?[33]

The *jurisprudence publique* of American constitutionalism teaches that corporations (and other groups) are private and accordingly not susceptible to constitutional norms. The operational code differs: Governments they are, despite the purblindness of Supreme Court Justices. If the state is in fact corporatist (see Chapter 2), it is anomalous indeed that the Constitu-tion is applied against only one part of the syzygetic merger of public and private power.

5. The Myth That Americans Are a Tolerant and Freedom-Loving People. This is one of the hardiest myths of American constitutionalism. We con-sider ourselves to be tolerant and free, believe that we value freedom of the press and academic freedom, and support the free exercise of religion and the right of assembly. The reality is otherwise, as Herbert McClosky and Alida Brill document in *Dimensions of Tolerance*.[34] They verify Professor Peter Bachrach's comment: "The illiberal and anti-democratic propensity of the common man is an undeniable fact that must be faced."[35] It has always been so, although we like to pretend otherwise. Law being culturally based rather than *a priori*, the harsh, even unpleasant, fact is that the constitutional limitations in the Bill of Rights and other provisions of the formal document are more hortatory admonitions than interdictions. They admonish government officers to act decently in the circumstances and thus are relative to the specific facts out of which constitutional disputes arise.

In language reminiscent of Erich Fromm's *Escape from Freedom*[36] and even of Fyodor Dostoevsky's "The Legend of the Grand Inquisitor,"[37] McClosky and Brill tell us that freedom is an unbearable burden for most people:

We are not convinced that the craving for freedom is inborn, much less that the tolerance of others and the notion of reciprocity of rights are inclinations natural to everyone. Although freedom has emerged in some parts of the world as a preferred condition, the desire for it scarcely represents the manifestation of an innate human trait. Of the many social practices invented to accommodate differences among people, none is more remarkable than freedom. . . . It is probably contrary to human impulse to endure, much less to encourage, deviant opinions or behaviors on the part of others, especially if their opinions and conduct are perceived as threatening to one's own interests and values, or, equally distressing, potentially hazardous to the social order and its cherished creeds and symbols.[38]

In sum: "Civil liberties are fragile and susceptible to the political climate of the time."[39]

That is just another way of stating what has been said above—the Constitution is relative to circumstances. Some credence can therefore be given to the comment of an astute English professor: "Societies are by nature authoritarian. Governments even more so."[40] To Professor J.A.G. Griffith of the London School of Economics, the widely held belief that sovereignty rests in the people who delegate it to the politicians to hold in trust for them is a "bit of nonsense"—a "cover-up for authoritarianism."[41] That is strong language, but any in-depth study of the history of American constitutionalism will reveal its accuracy. We are encouraged by the myth system to view the Constitution as a beneficent document that is responsible not only for our affluence but our domestic harmony. The constitutional order supposedly is responsive to reason rather than power, promotes the public interest, and permits change within a reassuring framework of continuity. Those beliefs are at least subject to severe questioning, if not outright rejection.

The idea of equality provides illustration. "The equal legal and moral status of free individuals was America's reason for independent existence." Yet at only comparatively rare—and then generally stormy—intervals has the idea of equality dominated American debates on major questions of policy.''[42] The formal Constitution contains a commitment to equality in the equal protection clause of the Fourteenth Amendment, but throughout American history may be discerned a woeful lack of public concern to put that commitment into public policy. That lack cannot be explained by saying that there had been sufficient advances so that there was little room for more. Americans have always preferred (at least, they have tolerated with little dissent) a caste system—*de jure* before the Civil War and *de facto* since then. Black Americans are the principal victims, but others exist. For blacks, the Second Reconstruction—the so-called civil rights revolution of the 1950s and 1960s—has come to an end. For others—many poor whites, many hispanics, native-born Indians, for example—a class system exists, with many imprisoned by the bondages of being in what is a growing "underclass." Nor is that all, as McClosky and Brill relate:

(Hard-won civil rights and liberties are not eternally safeguarded, but are highly vulnerable to assaults by strategically placed individuals and groups who find certain rights or liberties morally offensive, dangerous to safety and stability, and devitalizing to the political order.) Such assaults become especially threatening when the civil liberties under attack do not enjoy widespread popular support. This . . . is often . . . a result in great part of the failure of large segments of the population to have effectively internalized the the libertarian norms to which the American political culture, from the beginning, has been dedicated.[43]

If McClosky and Brill are correct, as I believe they are, what is one to conclude about their findings? Several conclusions may be suggested. First, there is a difference between the mass of the people and the elite structure, with the latter being in general more supportive of civil rights and liberties. (The elite, however, is supportive only to the extent that others' rights and liberties do not jeopardize its own position of power and prestige.) Second, today's conservatives, both the new right and the neo-conservatives, cannot be counted on to champion civil rights and liberties for everyone. Third, "single-issue" zealots may well force politicians to vote against newly won rights and liberties. (The ready example here is the continuing effort to reverse the Supreme Court's abortion decisions by political action.) Finally, the combination of the emergence of the "national security state" (the garrison state) and the burgeoning shrillness of the raw-meat conservatives (such as Patrick Buchanan, Orrin Hatch, Richard Viguerie, and Jerry Falwell) means that an anti-civil liberties point of view is being furthered and identified with Americanism, God, and virtue.

III.

Once seen as myths, the beliefs outlined above starkly indicate that orthodox constitutionalism is indeed dead. Constitutionalism, in the modern age, should be defined in non-normative terms. A constitutive act is one that structures government, for good or ill, without regard to a particular ideology. It refers to the ways that identifiable human beings in a given geographical area are organized. Even a totalitarian state, such as Nazi Germany or the Soviet Union, has a constitution.

Even so, *how* government and society are constituted is still an important question. For American constitutionalists, it is *the* important question. If, indeed, much of the knowledge about constitutionalism as it has been received and understood in the United States is based on myths, the time surely has come to develop a different and better way of looking at the problem.

A start can .be made in that direction by quoting James Madison in *Federalist No. 51*: "Justice is the end of government. It is the end of civil society. It ever has been and ever will be pursued until it be obtained, or until liberty is lost in the pursuit." Even if it is acknowledged, as it must be, that Madison's statement was written for propagandistic purposes, that does not mean that he was wrong. The meaning, for present purposes, is that serious thought about modern constitutionalism should be in terms of what government *should do*, rather than, as the orthodoxy would have it, what it *cannot or should not do*. The challenge posed by Leon Duguit many years ago should be confronted: "Any system of public law can be vital only so far as it is based on a given sanction to the following rules: First, the holders of power cannot do certain things; second, there are certain things they must do."[44] This is more than a semantic quiddity: The requirement is to fulfill the "must do" part of Duguit's formulation, to search, that is, for the affirmative duties of government—those obligations that the state speaking through its apparatus, government, owes to the populace (society).

Said differently, when one thinks about constitutionalism, today and in the future, that thought should be in terms of *taking human needs seriously*. The end of constitutional government is the achievement of social justice. Social justice is a form of distributive justice, concerned with the ways in which benefits are distributed in society through its major institutions, how wealth is allocated, personal rights are protected, and other positive benefits are divided among the people. Social justice thus is a conception under which a governmental structure is established that maximizes the fulfillment of basic human needs and human deserts. All of this must, however, be viewed within the framework of ecological constraints. In D. D. Raphael's terminology, the proposal here is to advance "prosthetic" over "conservative" justice.[45] According to Raphael, conservative justice has the object of preserving an existing order "of rights and possessions, or to restore it when any breaches have been made," whereas prosthetic justice aims at "modifying the status quo."[46] Modification of the status quo is precisely the requirement today.

No one can expect humans to participate in politics, which is what constitutions are all about, until certain basic human needs are satisfied. Human needs theory is not only a means of explaining certain political behavior but also a basis for judging politics and political institutions. One can validly argue that reasonably adequate satisfaction of human needs and deserts is the ultimate purpose of politics—and thus of constitutions. The further requisite, as noted, is that such satisfaction can come only within the constraints of the environment. This means that the society, if and when it comes, will require an equilibrating balance between *Homo sapiens* and the planet it occupies and dominates. Humankind must, contrary to the Judeo-Christian tradition and ethic, perceive that it is an integral part of nature, at one with it and not superior to it. To be contemptuous of nature is to invite disaster. One of the great tasks of modern constitutionalists is to help create such an equilibrium. The limited paradigm, based on Newtonian-Cartesian principles, underlying the Constitution of 1787 requires replacement with a new paradigm. The necessary balance is between humans and nature. This will require reordering of the very concept of constitutionalism.

I do not propose at this time to proceed further in developing the contours of a constitution of human needs and human deserts. That the American Constitution should change in that direction is a proposition that, to me, requires no argument. But since others doubtless will disagree with such a position, the argument must be made—at another time and another place.[47]

IV.

We live today in what seems to be a time of transition of myths. The old ones no longer suffice; they have deteriorated and are no longer functional. New ones have yet to arise from the collective unconscious of the people. This may be seen in the tedious debates currently in the law reviews about the nature and propriety of judicial review. That war of words is proof positive that the participants have little or nothing to learn from each other; they have exhausted the concept of orthodox constitutionalism. No one has emerged the clear winner on the merits, simply because no one has tried to say what the merits really are. Surely, however, a valid delineation of the merits will require cognizance of the total social and political context of the last part of the 20th century and the early 21st century. The debaters about judicial review should no longer look back to what was written in 1787; rather, they should consider what should be written in 1987.

The basic myth of constitutionalism should be viewed in conjunction with a more pervasive national myth, well stated by Frances FitzGerald: "The national myth is that of creativity and progress, of a steady climbing upward into power and prosperity, both for the individual and for the country as a whole. Americans see history as a straight line and themselves standing at the cutting edge of it as representatives for all mankind."[48] As "a nation with the soul of a church,"[49] the United States has always considered itself to have a special mission on Earth. Some try to resurrect the old myths of and about America, but the fact remains that the modern age is one of confusion and calamity; no truly thoughtful person can any longer believe that Americans are God's chosen people.

The requirement is for a new mythic structure, built around the basic idea that Earth is truly a shrinking planet, a global village, and that the peoples on it—of whatever faith or ideology—are all in the same boat and will sink or float together. We can hope, as hope we should, that such a structure will emerge from the detritus left from the smashing of old myths and the changes so apparent in the institutions constructed from that cultural base. Whether this will occur may well be the most portentous question that constitutionalists face in the latter part of the 20th century. It is the task and indeed the bounden duty of all who hold the proud title of citizen to help in the tortuous climb out of the slough of despond in which all the world is now mired. (Let no one be sanguine on that score.)

NOTES

1. S. Levinson, *"The Constitution" in American Civil Religion*, 1979 Supreme Court Review 123, 151.

2. *See*, for example, C. McIlwain, Constitutionalism: Ancient and Modern 21 (rev. ed. 1947); H. Arendt, On Revolution 143 (1965); C. Friedrich, *Constitutions and Constitutionalism*, 3 International Encyclopedia of the Social Sciences 318 (D. Sills, ed., 1968).

3. *See* the unsigned Comment, now known to be written by O. W. Holmes, *The Gas-Stokers; Strike*, 7 American Law Review 582 (1873).

4. J. Nowak, *Resurrecting Realist Jurisprudence: The Political Bias of Burger Court Justice*, 17 Suffolk University Law Review 549 (1983).

5. R. Dworkin, Taking Rights Seriously 147 (1977).

6. R. May, *Political Myth and Liberal Morality*, in W. Anderson (ed.), Rethinking Liberalism (1983).

7. R. Dworkin, *Does Law Have a Function?—A Comment on the Two-Level Theory of Decision*, 74 Yale Law Journal 640 (1965).

8. L. L. Fuller, *An Afterword: Science and the Judicial Process*, 79 Harvard Law Review 1604 (1966).

9. H. P. Monaghan, *Our Perfect Constitution*, 36 New York University Law Review 353 (1981).

10. D. Price, America's Unwritten Constitution: Science, Religion, and Political Responsibility (1983).

11. G. McConnell, Private Power and American Democracy (1966).

12. A. Bentley, The Process of Government (1908).

13. *See* Reynolds v. Sims, 377 U.S. 533 (1964).

14. *See* R. Parker, *The Past of Constitutional Theory—And Its Future*, 42 Ohio State Law Journal 223 (1981).

15. J. Nowak, *supra* note 4.

16. D. Price, *supra* note 10.

17. *Ibid*.

18. The Federalist No. 66.

19. W. Wilson, Constitutional Government in the United States (1908).

20. R. Neustadt, Presidential Power (1960).

21. J. Griffith, The Politics of the Judiciary (1977).

22. M. Shapiro, Courts: A Political and Comparative Analysis (1982).

23. *Ibid.*

24. *Ibid.*

25. 341 U.S. 494 (1951).

26. 360 U.S. 109 (1959).

27. 391 U.S. 367 (1968).

28. D. Price, *supra* note 10.

29. *Ibid.*

30. *Ibid.*

31. Dartmouth College v. Woodward, 4 Wheaton 518 (1819).

32. *See* A. Miller, *"Constitutionalizing" the Corporation*, 22 Technological Forecasting and Social Change 95 (1982); D. Ewing, Freedom Inside the Organization (1977).

33. A. Pekelis, *Private Governments and the Federal Constitution*, in M. Konvitz (ed.), Law and Social Action (1950).

34. H. McClosky and A. Brill, Dimensions of Tolerance: What Americans Believe About Civil Liberties (1983).

35. P. Bachrach, The Theory of Democratic Elitism (1967).

36. E. Fromm, Escape from Freedom (1940).

37. *See* F. Dostoevsky, The Brothers Karamazov.

38. H. McClosky and A. Brill, *supra* note 34.

39. *Ibid.*

40. J.A.G. Griffith, *The Political Constitution*, 42 Modern Law Review 1 (1979).

41. *Ibid.*

42. J. Pole, The Pursuit of Equality in American History (1978).

43. H. McClosky and A. Brill, *supra* note 34.

44. L. Duguit, Law in the Modern State (H. Laski trans., 1919).

45. D. D. Raphael, *Conservative and Prosthetic Justice*, 12 Political Studies 149 (1964).

46. *Ibid.*

47. *See* A. Miller, *Taking Needs Seriously: An Observation the Necessity for Constitutional Change*, Washington & Lee Law Review (1985). *See also* A. Miller, Moving Beyond Doomsday: An Inquiry into the Need for Constitutional Change (work in progress).

48. F. FitzGerald, Fire in the Lake (1972). *See also* J. Robertson, American Myth, American Reality (1980).

49. G. K. Chesterton, quoted in S. Huntington, American Politics: The Promise of Disharmony (1981).

CHAPTER 2

Defining the Constitution

In the popular wisdom, accepted by scholars and laymen, judges and lawyers alike, the Constitution is considered to be the document drafted in 1787 and 26 times amended. Some, particularly the judges, lawyers, and professoriate who are more than incidentally concerned with constitutional questions, concede an added dimension: the gloss that has been put on the document by decades of Supreme Court interpretation. A few of the more thoughtful go further and acknowledge that governmental officers other than Supreme Court Justices, such as members of Congress and the President, can and do at times make decisions of constitutional magnitude.

That this is a basically incomplete conception of America's actual fundamental law is the burden of Chapter Two. It is argued that the United States is governed by both a political and an economic Constitution, which are meeting and merging in a corporatist Constitution. The chapter goes beyond the evolution of the Constitution as seen in governmental decisions, and looks to the overall institutional structure of how Americans are in fact governed. This, however, is not a commentary on what is often called the "living" Constitution. That term refers to the ways in which specific constitutional provisions have evolved since 1789. Chapter 2 has a different perspective—that of delineating the underlying framework of the Constitution, a framework that must be understood before the specific decisions of the Supreme Court, Congress, and President can be fully comprehended.

The chapter was originally written as a response to a recent book by Professor Michael J. Perry, hence the references to that book in the text. But the discussion ranges far beyond what Perry has to say, to set forth some of the principles of the triadic constitutional order. In some respects, this essay complements Chapter 1; it also contains ideas that are discussed in subsequent chapters.

I. INTRODUCTION

Professor Michael Perry's *The Constitution, the Courts, and Human Rights*[1] is a longish essay that fits squarely into the mainstream of current constitutional commentary. He seeks to justify "human rights" decisions of the Supreme Court—in my judgment, successfully. In this paper, I do not wish to enter the controversy over "interpretivism" and "noninterpretivism," for I think the Court has always put content into nebulous constitutional language that has always been "noninterpretivist." Indeed, there is no way, as Justice White asserted in his dissenting opinion in *Miranda v. Arizona*,[2] for the Justices to do otherwise. The real and enduring problems of American constitutionalism transcend the current constitutional controversy. Those problems, as I will try to show, call for a conception of the Constitution that goes beyond the Document of 1787, its amendments, and the gloss the Supreme Court has placed upon those ancient words. We need, I believe, a thorough re-examination of the fundamental nature of American constitutionalism. A few years ago Professor Kenneth Dam called attention to our "fiscal constitution;"[3] I will maintain in this essay that Americans have a Political, an Economic, and an emergent Corporatist set of constitutions.

I do not agree with all that Perry says. For example, he thinks, as do Herbert Wechsler and divers others, that a "principled" decision is the *sine qua non* of constitutional adjudication.[4] One would think at

---

1. M. PERRY, THE CONSTITUTION, THE COURTS, AND HUMAN RIGHTS (1982).
2. 384 U.S. 436 (1966). Said Justice White:
[T]he Court has not discovered or found the law in making today's decision, nor has it derived it from some irrefutable sources; what it has done is to make new law and new public policy in much the same way that it has in the course of interpreting other great clauses of the Constitution. *This is what the Court historically has done. Indeed, it is what it must do and will continue to do until and unless there is some fundamental change in the constitutional distribution of governmental powers.*
Id. at 531. (White, J., dissenting) (emphasis added) (footnote omitted).
3. Dam, *The American Fiscal Constitution*, 44 U. CHI. L. REV. 271 (1977).
4. M. PERRY, *supra* note 1, at 25-29. *See* Wechsler, *Toward Neutral Principles of Consti-*

"Defining the Constitution" was originally published under the title of "Toward a Definition of 'The' Constitution" in 8 University of Dayton Law Review 633 (1983).

this juncture that Wechsler's muddled notions would have been given a decent burial, but apparently not.[5] Since I have elsewhere discussed such matters at some length, I do not propose to repeat what was said there.[6]

This essay, then, is a preliminary examination of an up-to-date definition of "the" Constitution and American constitutionalism. Constitutionalism in the United States is far more complex than many believe, certainly much more so than what is routinely presented to students by the professoriate and to the public by journalists. In large part, students and public alike are exposed to a set of myths about the Supreme Court and the Constitution; some bits of folklore about the judges who have the self-appointed task of interpreting the Document of 1787; more or less detailed analyses, as presented by law and political science professors, some judges in off-bench statements (and in their opinions), and a handful of journalists, employing a far too narrow framework of what those 101 men (plus one woman: Justice Sandra O'Connor) have said about the ancient instrument. The literature produced by that fairly small, identifiable group, though offered as constitutional "law" and thus as the *ne plus ultra* of American constitutionalism, in fact bears little resemblance to the immensely complicated politico-legal processes by which the nation is governed. A basic, and indeed indispensable, myth of that literature is that the Supreme Court is *the* authoritative interpreter of "the" Constitution. That simply is not accurate—on two scores: first, the Justices are not the only governmental officers with power to say, and say authoritatively, what the Constitution means (the Constitution in the sense of the Document); and second, there are numerous decisions of a constitutive nature in the American polity that do not receive judicial scrutiny. All of this will, I hope, become clearer in the ensuing discussion.

One other matter merits mention at this time: the intellectual imprisonment of most commentators (including, alas, Professor Perry) by the invisible bonds of the ideology of "legalism"—the belief that law is a discrete entity, separate and apart from the rest of society, an entity that can be fruitfully studied as such without reference to the politics and the economics of the social order. Law is considered to be "there." Most of the literature on the Supreme Court and the Constitution pro-

---

tutional Law, 73 Harv. L. Rev. 1 (1959). For another view, see A. Miller, The Supreme Court: Myth and Reality chs. 2-5 (1978).

5. A recent celebration of Wechsler is Greenawalt, *The Enduring Significance of Neutral Principles*, 78 Colum. L. Rev. 983 (1978). *Compare* Fiss, *Objectivity and Interpretation*, 34 Stan. L. Rev. 739 (1982).

6. *See* A. Miller, Toward Increased Judicial Activism: The Political Role of the Supreme Court (1982).

ceeds from the assumption, sociologically unsound, that law and the legal system and the State are not closely intertwined. That there is no there "there" (as Gertrude Stein once acidly described Oakland, California) should be obvious to all, but apparently is not. American constitutionalism cannot be understood as a "thing" separate from the political economy of the nation. In what follows, I assume the commonplace—that judges are lawmakers—and take my theme from a recent book by Martin Shapiro:

> If judges . . . are inevitably lawmakers, what happens to our proto-type of independence, preexisting legal rules, adversary proceedings, and dichotomous solutions, and more particularly, what happens to the substitution of legislation for legal rules consented to by the parties? In the first place, lawmaking and judicial independence are fundamentally incompatible. *No regime is likely to allow significant political power to be wielded by an isolated judicial corps free of political restraints. To the extent that courts make law, judges will be incorporated into the governing coalition, the ruling elite, the responsible representatives of the people, or however else the political regime may be expressed.*[7]

Should one doubt that judging is "closely associated with sovereignty or ultimate political authority,"[8] as Shapiro remarks, let him ponder for a moment the true meaning of *Dames & Moore v. Regan,*[9] the 1981 Iranian Hostage decision of the Supreme Court. That decision was by no means aberrational. It was, as I have said elsewhere, "a political decision by a political Court."[10]

One constitutional antiquarian, Justice Hugo L. Black, once asserted: "It is of paramount importance to me that our country has a written constitution."[11] Black denied the validity of what some call the "living" Constitution. Few join Black in that position, although some stoutly deny that some of the Court's decisions that make up part of the living or operative Constitution are legitimate. Black's simplistic view of "the" Constitution, thus, has its counterpart in the simplisms of some commentators—those, to take only one example, who strenuously maintain that the task of constitutional interpretation is to ascertain the intentions of those who drafted the Document.[12] It is a sad commentary on the state of scholarship that after almost 200 years of con-

---

7. M. Shapiro, Courts: A Comparative and Political Analysis 34 (1981).

8. *Id.*

9. 453 U.S. 654 (1981).

10. Miller, Dames & Moore v. Regan: *A Political Decision by a Political Court,* 29 UCLA L. Rev. 1104 (1982).

11. H. Black, A Constitutional Faith 1 (1968).

12. *E.g.,* R. Berger, Government by Judiciary (1977); Monaghan, *Our Perfect Constitution,* 56 N.Y.U. L. Rev. 353 (1981).

stitutional history there is no accepted method of judging, or accepted description of the nature of the judicial process. Small wonder, therefore, that Professor Richard Davies Parker can say that "[o]ur elders have brought constitutional theory to a crossroads."[13] Parker was not quite correct: constitutional theory, rather than being at a crossroads, is at a dead-end. The "elders" Parker mentions have led those who are concerned about constitutionalism into an intellectual cul-de-sac. More and more, the literature tends to be rehashes of ancient controversies, accompanied by the writers' value judgments—not unlike the lucubrations of medieval scholastics. One reason, I believe, for so much modern scholasticism is the failure to inquire into exactly what "the" Constitution in the United States is. Take, for instance, almost any issue of *The Supreme Court Review* or any of the annual *Harvard Law Review* summaries of the past term of the Court (or, for that matter, almost any law or political science journal article dealing with the Court and Constitution,) and one quickly perceives that "the" Constitution is the sacred Document so revered by Justice Black. That, put bluntly, is not enough.

"What is a constitution?" is a question not easily or quickly answered, save on a superficial and elementary level. High school civics texts, as well as Justice Black, provide that type of response. The Document of 1787 was written by a group of supermen since revered in America's history as the Founding Fathers, men assumed to have had a wisdom denied other mortals and who, consequently, should govern us from their graves. For many Americans, the Document has a mystical significance; it is an object of awe and reverence that projects a religious fervor to secular life, a unifying symbol around which Americans can rally. As the supreme law of the land, it is befogged by myths and belief-systems that give the ancient parchment a significance far transcending constitutions in other nations. Walton Hamilton rhetorically asked in 1938, in language that suggests some of the complexities of defining "the" Constitution:

> What is the Constitution? A writing set down on parchment in 1787 and some twenty-one times amended? Or a gloss of interpretation many times the size of the original page? Or a corpus of exposition with which the original text has been obscured? Or "the supreme law of the land"—whatever the United States Supreme Court declares it to be? Or the voice of the people made articulate by a bench of judges? Or an arsenal to be drawn upon for sanction as the occasion demands? Or a piling up of hearsay about its meaning in a long line of precedents? Or a

---

13. Parker, *The Past of Constitutional Theory—And Its Future,* 42 Ohio St. L.J. 223, 223 (1981).

cluster of abiding usages which hold government to its orbit and impose direction upon public policy? Or "a simple and obvious system of natural liberty" which even the national state must honor and obey? And is the Constitution engrossed on parchment, set down in the United States Reports, or engraved in the folkways of a people?

And last of all, has the United States a written or an unwritten Constitution?[14]

Even that statement, sophisticated as it is, falls considerably short of the mark. A more accurate definition is needed. For present purposes, the following shorthand definition is suggested: A constitution—*the* Constitution of the United States—is *a set of institutions,* both public *and* private, *by which society (human activity) is organized and directed.* Those institutions, furthermore, are both *licit* and *illicit.* The Constitution, moreover, consists of a set of *procedures* for making decisions and the *substantive* content of those decisions. Finally, it is both *written* and *unwritten, formal* and *living,* and *always in a state of becoming.*

Any social or political order consists of a "myth system"—a more or less clearly stated set of rules of behavior that purportedly guide human conduct—and an "operational code" that tells people when, by whom, and how certain things may be done *outside the myth system.* I take the labels from Professor Michael Reisman's *Folded Lies,*[15] a study of bribery. Reisman in turn drew from the work of Nathan Leites, who in 1951 published *The Operational Code of the Politburo.*[16] According to Reisman, the operational code is a private and unacknowledged set of rules that govern behavior. He distinguishes between what he calls *jurisprudence confidentielle*—"a set of confidential or secret theory and practice of law, known to a few key lawyers who sometimes perform legal functions in accord with it"—and *jurisprudence publique,* the "jurisprudence presented to the public and studied assiduously by students."[17] Further:

> *Jurisprudence confidentielle* is never expressed openly. High government lawyers and private practitioners who may advise the elite will be privy to secret agreements that they interpret; pleadings and arbitrations, sometimes rendered by judges of public courts acting in their private capacity, will be suppressed by agreement of the parties; opinions ren-

---

14. Hamilton, *Introduction,* in THE CONSTITUTION RECONSIDERED vii, xv-xvi (C. Read ed. 1938). *See generally* NOMOS XX: CONSTITUTIONALISM (J. Pennock & J. Chapman eds. 1979).

15. M. REISMAN, FOLDED LIES: BRIBERY, CRUSADES, AND REFORMS (1979). For a well-known state judge's application of Reisman's methodology, see R. NEELY, HOW COURTS GOVERN AMERICA (1981).

16. N. LEITES, THE OPERATIONAL CODE OF THE POLITBURO (1951).

17. M. REISMAN, *supra* note 15, at 12.

dered for corporations will be kept confidential; and vast amounts of legal material in the public sector will be classified. None of this *jurisprudence confidentielle* will be expressed by these same practitioners in the *jurisprudence publique*. . . . The *jurisprudence publique* is not a sham, for it may apply to some events and to certain groups; given the curious and almost sacramental role of generative logic in legal scholarship, *jurisprudence publique* can always be presented as a complete system of thought. But since it represents only a part of what is going on, it is inadequate as an explanatory or predictive tool.[18]

My intention here is not to develop a comprehensive theory of the *jurisprudence confidentielle* of the Constitution of the United States; but, rather, to pick up from Woodrow Wilson's comment in 1885—"The Constitution in operation is manifestly a very different thing from the Constitution of the books"[19]—and expand upon it. And I alter Reisman's concept from one of secret or confidential law, to law that is open and visible to all who would see. As used in this article, the operational code of "the" Constitution is synonymous with the "living" or "operative" constitutions.

"The" Constitution, properly perceived, consists of far more than the *jurisprudence publique* set forth in the coursebooks and textbooks studied in the law schools. A much larger fundamental law exists, and, indeed, is often considered to be part of the "natural" order of public affairs. However, since many of its institutions are nominally private, they are not considered to be part of the concept of American constitutionalism. It therefore is a form of hidden or invisible government—invisible only because of a consistent refusal to perceive the obvious. "The Emperor has no clothes," the little boy blurted out. That is not my point. Many of the Emperor's clothes can be easily seen, but only part of them are acknowledged as such.

Such a broad conception of constitutionalism runs counter to orthodox thinking. Most lawyers and political scientists see only the myth system and approach the subject along narrow lines, asserting that what is worth knowing about constitutionalism may be derived from historical study of a few documentary remnants and from analyses of Supreme Court decisions. They view the Court as the only important interpreter of the Document. When, however, the concept of constitutionalism is seen through larger and more accurate spectacles, it is readily perceivable that the province of constitutional law is much broader than the orthodoxy would have it. Some congressional and

---

18. *Id*. at 12-13.
19. W. Wilson, Congressional Government 30 (1885).

presidential decisions are of constitutional dimension.[20] Of even more significance, officers of the more important social groups—of which the giant corporations are the principal exemplar—also contribute to development of the constitutional norms by which Americans live. It is true those "private" norms are not set forth in familiar legal codes or even collected in law libraries. Nevertheless, they exist as a body of living or operative law; they are a part of the operational code of the American Constitution.[21]

Constitutionalism is like religion. It is an effort to bring coherency to seeming chaos, supplying a set of beliefs that seek to canalize human conduct. And like religion, constitutionalism has a normative dimension, as witness the following definitions (which, it will be shown, are faulty because they are incomplete):

1. *F.A. Hayek:* "Constitutionalism means that all power rests on the understanding that it will be exercised according to commonly accepted principles, that the persons on whom power is conferred are selected because it is thought that they are most likely to do what is right, not in order that whatever they do should be right. It rests, in the last resort, on the understanding that power is ultimately not a physical fact but a state of opinion which makes people obey."[22]

2. *Daniel Bell:* "The common respect for the framework of law, and the acceptance of outcomes under due process."[23]

3. *Charles McIlwain:* "Constitutionalism has one essential quality; it is a legal limitation on government."[24]

4. *Carl J. Friedrich:* Constitutionalism is "a kind of political order which contrasts sharply with nonconstitutional systems, such as a totalitarian dictatorship. In order to develop such a concept, a constitution must be defined in a way that indicates the features which make it contrast with other kinds of political order. These features come into view when we ask: What is the political function of a constitution? If

---

20. For Congress, the following statutes may be mentioned: The Judiciary Act of 1789, the Sherman Anti-Trust law, the Budget and Accounting Act of 1921, the Employment Act of 1946, the Civil Rights Act of 1964, the National Environmental Policy Act of 1969, and the Budget and Impoundment Control Act of 1974. These statutes concern the structure of government, and thus are constitutional in nature. As for the President, the prime example is perhaps the *de facto* war-making power of the Chief Executive. Even though the war-powers resolution of 1973 seems to limit that power, the fact remains that despite the Constitution, war-making has become an executive power. For the history, see A. SOFAER, WAR, FOREIGN AFFAIRS AND CONSTITUTIONAL POWER: THE ORIGINS (1976). (The second volume of this important study is now being written by H. B. Cox, Sofaer having become a federal judge.)

21. *Cf.* E. EHRLICH, THE FUNDAMENTAL PRINCIPLES OF THE SOCIOLOGY OF LAW (W. Moll trans. 1936).

22. F. HAYEK, THE CONSTITUTION OF LIBERTY 181 (1960).

23. Bell, *The End of American Exceptionalism,* 41 PUB. INTEREST 193, 193 (1975).

24. C. MCILWAIN, CONSTITUTIONALISM: ANCIENT AND MODERN 21 (rev. ed. 1947).

that question is asked, the constitution is seen as a process by which certain political objectives are realized."[25] Professor Friedrich goes on to maintain: "Only those parts of politics which can be expressed in legal rules can be reflected in a constitution. Behind the formal organization, an informal one will always operate. It is an essential part of the living constitution, which could not function without it."[26]

My point is that formal and informal organizations must be recognized in an accurate exposition of constitutionalism and that the concept should not be limited to notions of limitations on government. It will be noted that the quoted definitions, which are variations on the orthodoxy, all invoke the idea of limiting public government. That, however, is far too narrow a conception. Surely a totalitarian nation has a constitution, even a written one as in the U.S.S.R. Constitutions and constitutionalism are, to be sure, both descriptive and prescriptive. But their prescriptions, their rules of law, by no means run in one direction. The quoted passages are illustrative of the "prevalently liberal, antiauthoritarian inspiration of the nineteenth-century constitutional state,"[27] the public law of which had two principal aspects: positive law being changeable, vested rights are constitutional proscriptions; and citizens have correlative public rights, "constitutional" in nature, in the public sphere. The problem with that view may be simply stated: If anything has been learned about how written constitutions and their putative limitations on government operate in reality, it is that they are relative to circumstances. A principle of constitutional relativity runs throughout American history.[28] The limitations the orthodoxy perceives in constitutionalism are more apparent than real. Government in the United States is now, has always been, and will always be precisely as strong as conditions necessitate. Necessity is the mother of constitutional law.

Moreover, the "legal rules" Friedrich mentions are sufficiently ambiguous to make it possible not only to contend that the "private law" of the American economy is a substantial part of the Economic Constitution, but also to maintain that the way important societal decisions are actually made—often a part of the *jurisprudence confidentielle*—must be included in the notion of legal rules. As Brian Sedgemore said about Great Britain: "Two things only can be said with

---

25. Friedrich, *Constitutions and Constitutionalism,* 3 INT'L ENCY. SOC. SCI. 318, 319 (D. Sills ed. 1968).

26. *Id.* at 325.

27. G. POGGI, THE DEVELOPMENT OF THE MODERN STATE: A SOCIOLOGICAL INTRODUCTION 104 (1978).

28. *See* A. MILLER, DEMOCRATIC DICTATORSHIP: THE EMERGENT CONSTITUTION OF CONTROL (1981).

certainty about Parliamentary democracy in Britain today. First, effective power does not reside in Parliament. Secondly, there is little that is democratic about the exercise of that power."[29] So it is in the United States.

Finally, certainly there is much more to constitutionalism than what Friedrich calls "the first and foremost objective" of a constitution: "that of protecting the individual member of the political community against interference in his personal sphere of genuine autonomy."[30] The self is to be safeguarded, but only by limiting public government. That is the essence of the orthodoxy. Interference with the self, however, can come from elsewhere—from the power centers of the Economic Constitution. Protection, furthermore, has both negative *and* positive (affirmative) characteristics—negative in the sense of guarding against harm, and positive in the sense that government has a responsibility to create the conditions that will permit the full flowering of the self.

II. The Political Constitution

Lawyers specifically and Americans generally are inflicted, as has been said, with a peculiar mental handicap. They insist upon viewing law as a discrete entity separate from the warp and woof of society. The fact is that law and the State are closely intertwined, with law being, in Professor Burns Weston's terminology, "legitimized politics."[31] In the constitutive process, the political economy is the very stuff of constitutional law. The Supreme Court in its constitutional, and perhaps in all, decisions, articulates juristic theories of politics. Because of the hyper-legalistic bent of American thought and practice, the Constitution and constitutionalism are seen as a species of law—the highest law, perhaps, but law nonetheless—rather than as pronouncements of political theories and statements of social ethics. Lawyers, however, know little about political theory and next to nothing about social ethics; but the accident of history that gave them a monopoly on judging in *constitutional* matters has been carried over to the present day. (I have suggested elsewhere that the lawyers' monopoly on Supreme Court appointments should be broken.)[32]

If constitutions and constitutionalism are defined fully and accurately, they should be viewed sociologically (functionally). What, that

29. B. Sedgemore, The Secret Constitution: An Analysis of the Political Establishment 11 (1980).

30. Friedrich, *supra* note 25, at 319.

31. Weston, *The Role of Law in Promoting Peace and Violence: A Matter of Definition, Social Values, and Individual Responsibility,* in Toward World Order and Human Dignity 114, 117 (1976).

32. A. Miller, *supra* note 6, ch. 11.

is, is their social purpose? As we have seen, most commentators define the terms normatively. Thus, Professor Walter F. Murphy: "The fundamental value that constitutionalism protects is human dignity."[33] Murphy differentiates between "two quite different political theories—democracy and constitutionalism. The democratic genes stress popular rule and processes to effectuate that rule. The constitutional genes emphasize individual liberty and limitations on government power, even when it is responding to public opinion."[34] That distinction need not be accepted. Murphy's view is too narrow. Constitutions refer to ways that identifiable humans order their affairs; the word also has substantive content beyond the organizational, but not for any specific set of values.

Indeed, how can any one set of public values be said to be the sole standard of constitutionalism? The normative (orthodox) view of that concept should be seen for what it is: a consequence of what Walter Prescott Webb called the Great Discoveries of the post-Columbian era.[35] For the first time in Western history—for that matter, in the history of mankind—all things seemed possible to people of good will; and certainly many things not theretofore possible did become thinkable and even do-able. In one brief moment of planetary history, and then only in a limited geographical area, economic well-being and human freedom on a widespread scale became realizable. Normative constitutionalism, in sum, is a product of what Webb called the "400-year boom." In that, Webb extended Frederick Jackson Turner's frontier theory[36] from the United States to what he called the "Metropolis"—Western Europe. That boom has ended, and with it the orthodox notion of constitutionalism.

"It is ironic," Professor Sanford Levinson asserts, "that a culture which has experienced a centuries-long 'melancholy, long-withdrawing roar' from religious faith can believe so blithely in the continuing reality of citizens organized around a constitutional faith. The 'death of constitutionalism' may be the central event of our time just as the 'death of God' was that of the past century."[37] Levinson cannot be accurate when one considers constitutionalism sociologically; he is really talking about the death of orthodox constitutionalism. Only when the concept is viewed normatively, as apparently Levinson does, can it be argued that it is either dead, as he says, or dying. There can be little

---

33.   Murphy, *An Ordering of Constitutional Values,* 53 S. CAL. L. REV. 703, 758 (1980).
34.   *Id.* at 758.
35.   W. WEBB, THE GREAT FRONTIER (1952).
36.   F. TURNER, THE FRONTIER IN AMERICAN HISTORY (1920).
37.   Levinson, *"The Constitution" in American Civil Religion,* 1979 SUP. CT. REV. 123, 151.

question that "the" Constitution of the United States is tilting toward authoritarianism, and thus is undercutting constitutionalism as a limitation on government.[38] Perhaps it was always actually authoritarian—in its operational code—and that has merely become apparent, merging with the myth system, in recent years. Professor John Griffith of the London School of Economics so contends: "Societies are by nature authoritarian. Governments even more so."[39] The widely-held belief that sovereignty resides in "the people" who delegate it to the politicians to hold in trust for them is, for Griffith, a "bit of nonsense"—a "cover-up for authoritarianism."[40] Whether Griffith is entirely correct may be debatable, although his contention is verified, as we have said, by Brian Sedgemore (based on Sedgemore's experience in Parliament). Today, constitutionalism is dead only in the sense that authority, the faith in the benevolence of which is essential to the workings of liberal democracy, is being replaced, slowly but surely, by a form of authoritarianism. (By no means is it certain that there will ever be a swing back. Quite the contrary). Griffith goes on to say (about the British constitution):

> It is still quite common to hear the constitution described—even lovingly described—as a piece of machinery cleverly and subtly constructed to enable the will of the people to be transmitted through its elected representatives who make laws instructing its principal committee the Cabinet how to administer the affairs of the State, with the help of an impartial civil service and under the benevolent wisdom of a neutral judiciary. Not only is this explanation given to thousands of school children but . . . it also finds its way—in a more sophisticated form—into the curricula of some institutions of further and higher learning.[41]

If one substitutes "the Executive" for "the Cabinet" in that statement, Griffith's remarks are obviously applicable to the United States.

Seen as a sociological construct, constitutionalism and a constitution require answers to the following questions: *Who* makes *societally important decisions, how,* and with *what effects?* The unit for study is the decision of societal importance, one that when made may be directed, to be sure, toward one person alone (as in the sentencing of a person to prison) but that has a wider importance. Lawyers have a way of squaring the circle, of doing the logically impossible by inferring a general principle from one particular; hence, even individual decisions

---

38. *See* A. MILLER, *supra* note 28. *See also* K. PHILLIPS, POST-CONSERVATIVE AMERICA (1982).
39. Griffith, *The Political Constitution,* 42 MOD. L. REV. 1, 2 (1979).
40. *Id.* at 3.
41. *Id.* at 5-6.

have a collective significance.

What, then, is the Political Constitution? The following exposition is more suggestive than comprehensive. A beginning may be made with a recent statement of Professor Myres S. McDougal:

> Our constitution can be observed to be not merely the document of 1789 [sic], however important, or a diffuse mass of contemporary expectations about the requirements of decision, but rather a continuous process of communication and collaboration, beginning before 1789 and coming down to date, which establishes and maintains the basic features of authoritative decision in the body politic. It is the totality of this cumulative process of communication and collaboration, and not any single component, which identifies authoritative decision-makers, projects basic community policies, allocates competences and balances effective power as between different branches of government, authorizes procedures for the making of different types of decisions, and thereby secures the flow of prescriptions which we commonly decide as constitutional law.
>
> . . . .
>
> Every feature of this process, including all the many different communicators and communicatees who participate in it at many different times, affect the content of the constitutive prescription emerging from the process. . . . The whole community, operating through many different official and private spokesmen in multiple channels of communication and influence, constitutes [a] continuing constitutional convention.[42]

That is far too diffuse and abstract. To be sure, McDougal is correct in maintaining that "the" Constitution is more than the original document plus amendments; but after that assertion his exposition suffers. Much more specificity is required. His message may be summed up tersely: Each generation of Americans writes its own constitution. In that, he is correct.

The Political Constitution is the visible part of American constitutionalism, seen in the Document of 1787 and in the numerous interpretations by the Supreme Court, Congress, and the President. It may also be seen in the many silences of the Document (most of which have been made explicit by subsequent political action). At the barest minimum, the Political Constitution establishes a structure of government—in the tripartite division of powers of the national government and in the spatial split between that government and the states. Add the Bill of Rights—a putative set of limitations on public government. The Political Constitution also is a theological instrument, the principal evidence of America's civil religion of Americanism (or nationalism or

---

42. M. McDougal, The Application of Constitutive Prescriptions: An Addendum to Justice Cardozo 29 (1978).

patriotism).[43] And finally, its institutions routinely interact with those of the Economic Constitution. Each constitution has a number of basic principles. Those for the Political Constitution are set forth here; the next section develops the principles of the Economic Constitution.

The first principle is that the Political Constitution is bifurcated. It will be recalled that Woodrow Wilson, writing in 1885, noted the difference between the Constitution "in operation" and that "of the books."[44] Formal constitutional law says, or at least appears to say, one thing, but reality is often different. Examples are easily found. In plain language, the Document provides for a way of electing presidents; but since almost the beginning that way has been supplanted by the operative Constitution's method—political parties (not named in the Document), with electors of the Electoral College voting in accordance with the popular vote in each state rather than for the person considered to be best qualified. "The American method of selecting the president is one thing in the written constitution, and another in the actual constitution."[45] So wrote Arthur Bentley in 1908. Going to war, or at least the calculated use of violence in other lands, has become presidential—despite the clear language of article I that it is the prerogative of Congress. The first amendment speaks in absolute terms and is directed only toward Congress: "Congress shall make no law . . . ."[46] In fact, the amendment is far from absolute and also binds the states.

"The" Constitution is bifurcated for several reasons. First, there are many silences in the original constitutive instrument, silences that have had to be filled by political and judicial action. Second, some of the Document's provisions have not worked out in practice (e.g., election of the President), so they have been amended *sub silentio*. Third, all of the litigable parts of the Document are couched in terms of high-level abstraction, so that a series of interpretations must be made to accommodate nebulous language to new factual (and social) situations. Finally, other centers of actual governing power have appeared since 1787, so that Americans today are governed as much, perhaps more, by ostensibly private groups than by public government itself.

The gap between the formal and the living (or operative) law is the difference between the myth system (the precepts of the written Document) and the operational code (what actually occurs in society). Whatever the labels, it is clear beyond doubt that "the" Constitution is

---

43. *See* LEVINSON, *supra* note 37. *Compare* S. HUNTINGTON, AMERICAN POLITICS: THE PROMISE OF DISHARMONY 30 (1981).

44. W. WILSON, *supra* note 19, at 30.

45. A. BENTLEY, THE PROCESS OF GOVERNMENT, A STUDY OF SOCIAL PRESSURE 295 (1908).

46. U.S. CONST. amend. I.

more unwritten than written. Americans today are tied to the Document of 1787 only symbolically or metaphorically.

The second principle is that the Constitution of 1787 is only ostensibly one of rights and limitations; in fact, it is one of powers and of control. The "nineteenth-century constitutional state"[47] was, and is, in fact a part of the myth system. Government, as Franz Neumann cogently pointed out, has always been precisely as strong as conditions of succeeding generations of Americans required:

> No society in recorded history has ever been able to dispense with political power. This is as true of liberalism as of absolutism, as true of laissez faire as of an interventionist state. No greater disservice has been rendered to political science than the statement that the liberal state was a "weak" state. It was precisely as strong as it needed to be in the circumstances. It acquired substantial colonial empires, waged wars, held down internal disorders, and stabilized itself over long periods of time.[48]

The term "the liberal state" in that quotation refers, not to modern liberalism (which is interventionist), but to the liberalism of John Stuart Mill, and others who espoused the "negative, nightwatchman state."

Seeming constitutional absolutes, as in the Bill of Rights and the thirteenth amendment, have always been interpreted by judges and others to be more cautionary admonitions to act reasonably in the circumstances than interdictory rules of law. What is reasonable, furthermore, becomes in the last analysis what the Supreme Court, sitting as a little lunacy committee, considers the circumstances to warrant. For example, both the first and thirteenth amendments speak in unqualified terms, but both have been interpreted not to mean what they say. Congress and the states can constitutionally make *some* laws abridging freedom of expression; and neither compulsory military service nor jury duty are proscribed by the thirteenth amendment.

By focusing on Supreme Court decisions, lawyers and others have traditionally viewed the Document of 1787 as one of rights or limitations. Perhaps the most influential constitutional textbook of the nineteenth century was Cooley's *Constitutional Limitations*.[49] That conception of history ignores the numerous affirmative subventions by government into societal affairs, principally to help develop and exploit the new lands of the west—pursuant to principles of government articulated by Alexander Hamilton in, among other writings, his famous

---

47. G. POGGI, *supra* note 27, at ch. V.
48. F. NEUMANN, THE DEMOCRATIC AND THE AUTHORITARIAN STATE 8 (1957).
49. T. COOLEY, A TREATISE ON THE CONSTITUTIONAL LIMITATIONS (4th ed. 1878).

Report on Manufactures.[50] It also is oblivious to such encroachments on individual freedom as the Alien and Sedition Acts of 1798,[51] many actions taken by Lincoln to quell what he maintained was a rebellion against the Union, and the oft-times savage repression of dissent.[52] Finally, the orthodoxy does not acknowledge that many outwardly limitative laws and constitutional proscriptions were *administered* contrary to their letter as well as to their spirit. Although it is true that at times the Court is "free to go behind the face of the law and inquire into the fairness of its actual enforcement,"[53] that practice began only in 1886 with *Yick Wo v. Hopkins,*[54] and by no means is it an invariable practice. Even that sporadic inquiry into the fairness of enforcement has been greatly diluted, in equal protection cases at least, by the Justices' discovery that plaintiffs alleging discrimination must prove a subjective intent by the administrator to do so.[55]

It would have been difficult to convince black Americans who had been freed from slavery that the Document of 1787 was one of *their* personal rights or one of limitations on governments at all levels, when, as was the fact, those very governments kept them in a rigid *de facto* caste system of peonage. The reason for the purblindness that enables scholars to speak of a Constitution of Rights (or of Limitations) is easy to locate: lawyers use tunnel vision and believe that Supreme Court decisions are the sole means of articulating what the Constitution means. Among other matters, the Justices never ruled on subsidies by government for economic development, the constitutionality of the Alien and Sedition Acts, the caste system imprisoning most blacks with invisible chains, or the brutal treatment of native Indians. But the Justices did sustain Lincoln's extraordinary, even extralegal, actions during the Civil War, and did not object to savage treatment of the nascent trade union movement after that war. Capital—the business corporation—could collectivize itself and receive government largesse, but labor—the working class—was long denied the right to act in concert; and government aid to it, as in wage and hour laws, was for years invalidated by a Supreme Court that in fact was an arm of the capital-owning class.

---

50. X THE PAPERS OF ALEXANDER HAMILTON 1 (H. Syrett ed. 1966). *See* J. MILLER, ALEXANDER HAMILTON AND THE GROWTH OF THE NEW NATION ch. 19 (1959).

51. The Alien & Sedition Act of 1798, ch. 58, 1 Stat. 570.

52. Discussed in A. MILLER, *supra* note 28. *See also* Miller, *Reason of State and the Emergent Constitution of Control,* 64 MINN. L. REV. 585 (1980).

53. E. CORWIN, THE CONSTITUTION AND WHAT IT MEANS TODAY 417 (rev. by H. Chase & C. Ducat, 13th ed., 1973).

54. 118 U.S. 356 (1886).

55. *See* Binion, *The Disadvantaged Before the Burger Court,* 4 L. & POL'Y. Q. 37 (1982); Soifer, *Complacency and Constitutional Law,* 42 OHIO ST. L.J. 383 (1981).

That limited vision about constitutionalism still prevails in large part. Much, perhaps most, scholarly treatment of the Constitution today is a form of reductionism; it consists of detailed, at times readable, analyses of specific Supreme Court decisions. Dozens of books and hundreds of essays have been and are being published, almost none of which takes a truly functional view of the Court and Constitution. Judicial opinions are parsed with an intensity similar to the medieval Scholastics who spent endless hours in futile disputations over the meaning to be given to Aristotle and other ancients. Few scholars, today or yesterday, are prepared to acknowledge that constitutional law when perceived broadly, and correctly, was—in the past, is now, and will continue to be—instrumental rather than interdictory. Law, however created, is a purposive human endeavor; and the correct question to ask about Supreme Court decisions is this: *cui bono?* Who benefits in fact from them? I have discussed this question elsewhere,[56] so will content myself with citing a passage from Professor Morton Horwitz that seems to be relevant to constitutional law as well as the common law about which he wrote:

> By 1820 the legal landscape in America bore only the faintest resemblance to what existed forty years earlier. While the words were often the same, the structure of thought had dramatically changed and with it the theory of law. Law was no longer conceived of as an eternal set of principles expressed in custom and derived from natural law. Nor was it regarded primarily as a body of rules designed to achieve justice only in the individual case. Instead, judges came to think of the common law as equally responsible with legislation for governing society and promoting socially desirable conduct. The emphasis on law as an instrument of policy encouraged innovation and allowed judges to formulate legal doctrine with the self-conscious goal of bringing about social change.[57]

The point is that the nineteenth-century Constitution—the Document of 1787 as interpreted—was teleological, goal-seeking. Only a few official actions were limited; in the main, those that were seen to trample on "vested rights" of money and property.

Some commentators, notably Professor Edward S. Corwin, whose mind was only partially corrupted by legalism, have perceived in part a more accurate picture of the Constitution. In 1951, Corwin called attention to the overt emergence of a "constitution of powers in a secular state,"[58] building upon judicial approval of New Deal programs for that conclusion. He surely was accurate then. Had he extended his

---

56. A. MILLER, *supra* note 6.

57. M. HORWITZ, THE TRANSFORMATION OF AMERICAN LAW, 1780-1860, at 30 (1977).

58. E. CORWIN, A CONSTITUTION OF POWERS IN A SECULAR STATE (1951).

analysis back into American history, however, he would have seen that government was always one of "powers" when conditions were considered by ruling elites to warrant the exercise of powers. Since 1951, and perhaps earlier, still other types of powers have become evident and have been employed—again with judicial approval: those that validate controls on human behavior, controls that emanate from public and private governments. One can now correctly speak about an emergent "Constitution of Control"—a development which marks a sea change in the nature of "the" Constitution. In briefest terms, crisis government is becoming the norm.[59]

No formal announcement has been made of the change; but none need be. The Constitution of Control is a logical inference from a series of official decisions coming from the courts, Congress, the Executive Branch, and the private governments of the nation. Only a few illustrative instances need be mentioned. For courts, censorship of the press in the *Progressive*[60] case; the alleged but not actual victory in the *Pentagon Papers*[61] case; and *Haig v. Agee*,[62] upholding cancellation of a dissident's passport are evidence enough. Congress legislated discretionary wage and price controls,[63] used by President Nixon but now off the books, and in the National Emergencies Act[64] lent congressional approval to the use of emergency powers by the Executive. The President has committed military services in such places as Korea, Vietnam, and the Dominican Republic—all without express congressional mandate, and all part of the undeclared World War III with the Soviet Union, which began in 1944.[65] The National Security Agency routinely intercepts *all* overseas telephone and cable messages coming from the United States, a procedure that has received judicial approval as a "state secrets privilege."[66] And the private governments of the nation

---

59. *See* Miller, *Constitutional Law: Crisis Government Becomes the Norm,* 39 Ohio St. L.J. 736 (1978).

60. United States v. The Progressive, Inc., 467 F. Supp. 990 (W.D. Wis. 1979). *See* Cheh, *The Progressive Case and the Atomic Energy Act: Waking to the Dangers of Government Information Controls,* 48 Geo. Wash. L. Rev. 163 (1980).

61. New York Times Co. v. United States, 403 U.S. 713 (1971).

62. 453 U.S. 280 (1981).

63. Economic Stabilization Act of 1970, Pub. L. No. 91-379, 84 Stat. 799 (expired Apr. 30, 1974).

64. Pub. L. No. 94-412, 90 Stat. 1255 (1976) (codified at 50 U.S.C. ch. 34, §§ 1601, 1621-22, 1631, 1641, 1651 (Supp. II 1978)). *See* Slater, The National Emergencies Act of 1976—End of Emergency Government? (1978).

65. *See* Kenworthy, *Reagan Rediscovers Monroe,* 2 Democracy 3 (1982). "[W]e are in the third phase of World War III. . . . " *Id.* at 80. World War III is a "cold war," and is fought on the periphery of the major contestants, and often with surrogates. World War III can be said to have begun in 1944, once the defeat of Nazi Germany seemed assured. *See* Dugger, *On to World War IV?,* The Progressive, June 1982, at 20.

66. Halkin v. Helms, 598 F.2d 1 (D.C. Cir. 1978). *See* Hayden v. National Security

routinely "legislate" the terms and conditions of the contracts of adhesion that make up the bulk of the promissory transactions between individuals and corporations.

More evidence could be cited, but heeding William of Occam, need not be. Constitutional rights and limitations still exist, to be sure, at least on paper, but the overriding criterion of public policy is a conception of the "public" or the "national" interest. The myth system speaks in terms of the Document of 1787, in words of limitation, but the operational code, now as always, is one of powers and increasingly of control. I am not suggesting that the State is always able to enforce *its* conception of the national interest, but I am saying that the individual *qua* natural person is insignificant in the constitutional order.

The third principle is that America has a government ruled by politics, rather than interdictory law. Only by an indefensible fiction can decisions on the constitutionality of governmental actions be said to be either logical derivations from the constitutional text or latter-day discoveries of the intentions of those who wrote the Document of 1787. On the contrary, those who exercise governing authority, including the Supreme Court and other interpreters of "the" Constitution, are limited mainly by the political process. Despite the myth system, decisionmakers in general can do whatever politics permits. Some learned professors to the contrary, that is not "nihilism," but simply stating the obvious.[67] Like it or not, power rather than law is supreme—always has been and likely always will be. We may not like that, but it is something with which we have to live.

Illustrative Supreme Court decisions are legion. One will suffice: the recent Iranian hostage case[68] in which the Court validated President Carter's transmutation of a species of property—the claims of the plaintiff, Dames & Moore, against Iran—into a "bargaining chip" for public use in negotiations. The decisions, taken as a whole, exemplify Professor Griffith's observation that

> law is not and cannot be a substitute for politics. This is a hard truth, perhaps an unpleasant truth. For centuries political philosophers have sought that society in which government is by laws and not by men. It is an unattainable ideal. Written constitutions do not achieve it. Nor do Bill of Rights or any other device. They merely pass political decisions out of the hands of politicians and into the hands of judges or other persons. To require a supreme court to make certain kinds of political

---

Agency, No. 78-1728 (D.C. Cir. Oct. 29, 1979); *In re* Halkin, 598 F.2d 176 (D.C. Cir. 1978).

    67. See Fiss, *supra* note 5, for assertions that some constitutional commentators are "nihilists." To the same effect, see J. ELY, DEMOCRACY AND DISTRUST (1980).

    68. Dames & Moore v. Regan, 453 U.S. 654 (1981).

decisions does not make those decisions any less political.[69]

In *Dames & Moore,* Justice Rehnquist writing for the Court, sustained the President's executive agreement, choosing harsh international reality over abstract constitutional (legal) norms. He crafted his opinion in familiar lawyers' language, but it—both the decision and the opinion—reeks with the odor of compromise forced by necessity.[70] Principle (the idea of law as it has been received and understood), as usual, gave way to *realpolitik.* In the last analysis, the Court had no other choice. To invalidate President Carter's hurried deal would have placed the conduct of American external relations in an intolerable position. The decision thus classically exemplifies Professor Martin Shapiro's previously quoted comment: "No regime is likely to allow significant political power to be wielded by an isolated judicial corps free of political restraints."[71] The key word there is "isolated." I do not say that the Court does not wield political power—of course it does—but I do say that it does so as a constituent part of the governing coalition—in fact, though not in theory, as an arm when the need arises of the avowedly political branches of government. Machiavelli maintained that "[a] republic or a prince should ostensibly do out of generosity what necessity constrains them to do."[72] My suggestion is that a republic—the United States—purports to do under the law what brute political necessity requires that it do. Put even more bluntly, *Dames & Moore* is a pure example of a political Hobson's Choice; the Justices not only had to take the first horse in Mr. Hobson's livery stable, it was the only horse there.

The larger point is that, when all is said and done, politics and politics alone, not interdictory law, determines the thrust and measure of significant governmental action. The decisions may be couched in familiar legal form—statutes, judicial decisions, executive orders—but that is merely the counterpane of what, after Professor Horwitz, is an "instrumental conception" of constitutional law.[73] Americans live under the Constitution, or at least seem to do so, but the Document at most is the principal artifact of the myth system of the American polity. Even as interpreted by the Supreme Court, it does not reflect the realities of socio-economic life. *Dames & Moore* was not the first (and certainly will not be the last) time the realities of politics collided with apparently clear constitutional precepts—with politics emerging the victor. A

---

69. Griffith, *supra* note 39, at 16.
70. *See* Miller, *supra* note 10.
71. M. SHAPIRO, *supra* note 7, at 34.
72. N. MACHIAVELLI, THE DISCOURSES, I.51 (L. Walker trans. 1950).
73. *See* M. HORWITZ, *supra* note 57 and accompanying text.

form of *realpolitik* has always prevailed both externally *and* domestically. Despite orthodox theory to the contrary, the Constitution is relative to circumstances. Government in the United States has, thus far at least, been able to meet successfully every emergency that has arisen.

The Supreme Court goes along, because it is "an essential part of the system of government," with a function to underpin "the stability of that system" and to protect it by resisting "attempts to change it."[74] Said somewhat differently, judges in the United States and particularly those on the Supreme Court are governmental officers with the mission of protecting the existing political order against undue change—and thus to shelter those who control and benefit most from that order. Although cast in the legalisms familiar to lawyers, Supreme Court opinions justifying or rationalizing decisions are political documents written by a group of political Justices. That, to be sure, tends to make judicial independence (from the governing coalition) a part of the myth system, but not part of the operational code of the United States. When matters of important State policy are concerned, the Supreme Court and courts generally should be seen as arms of the State, different only in appearance but not in type from the legislative and executive branches of government. Furthermore, there is far more discretion routinely exercised by all government officers, including judges, than most people—especially those who unthinkingly parrot the slogan of a "government of laws, not of men"—realize. The rules that bind governmental behavior are to be found at the lowest levels, and then mainly in the myth system. Justice William J. Brennan expressed the judicial posture in these words:

> Under our system, judges are not mere umpires, but, in their own sphere, lawmakers—a co-ordinate branch of *government*. While individual cases turn upon controversies between parties, or involve particular prosecutions, court rulings impose official and practical consequences upon members of society at large. Moreover, judges bear responsibility for the vitally important task of construing and securing constitutional rights.[75]

Justice Brennan expanded that idea in a footnote:

> The interpretation and application of constitutional and statutory law, while not legislation, is lawmaking, albeit of a kind that is subject to special constraints and informed by unique considerations. Guided and confined by the Constitution and pertinent statutes, judges are obliged to be discerning, exercise judgment, and prescribe rules. Indeed, at times

---

74. J. GRIFFITH, THE POLITICS OF THE JUDICIARY 213 (1977) (paperback ed.). *See* Miller, *The Politics of the American Judiciary,* 49 POL. Q. 200, 201 (1978).

75. Richmond Newspapers, Inc. v. Virginia, 448 U.S. 555, 595 (1980) (Brennan, J., concurring).

judges wield considerable authority to formulate legal policy in designated areas.[76]

In that extraordinary statement, Justice Brennan went far to buttress the validity of the third principle.

The fourth principle is that questions of political economy are usually presented as questions of law and dealt with by lawyers and lawyer-judges. The United States is the most legalistic of all nations. No other country, certainly none with any substantial power, allows public policies to be set in lawsuits between private parties or between government and an individual person. The classic example came in the 1930s when national monetary policy was formally established in a Supreme Court decision between two private litigants in a dispute over the princely sum of $15.60.[77] Some Europeans, bemused by the decision, were unable to understand why the United States could allow a bare majority of nine lawyer-judges to pronounce policy in a matter of such national importance. That decision is yet another example of a political decision by a Court that was, in fact, a part of the governing coalition.[78]

Although monetary policy has now become completely politicized and, thus, is no longer a matter of judicial cognizance, Alexis de Tocqueville's well-known observation that in the United States many political questions ultimately come before the courts still remains accurate. It can be extended to say that under the formal Constitution—under, that is, the myth system—problems of political economy, and thus of the constitution of American society, are routinely handled by lawyers, whether as advisers to the Executive, as judges, as members of Congress, or as officials in the bureaucracy. Lawyers provide the means to legitimize decisions made under the operational code, by obtaining for them the imprimatur of officiality.

The fifth principle is that the State is the primary entity or institution. Even though it is an abstraction—no one can lay hands on the State—it nonetheless exists as the fundamental source of all of the rights and privileges, duties and responsibilities of the citizenry. The State should be distinguished from *government,* which is the apparatus of the State; and from *society,* which is the congeries of groups and individuals that are ruled through government by the State. Under

---

76. *Id.* at 595 n.20.

77. Norman v. Baltimore & Ohio R.R. Co., 294 U.S. 240 (1935).

78. *Norman,* along with Perry v. United States, 294 U.S. 330 (1935); Nortz v. United States, 294 U.S. 317 (1934) and United States v. Bankers Trust Co., 294 U.S. 240 (1935) were heard by the Court together and are commonly referred to as the "Gold Clause Cases." For a discussion of this famous dispute, see R. JACKSON, THE STRUGGLE FOR JUDICIAL SUPREMACY (1941).

"the" Constitution, the State is sovereign—despite the rhetoric about popular sovereignty.

After the break-up of the Roman Empire, the Church, together with decentralized political units, exercised dominion over the remnants. One result was the Holy Roman Empire, a curious combination of ecclesiastical and political authority. Out of that chaos, that partial anarchy, emerged the pattern of relationships among increasingly autonomous States, which in time became nation-states, each of which claimed sovereignty in the sense of ultimate and unappealable power over designated territory and its populace. The Peace of Westphalia (1648) was the cornerstone of what became the modern system. What today seems to be the natural order of affairs, the nation-state, had its origin less than 400 years ago. Professor Leo Gross described the development in these terms:

> [A] new system characterized by the coexistence of a multiplicity of states, each sovereign within its own territory, equal to one another, and free from any external earthly authority [came into existence]. The idea of an authority or organization above the sovereign states is no longer. . . . This new system rests on international law and the balance of power, a law operating between rather than above states. . . . [T]he idea of an international community became an almost empty phrase and where international law came to depend upon the will of states concerned with the preservation and expansion of their power. . . .[79]

Within this system, each nation-state is a discrete geographical entity having one and only one goal: the pursuit and enhancement of its own interests. In the post-World War II period, more nation-states, some tiny unto insignificance, have been formed than ever before. About 160 exist at the present time—more than three times as many as when the United Nations was created in 1945.

Since its inception, the single most important characteristic of the United States has been unitary internal sovereignty. All societal activities involving the "authoritative allocation of value"[80] are performed by authority of a single decision center—the State itself (as expressed or implied in the Document of 1787)—without regard to whether those actions may be differentiated (in the federal system) or seemingly private. As Gianfranco Poggi has put it, "no individual or corporate body can engage in activities of rule except as an organ, agent, or delegate of the state; and the state alone assigns and determines the extent of those

---

79. Gross, *The Peace of Westphalia,* 1648-1948, in INTERNATIONAL LAW AND ORGANIZATION: AN INTRODUCTORY READER 54, 55, 64 (R. Falk & W. Hanrieder eds. 1968) (footnote omitted).

80. D. EASTON, THE POLITICAL SYSTEM (1953), *quoted in* G. POGGI, *supra* note 27, at 92.

activities according to its own rules, backed by its own sanctions."[81] Even though the people are considered under the myth system to be the ultimate depository of sovereignty, the State is monistic. It is one unit, with a single currency and a national language and a legal system that, although divided into parts in the federal system, is in fact unified.

Sovereignty in the United States lies in the State, not in the people. Although a disembodied entity existing only in contemplation of law, the unitary State is sovereign, with a governmental triad being its apparatus. The slogan of popular sovereignty, to be sure, is often employed; but it is a rhetorical device to organize and placate the people. The "We, the people"[82] statement in the preamble to the Document should not—cannot—be taken literally. To paraphrase Lincoln, we have a government *of* the people, but not *by* the people and not always *for* the people, if the word "people" means the populace at large.

The sixth principle is that the State is corporatist. A half-century ago Mihail Manoilesco maintained that "[t]he twentieth century will be the century of corporatism just as the nineteenth was the century of liberalism."[83] So it seems to be, although the term is seldom used as such. In the United States, corporatism, to use Philippe C. Schmitter's useful categorization, tends to be *societal* rather than *state.*[84] It is the successor to political pluralism that for decades was the prevailing ideology of political scientists (and still is the ideology of such legal scholars as Alexander Bickel and John Hart Ely). Since I have discussed my belief that the United States is indeed a corporate State at some length elsewhere,[85] and since America as an exemplar of societal corporatism will be the focus of attention in the conclusion to this essay, no further exposition is required at this time. Suffice it only to say that corporatism under "the" Constitution of the United States is a joinder of the political power of public government with the economic power of private governments—that is, of the institutions of the Political and Economic Constitutions—and a consequent formation of a metaphysical entity, the Corporate State, that transcends both fundamental laws. Thus, the State is what we will call a "super-group person."[86]

The seventh principle is that government, as the apparatus of the State, is apparently but not actually one of splintered powers. One of

---

81. G. POGGI, *supra* note 27, at 92.

82. U.S. CONST. preamble.

83. M. MANOILESCO, LA SIÈCLE DU CORPORATISME (rev. ed. 1936), *quoted in* Schmitter, *Still the Century of Corporatism?*, 36 REV. OF POL. 85, 85 (1974).

84. Schmitter, *supra* note 83.

85. A. MILLER, THE MODERN CORPORATE STATE: PRIVATE GOVERNMENTS AND THE AMERICAN CONSTITUTION (1976).

86. The term comes from Otto von Gierke. *See infra* note 153 and accompanying text.

the consequences of the rise of societal corporatism is the progressive blurring of lines of authority and political power set forth in the Document of 1787. Three lines of development are discernible: in the federal system, in the separation of powers, and in the supposedly discrete domains of public and private. Popular wisdom accepts the notion, stated in classic terms by Justice Louis D. Brandeis, that the national government's powers were split to better protect liberty: "The doctrine of the separation of powers was adopted by the Convention of 1787, not to promote efficiency [in government] but to preclude the exercise of arbitrary power."[87] That sentiment was echoed in 1965 by Chief Justice Earl Warren: "[S]eparation of powers was obviously not instituted with the idea that it would promote governmental efficiency. It was, on the contrary, looked to as a bulwark against tyranny."[88]

What was obvious to Brandeis and Warren, however, has now been refuted, at least in part, by modern scholarship. Louis Fisher, for example, has convincingly argued that a separate Executive was created by the 1787 Convention *to promote efficiency,* precisely because government under the Articles of Confederation was demonstrably inefficient.[89] America had congressional government under the articles, which led the "runaway" Convention to establish an independent Executive. Brandeis and Warren unthinkingly repeated the propaganda of James Madison, who in *The Federalist No. 51* said:

> But the great security against a gradual concentration of the several powers in the same department, consists in giving to those who administer each department the necessary constitutional means and personal motives to resist encroachments of the others. The provision for defence must in this, as in all other cases, be made commensurate to the danger of attack. Ambition must be made to counteract ambition. The interest of the man must be connected with the constitutional rights of the place. It may be a reflection on human nature, that such devices should be necessary to control the abuses of government. But what is government itself, but the greatest of all reflections on human nature? If men were angels, no government would be necessary. If angels were to govern men, neither external nor internal controls on government would be necessary. In framing a government which is to be administered by men over men, the great difficulty lies in this; you must first enable the government to control the governed; and in the next place oblige it to control itself.[90]

Madison saw matters somewhat differently from other prominent figures of the age, perhaps because *The Federalist Papers* were written

87. Myers v. United States, 272 U.S. 52, 293 (1926) (Brandeis, J., dissenting).
88. United States v. Brown, 381 U.S. 437, 443 (1965).
89. *See* L. FISHER, PRESIDENT AND CONGRESS: POWER AND POLICY 1-27 (1972).
90. THE FEDERALIST NO. 51, at 337 (J. Madison) (Mod. Libr. ed. 1937).

to convince people of the essential benevolence of the new constitution. James Wilson's views are particularly apposite:

> In planning, forming, and arranging laws, deliberation is always becoming, and always useful. But in the active scenes of government, there are emergencies, in which the man, as, in other cases, the woman, who deliberates, is lost. . . . But, can either secrecy or despatch be expected, when, to every enterprise, mutual communication, mutual consultation, and mutual agreement among men, perhaps of discordant views, of discordant tempers and of discordant interests, are indispensably necessary? How much time will be consumed! and when it is consumed; how little business will be done! . . .
>
> If, on the other hand, the executive power of government is placed in the hands of one person . . . is there not reason to expect, in his plans and conduct, promptitude, activity, firmness, consistency, and energy?[91]

Under the Articles of Confederation, government was seriously faulty because powers were *not* separated, resulting in ineffectual government.

The original intentions, therefore, were quite different from what is set forth in a few scattered Supreme Court opinions and in much of the political science literature. That, however, is not the real point, which is that *powers were not really separated in fact, and each branch of the national government exhibits separate institutions sharing powers. Accordingly, the myth system to the contrary notwithstanding, the praxis among the three branches is cooperation rather than conflict.* Throughout American history, with some instances to the contrary, officers in Congress, the Executive Branch, and the judiciary have tended to act as one. The national government is multiheaded. In theory, no one of the branches is preeminent. In fact, the tendency is toward Executive hegemony, with the Executive—consisting of both the presidency and the bureaucracy—sharing power with Congress. (The courts have become not only "the least dangerous branch," but also the least important branch—although, again, the myth system says otherwise.)

"Separation of powers" as separate institutions sharing power have all but smashed the Brandeis-Warren conception. Woodrow Wilson knew this as long ago as 1908, when he wrote that "warfare" between Congress and the President would be "fatal."[92] (Even then Wilson paid scant attention to the Supreme Court.) Separation of powers in fact means that a complex web of routine interactions between President, Congress, and interest groups exists. Ever increasingly, the norm is

---

91. *Quoted in* Sharp, *The Classical Doctrine of "The Separation of Powers,"* 2 U. CHI. L. REV. 385, 413 (1935).

92. W. WILSON, CONSTITUTIONAL GOVERNMENT IN THE UNITED STATES (1908).

cooperation.

It could scarcely be otherwise. No nation, let alone a superpower, can long afford to have the powers of government splintered. Paralysis would be the result, at a historical moment when the ability to take action has never been more needed. Some built-in structural problems may still exist, to be sure, as the well-known Washington lawyer Lloyd Cutler recently argued.[93] Battle they may, at least in the media, but Congress and the President (and the bureaucracy) cooperate more than they conflict.[94] Compromises of course are the result; but the important matter to perceive is that, as badly as it works, the tasks of government do get done. The problem is to get them done better—and that is a major challenge that constitutional lawyers face at this time. I argue elsewhere that fundamental alterations in the governments established by the Political Constitution will help attain a sustainable society.[95] Cutler, in advocating change in the separation of powers, hits only one symptom of a deep-seated, pervasive malaise in the governmental process. The problem is systemic, and the Band-Aid Cutler recommends will do little toward attainment of a more humane, or sustainable, society.

As with the so-called "doctrine" of separation of powers, which is not a doctrine but an unrealized political theory, so too with the principle of federalism. Political power in the United States is apparently split spatially between the central government and fifty states. The original theory was that the federal government possesses only limited, delegated powers; but that theory has long since lost its potency. Federalism was supposed to be "dual," with the dominant segment being the states. Power has slowly accreted to the national government, a process that began early in the nineteenth century, and the system has so changed that there can be no question today that the general government is preeminent. Regardless of how often politicians, such as President Reagan, speak of a "new" federalism, a superpower in the nuclear age, dominated economically by supercorporations and technologically knit together by communications and transportation, simply cannot brook the diversity and decentralization of dual federalism. What Harold Laski once called the "inexpugnable" variety of America is fast vanishing.[96] A continental-sized nation, with a central income tax, multistate economic organizations, and with commitments all over the planet and reaching far out into space, will not—cannot—revert to the

---

93. Cutler, *To Form A Government*, 59 FOREIGN AFF. 126, 127 (1980).

94. *Cf.* J. SUNDQUIST, THE DECLINE AND RESURGENCE OF CONGRESS (1981).

95. A. MILLER, GETTING THERE FROM HERE: CONSTITUTIONAL CHANGES FOR A SUSTAINABLE SOCIETY (work in progress).

96. Laski, *The Obsolescence of Federalism*, 98 NEW REPUBLIC 367 (1939).

purported halcyon days of a small-shop, agriculturally dominated society.

"Cooperative" federalism is the consequence, with the states ever more becoming administrative districts for centrally established policies. Those policies emanate from both the organs of public government (Congress, the Executive, the Supreme Court) and from the institutions of the nationwide private governments of the country (of which the giant corporations are the principal exemplar). The United States, in sum, has become a "united state"—[97] and there is no likelihood of reversion to the *status quo ante*. The problems of public policy are *national* more than local, and will be resolved, if, indeed, they are resolved, by *national* (uniform) policies. The meaning, for present purposes, is that the line of demarcation between national and state power and authority is being extinguished. As with separation of powers, cooperation is the norm.

The same pattern is visible in the activities of institutions in the public and private sectors of the nation. Inasmuch as this is but another way of stating that the United States exemplifies societal corporatism—even State corporatism at times—further discussion will be deferred until the final section of this essay.

The eighth principle is that within the tripartite division of powers of the central government, the Executive Branch is becoming dominant. That branch consists of two main segments—the office of the presidency, made up of over 5000 men and women who cluster around the Chief Executive and who constitute the nerve center of government (to the extent that such a center exists); and the federal bureaucracy. The latter has three segments: the civilians in the public administration, headed by political appointees; the military services; and an "external" bureaucracy, consisting of employees of nominally private organizations that continuously contacts and contracts with the government. Although the three branches are supposedly "equal in origin and equal in title,"[98] since the beginnings of the republic the presidency has steadily gained actual power vis-à-vis both Congress and the courts. Once again, the gap between the pretenses of the myth system and the realities of the operational code may be perceived.

The Document of 1787 speaks cryptically. Article II begins: "[t]he executive Power shall be vested in a President of the United States of America."[99] Nowhere is "the executive power" defined. The office was left to gather power from experience. As the United States moved from

---

97. T. Lowi, The End of Liberalism 295 (2d ed. 1979).

98. Gordon v. United States, 117 U.S. 697, 701 (1864).

99. U.S. Const. art. II, § 1, cl. 1.

an underdeveloped nation, dependent upon capital and cheap labor from Europe and struggling to eke out an existence from the fabulous but nonetheless forbidding riches of an unexploited continent, to emergence in this century as *the* superpower of the world (at least for a time—about 1945 to 1970), the need for presidential leadership in government became ever more apparent. Those presidents considered to be the "best" are the ones who were also the strongest, who by one means or another assumed the power of direction of the nation. Examples are easily found: Washington, Jackson, Lincoln, Theodore Roosevelt, Wilson, Franklin Roosevelt, Truman—to name them chronologically.

The delphic terms of the Document of 1787 permit a President to be as "big" as he wishes; or, rather more precisely, to be as big as the political process allows. And that is exactly what all modern presidents (since Franklin Roosevelt) have been—or at least have tried to be. There will be no more Buchanans in the White House. The twentieth century, and the future so far as it can be foreseen, belongs to the Executive. In this country and all others of any consequence, government is ever increasingly dominated by the Executive. Given the state of socioeconomic and technological affairs, it could not be otherwise. Add the all-too-obvious psychological need, noted in classic terms by Fyodor Dostoevsky in *The Grand Inquisitor*,[100] of people for miracle, mystery and authority, and it may quickly be seen that the President is the High Priest—the closest thing to an American Pope—of our civil religion of nationalism (or Americanism or patriotism). I do not suggest that the President *qua* Chief Executive can do whatever he pleases. What Professor Thomas Cronin calls the "textbook" presidency is, as Cronin shows, a myth.[101] What is suggested is that among the three branches of government, the Executive—the presidency plus the bureaucracy—is by any criterion the strongest. That the trend toward aggrandizement of executive power will not only continue but accelerate seems to be about as safe a prediction as one can make about governmental affairs.

When one speaks about the presidency, four facts should be borne in mind. First, the President is both Chief of State and Head of Government; that makes the United States unique among the major powers of the world. It is as if Great Britain combined the office of the sovereign (the Queen) with that of the Prime Minister. Centering both functions in one person adds enormously to the prestige of the office and to the actual power of the President. Second, the presidency is both one

---

100. F. DOSTOEVSKY, THE GRAND INQUISITOR (J. Wasserman ed. 1970).
101. T. CRONIN, THE STATE OF THE PRESIDENCY (1975). *See also* R. PIOUS, THE AMERICAN PRESIDENCY (1979).

man and the Executive Offices of the President (E.O.P.), the 5000-plus people who surround the President. The E.O.P. consists of both the "inner" presidency—the man in the Oval Office plus the 1200 or so people immediately around him—and the "outer" presidency—those who occupy the offices that make up the sprawling complex that surrounds the White House. Those men and women are the locus of power in American government, to the extent that one exists. Some of them wield immense power, simply because they can invoke the name of the President when they speak. Third, because of the growing complexity of society and thus of the tasks of government, there is simply no way that Congress—two committees of 100 and 435 people—can govern in any systematic and comprehensive manner. Even given the will to rule, characteristics which by no means are in high supply in Congress, an individual member does not have the time to keep abreast of all of the manifold details of governance. Indeed, it is impossible to know more than cursorily what is in each of the 400 or so public laws enacted each session by Congress. Hence, vast delegations of legislative power are made to the Executive (and even at times to the courts and to private parties), which brings up the fourth fact: The Executive Branch is a congeries of agencies, bureaus, and departments over which the President rules as titular (and in most instances as legal) head, but which in fact often are independent fiefdoms with which even the White House has to "negotiate treaties."[102] The public administration—the bureaucracy—is a headless fourth branch of government. Nominally executive (or at least administrative), that branch has formal authority over the implementation of many of the public policies of the Political Constitution.

To the visible bureaucracy of the public administration there should be added the military services, which administer what is perhaps the most important aspect of American public policy (national security), and also a number of purported private organizations—corporations, universities, etc.—that through the medium of contracts and grants have created an "external bureaucracy."[103] Any description of the Executive must include this dimension as well as those in the civil service and the military departments. (The external bureaucracy is substantial evidence of the close and continuing links between the institutions of the Political and Economic Constitutions.)

The ninth principle is that the Political Constitution is always in

---

102. *See* A. MILLER, PRESIDENTIAL POWER IN A NUTSHELL (1977); R. NEUSTADT, PRESIDENTIAL POWER (2d ed. 1976).

103. *See* Miller, *Administration by Contract: A New Concern for the Administrative Lawyer,* 36 N.Y.U. L. REV. 957 (1961).

a state of becoming. It is malleable. Its terms are more invitations for debate than preordained dispositions of present-day problems. The meaning is clear: despite being silent on the point, the Document of 1787 delegated power to succeeding generations of Americans to write their own constitutions. True, the words remain the same, but the meanings given to that language change through time. One has a good legal mind when he can understand that meanings given to unchanging words can be altered through time. They are reflective of the conditions in which they are used. Since social conditions are constantly in flux, there should be little wonder that the ancient words receive differing interpretations.

Thus, adaptability characterizes the Document, but it is far from complete. Enormous societal changes, domestic and external, have thus far been accommodated within an instrument written almost two centuries ago for a far different nation that existed in a far different world. The ability to adapt, however, appears to have about run its course. Except in times of widely acknowledged emergency or crisis conditions, such as total war (for example, the Civil War and World War II) or severe economic depressions (as in the 1930's)—in which events the ostensible rigidities of the formal Constitution are silently shelved "for the duration"—the Political Constitution has built-in provisions that have become positive barriers to achievement of both efficiency and accountability in government. It is out of phase with the demands that Americans (as well as peoples the planet over) are making of the governments created by the Document. In sum, the Political Constitution has gone about as far as it can go. Systemic change is required. Its evolution within the framework set down in 1787 is coming to an end. Although it has been and still is always in a state of becoming, that "becoming" has now forced politico-economic institutions into a cul-de-sac. They are not sufficient to meet the present and emergent needs.[104]

The tenth principle is that government, as the apparatus of the State, has a monopoly on the legitimate use of violence. This is a self-evident proposition, requiring no extended discussion. The key word is "legitimate"; other sources of violence, of course, exist, but none that has the imprimatur of legitimacy. Indeed, those illicit uses of violence are subjected to punishment by the State. Governmental violence runs on a continuum from war to individual punishment (capital punishment being the extreme). I am not suggesting, it should be mentioned, that all use of violence by governmental officers is legitimate. Some examples of extralegal violence are also, albeit rarely, punishable by the

---

104.   *See* Sundquist, *The Crisis of Competence in Government,* in Setting National Priorities: Agenda for the 1980s 531 (J. Pechman ed. 1980). *See also* Cutler, *supra* note 93.

State.[105]

The eleventh principle is that formal as well as actual political power resides in narrow elite structures, which exercise control over segments of public policy. Professor Grant McConnell has stated the matter well:

> [A] substantial part of government in the United States has come under the influence or control of narrowly based and largely autonomous elites. These elites do not act cohesively with each other on many issues. They do not "rule" in the sense of commanding the entire nation. Quite the contrary, they tend to pursue a policy of noninvolvement in the large issues of statesmanship, save where such issues touch their own particular concerns. . . .
>
> [The distinction between the public and the private] has been compromised far more deeply than we like to acknowledge. . . .
>
> [T]he very idea of constitutionalism sometimes seems to be placed in question.[106]

McConnell is far from alone. Public policy, as enunciated in the United States, all too often is the product of the "subgovernments" or the "iron triangles" of government.[107] One leg of the triangle is the appropriate congressional committee, another is the administrative agency, and the third is the relevant interest group. The interactions of these groups produce policies that affect—perhaps within narrow areas—all Americans. Since here, again, there may be seen the interplay between the institutions of the Political and Economic Constitutions, further discussion will be deferred to Section IV of this essay.

The consequence is a paradox, which is the twelfth principle: *The political order labeled pluralism, established by the Political Constitution, is bankrupt in theory and practice.* Pluralism, the political theory that out of the clash of decentralized interest groups in American society comes the public good, is a version of Adam Smith economics transferred to politics and writ large. It is no more valid there than it is in economics. Since Arthur Bentley published *The Process of Government*[108] in 1908, pluralism has largely been the operative ideology of students of politics (it still is for many lawyers).[109] Its basic shortcomings have, however, become all too evident in recent years. Pluralism "worked" during the nineteenth century, as Bentley noted and as David

---

105. *E.g.*, Bivens v. Six Unknown Named Agents, 403 U.S. 388 (1971).

106. G. McConnell, Private Power and American Democracy 339, 361-62 (1966).

107. *See* D. Cater, Power in Washington (1964). *Compare* Heclo, *Issue Networks and the Executive Establishment,* in The New American Political System 87 (A. King ed. 1978).

108. A. Bentley, *supra* note 45.

109. *See e.g.*, A. Bickel, The Supreme Court and the Idea of Progress (1970); J. Ely, Democracy and Distrust (1980).

Truman iterated as late as 1951;[110] but it worked *only* because there was but one dominant group—the corporate class; the moneyed and propertied. By the 1970s, pluralism was widely perceived as intellectually bankrupt, paradoxically, because it was successful. Other groups arose—labor unions, farmers' leagues, veterans' legions, and the like—at a time when economic growth seemed to be a permanent attribute of the political economy. (I have elsewhere called that time, from roughly 1945 to 1970, the true Golden Age of America.)[111] Those groups successfully fought for and managed to capture the relevant segments of government (administrative agency; Congressional committee).

That development—the fulfillment of the demands of new groups for "entitlements"—occurred at a time when economic growth began to slow and even to cease and when, as a consequence, the ecological trap began to close. Politics became a zero-sum game, one in which for every winner there must be a loser. Those outside of a dominating group (over a segment of public policy) are left behind—the precise reason why they go to court in attempts to have perceived and felt shortcomings rectified (and thus the reason why John Hart Ely advocates a "representation-reinforcing" theory of constitutional review).[112]

The manifest failure of pluralism, acknowledged by perceptive political scientists but thus far denied by most academic lawyers, by itself poses grave challenges to the normative concept of constitutionalism. But that is not all. Another harsh fact must be added, namely, that under pluralism there is no possible way, save perhaps in widely-acknowledged emergencies, for the "national" or the "public" interest—the interests of the nation as a unified collective—to be realized. One, therefore, can readily see that the Political Constitution is badly out of phase with the pressing needs of the era. (So is the Economic Constitution, as we will see.) The cruel paradox of pluralism being a failure, principally because it has been so successful, must be confronted by anyone who would think seriously about constitutionalism in America. It is precisely that paradox that causes such leading neoconservative writers as Professor Samuel P. Huntington to lament what he calls the "ungovernability" of modern democracies.[113]

The thirteenth principle is that the individual is only apparently the sole political actor. Although the Document of 1787 recognizes

---

110. D. TRUMAN, THE GOVERNMENTAL PROCESS (1951).

111. A. MILLER, *supra* note 28, at ch. 3. The golden age, of course, was far from that for those who fought and died in Korea and Indo-China.

112. J. ELY, *supra* note 109.

113. Huntington, *The United States*, in M. CROZIER, S. HUNTINGTON, & J. WATANUKI, THE CRISIS OF DEMOCRACY (1975).

only two juridical entities—government and the natural person—that conception has been overtaken in the operative or living Constitution. The operational code of American constitutionalism recognizes, as has already been said, that an elite structure promulgates public policies.[114] The thirteenth principle is the corollary: the decline in importance of the individual. In economics, in politics, in social affairs generally, it is the group rather than the individual that is dominant. Individualism as a concept, even an ideology, was a late-bloomer: It does not antedate the French Revolution; and in many respects it is a "natural" by-product of the Great Discoveries, coming into being at a time when the bonds which theretofore had constricted the activities of all (except perhaps a tiny few of the best-advantaged) had been thrown off.

Because of the influence of John Locke and others who did not acknowledge the ecological basis of human freedoms, law in America was long predicated upon notions of individualism. Contract law provides the classic illustration; as does tort law. Even constitutional law was not immune, a development that reached its apotheosis when the Supreme Court read Social Darwinism into the Constitution. As long ago as the turn of the century, individualism began to die. It became anachronistic when, in the words of John D. Rockefeller early in the twentieth century, "large-scale organization had revolutionized the way of doing business and when individualism had gone, never to return."[115] Arthur Bentley, as has been said, noted the change in 1908.

Not all vestiges of individualism have vanished. Some intellectual Neanderthals still parrot the words of Adam Smith. Of more importance, the very nature of individualism was transmogrified by the Supreme Court when in 1886 it casually asserted that the corporation—a disembodied collective—was a person within the meaning of the fourteenth amendment.[116] That bit of judicial legerdemain keeps the notion of individualism alive, but in the strangest way: all persons are equal under the law, but some constitutional persons—those collectives called business corporations—are more equal than others. The theory of corporate personality collides with the reality of vastly disproportionate economic—and thus political—power of giant companies (and other social groups) and the lonely individual, the naked ape who stands alone and faces a fearful congeries of bureaucracies both public and private. The natural person as the sole constitutional political actor has been supplanted by the group. Modern man is bureaucratized man: he spends his life as a member of groups and, indeed, is wellnigh meaning-

---

114. *See e.g.,* P. BACHRACH, THE THEORY OF DEMOCRATIC ELITISM: A CRITIQUE (1967).
115. *Quoted in* 1 A. NEVINS, JOHN D. ROCKEFELLER 622 (1940).
116. Santa Clara County v. Southern Pac. Ry., 118 U.S. 394 (1886).

less and purposeless outside of groups. (The rare hermit may provide the exception that provides the rule.) Even the entrepreneur who believes that only his own effort, abetted by his property, has enabled him to be successful is wholly dependent upon society—the ultimate group. There are not—there cannot be—any Robinson Crusoes in the modern age. L.T. Hobhouse stated the point in these words:

> The organizer of industry who thinks that he has "made" himself and his business has found a whole social system ready to his hand in skilled workers, machinery, a market, peace, and order—a vast apparatus and a pervasive atmosphere, the joint creation of millions of men and scores of generations. Take away the whole social factor and we have not Robinson Crusoe, with his salvage from the wreck and his acquired knowledge, but the naked savage living on roots, berries, and vermin. *Nudus intravi* should be the text over the bed of the successful man, and he might add *sine sociis nudus exirem.*[117]

The death of individualism can be perceived through all fields of law—private law as well as public law. Man, as Aristotle said, is a political animal; that means he is a social animal, unable to exist without the trappings of group life—of, that is, the institutions of civilization.

The fourteenth principle is that Reason of State (the "national interest") is the overriding value of the Political Constitution. The principal goal is survival of the State, and thus ultimately the survival and furtherance of the interests of those who control the State and who profit most from societal activities.

Reason of State, "the State's first law of motion,"[118] has been defined as "the doctrine that whatever is required to insure the survival of the State must be done by the individuals responsible for it, no matter how repugnant such an act may be to them in their private capacity as decent and moral men."[119] That definiton does not go far enough. One of the great silences of the Document of 1787, Reason of State is applicable to more than survival alone; it is perceivable in other guises as well: whenever the basic interests of the State and of those who under the operational code control the State are perceived to be jeopardized, whether from external dangers or internal turmoil. In orthodox constitutional theory, the label "Reason of State" is not employed; rather,

---

117. L. Hobhouse, The Elements of Social Justice 140-41 (1922). *See also* A. Berle, Power Without Property: A New Development in American Political Economy 4 (1959); W. Galston, Justice and the Human Good ch. 6 (1980).

118. F. Meinecke, Machiavellism: The Doctrine of Raison d'Etat and Its Place in Modern History 1 (D. Scott trans. 1957).

119. C. Friedrich, Constitutional Reason of State: The Survival of the Constitutional Order 4-5 (1957).

the principle travels under the banner of "national security" and even the "national" or "public" interest. The terms are roughly synonymous even though they have never been adequately defined. We are thus left with the parlous condition of a constitutional silence being so nebulous that no one quite knows what it precisely means. That permits maximum discretion of those in government who can invoke it. Professor Alfred Vagts once observed that "there is in the American system of government and politics no fixed or final arbiter on the question of what constitutes national interest"[120]—which was not quite correct. The State, speaking through government, is that "fixed and final arbiter."[121] Vagts should have qualified his statement to indicate that within the triad that makes up the national government, each branch can and does make national interest decisions—usually, as has been said, by working in concert.

Admiral Alfred T. Mahan, the American philosopher of sea power, wrote in 1898:

> Self-interest is not only a legitimate, but a fundamental cause for national policy; one which needs no cloak of hypocrisy. As a principle it does not require justification in general statement, although the propriety of its application to a particular instance may call for demonstrations. . . . Not every saying of Washington is as true now as it was when uttered, and some have been misapplied; but it is as true now as ever that it is vain to expect governments to act continuously *on any other ground than national interest.*
>
> It follows from this directly that the study of interests—international interests—is the one basis of sound, provident policy for statesmen. . . . Governments are corporations, and corporations have no souls . . . [they] must put first the interests of their own wards . . . their own people.[122]

Again, Mahan was not quite correct. It is not, as he suggests, the interests of all the people that are protected by invoking the national interest (Reason of State), but the interests of those who profit most under the operational code by invocations of a societal interest. Mahan also failed to perceive that the national interest had its twin insofar as domestic affairs are concerned in the concept of the public interest.

The public interest has never been defined, although it is often invoked. President John F. Kennedy once maintained that the public interest was larger than the arithmetical sum of the private interests of the people of the nation, a sentiment echoed by President Jimmy

---

120. Vagts, *Introduction,* to C. BEARD, THE IDEA OF NATIONAL INTEREST xiii, xxii (1934).
121. *Id.*
122. *Quoted in* C. BEARD, *supra* note 120, at 1-2 (footnote omitted).

Carter in his farewell address.[123] The public interest is to the bureaucracy what due process is to the judiciary: it is a wellnigh illimitable grant of authority—often by constitutional and statutory silences—for governmental officers to act with discretion, to act, that is, with little or no external standards limiting their judgment. The Supreme Court goes along. The *Barenblatt*[124] case provides a classic example. There Justice John M. Harlan invoked the national or public interest (that is, Reason of State), although he did not use those labels (he employed the term "the interests of society" instead), to enable Barenblatt to be jailed for refusing to testify before Congress.

Although Reason of State is preeminent so far as official action is concerned, *the fifteenth principle is that private property, and the protection of it, is the highest in the hierarchy of personal values under the Political Constitution.* This principle, as with the sixteenth—*that propaganda is routinely employed by government and it is the function of the mass media to be instruments of that propaganda for government*—will be discussed in Section III, dealing with the principles of the Economic Constitution.

The seventeenth principle is that the State and religion (but not the Church) are closely connected. "We are a religious people, whose institutions presuppose a Supreme Being,"[125] Justice William O. Douglas once remarked. That may well be, for despite the separation of church and State under the formal Constitution as interpreted by the Supreme Court, the operational code not only provides for subventions by government for religious entities, but also enables routine interactions between government and religion. Perhaps the major subsidy for religion is the tax exemption for church property; but many others exist: school books are purchased and buildings are financed for parochial schools, for example. Through a neat bit of judicial casuistry, those are rationalized as aids to the student, not to a church—a distinction without a true difference.

That government and religion are closely interlocked may be seen throughout the federal government—chaplains in the Senate and in the armed services; prayer breakfasts in the White House; and even in the public sessions of the Supreme Court, which are opened by a functionary bellowing "God Save This Honorable Court!" Those are a few examples of a far larger pattern. Furthermore, the State and religion come even closer together when the Document of 1787 is perceived, as

---

123.   Kennedy's statement may be found in N. Y. Times, Mar. 8, 1962, at 14, col. 5; Carter's in Miami Herald, Jan. 15, 1981, at 17A.
124.   Barenblatt v. United States, 360 U.S. 109 (1959).
125.   Zorach v. Clauson, 343 U.S. 306, 313 (1952).

it should be, as the chief artifact of the American civil or secular religion of Americanism and patriotism. That makes the Justices priests of a modern Delphic Oracle, vested with authority under the operational code to put meaning into the terms of the Document.

"Every tribe," Max Lerner remarked in 1937, "clings to something which it believes to possess supernatural powers, as an instrument for controlling unknown forces in a hostile universe."[126] The United States fits that model:

> In fact the very habits of mind begotten by an authoritarian Bible and a religion of submission to a higher power have been carried over to an authoritarian Constitution and a philosophy of submission to a 'higher law'; and a country like America, in which its earliest tradition had prohibited a state church, ends by getting a state church after all, although in a secular form.[127]

That much is obvious, or at least should be obvious, to any who would see: the Document of 1787 is a theological instrument. As long ago as 1838, Abraham Lincoln maintained there should be conscious adherence to the "political religion of the nation . . . reverence for the laws."[128] And all who saw her on television will recall the stirring words of Representative Barbara Jordan, just before voting on the impeachment of President Richard Nixon: "My faith in the Constitution is whole, it is complete, it is total, and I am not going to sit here and be an idle spectator to the diminution, the subversion of the Constitution."[129] That is a pure religious statement.

Whether defined as Americanism or patriotism or, in Lincoln's words, "reverence for the laws," there can be little question that the Document of 1787 is the principal artifact of the civil religion of the United States. As such, constitutionalism shares with organized religion the effort of Americans to bring coherence into a chaotic world. Were some means available to measure the relative importance of the two, there could be little doubt that civil religion is far more important than organized religion. Justice Felix Frankfurter perhaps stated the point when he said that even "one who has no ties with any formal religion . . . the feelings that underlie religious forms for me run into intensification of my feelings about American citizenship."[130] The sepa-

---

126. Lerner, *Constitution and Court as Symbols*, 46 YALE L.J. 1290, 1294 (1937).

127. *Id.* at 1294-95.

128. A. LINCOLN, *The Perpetuation of Our Political Institutions*, in THE POLITICAL THOUGHT OF ABRAHAM LINCOLN 16-17 (1961 ed.).

129. *Quoted in* Levinson, *The Specious Morality of the Law*, HARPER'S MAGAZINE, May 1977, at 35.

130. *Quoted in* Levinson, *"The Constitution" in American Civil Religion*, 1979 SUP. CT. REV. 123, 150-51. *See also* H. HIRSCH, THE ENIGMA OF FELIX FRANKFURTER (1981); B. MUR-

ration between church and State in America, moreover, provided a way for the employment of many of the ideas and even the symbols of organized religion into politics. Professor Samuel P. Huntington maintains that the consequence

> was to give the nation many of the attributes and functions of a church. The United States is, indeed, as G.K. Chesterton said, "a nation with the soul of a church." Fifty years later another European observer could also observe, "You don't have a country over there, you have a huge church." The point is well taken. Just as Americanism as an ideology is a substitute for socialism, at the same time that it incorporates some socialist values, so Americanism as a creed constitutes a national civil religion. The United States, Chesterton said, "is founded on a creed" that "is set forth with dogmatic and theological lucidity in the Declaration of Independence." The Declaration and the Constitution constitute the holy scripture of the American civil religion. . . . Like other religions, the American civil religion has its hymns and its sacred ceremonies, its prophets and its martyrs. It also has its mission: to create "a city on a hill," "the last best hope of earth," and to bring about a "new heaven and new earth" through its "errand in the wilderness" of the world."[131]

In sum, the Constitution in the sense of the formal document drafted in 1787 and only twenty-six times amended is *the* true religion of the American people. The operational code of the United States thus comes close to making the nation a theocracy.

The eighteenth, and final, principle is that the institutions of the Political Constitution routinely interact with those of the Economic Constitution. That pair of institutions complement each other; they cooperate routinely—much more than they conflict. Since, however, that cooperation falls under the purview of the Economic Constitution, further discussion will be deferred to Section III of this article.

To conclude this section: Paraphrasing Brian Sedgemore in his comments about government in Great Britain, only two things can be said with certainty about representative democracy in the United States today. First, it is clear beyond peradventure of doubt that effective power does not reside in the people's representatives (those Perry calls "electorally accountable" officials). Secondly, there is little that is democratic about the exercise of that power. Expressed another way, political power under the operational code of the United States is far more important than that set forth in the myth system—the Document of 1787, as amended and construed. To understand "the" Constitution

---

PHY, THE BRANDEIS/FRANKFURTER CONNECTION (1982); Levinson, *The Democratic Faith of Felix Frankfurter,* 25 STAN. L. REV. 430 (1973).

131. S. HUNTINGTON, AMERICAN POLITICS: THE PROMISE OF DISHARMONY 159 (1981) (footnote omitted).

one must first distinguish between those two systems; then go on to see that the Political Constitution has its parallel in the Economic Constitution; and finally perceive that the two are interlocked in the Corporatist Constitution.

III. THE ECONOMIC CONSTITUTION[132]

Prescient observers have for some time noted that a new constitutional structure of industry and government is emerging. Adolf Berle, building on the works of John P. Davis, was one of the first. Others include Alexander Pekelis, Max Lerner, Arthur Bentley, Leicester Webb, Walton Hamilton, Edward Mason, and Earl Latham.[133] Although written as a statement of economics only, John Kenneth Galbraith's *The New Industrial State*[134] is essentially a statement of the new constitutionalism. These writers, prominent as they are, have thus far largely been voices crying in a wilderness of orthodoxy. Furthermore, the new constitutional structure is not really novel. This section is devoted to what is perhaps the largest silence of the Document of 1787—the operations and institutions of the American economy. To most observers, the notion of an Economic Constitution will seem odd. Certainly it does not fit within the framework of thought of most constitutional lawyers. Constitutions deal with what is considered to be a purely political concept—power. Even though it has been known since John R. Commons published *Legal Foundations of Capitalism*[135] in 1924 that two types of power exist, physical (the State) and economic (property or business), the orthodoxy consigns power to public government only. Commons also suggested that a third type of power existed—moral power; but whether that is so may well be doubted.[136]

The Constitution says little about economics, probably because the economic order was taken for granted by those who controlled the 1787 convention. The federal government has the power to tax, spend, and regulate interstate commerce. Beyond that, only a few fiscal issues were

---

132. This section draws heavily on Chapter 9 of A. MILLER, TOWARD INCREASED JUDICIAL ACTIVISM: THE POLITICAL ROLE OF THE SUPREME COURT (1982); a version of that chapter appears in Miller, *The American Economic Constitution,* THE CENTER MAG. July-Aug. 1982, at 17.

133. *See* A. BENTLEY, *supra* note 45; A. BERLE, POWER WITHOUT PROPERTY (1959); A. BERLE, THE 20TH-CENTURY CAPITALIST REVOLUTION (1954); J. DAVIS, CORPORATIONS (1897); W. HAMILTON, THE POLITICS OF INDUSTRY (1957); E. LATHAM, POLITICAL THEORIES ABOUT MONOPOLY POWER (1957); M. LERNER, AMERICA AS A CIVILIZATION (1957); E. MASON, THE CORPORATION IN MODERN SOCIETY (1959); A. PEKELIS, LAW AND SOCIAL ACTION 91-127 (M. Konvitz ed. 1950); L. WEBB, LEGAL PERSONALITY AND POLITICAL PLURALISM (1958). *See also* Miller, *The Corporation as a Private Government in the World Community,* 46 VA. L. REV. 1539 (1960).

134. J. GALBRAITH, THE NEW INDUSTRIAL STATE (1967).

135. J. COMMONS, LEGAL FOUNDATIONS OF CAPITALISM (1924).

136. *Id.* at 47-64.

set forth, leaving the respective powers of the federal and state governments to gather content from experience. That experience, however, was not left to chance. An obligations-of-contracts clause was included in the document, and in 1791 a due process clause and an eminent domain provision were added—all protective of wealth and property. Since the beginnings, American policymakers have followed principles stated by Alexander Hamilton. Hamilton, the true father of the operative, and at times the formal Constitution, maintained there were no limits on Congress' power to spend. The Supreme Court has agreed. A consistent thread of policy has run through government-business relationships throughout American history: government aid to business. When President Calvin Coolidge observed that the business of the United States is business he was merely stating the commonplace—a part of the "given" of the American constitutional order.

The concept of the Economic Constitution is based upon the bedrock proposition that the American economy is, and always has been, a system of power. Power, a political concept, is fundamental to an understanding of American constitutionalism. It is a slippery term requiring definition. For present purposes, it will be taken to mean the ability or capacity to make decisions affecting the values of others, to impose deprivations or bestow rewards so as to control the behavior of others. The suggestion is not that one who exercises power need also be able to employ actual physical coercion over another. As Commons saw, the sanctions through which power is wielded can be, and usually are, much more subtle. They are economic or psychological, or both, and can be direct or indirect.

The Document of 1787 allocates *formal* power; the Bill of Rights, added in 1791, was an effort to limit that power. Informal, unofficial, private power relations are not mentioned (except for the thirteenth amendment's prohibition against involuntary servitude). The greatest and most eloquent silence of the Constitution is concerned with the organization and management of the economy into an informal system of power relations. That system consists of at least two coexistent economies: one, by far the larger quantitatively, made up of small business; and the other, smaller in number but qualitatively much more important, being the giant multistate, and increasingly multinational, corporations. Both segments are important, but our interest herein lies principally in the latter. These are the firms that set the tone for the entire political economy of the nation, the companies that have helped create a national common market—a single economic system superimposed on a decentralized political order, the super-corporations that have become major actors in the world economic order.

The Economic Constitution has two fundamental principles: contract and property. Contract is the appropriate legal instrument for effectuating a private-enterprise economy. The protection of property, according to John Locke, the intellectual father of the Constitution, was the reason for the formation of governments.[137] Professor Charles E. Lindblom has observed that "property is a system of authority established by government."[138] If that is so, then private law is the legal system of the Economic Constitution. Private law is law, not because of any inherent qualities or natural order of things, but because the State recognizes it as such. It is, in other words, a form of delegation of power from the State to private individuals and the organizations they form.

My point is that the economy exists—capitalism exists—only because it is permitted by the State. Capitalism, itself a system of power, is derivative rather than autonomous or *a priori*. "The possession of capital is a legally and politically protected means to the creation and reproduction of de facto relations of domination between individuals belonging to different classes."[139] There is an apparent, but not actual, contradiction here: The State, which is the source of all power relations within the nation, guarantees power relations that emanate from the ownership of capital.

Private control over capital in the United States is possible only because it is permitted by the State, not because of any natural or inherent right to it. That means the power exercised by private capital is a tacit but very real delegation of governing power from the State. The State—not mentioned in the Document of 1787—is a legal abstraction consisting of a public and a private sector that operates as a machine whose parts mesh. "The State organization reaches deep into the personal existence of man, forms his being."[140] For example, as Max Weber has argued, it shares with religion the ability to impart meaning to death. "The warrior's death on the battlefield," Weber suggests, "is a consecrated one, a consummation vibrant with elevated feeling. Has not the nineteenth-century State appealed all too often all too successfully to such motifs in order to send young men willingly to die (and to kill)?"[141]

The private law of the Economic Constitution meshes with the public law of the Political Constitution. Public law gives direction for

137. *Quoted in* Gramm, *Industrial Capitalism and the Breakdown of the Liberal Rule of Law,* 7 J. Econ. Issues 577, 599 n.17 (1973).

138. C. Lindblom, Politics and Markets: The World's Political Economic Systems 8 (1977).

139. G. Poggi, *supra* note 27, at 94-95.

140. Hermann Heller, a German scholar, *quoted in id.* at 99.

141. *Id.* at 99-100.

the operation of the official organs of government, and private law establishes frameworks for the activities of persons, natural and artificial, pursuing their own interests. They are two parts of one legal system—that of the American version of the corporate State. Private interests are only apparently autonomous. They can be pursued only because they do not conflict with the interests of the State itself. Those private interests are manifested through the law of obligations (both contract and tort), of property, and of corporations. In this manner, the State provides a system of private agreements which establishes horizontal arrangements between constitutional persons, a system for the enforcement of liability for private wrongs, and a set of rules for the governance of private corporations. The State's law-enforcement apparatus is placed at the disposal of persons involved in any of those matters. Indeed, without the authority of the State behind it, private law could not exist.

Under the liberal theory of the rule of law (which is predominant throughout the law schools), those horizontal transactions—promissory and otherwise—are governed by a neutral body of rules that are impartially administered. Although it has long been discredited, that theory lingers on. Sir Henry Maine asserted in 1861 that the movement of "progressive" societies was from status to contract.[142] However, that proposition was invalid when made. Necessitous men cannot be free men; the notion of arms-length bargaining in nineteenth-century contract law was more fantasy than fact. Under the labor contract, for example, an individual sold his time and energy in exchange for a wage. When business collectivized in the drive for incorporation, the bargaining power of the individual worker was by no means equal to that of the enterprise. Even so, the law assumed that it was—as it did in tort law, where during the nineteenth century the dreadful costs of industrial accidents fell in large part on those least able to pay: the workers. Judges obligingly invented rules of assumption of risk, contributory negligence, and the fellow-servant concept to insulate corporate enterprise from the human costs of industrialization.[143] This was the private-law counterpart to the Supreme Court's invalidation of legislation aimed at ameliorating conditions of the working class.[144]

Those laws were far from neutral. Judges and the law they promulgated were class-oriented, in favor of the moneyed and propertied. Oliver Wendell Holmes, before he became an Associate Justice,

---

142. H. MAINE, ANCIENT LAW (1861).

143. *Cf.* Schwartz, *Tort Law and the Economy in Nineteenth-Century America: A Reinterpretation,* 90 YALE L.J. 1717 (1981).

144. *E.g.,* Lochner v. New York, 198 U.S. 45 (1905). *Lochner* is the best known of the so-called "economic due process" decisions.

recognized that fact. In 1873 he wrote that the idea the law was neutral, impartially imposed by judges, "presupposes an identity of interest between the different parts of a community which does not exist in fact."[145] Discussing prosecution of gas-stokers who went on strike in London, Holmes asserted that not only was there no unity in law as a whole, but there was a lack of unity at the social level that eventually was translated into law. That statement was almost completely unheeded. However, it struck a mortal blow to the liberal theory of the rule of law, with its assumptions of known general rules, applied impartially, which theoretically produce effects that benefit all. Holmes maintained that the decisions of courts represented the interests of the strongest in society.

> [W]hatever body may possess the supreme power for the moment is certain to have interests inconsistent with others which have competed unsuccessfully. The more powerful interests must be more or less reflected in legislation [and judicial decisions]; which, like every other device of man or beast, must tend in the long run to aid the survival of the fittest.[146]

That, to be sure, is a bleak and despairing jurisprudential universe. But, can it be said that he was wrong—or, indeed, that he was wrong when he wrote in 1881: "[t]he first requirement of a sound body of law is, that it should correspond with the actual feelings and demands of the community, whether right or wrong"?[147]

Corporation law provides an illustration. Originally, corporations were franchised by government for limited purposes and set periods of time. As Henry Carter Adams said in 1886:

> Corporations originally were regarded as agencies of the state. They were created for the purpose of enabling the public to realize some social or national end without involving the necessity of direct governmental intervention. They were in reality arms of the state, and in order to secure efficient management, a local or private interest was created as a privilege or property of the corporation. A corporation, therefore, may be defined in the light of history as a body created by law for the purpose of attaining public ends through an appeal to private interests.[148]

---

145. Comment, *The Gas-Stokers' Strike*, 7 AM. L. REV. 582, 583 (1873). *See* Tushnet, *Truth, Justice, and the American Way: An Interpretation of Public Law Scholarship in the Seventies*, 57 TEX. L. REV. 1307 (1979).

146. Comment, *The Gas-Stokers' Strike, supra* note 145, at 583.

147. O. W. HOLMES, THE COMMON LAW 36 (1881), *quoted in* G. GILMORE, THE AGES OF AMERICAN LAW 49 (1977). Holmes did not define a "sound body of law." Whatever that term means, surely in constitutional, as well as other questions, there is a need to recognize standards of judgment external to both judges and "the community."

148. H. ADAMS, RELATION OF THE STATE TO INDUSTRIAL ACTION, AND ECONOMICS AND JURISPRUDENCE 145 (1954).

We have strayed far from that conception. Corporations still must be chartered, but their goal is single-minded: the pursuit of profit. Only by happenstance do their actions attain the public good. In other words, the State permits private greed, perhaps on the assumption that Adam Smith, whose *The Wealth of Nations*[149] was published in 1776 and was widely read in America, was correct in his benign view of the "invisible hand" that was supposed to transform personal greed into public good. The Document was written, however, when corporations were not the usual mode of doing business (only about 300 existed in all the United States as late as 1800). However, the silences of the Constitution provided ample room for capital to operate. The State helped in the accumulation of even more capital, resulting in a system of corporate capitalism. "Under capitalism the economy does not operate within the social sphere simply as 'one' factor among and coordinate with others; rather, it imperiously *sub*ordinates or otherwise reduces the independent significance of all other factors, including religion, the family, the status system, education, technology, science, and the arts."[150] In net, the economic system is a system of power—and that means that it should be considered in constitutive terms.

Corporate capitalism involves the domination by a capital-owning class over other social groups and, of course, over individual persons. That class also has managed to dominate large segments of government. It routinely interacts with and greatly influences the institutions of the Political Constitution. A class society is the inevitable consequence of corporate capitalism. To uphold it, the Supreme Court and other governmental organs managed for decades to exclude from the formal political process the claims and demands of groups which may have wanted to abolish capital ownership, modify the distribution of wealth, or interfere with the accumulation of profits. In other words, property was protected: it was, and still is, highest in the hierarchy of values guarded by the formal Constitution.

Other groups, economic and otherwise, were able to attain formal political power through the spread of the franchise and, more importantly, through the greatly increased productivity of labor. This process was accelerated by the Supreme Court's validation of New Deal measures, beginning with the *Jones & Laughlin*[151] decision in 1937. The labor unions and farmers' leagues became entities politicians had to reckon with. These changes occurred during America's true "golden age"—the time from 1945 to about 1970. As has been discussed previ-

---

149. A. Smith, The Wealth of Nations (Mod. Libr. ed. 1937).
150. G. Poggi, *supra* note 27, at 120-21.
151. NLRB v. Jones & Laughlin Steel Corp., 301 U.S. 1 (1937).

ously, by the 1980's this development has resulted in the cruel paradox that political pluralism is a failure in the United States precisely because it has been so successful. With a diminishing economic pie, as more and more groups proliferate and make demands, the divergence of interests is proving to be unworkable.[152]

The point, however, is that when the public legal order recognized under the Political Constitution the right of capital to collectivize itself—and then equated the collective with a natural person—something new under the constitutional sun came into being. By now it has become utterly clear that the economy of the corporate behemoths is a system of power, made up of quasi-polities, each with a constitutional system of its own. Those supercorporations are at once economic entities, sociological communities, political orders, and legal persons. A new social order has been created in the past 100 years—a form of neo-feudalism. In many respects, the State is subordinate to the economic process. It is deeply involved in economic tasks, seeking to help business growth while simultaneously trying to ameliorate the excesses of corporate collectivism. The consequence is that the line between politics and economics has in fact, although not in theory, been all but erased. Politics and economy syzygetically exist, making up one overarching whole: the American form of corporatism.

That means that sovereignty in the United States lies, not in the people as the myth system would have it, but in the State. The "visible" sovereign is "the" United States, which in turn is a triad of legislative, executive, and judicial powers; and the "invisible" sovereign lies in the system of private governments that exist as "worms in the entrayles" of the body politic. Since sovereignty, defined as ultimate power, is itself indivisible, that means the two types of American sovereignty are conjoined into what was termed by Otto Gierke as a "super-group-person."[153]

What, then, are the characteristics of the Economic Constitution? My thesis comes from Adam Smith: "Civil government, so far as it is instituted for the security of property, is in reality instituted for the defense of the rich against the poor, or of those who have some property against those who have none at all."[154] The putative "father" of the American Constitution, John Locke, said that "government has no

---

152. *Compare* T. Lowi, The End of Liberalism (2d ed. 1979) *with* L. Thurow, The Zero-Sum Society (1980) and R. Dahl, Dilemmas of Pluralist Democracy (1982). *See also* Beer, *The Idea of the Nation,* New Republic, July 19 & 26, 1982, at 23.

153. O. Gierke, Natural Law and the Theory of Society, 1500-1800 (E. Barker trans. 1933).

154. A. Smith, *supra* note 149, at 674.

other end but the preservation of property."[155] James Madison restated that thought in *Federalist No. 10*. There can be little question that the Founding Fathers believed in Smith and Locke, whose views have, indeed, prevailed since the beginnings.

The first principle of the Economic Constitution has already been stated and discussed: *The economy in the United States is a system of power* which has significant political consequences for the American people.

The second principle is that governing power was delegated from the State to the owners of property (the capitalists). Rather than being explicit, this delegation was left to inference and to subsequent legislation and judicial decisions. Although the economic order, as Karl Polanyi has shown,[156] was entirely isolated from the jurisdiction of the formal Constitution, protection of private property was so high in the hierarchy of values that it can be viewed as a part of the fundamental law.

The delegation of power to organizations is to be inferred from the Document itself. (It remains true that *formal* political power cannot be transferred from the legislature to private parties. We speak now of the exercise of *informal* power, in the operational code of the American Constitution.) What was *not* said in the 1787 instrument is as important as what *was* said. For centuries the State has succeeded in asserting that it is the sole source of all power relations—all *licit* power relations, that is—within the nation. Nothing can exist without its permission, express or tacit. The Founding Fathers cleverly created an elitist document, in which the State is preeminent under the Political Constitution, while simultaneously making implicit provision for a "self-regulating market economy." Such a system, according to Polanyi, is "nothing less than the institutional separation of society into an economic and political sphere."[157] Therefore, "human society" in a market economy is an "accessory of the economic system." The tail wags the dog.

It is important to realize that the market economy and its political counterpart, liberal representative democracy, was the consequence of *the* major new social force that developed in the Western world—the enormous wealth pouring into Europe following the great discoveries. In *The Great Frontier*,[158] Walter Prescott Webb has shown the immense impact that new wealth and new land had upon old institutions.

---

155. *Quoted in* Gramm, *supra* note 137, at 599 n.17.
156. K. POLANYI, THE GREAT TRANSFORMATION 225-26 (1944).
157. *Id.* at 71.
158. W. WEBB, THE GREAT FRONTIER (1952).

It is also important to realize that the "400-year boom" produced by those discoveries has now run its course; and that, accordingly, humankind in the Western world, not excluding the United States, is back in the ecological trap that characterized the pre-modern world. The portents of that development are the realities of today. Humankind finds itself not in a crisis, but in the "crisis of crises"—in a climacteric, a sea change in the way in which *Homo sapiens* confronts the environment. Perceptive observers have long known this, as evidenced in the following statement:

> The consumption of energy from fossil fuels . . . is a "pip" [on a graph] rising sharply from zero to maximum, and almost as sharply declining, representing but a moment of human history. . . . The release of this energy is a unidirectional and irreversible process. It can only happen once, and the historical events associated with this release are necessarily without precedent, and are incapable of repetition.[159]

The Document of 1787 came at a propitious time. It could not have failed: the environment was favorable. "The extraordinary affluence of the United States has been produced by a set of fortuitous, nonreplicable, and nonsustainable factors."[160] The consequences for American constitutionalism are enormous.

The American economy has always operated as a privilege from the State, and thus as a tacit delegation of power. "[T]he courts," Robert L. Hale observed in 1935, "have been blind to the fact that much of private power over others is in fact delegated by the state, and that all of it is 'sanctioned' in the sense of being permitted."[161] This power permeates the entire economic system. Those who wrote the Document of 1787 were by and large the rich and well-born who dominated government:

> Their power was born of place, position, and fortune. They were located at or near the seats of government and they were in direct contact with legislatures and government officers. They influenced and often dominated the local newspapers which voiced the ideas and interests of commerce and identified them with the good of the whole people, the state, and the nation. The published writing of the leaders of the period are almost without exception those of merchants, of their lawyers, or of politicians sympathetic with them.[162]

---

159. Hubert, *Energy From Fossil Fuels,* 109 SCIENCE 103, 108 (1949).

160. R. MILES, AWAKENING FROM THE AMERICAN DREAM: THE SOCIAL AND POLITICAL LIMITS TO GROWTH 224 (1976).

161. Hale, *Force and the State: A Comparison of "Political" and "Economic" Compulsion,* 35 COLUM. L. REV. 149, 199 (1935).

162. M. JENSEN, THE NEW NATION 178 (1950).

Those men wanted and got a free hand in commerce, accompanied by the repression of attempts by the poor and disadvantaged to better themselves. They knew a strong national government would be the best protector of their interests, and drafted the Constitution accordingly. Targeting Congress and the judiciary, and employing the principle of federal supremacy written into Article VI, they made the United States a "united State." The Document settled a revolution. "What was at stake for Hamilton, Livingston, and their opponents, was more than speculative windfalls in securities; it was the question, what kind of society would emerge from revolution when the dust had settled, and on which class the political center of gravity would come to rest."[163] By the twenty-twenty vision of hindsight, we know society was to be business dominated, and the moneyed and propertied class would control the levers of political power. That makes the Constitution of 1787 a counterrevolutionary instrument—elitist rather than populist.

The third principle is that the State established mechanisms of law without which the propertied class could not rule.

The fourth principle is that public power, the power of the Political Constitution, was and is employed to further the ends of the beneficiaries of the Economic Constitution.

The fifth principle is that society, as distinguished from both the state and government, was and is made up of classes.

The sixth principle is that the law, as enunciated by courts, is far from neutral; it has a class bias, toward those with property.

Since these principles overlap, they will be discussed together. Under the third principle, the private law of contracts and torts, of property and of corporations was, in the nineteenth century and to a large extent still is, the means by which the poor and economically disadvantaged are kept "in their places." This paralleled the Supreme Court's protection of money and property under both the obligations-of-contracts and due process clauses. The power of the State, operating through its apparatus, the government, was placed at the disposal of the moneyed class. Robert L. Hale stated the consequences:

> [I]t is so seldom recognized that when the state is enforcing contract and property rights at common law it is using its compulsory powers to effectuate the wills of private persons, and doing so in a manner which forces other private persons to forego the exercise of liberties which the state could not constitutionally deny them in furtherance of any legislative policy of its own. . . .[164]

---

163. S. Lynd, Class Conflict, Slavery and the United States Constitution 113 (1967).

164. Hale, *Our Equivocal Constitutional Guaranties,* 39 Colum. L. Rev. 563, 576 (1939).

Similarly, the judge-made rules of tort law forced the workers—those least able to do so—to bear the brunt of the costs of industrialization. And so also with contracts of adhesion, which are far from arms-length transactions. Those contracts, which generally emanate from the corporate behemoths, are another tacit delegation of power to those firms to legislate the terms of promissory obligations. Those who enter into such agreements exemplify a remark of Justice Holmes:

> In order to enter into most of the relations of life people have to give up some of their constitutional rights. If a man makes a contract he gives up the Constitutional right that previously he had to be free from the hamper that he puts upon himself. Some rights, no doubt, a person is not allowed to renounce, but very many he may. . . . Every contract is the acceptance of some inequality.[165]

Although corporations are constitutional persons—in the eyes of the law, the same as natural persons—the sheer economic strength of corporate giants enables them to issue standardized contracts on a take-it-or-leave-it basis. (When one leaves it, he usually learns that he must deal on roughly the same terms with some other private government.)

Corporations as constitutional persons have contributed greatly to the thin fiction that the firms—particularly the giants—are "private." It is quite obvious they are not private, save that their shares are often owned by natural persons. They are collectives; as such, they have governing power: "[a] corporation is government through and through. . . . Certain technical methods which political government uses, as, for instance, hanging, are not used by corporations, generally speaking, but that is a detail."[166] Arthur Bentley wrote that in 1908, yet three-quarters of a century later the lawyer-judges on the Supreme Court still stoutly refuse to acknowledge what all but the willfully blind can see.

As for the fourth principle, the Economic Constitution, illustrating Hamiltonian principles, permitted—perhaps commanded—massive public aid to private business. The United States has always been a welfare State for the affluent. The federal government, now and in the past, may be likened to a great recumbent sow, with dozens of teats to each one of which is attached some recipient of largesse from the national treasury. Billions of dollars are disbursed each year in the form of grants, direct subsidies, or otherwise. Even the Queen of England has received $68,000 for not producing anything on her plantation in

See also Cohen, *Property and Sovereignty,* 13 Cornell L.Q. 8 (1927).

165. Power Mfg. Co. v. Saunders, 274 U.S. 490, 497-98 (1927).

166. A. Bentley, *supra* note 45, at 268.

Mississippi![167]

As Matthew Josephson noted in 1934:

> [T]his benevolent government handed over to its friends or to the astute
> first comers . . . all those treasures of coal and oil, of copper and gold
> and iron, the land grants, the terminal sites, the perpetual rights of
> way—an act of largesse which is still one of the wonders of history. To
> the new railroad enterprises in addition, great money subsidies totaling
> many hundreds of millions were given. The Tariff Act of 1864 was in
> itself a sheltering wall of subsidies; and to aid further the new heavy
> industries and manufactures, an Immigration Act allowing contract la-
> bor to be imported freely was quickly enacted; a national banking system
> was perfected. . . . Having conferred these vast rights and controls, the
> . . . government would preserve them . . . so as to "curb the many who
> would do to the few as they would not have the few do to them."[168]

The close connection between government and private enterprise is not
noted in constitutional law books, perhaps because it was never litigated. The largesse Josephson mentioned came from statutory action,
by both Congress and state legislatures, and thus is not constitutional
law in the eyes of most lawyers. Surely, however, it is a part of the
constitutive process of the United States, particularly since the institutions of the Economic Constitution have widely and deeply affected the
organs of the Political Constitution. For example, the regulatory movement so often attributed to populism and the program of progressives
early in this century was in fact a successful effort by the business community to help stave off the destructive effects of too much competition.[169] The myth is to the contrary, to be sure, but it is just that, a
myth.

Those who wrote the Document of 1787 got the type of government they desired. Chief Justice John Marshall and colleagues saw to
that. Congress, too, was the quite willing ally of the propertied class, a
class that simply did not like democracy as such. As Alexander Hamilton said in the 1787 convention:

> All communities divide themselves into the few and the many. The first
> are the rich and the well-born, the other the mass of the people. The
> voice of the people has been said to be the voice of God; and however
> generally this maxim has been quoted and believed, it is not true in fact.
> The people are turbulent and changing; they seldom judge or determine
> right. Give therefore to the first class a distinct, permanent share in gov-
> ernment. They will check the unsteadiness of the second, and as they

---

167. N.Y. Times, July 11, 1973, at 17, col. 1. *See* M. PARENTI, DEMOCRACY FOR THE FEW
77 (3d ed. 1977).

168. M. JOSEPHSON, THE ROBBER BARONS 52 (1934) (footnote omitted).

169. *See* G. KOLKO, THE TRIUMPH OF CONSERVATISM (1967).

cannot receive any advantage by a change, they therefore will ever maintain good government.[170]

The Constitution of 1787 did just that: it did not permit the propertyless majority to act in concert against the established social order.

Socialism for the affluent has always characterized American government, but has seldom been controversial. Those Hamilton called "the rich and well-born" have always been able to suckle at the teats of the recumbent sow, the federal treasury. Only when welfareism is aimed at alleviating some of the distresses of the poor and the disadvantaged do the programs become controversial. That is so even though such programs are neither income nor wealth distributive. The same small percentage of people control the same large amount of wealth today as in the past. True, more people were able to sup at the groaning table of opulence during the post-World War II period, but that was because of rising levels of productivity accompanied by the realization that mass discontent could be diverted and distracted, and even mollified, by welfare programs.

The meaning is clear: the United States has always been a class society, the myth to the contrary notwithstanding. That is the fifth principle of the Economic Constitution. Certainly, classes are not mandated by law; and the American ethos and myth structure militate against them. Nonetheless, they exist, and are protected by the State as a derivation from the disproportionate wealth between the few and the many. The drafters of the Constitution were quite aware of the stratified nature of American society, and they produced an instrument that helped to perpetuate it. Of course, social mobility has always occurred, and still does, in some degree. Some were and are able to bootstrap their way to become a part of the rich. They may not have been "well-born," but being rich meant that their children are.

Furthermore, through a subtle legitimation process the dominant class is able to assert that it is representative and an advocate of all the people. The governing class rules by identifying with the people—with the myths and legends of democracy and popular sovereignty. The people generally are convinced, by one means or another, that their interests and those of the ruling class are identical. One of the functions of the American mass media is to persuade the people to accept our system as it is defined by the elite. Max Weber knew this when he observed that privileged groups have the ability "to have their social and economic positions 'legitimized'." Weber said: "They wish to see their positions transformed from a purely factual power relation into a cos-

---

170. 1 RECORDS OF THE FEDERAL CONVENTION (M. Ferrand ed. 1927), *quoted in* M. PARENTI, *supra* note 167, at 44.

mos of acquired rights, and to know that they are thus sanctified."[171] The man of position and fortune is seldom satisfied with merely being fortunate; he knows that if his property is to be secure it must have legitimacy in society. That is, the man of fortune

> needs to know that he has a *right* to his good fortune. He wants to be convinced that he 'deserves' it, and above all, that he deserves it in comparison with others. He wishes to be allowed the belief that the less fortunate also merely experience his due. Good fortune thus wants to be 'legitimate' fortune.[172]

And further: "Strata in solid possession of social honor and power usually tend to fashion their status-legend in such a way as to claim a special and intrinsic quality of their own, usually a quality of blood."[173] A status-legend is a myth that both soothes the consciences of the rich and serves to sanctify their dominance in a class-ridden and unequal society. One way that status-legends are perpetuated (and perpetrated) is through the basic myth of the American legal system—the rule of law, impartially created and administered.

That suggests the sixth principle—that the law is distinctly not a neutral force in society. I have already mentioned Holmes' challenging comment in 1873 about the nonneutrality of the law, a comment that has never been satisfactorily answered. The tough-minded Holmes saw that all participants in legal affairs are struggling to win their self-interests. One may hope that compassion will temper self-interest, but "[a]ll that can be expected from modern improvements is that legislation should easily and quickly, yet not too quickly, modify itself in accordance with the will of the *de facto* supreme power in the community."[174] Surely Holmes was correct, which means the liberal theory of the rule of law is completely discredited. Under that theory, the assumption is that *general* rules, applied *impartially*, will produce effects beneficial to all of society. Professor Mark Tushnet has maintained that "law in a class society [such as the United States] is one form of the incomplete hegemony of the ruling class."[175] Or, in Holmes' words, law is "a means by which a body, having the power, puts burdens which are disagreeable to them on the shoulders of somebody else."[176] And Professor Jerold Auerbach in his brilliant book *Unequal Justice*[177] has

---

171. M. WEBER, *The Meaning of Discipline,* in FROM MAX WEBER: ESSAYS IN SOCIOLOGY 262 (H. Gerth & C. Mills eds. 1958).
172. *Id.* at 271.
173. *Id.* at 276.
174. Comment, *The Gas-Stokers' Strike, supra* note 145, at 583.
175. Tushnet, *supra* note 145, at 1346.
176. Comment, *The Gas-Stokers' Strike, supra* note 145, at 584.
177. J. AUERBACH, UNEQUAL JUSTICE (1976).

maintained—persuasively, in my view—that the criminal law is a means by which the poor and disadvantaged are controlled.

It will not do to shrug off such comments and proceed on ancient but faulty assumptions about the neutrality of law and the legal process. The hegemony of the ruling class may be incomplete, but that should not be taken to mean that the ultimate beneficiaries of the legal system are not Hamilton's "rich and well-born."

The seventh principle is that *the State intervenes when necessary to correct imperfections in the market economy*. That means institutions of the Economic Constitution, corporations and others (such as farmers), can draw upon organs of the Political Constitution for assistance. The consequence is one we have already adumbrated: the merger of the two constitutions into one over-arching entity, the super-group-person called the Corporate State.

The measures taken to combat the Great Depression clearly show that State intervention in the economy is not only necessary but welcome. President Franklin D. Roosevelt's New Deal, despite fervent beliefs to the contrary, was a means of preserving the system of corporate capitalism at minimum cost to those with wealth. It was not so much the misery of millions that motivated and brought government aid as it was the threat of social and political turmoil. Roosevelt's administration was primarily dedicated to business recovery rather than social reform. Although the rhetoric was otherwise, the reality of the New Deal was its service to corporate capitalism. Social discontent was defused by a series of programs aimed at alleviating the worst aspects of poverty. The New Deal is now commonly recognized as a failure. Barton J. Bernstein, writing of the conservative achievements of liberal reform, concluded:

> The New Deal failed to solve the problem of depression, it failed to raise the impoverished, it failed to redistribute income, it failed to extend equality and generally countenanced racial discrimination and segregation. It failed generally to make business more responsible to the social welfare or to threaten business's pre-eminent political power. In this sense, the New Deal, despite the shifts in tone and spirit from the earlier decade, was profoundly conservative and continuous with the 1920s.[178]

Only the coming of a war economy enabled the nation to pull itself out of the swamp of economic misery afflicting so many Americans.

After the Second World War, however, the United States entered into its true golden age. It was a time when all things seemed possible and, indeed, many were. It was a time of economic abundance; a time

---

178. Bernstein, *The New Deal: The Conservative Achievements of Liberal Reform*, in Towards A New Past 264-65 (B. Bernstein ed. 1968).

of enhancement of civil rights and liberties. The connection between economic growth—the age of abundance—and furtherance of human rights has been little noted and never analyzed. Surely it can be said, nonetheless, that there is *some* causal connection—and *some* causal connection between today's diminution of rights, as seen through Supreme Court eyes, and the end of America's golden age. The Nixon Court knows this, at least intuitively, and is once more placing property rights first, this time under the leadership of Justice William Rehnquist.[179]

The seventh principle of the Economic Constitution may also be seen historically, in the way the Army was used to quell labor disputes and other civil disorders which threatened the corporate class. Jerry M. Cooper has concluded that military leaders tried to exploit civilian fears of a disorderly working class to further the Army's interests. Troops were used to police labor troubles.

> Conflicts over the rights of property in contrast with the needs of individuals, inevitably . . . engendered social turmoil. The advocates of property and the new values [of corporate capitalism] . . . controlled the agencies of government and hence the institutions of social control. Police, the National Guard, and the Army were committed to maintaining existing power relationships in the name of law and order.[180]

Cooper's focus was upon the nineteenth century; surely, however, the same pattern may be seen in this century.

The Pullman strike during the 1890's classically illustrates how corporate capitalists were able to call upon both the courts and the Executive for assistance. The President broke the strike through use of federal troops. And the Supreme Court went along: *In re Debs*[181] is a prime example of the judiciary in effect becoming an arm of the business class. (The law the Justices created in *Debs* was tailored to the circumstances, as the Senate Watergate Committee learned in its abortive effort to obtain the infamous White House "tapes.")[182]

International economic matters reveal a similar pattern. Corporate managers have long been able to define the axiomatic in American foreign economic policy. For example, it is axiomatic that force be used to help American business abroad. Witness a statement by General Smed-

---

179. See Fiss & Krauthammer, *The Rehnquist Court,* NEW REPUBLIC, Mar. 10, 1982, at 14, 21; Miller, *Divisive Rancor on the Supreme Court,* Miami Herald, July 4, 1982, at 4E; Van Alstyne, *The Recrudescence of Property Rights as the Foremost Principle of Civil Liberties: The First Decade of the Burger Court,* LAW & CONTEMP. PROBS., Summer 1980, at 66.

180. J. COOPER, THE ARMY AND CIVIL DISORDER xiv-xv (1980).

181. 158 U.S. 564 (1895).

182. Senate Select Comm. on Presidential Campaign Activities v. Nixon, 366 F. Supp. 51, 55 n.5 (D.D.C. 1973).

ley D. Butler, former commander of the Marines:

> I spent thirty-three years and four months in active service as a member of our country's most agile military force—the Marine Corps. . . . And during that period I spent most of my time being a high-class muscle man for Big Business, for Wall Street, and for the bankers. In short, I was a racketeer for capitalism. . . . Thus I helped make Mexico and especially Tampico safe for American oil interests in 1914. I helped make Haiti and Cuba a decent place for the National City Bank boys to collect revenues . . . . I helped purify Nicaragua for the international banking house of Brown Brothers in 1909-1912. I brought light to the Dominican Republic for American sugar interests in 1916. I helped make Honduras right for American fruit companies in 1903. In China in 1927 I helped see to it that Standard Oil went its way unmolested.[183]

The pattern still continues. For example, whether the lives of American hostages in Iran were the first priority of government has been doubted. The decision to freeze Iranian assets "was not a desire to punish Iran for taking the hostages, but fear that a sudden withdrawal of those assets might set off a major currency and banking crisis for the United States." Private banks, such as Citibank and Chase, "stood to lose a lot of money if Iran repudiated its debt."[184]

Control over the levers of political power is aided by the eighth principle: *The mass media of communication are privately owned and are the principal instruments of propaganda in the United States.* "Not the gun but the word is the symbol of authority."[185] To gain public acceptance, those with wealth and property must be able to control or greatly influence the flow of information to the people.

The American mass media—the three television networks, the major news magazines, the handful of important newspapers—all have similar functions: in essence, making a profit for the owners, helping to sell consumer goods through advertising, and helping to socialize the people by a flow of news and opinions that supports corporate capitalism and the "American way." Other publications of course exist, but they have small circulations and little impact on public opinion. Furthermore, despite the seemingly absolute language of the first amendment, publications considered to be dangerous to the State's interests have been and are suppressed by one means or another.[186]

---

183. *Quoted in* S. Lens, The Forging of the American Empire 270-71 (1971).

184. Lissakers, *Money and Manipulation,* Foreign Policy, Fall 1981, at 107, 114. *See also* A. Sampson, The Money Lenders (1981).

185. C. Lindblom, Politics and Markets 52 (1977).

186. Several well known first amendment cases evidence this. *See* Haig v. Agee, 453 U.S. 280 (1981); Snepp v. United States, 444 U.S. 507 (1980); Dennis v. United States, 341 U.S. 494

The net result is a virtual monopoly of effective or influential expression in the United States, held by those who are themselves part of the Establishment and thus oriented toward preservation of the system of corporate capitalism. Far from being in an adversarial relationship, government (public or private) and the media are in fact close allies.[187] Almost no serious criticism of much of the public or private government of the nation appears in the mass media. There are exceptions, of course, but they tend to be rare rather than routine. Despite belief to the contrary, the *Washington Post* did not bring down President Nixon; it was only one of at least three, perhaps, four important actors in Watergate. For example, had the Senate Committee not discovered the existence of the Nixon tapes, he would doubtless have stayed in office. Since Watergate, the media have been anything but zealous in their relationship with government. Being part of the Establishment themselves, media personnel generally share the assumptions, ethos, expectations, and aspirations of the dominant group in society.

The ninth principle is that the institutions of the Economic Constitution operate with a high degree of secrecy. Professor Samuel P. Huntington maintains that "[t]he coexistence in America of the anti-power ethic with inequality in power gives rise to what may be termed the 'power paradox': effective power is unnoticed power; power observed is power devalued."[188] There is no Freedom of Information Act for corporations. Nor do the media deal with more than the occasional: the media managers resolutely eschew viewing corporations as centers of economic power. That means in the United States, and elsewhere, there is a lot of "democratic make-believe."[189]

The tenth principle is that the institutions of the Economic Constitution are not subject to the limitations of the Political Constitution. The Economic Constitution, as the Political Constitution, is an expression of a system of powers rather than limitations. The only difference between the two fundamental laws is that public officials are purportedly limited by the Constitution, while officers of the private governments are not. As we have seen in Section II, politics rather than

---

(1951); Gitlow v. New York, 268 U.S. 652 (1925); Schenck v. United States, 249 U.S. 47 (1919); United States v. The Progressive, Inc., 467 F. Supp. 990 (W.D. Wis.), *appeal dismissed,* 610 F.2d 819 (7th Cir. 1979).

187. *See* R. Cirino, Don't Blame the People (1972); J. Herbers, No Thank You, Mr. President (1976); P. Knightley, The First Casualty (1975); P. Lazarsfeld & R. Merton, Mass Communications, Popular Taste, and Organized Social Action, *cited in* N. Chomsky, For Reasons of State 205 (1973). *But cf.* J. Barron, Public Rights and the Private Press (1981).

188. S. Huntington, *supra* note 131, at 75.

189. Bay, *Access to Human Knowledge as a Human Right,* in Government Secrecy in Democracies 22 (I. Galnoor ed. 1977).

interdictory law tends to be the controlling influence over public officials. A difference may be seen, no doubt, between those at the highest and those at the lowest levels of office, with discretion within political limits characterizing the former much more than the latter. R.M. Hartwell of Oxford University has said it well:

> If individualism was the motivating spirit of the Renaissance, rationalism the guiding principle of the Enlightenment, and laissez-faire that of the industrial revolution, politicization is the prevailing characteristic of our age. *Politicization,* however, is a relatively new word in the vocabulary of politics. Politicization can be defined as that now pervasive tendency for making all questions political questions, all issues political issues, all values political values, and all decisions political decisions. As Julien Benda observed as early as 1927: "The present age is essentially the age of politics." Half a century later almost all social phenomena have become politicized, and almost all social problems are assumed to have only political solutions.[190]

In sum, "the" Constitution of the United States has been politicized. Whether we like it or not—and I do not—the power of the State is all-pervasive, with the State being a super-group-person consisting of the joinder of political and economic power.

To be sure, under the Political Constitution there is at least nominal attention accorded constitutional limitations. But under the Economic Constitution, corporate managers are self-appointed oligarchs responsible to no one but themselves. No Bill of Rights or fourteenth amendment applies to them, the Supreme Court being unwilling to recognize what should be plain to all: the social power of corporate managers. It would be quite easy for the Justices to define the state-action concept to include private governments; but, other than an occasional decision such as *Marsh v. Alabama,*[191] they have not done so. John F. Davis said in 1897 that Americans are "governed more by corporations than by the State" and that corporations "are the major part of the mechanism of government under which they live."[192] That knowledge has not yet penetrated the Marble Palace.

Inequality in the economic sphere is largely taken for granted, as compared with the efforts, thus far largely futile, to further equality in the political sphere. The reason for this, according to Robert F. Hale, is that "[e]quality before the law . . . is not consistent with unequal property rights."[193] And further:

---

190. Hartwell, *Introduction* in THE POLITICIZATION OF SOCIETY 7, 14 (K. Templeton, Jr., ed. 1979) (emphasis in original).

191. 326 U.S. 501 (1946).

192. J. DAVIS, CORPORATIONS 268 (1897) (1961 paperback ed.).

193. Hale, *Economics and Law,* in THE SOCIAL SCIENCES AND THEIR INTERPRETATION 131

> The premise of legal equality . . . [is] in fact fallacious, for legal rights, privileges, and duties depend on property rights and these depend on the law. Each person has a legal duty not to infringe any other person's property rights, a privilege to use what he himself owns and a right to exclude everyone else therefrom except on his own terms. These statements, however, are empty abstractions until it is specified to what particular objects the property rights of each attach; when it is so specified, the specious equality disappears. . . . The respective legal rights of A and B are equal only in the most formal and empty sense. . . . The ultimate economic position of each person is not so rigidly predetermined at birth as in the feudal system, but the law still imposes vastly unequal handicaps.[194]

Formal equality under the Political Constitution, insofar as it has been attained, is largely meaningless because of the manifest inequalities permitted under the Economic Constitution.

The consequence is that the institutions of the Economic Constitution are profoundly undemocratic. However one defines the word "democracy," by no criterion are corporations and other economic entities democratic. They are authoritarian, exemplifying Michels' "iron law of oligarchy."[195] The further consequence is that the authoritarianism of the Economic Constitution—which is a part of the operational code of "the" American Constitution—tends to influence the behavior of the institutions of the Political Constitution.

The eleventh principle is that of citizenship. Two points merit mention. First is the way in which corporations, particularly the giants, appear to owe allegiance to no nation-state. This becomes of special significance because so many of the supercorporations have become international.[196] Second is the fact that the allegiance of corporate managers seems to run more to the enterprise than to the nation-state. The identifications and loyalties—the bundle of rights and duties subsumed under the concept of citizenship—attach in the first place to the firm. Corporate managers and others operate under a theory of *raison de groupe,* similar to the way that officers of the Political Constitution operate under a theory of *raison d'etat.* The welfare of the firm is the *summum bonum,* with the executives often acting on pure Machiavellian principles.[197]

The final principle is that the governing institutions of the Eco-

---

(W. Ogburn & A. Goldenweiser eds. 1927).

194. Hale, *Labor Law, Anglo-American,* 8 ENCY. SOC. SCI. 669 (1932).

195. Michels' famous "iron law" may be found in R. MICHELS, POLITICAL PARTIES (1915).

196. *See, e.g.,* Miller, *The Multinational Corporation and the Nation-State,* 7 J. WORLD TRADE L. 267 (1973).

197. A. MILLER, DEMOCRATIC DICTATORSHIP: THE EMERGENT CONSTITUTION OF CONTROL 99-103 (1981).

nomic Constitution are markedly similar to those of the Political Constitution. The corporation is a political order, both in its internal operations and in its relationships with other economic entities and with public government. Supercorporations should be studied as political institutions as well as commercial or economic enterprises. They are also sociological communities.

Consider, for example, the widespread use of private judiciaries. Labor arbitration is a clear example, as is the employment of arbitrators in international economic affairs. Most disputes concerning multinational corporations are settled by private courts. Consider, too, the increasing use of private police forces—security forces—which can be likened to private armies. In addition, there is frequent use of intelligence forces, particularly in the area of industrial espionage. The supercorporations also have their own constitutions, either in the corporate charter and by-laws or in the collective bargaining agreement with a labor union.

To conclude this section: If we want to think critically and intelligently about "the" Constitution, we must include the dimension of the Economic Constitution. Like it or not, the economy *is* a system of power—and thus constitutive in nature. John P. Davis pointed out that during the sixteenth century a change took place that has had great influence on the way corporations are perceived.

> The standpoint from which all institutions were viewed was shifted from society as a whole to the individual. Social forces were conceived as moving from below and not from above. The destruction of tradition and the elevation of reason was one phase of the change. To be sure, the view was not to find full expression in philosophy until the eighteenth century, but the Reformation was a practical application of it. Private contract largely superseded status in the determination of social relations. Corporations were viewed not so much as divisions of society as associations of individuals. They were now enlarged individuals, not reduced societies.[198]

A major task of constitutional scholars today, and thus of the Supreme Court, is to recognize in formal constitutional theory that corporations, the dominant institution of the Economic Constitution, are more divisions of society than associations of individuals. They are a substantial part of the operational code of "the" Constitution.

IV. THE CONSTITUTION OF THE THIRD "ISM": CORPORATISM

And so I end where I began. Perry is correct, but only as far as he goes—which is not nearly far enough. We will never have an adequate theory of judicial review until there is a full understanding of what is

---

198. J. DAVIS, *supra* note 192, at 246.

meant by "the" Constitution. That means the theory must be one of the third "ism"—not capitalism and not socialism, but corporatism. Recall: "The twentieth century will be the century of corporatism just as the nineteenth was the century of liberalism."[199] Constitutional commentators have not yet confronted that, either to refute it or to analyze it or even to note it.[200] In this concluding section, some general observations about American corporatism are proffered. My theme comes from an important article by Phillippe C. Schmitter:

> Societal corporatism is found imbedded in political systems with relatively autonomous, multilayered territorial units; open, competitive electoral processes and party systems; ideologically varied, coalitionally based executive authorities—even with highly "layered" or "pillared" subcultures . . . . Societal corporatism appears to be the concomitant, if not ineluctable, component of the postliberal, advanced capitalist, organized democratic welfare state. . . . [201]

Schmitter distinguishes societal corporatism from State corporatism, which he defines as polities

> associated with political systems in which territorial subunits are tightly subordinated to central bureaucratic power; elections are nonexistent or plebiscitary; party systems are dominated or monopolized by a weak single party; executive authorities are ideologically exclusive and more narrowly recruited and are such that political subcultures based on class, ethnicity, language, or regionalism are suppressed.[202]

My suggestion is that the United States has traveled well down the road toward societal corporatism, and that at times it has overtones of State corporatism. Pluralism is in decay as the operative ideology of American politics and political scientists, and with it much of the theory of liberal democracy.[203] John Maynard Keynes, with uncanny prescience, foresaw in 1925 that "the government will have to take on many more duties which it has avoided in the past." The goal, he said, was to exercise "directive intelligence . . . over the many intricacies of private business, yet . . . leave private initiative and enterprise unhindered."[204] Specifically, he noted the need for control over currency and credit, widespread dissemination of data relating to business, and

---

199. Schmitter, *supra* note 83, at 85.

200. *But see* A. MILLER, THE MODERN CORPORATE STATE: PRIVATE GOVERNMENTS AND THE AMERICAN CONSTITUTION (1976).

201. Schmitter, *supra* note 83, at 105.

202. *Id.*

203. *See, e.g.,* R. DAHL, DILEMMAS OF PLURALIST DEMOCRACY (1982); H. KARIEL, THE DECLINE OF AMERICAN PLURALISM (1961).

204. Keynes, *Am I A Liberal?,* in ESSAYS IN PERSUASION 331 (1931) (reprint of speech delivered in 1925).

judgments as to the scale on which the community should save, the scale on which the savings should go abroad, and rationalization of investment markets. In sum, he advocated societal corporatism—precisely what has come about in the United States and some Western nations:

> I believe that in many cases the ideal size for the unit of control and organization lies somewhere between the individual and the modern state. I suggest, therefore, that progress lies in the growth and recognition of semi-autonomous bodies within the state—bodies whose criterion of action . . . is solely the public good as they understand it, and from whose deliberations motives of private advantage are excluded, though some place it may still be necessary to leave, until the ambit of man's altruism grows wider, to the separate advantage of particular groups, classes, or faculties—bodies which in their ordinary course of affairs are mainly autonomous within their prescribed limitations, but are subject in the last resort to the sovereignty of democracy expressed through Parliament. I propose a return, it may be said, towards medieval conceptions of separate autonomies.[205]

What Keynes did not see was that "the sovereignty of democracy expressed through parliament" (or Congress) has become, not "the last resort" but often the prisoner of those "semi-autonomous bodies within the state."

The modern State and modern interest groups—corporations, unions, farmers leagues, veterans legions, and the like—seek each other out. Andrew Shonfield has shown in his magisterial *Modern Capitalism*[206] that the State seeks to foster maximum employment, promote economic growth, curb inflation, smooth out business cycles, regulate conditions of work, help alleviate individual economic and social risks, and resolve labor disputes. This, Shonfield calls corporatist: "[t]he major interest groups are brought together and encouraged to conclude a series of bargains about their future behaviour, which will have the effect of moving economic events along the desired path."[207] (How far that can be done in fact is by no means certain. It may be, as David Ehrenfeld maintains, "the arrogance of humanism" for humans to think that they can rationally guide and control their affairs.)[208]

Time and space permit only an adumbration of the idea of American corporatism. In a longer essay published in 1976, I ventured a pre-

---

205. *Id.* at 313-14.
206. A. Shonfield, Modern Capitalism: The Changing Balance of Public and Private Power 231 (1965).
207. *Id. See* Schmitter, *supra* note 83, at 112-15.
208. D. Ehrenfeld, The Arrogance of Humanism (1978).

liminary definition of the "corporate State, American style."[209] There is little reason to vary that evaluation today; if anything, events since 1976 have produced additional evidence that Americans are moving toward, and in significant respects have already reached, the third great "ism." This was and is being done when liberal democracy and normative constitutionalism are still the operative belief-systems of most constitutional commentators—and to the extent the Justices have a discernible philosophy, of the Supreme Court also.

Professor Howard J. Wiarda has suggested in an important essay that much of the debate about capitalism and socialism, or between liberals and their critics, is irrelevant and misses the point. To him, the issue in last analysis is what form American corporatism will take:

> [I]t is time for Americans . . . to begin putting away their narrow and ethnocentric biases, to terminate the literature and thinking that sees the United States as superior and more 'developed' not only in the economic sense (also now questionable in a way it wasn't a decade ago) but politically, socially, and morally as well, and to begin comprehending our own conditions in the light not of some ancient and now largely imaginary or mythical liberal model but from a truly comparative perspective and in the light of the European-Iberic-Latin corporatist model which socially and politically we now also approximate.[210]

The "liberal model" Wiarda mentions is of classical liberalism—that of John Stuart Mill and others—epitomized, for example, in the Supreme Court's marketplace-of-truth theory of the first amendment. It is part of the inarticulated assumptions of much, perhaps most, constitutional commentary, including Professor Perry. Perry illustrates a modern version of Holmes' comment in 1899: "I sometimes tell law students that the law schools pursue an inspirational combined with a logical method, that is, the postulates are taken for granted upon authority without inquiry into their worth, and then logic is used as the only tool to develop the results."[211] Eighty-three years later, that statement remains sound. What is important in constitutional commentary are the postulates—the premises—that are taken for granted. Professor Perry seems to adhere to these postulates: (a) the United States is a representative democracy; (b) whatever was done in the past, particularly by the Supreme Court, has a special significance, so that it carries with it the presumption that it should be repeated today; (c) those who drafted

---

209. A. MILLER, *supra* note 200.

210. Wiarda, *The Latin Americanization of the United States*, 7 NEW SCHOLAR 51, 84-85 (1979). Wiarda also says: "The issue is no longer liberalism or something else but rather what form corporatism will take." *Id.* at 84.

211. O. W. HOLMES, *Law In Science and Science In Law*, in COLLECTED LEGAL PAPERS 238 (1920).

the Document of 1787 had a special wisdom and a rare prescience: they acted not only for themselves but for generations yet unborn; (d) lawyers are uniquely qualified to discern and articulate the meaning of the words written in 1787; (e) national uniformity in policy is a "good"; (f) in America, process is what counts: "deliberation is about means and presupposes that the problem of ends has been settled";[212] (g) man is capable through the exercise of reason of moving steadily toward perfecting the good life; (h) there is no problem, however novel or complex, that cannot be handled within the confines of the Document of 1787—even though most constitutional decisions, says Perry, are "noninterpretive" in nature; and (i) there is such a thing as a pure legal problem, separate and apart from the political economy of the nation.

Other postulates may exist, but those will suffice to show the pattern. Professor Perry's exposition is valid to the extent the postulates are valid. I believe that most, perhaps all, of them are faulty, at least in part. One is singled out for discussion here—the last one listed.

A.   The Socioeconomic Context

Any perusal of the writings on constitutionalism, constitutional law, and the Supreme Court soon makes one fact stand out clearly: most disquisitions are exercises in intellectual abstraction, without reference to the political economy and other relevant data. Such preoccupation with what judges—a few hundred middle-aged or elderly men, plus a few women—have had to say about constitutionalism is a form of legal reductionism.[213] Without adequate contextual analyses, most commentary is fatally flawed (including Professor Perry's). For most commentators, history seems to have begun with the "immaculate conception" of the Constitution of 1787 and the government formed under it in 1789. Little of constitutional importance is thought to have happened before that time. On occasion some reference is made to the colonial experiences and even to smidgens of English history, but those references are at best mere simulacra. Not even the Articles of Confederation receive adequate attention. The result is a mountain of commentaries that exemplify legalism. We have a plethora of doctrinal exegeses of nebulous constitutional language, resembling medieval Scholastics arguing endlessly over Aristotle and other ancients and modern divines interpreting the sacred texts of the Bible, the Talmud, and the Koran. The time has come—indeed, it is long past—when

---

212.   Y. SIMON, PHILOSOPHY OF DEMOCRATIC GOVERNMENT 123 (1951).

213.   *See* Miller, *Reductionism in the Law Schools, or, Why the Blather About the Motivation of Legislators?*, 16 SAN DIEGO L. REV. 891 (1979).

modern-day Scholasticism should be replaced by studies that view constitutions and judicial review in the total socioeconomic context.

At this time I do not intend to do more than mention a major factor that seems to be indispensable in analyzing the nature and direction of American constitutionalism today. What follows immediately below is based upon one bedrock proposition: that normative constitutionalism and its institutions—the private enterprise system, liberal democracy, attention to limitations on government—are derived from the Great Discoveries of the sixteenth and seventeenth centuries and the consequent wealth that poured into Western Europe and its colonies, including the United States. As a corollary, the unique socioeconomic conditions following the Great Discoveries have now vanished. If that be so—and I do not think it can be gainsaid—then the assumptions of orthodox constitutional commentary listed above are demonstrably faulty. The task, therefore, of constitutional scholarship is to develop a theory and policy appropriate for the modern age and the foreseeable future.

It is futile beyond measure to argue "interpretivism" versus "noninterpretivism."[214] To answer Thomas Grey: of course we have an unwritten Constitution. To answer Munzer and Nickel: of course the Constitution means something different today from what it meant in the past.[215] The Constitution has always been relative to circumstances. To be sure, the words remain the same but their content changes through time. Even a number of silences have been filled by governmental action. It could not be otherwise. Government is not a static system: it is organic; a process, Darwinian and Einsteinian rather than Newtonian.[216] All governments are Darwinian, whether or not they have written fundamental laws and whether they are democratic or authoritarian. Molded by their environments, their decisions are reflections of social conditions.

What, then, are the relevant circumstances to which the Constitution must adapt? During the past 300 years many institutions that Americans consider to be the natural order of human affairs were born: representative democracy, capitalism, individualism. Were one to ask

---

214.   Professor Philip Kurland calls them "pedantic expressions," and I agree. *See* Kurland, *Curia Regis: Some Comments on the Divine Right of Kings and Courts "To Say What the Law Is,"* 23 ARIZ. L. REV. 581, 586 (1981). My point, however, is different: The Supreme Court has always been "noninterpretivist"; those who dislike such activism are making "should" or "ought" statements. My position is set forth in Miller, *In Defense of Judicial Activism,* in SUPREME COURT ACTIVISM AND RESTRAINT 167 (S. Halpern & C. Lamb eds. 1982).

215.   Grey, *Do We Have an Unwritten Constitution?,* 27 STAN. L. REV. 703 (1975). Munzer & Nickel, *Does the Constitution Mean What It Always Meant?,* 77 COLUM. L. REV. 1029 (1977).

216.   *See* W. WILSON, CONSTITUTIONAL GOVERNMENT IN THE UNITED STATES (1908).

why they appeared at roughly the same time and in a quite limited geographical area, what answer would be forthcoming? Even if we accept, as surely we should, that there is no simple and complete explanation of any social phenomenon,[217] let alone a set of them, history does provide a principal determinant. It is emphatically not an example of *post hoc, ergo propter hoc* reasoning to maintain that the Great Discoveries were the prime mover in normative constitutionalism and its institutions. Wealth in untold amounts poured into the "Metropolis"—Western Europe—and seemingly endless land became available to the hard-pressed peoples of Europe. They were able to escape the "ecological trap," with its concomitant authoritarian institutions, that had imprisoned them in a rigid caste system since time immemorial.

With the Great Discoveries, a static society gave way to one of permanent revolution. The ancient and the medieval worlds were closed. Space, rather than being infinite, was considered to be a solid sphere in which the stars were embedded. Time, too, was finite: To medieval man the world was about 4000 years old and was to end in a short time. Learning was limited: people believed the final truth of all subjects had already been written by the ancients—Aristotle, Plato, Euclid, and others. The Bible as Holy Writ was the ultimate truth for religion and for cosmology. Those who thought and wrote did so within a closed body of knowledge; they were confined to refining already known concepts. The universe was anthropocentric: earth was its center and man was the special creature of an all-knowing and all-wise God. It was an authoritarian age—in economics, in politics, in religion.

Then came the Great Discoveries, which opened space and time and eventually the mind of man. Massive social changes began to appear, slowly at first, but accelerating with the advent of the scientific-technological revolution (of which the industrial revolution was the first part). "Revolution"—social revolution—as Romano Guardini has said, has become "a perpetual institution."[218] The underlying assumptions, the metaphysic, of society were fundamentally altered. Human life on earth, rather than being thought of as a prelude to heaven or hell, became an end in itself. The idea of progress flowered. In Charles Beard's words, it became possible "to think of an immense future for mortal mankind, of the conquest of the material world in human interest, of providing the conditions for a good life on this planet without reference to any possible hereafter."[219] Rather than living in the final age, hu-

---

217. *See* E. NAGEL, THE STRUCTURE OF SCIENCE: PROBLEMS IN THE LOGIC OF SCIENTIFIC EXPLANATION (1961).

218. R. GUARDINI, THE END OF THE MODERN WORLD: A SEARCH FOR ORIENTATION 44 (1956).

219. Beard, *Introduction,* in J. BURY, THE IDEA OF PROGRESS: AN INQUIRY INTO ITS ORI-

mankind saw itself as participating in a process of progressive improvement of the human lot. People became optimistic, rather than having a "sombre melancholy." Humans, through the application of reason, were believed to be able to know and to solve all problems. Faith in an all-wise and benevolent God was eventually subtly transferred to faith in scientists and technologists, who were (and are) considered to be able to create technological "fixes" that would ameliorate the harshness of life. Politics changed; the nation-state became the characteristic form of political order. Economics went from mercantilism—a statist economy—to laissez-faire (private enterprise capitalism)—although the State was still important as a protector of and simulant to business. The individual human being was perceived as the basic unit of society, a belief that crept into the dominated law and legal institutions. The Constitution of 1787 reflected the new views about life. In short, the "modern age" was born. Allen Wheelis observes:

> The vision of the Modern Age is a Promethean leap in pride. While it does not usurp God's role, does not yet claim omnipotence for man, it makes a point of recognizing no limits. It alleges that the universe moves by forces which are blind, that man, therefore, possesses mind at the summit. No intelligence, no planning, no consciousness operates above him, and nothing, therefore, can set a priori limits to what he may think, accomplish, understand. The universe is vast, mysterious, hazardous, but as it is a machine, functions by law, man may aspire to know it and control it.[220]

That age no longer exists.

My point is not that a direct causal connection existed between all of the developments listed above and the Great Discoveries; but, rather, that it was only after those Discoveries that the new institutions and beliefs came into being. An environment was provided in which new ideas and concepts could flourish. Adam Smith, writing in 1776, saw a connection:

> The general advantages which Europe, considered as a great country, has derived from the discovery and colonization of America, consist, first, in the increase of its enjoyments; and secondly, in the augmentation of its industry.
>
> The surplus produce of America, imported into Europe, furnishes the inhabitants of the great continent with a variety of commodities which they could not otherwise have possessed. . . .
>
> The discovery and colonization of America . . . have contributed to augment the industry, first, of all the countries which trade to it directly

---

GIN AND GROWTH (1955), *quoted in* A. WHEELIS, THE END OF THE MODERN AGE 15 (1971).
220. A. WHEELIS, THE END OF THE MODERN AGE 6-7 (1971).

Defining the Constitution   87

. . . and, secondly, of all those which, without trading to it directly, send, through the medium of other countries, goods to it of their own produce.[221]

Without the wealth of the Great Discoveries, modern capitalism could not have flourished; its political counterpart, liberal democracy, would never have come into existence; and normative constitutionalism would have been at best a wistful dream. What had been abnormal before the Discoveries became normal—but only for a small segment of the planet. To repeat: normative constitutionalism is limited in time and space—in time to the past 300-plus years, and in space to Western Europe and some of its former colonies (particularly the United States).

There is no need to buttress the uniqueness of the modern era. Walter Prescott Webb in one of the most important, albeit little noticed, books of this century has provided ample data to show the modern age is "an abnormal age, and not a progressive orderly development which mankind was destined to make anyway."[222] In *The Great Frontier,* Webb perceived that frontier as "one of the primary factors in modern history. . . . [T]he sudden acquisition of land and other forms of wealth by the people of Europe precipitated a boom on Western civilization. . . . [T]hat . . . boom lasted as long as the frontier was open, a period of four centuries."[223] The Great Frontier closed during the first part of this century. The bulk of public lands had disappeared. An enormous increase in population has made the density per square mile, both in Europe and in the new world, "on average greater than the density was in Europe in 1500."[224]

Webb's analysis and conclusions seem to be irrefutable. Some questions which they present include: (a) do institutions which matured during the 400-year boom, which reflected and were adapted to those conditions, require alteration now that the frontier has closed? and (b) is there somewhere, somehow, a modern substitute for that boom? The short answers to those questions may be simply stated: (a) yes, those institutions—economic, political and philosophical—must be thoroughly examined anew to determine how they should be changed to fit a radically different social milieu; and (b) no new frontier of comparable significance is in the offing. Outer space—whether within or without the solar system—cannot, under any reasonably foreseeable set of

---

221. A. Smith, The Wealth of Nations 92 (E. Cannan ed. 1904).

222. W. Webb, *supra* note 158, at 14.

223. *Id.* at 413.

224. *Id. See* D. Potter, People of Plenty: Economic Abundance and the American Character (1954).

circumstances, become a substitute for the Great Discoveries. On the contrary, rather than providing new resources and new lands, space exploration and settlement (even if theoretically possible) will be an enormous drain on planetary resources. Some consider science to be an endless frontier, and to the extent new scientific discoveries and technological "fixes" can help develop an environment comparable to that of the 400-year boom, there is validity in that idea. But science, too, is resource-draining, and even some thoughtful scientists concede that technological "fixes" will not do the necessary job.[225] Furthermore, science cannot create matter; it cannot make something out of nothing. And we have learned in recent years that entropy is a universal law that cannot be repealed.[226]

In sum, then, what has seemed to be normal during all of American history—economic growth, relative peace, seemingly inexhaustible resources, the idea of progress and of the perfectability of man—has in dour fact actually been abnormal. Abnormal, that is, in the sense of how people lived prior to the Great Discoveries, and how people lived outside of Europe and a few other nations since those Discoveries. The Golden Age for Western Man started about 1600 and lasted until about 1970, when institutions honored by time began to become unraveled. Immense strains created by burgeoning population and rapid depletion of resources have set man back in the man-land ratio worse than where it was in 1650. In the West, population density in 1500 was about 26.7 people per square mile. By 1940 that figure had become 34.8 per square mile.[227] Only technological growth enabled humans to have a relatively abundant economy (and then often at the expense of the poverty-rows of the Third World). The question is whether that can continue. My answer is that it cannot. The ecological trap is once more closing.[228]

The pity is that constitutional commentators, including Professor Perry, simply ignore the historical socioeconomic context in which the ideas of normative constitutionalism arose. If, however, one accepts, at least as a working hypothesis, that American history was in fact aberrational—a unique set of fortuitous and nonreplicable circumstances—then it becomes somewhat easier to view American constitutionalism in a more accurate perspective. I have suggested above that

---

225. *See* Weinberg, *Social Institutions and Nuclear Energy,* 177 SCIENCE 27 (1972). *See generally* McDermott, *Technology: The Opiate of the Intellectuals,* in TECHNOLOGY AS A SOCIAL AND POLITICAL PHENOMENON 78 (P. Bereano ed. 1976).

226. *See* J. RIFKIN, THE EMERGING ORDER: GOD IN THE AGE OF SCARCITY (1979).

227. W. WEBB, *supra* note 158, at 13-28.

228. *See generally* P. EHRLICH, A. EHRLICH & J. HOLDREN, ECO-SCIENCE: POPULATION, RESOURCES, ENVIRONMENT (rev. ed. 1977).

"the" Constitution has become corporatist in some degree, and that this trend will continue. To the extent that is valid, much current constitutional commentary is irrelevant; it badly—sadly—misses the point of the nature of the Constitution today. Constitutions are concerned with *power*—who has it, who exercises it, for whose benefit, in what circumstances. What follows states with little discussion some of the principal aspects of the American version of corporatism.

B. Societal Corporatism

However one characterizes the socioeconomic environment in which constitutional mechanisms operate, it is indubitably clear that abstract discussions of constitutionalism do not suffice. Little truly useful comes from the verbal battles of academics today. Contrary to Professor Perry, I agree with Paul Brest in his claim that "the controversy over the legitimacy of judicial review in a democratic polity—the historic obsession of normative constitutional law scholarship—is essentially incoherent and unresolvable."[229] The war of words among constitutional theorists consists mainly of assertions and counter-assertions unrelated to either historical or contemporaneous context. That simply is not enough.

I do not suggest, of course, that there is general agreement on the history or the contemporary "climacteric" of humankind. There are those who think that all will be well, that the species will be able to muddle through the present time of troubles. Herman Kahn and Julian Simon are prominent examples of that mind-set.[230] Simon believes that increased and increasing population, rather than being a disaster as Paul Ehrlich and others think, is "the ultimate resource."[231] Kahn's roseate views of the future are well known. E.J. Mishan and Eric Ashby, among others, disagree; Harrison Brown and Lester Brown add to the gloom.[232] Only the future will reveal who is correct—the cautious optimists, such as Kahn, or the despairing pessimists. My own view is that Kahn and Simon are dead wrong.

---

229. M. PERRY, *supra* note 1, at x. Brest, *The Fundamental Rights Controversy: The Essential Contradictions of Normative Constitutional Scholarship*, 90 YALE L.J. 1063 (1981) (footnote omitted).

230. H. KAHN, THE COMING BOOM (1982); H. KAHN, W. BROWN & L. MARTEL, THE NEXT TWO HUNDRED YEARS: A SCENARIO FOR AMERICA AND THE WORLD (1976); J. SIMON, THE ULTIMATE RESOURCE (1981).

231. To Simon, increasing population is an unmitigated good. For Ehrlich's views, see the detailed study cited *supra* note 228.

232. E. ASHBY, RECONCILING MAN WITH THE ENVIRONMENT (1978); H. BROWN, THE HUMAN FUTURE REVISITED (1978); L. BROWN, THE TWENTY-NINTH DAY (1978); E. MISHAN, THE ECONOMIC GROWTH DEBATE: AN ASSESSMENT (1977). *See also* W. OPHULS, ECOLOGY AND THE POLITICS OF SCARCITY: PROLOGUE TO A POLITICAL THEORY OF THE STEADY STATE (1977).

That, however, is not my present point—which is that disputations about constitutions and judicial review are valueless absent continuing careful attention to the environment in which those human institutions operate. In that sense, the greatest barrier to more meaningful discussions of constitutionalism is the gaggle of the professorial elite who have a vested interest in present ways—those who author the standard coursebooks used in law and political science classes. I am not saying those books and articles serve no useful purpose; of course, they do—but only within a severely constricted framework. That frame of reference is the adversary system, whereby the problems of *meum* and *tuum* are presented to the Supreme Court, which then transmutes them into general norms. That, however, is pure vocationalism, a process in which keen minds are sharply honed to "think like lawyers."[233] My contention is that attention to the minute details of constitutions and judicial review does little to further understanding of either institution. Our goal should be increased *understanding* of the Constitution and Court, rather than the limited task of being better able to *predict* the course of judicial decision (although greater understanding will doubtless lead to more accurate predictions). As Lon Fuller wrote in 1966:

> There may be said to exist two philosophies of science. The one sees the aim of science as *understanding*; the other as *prediction*. The first regards prediction as a by-product of understanding; we acquire the ability to predict events as our minds penetrate into the causes that underlie the happenings of nature. The adherents of the opposed theory see "understanding" as an illusory, metaphysical trapping superfluously tacked on the essential goal of acquiring predictive knowledge.[234]

There is a pressing need for an accurate perception of the nature of the Constitution and Court as politico-legal institutions in a broad social matrix before predictions of what the Court will do or assertions about what it should do can be made. Neither law nor legal institutions are homeless, wandering ghosts; they are significant aspects of human endeavor, serving identifiable purposes and furthering the causes of equally identifiable people.

To understand modern constitutionalism requires at the outset the recognition that it ever increasingly exemplifies the third great "ism": corporatism. What, then, are the characteristics of corporatism? Several may be suggested. The following do not exhaust all of the aspects

---

233. *Cf.* Levinson, *Taking Law Seriously: Reflections on "Thinking Like a Lawyer,"* 30 STAN. L. REV. 1071 (1978). In my own, perhaps jaundiced view, legal education is a form of brain damage; and "thinking like a lawyer" is often a disaster.

234. Fuller, *An Afterword: Science and the Judicial Process,* 79 HARV. L. REV. 1604, 1623-24 (1966) (emphasis in original).

of the emergent form of American corporatism, but they will suffice to show its general outlines.

The first principle is that there is a fusion of political and economic power in society. This is occurring in two ways. First, the supercorporations and other decentralized organizations in the pluralistic order are themselves political in nature. They are private governments for the corporate communities—for corporations, the stockholders, the employees (management and blue collar), those who buy from it, those who supply it and lend to it, and those whose lives are affected by its actions.[235] Second, political and economic power merge in the formulation of public policies, through the operation of the "subgovernments" or the "iron triangles" of Washington. The terms refer to the symbiotic relationships between congressional committee, administrative agency, and affected interest group. In sum, the institutions of the Political Constitution are meeting and merging with those of the Economic Constitution.

The second principle is that the group is the basic unit of society. Although the Document of 1787 recognizes only two entities—the natural person and government—the "organizational revolution"[236] has produced a society in which the group is dominant. Both in politics and in economics, the lone individual counts for little. Even in the Supreme Court's constitutional decisions, a person is important only because the Court is not a self-starter; it cannot reach out and seize policy issues for decisions, but must await the accident of litigation. Once the process starts, and particularly once a given case is accepted for decision on the merits, the litigant becomes insignificant. Those 150 plus Supreme Court decisions made each term are for development of "the law," or, in other words, for larger legislative purposes. One example will suffice: Clarence Gideon was important to law not as a person who had been treated shabbily by the State of Florida, but because his situation exemplified a large category of persons throughout the nation. *Gideon's Case,*[237] accordingly, was a *de facto* class action, although not brought as such.

The third principle is that the State is a metaphysical entity—a "super-group-person"—larger than the arithmetical sum of its parts (public and private governance). As has been previously suggested, the State is sovereign in the United States, and is recognized as such by

---

235. *See* W. GOSSETT, CORPORATE CITIZENSHIP (1957); W. HARMAN, THE WORLD PROBLEMATIQUE: THE CHANGING ROLES OF BUSINESS (Woodlands Occasional Paper No. 1, 1981).

236. K. BOULDING, THE ORGANIZATIONAL REVOLUTION (1953).

237. Gideon v. Wainwright, 372 U.S. 335 (1963). *See* A. LEWIS, GIDEON'S TRUMPET (1964).

the Supreme Court. And the State is to be distinguished from both its apparatus, government, and those who are ruled, society. The State as "group-person" is a conception based on Otto von Gierke's analysis of society. To him, "groups were real persons—real 'unitary' persons, existing over and above the multiple individual persons of which they were composed."[238] Just as corporations are constitutional persons by Supreme Court fiat, so too with the State: It is, as Ernest Barker said, "a sort of higher reality, of a transcendental order, which stands out as something distinct from, and something superior to, the separate reality of the individual"[239]—and, one might add, the separate realities of government and social groups. Barker goes on to point out the dangers of such a view:

If we make groups real persons, we shall make the national State a real person. If we make the State a real person, with a real will, we make it indeed a Leviathan—a Leviathan which is not an automaton, like the Leviathan of Hobbes, but a living reality. When its will collides with other wills, it may claim that, being the greatest, it must and shall carry the day; and its supreme will may thus become a supreme force. If and when that happens, not only may the State become one real person and the one true group, which eliminates or assimilates others: it may also become a mere personal power which eliminates its own true nature as a specific purpose directed to Law or Right.[240]

Even a cursory survey of American policy in recent decades will quickly reveal that the State does indeed "carry the day," and that, accordingly, it is preeminent. Any number of Supreme Court decisions of recent as well as ancient vintage will show that the Justices are willing allies in that development.[241] We may not like that—I do not—but it would be puerility compounded to deny it.

The fourth principle is that the Supreme Court is an arm of the State. This principle follows from the third, and need not be expanded.[242]

The fifth principle is that "communitarianism" has replaced individualism. I take the term *communitarianism* from Professor George Lodge's recent book, *The New American Ideology.*[243] "America,"

238. O. GIERKE, NATURAL LAW AND THE THEORY OF SOCIETY, 1500-1800, at xxix (E. Barker trans. 1933).
239. *Id.* at xxxi.
240. *Id.* at lxxxv.
241. One example should suffice, although there are divers others: Dennis v. United States, 341 U.S. 494 (1951) (legitimized thought control).
242. *Compare* J. GRIFFITH, THE POLITICS OF THE JUDICIARY (1977) *with* M. SHAPIRO, COURTS: A COMPARATIVE AND POLITICAL ANALYSIS (1981).
243. G. LODGE, THE NEW AMERICAN IDEOLOGY (1975).

Lodge maintains, "now appears to be heading into a return to the communal norms of both ancient and medieval worlds," noting that "our atomistic, individualistic ideology constitutes a fundamental aberration from the historically typical norm."[244] Lockean individualism, the ideology that permeates much of constitutional commentary, is being replaced—whether we like it or not—by the new ideology. In many respects, Lodge's ponderous label of communitarianism is synonymous with the more familiar word, "corporatism." In any event, the individualistic basis of law, both private and public, is rapidly vanishing. Individualism as such is simply not possible in a society dominated by huge public and private bureaucracies. (The occasional hermit merely proves the rule.)

The sixth principle is that corporatism is mercantilist. Mercantilism was the economic theory appropriate for the medieval period, the time of feudalism and the first beginnings of nationalism, the period of roughly the fifteenth to the eighteenth centuries. It had five primary characteristics: It was nationalistic; it saw in gold and other precious metals an important economic force; it promoted exports over imports; it limited imports by tariffs and nontariff barriers to trade; it was both an economic and a political policy. The economic objective was a favorable balance of trade, or at least a balance of trade, whereas the political goal was a balance of power. Mercantilism gave way to classical economics and the notion of a natural equilibrium.

It takes no special insight to perceive parallels between mercantilism and the economic system of today. Other than the fact that major currencies have been cast adrift from gold as a standard, the modern age may accurately be termed neo-mercantilistic in nature. Certainly the other characteristics of the older version are plainly evident in American public policies. I do not say this is an abrupt shift from past policy: quite the contrary. The mercantilist tendencies, however, have been accentuated in recent years.

The seventh principle is that society is bureaucratized. This principle is, to be sure, one of the commonplaces of the day. Bureaucracy exists, and is dominant, yet learned constitutional scholars still write and speak in terms of individualism (which is giving way to communitarianism). Max Weber is the seminal thinker in this area. More than sixty years ago he observed:

The bureaucratization of society will, according to all available knowledge, some day triumph over capitalism, in our civilization just as in

---

244. *Id.* at ch. 6. It will not do to shrug off such a view, for Lodge, himself a pillar of the "Northeastern Establishment" is on the faculty of that central organ of the business establishment, the Harvard Business School.

ancient civilizations. In our civilization also the 'anarchy of production' will be supplanted in due course by an economic and social system similar to that typical of the Late Roman Empire, and even more so of the 'New Kingdom' in Egypt or the sway of the Ptolemies.[245]

Once rapid capitalist expansion had halted, the dynamism of capitalist competition gave way to bureaucratic techniques of regulating the economy. Weber may have been overly pessimistic at the time he wrote (*circa* 1920), but who can say that he did not presciently envisage the shape of things to come. Even though he maintained that charismatic leadership could be a creative revolutionary force that would help alleviate the problems he saw, Weber nevertheless maintained that in the long run "the seemingly irresistible advance of routinization, rationalization and bureaucratization"[246] would be dominant. As of 1983—and for the future insofar as it can be foreseen—that domination is becoming ever increasingly obvious.

In modern times, Jacques Ellul takes Weber a giant step further. Focusing on what he calls "technique," he notes, "the transition from the individualist to the collectivist society."[247] Ellul defines *technique* as more than machines, technology, or procedures for attaining an end. "In our technological society, technique is the *totality of methods rationally arrived at and having absolute efficiency* (for a given stage of development) in *every* field of human activity. Its characteristics are new; the technique of the present has no common measure with that of the past."[248] Technique imposes centralism upon the economy. In politics, the technocrat perceives the State as an enterprise providing services that must function *efficiently*. And efficiency requires administration (bureaucracy).

The eighth principle is that a growing social stratification characterizes the Corporate State. Society in America is ever increasingly one of a managerial elite structure at the top, those who have expert knowledge, with a larger and larger underclass.[249]

The ninth principle is that universities, rather than being centers of independent knowledge, are "service stations" for the institutions of corporatism.[250]

245.   W. MOMMSEN, THE AGE OF BUREAUCRACY: PERSPECTIVES ON THE POLITICAL SOCIOLOGY OF MAX WEBER 99 (1974).

246.   *Id.* at 103.

247.   J. ELLUL, THE TECHNOLOGICAL SOCIETY 305 (J. Wilkinson trans. 1964) (paperback ed.).

248.   *Id.* at xxv.

249.   *See* J. BURNHAM, THE MANAGERIAL REVOLUTION (1941); M. PARENTI, DEMOCRACY FOR THE FEW (3d ed. 1980); M. PARENTI, POWER AND THE POWERLESS (1978).

250.   *See, e.g.,* M. BARITZ, THE SERVANTS OF POWER: A HISTORY OF THE USE OF SOCIAL SCIENCE IN AMERICAN INDUSTRY (1960); J. RIDGEWAY, THE CLOSED CORPORATION: AMERICAN

The tenth principle is that the distinction between law and politics is disappearing.[251]

The last three principles of corporatism will be discussed together. The eighth and tenth principles have been discussed previously. There is little need to do more than suggest that a permanent underclass is being produced in the United States and that the storied Rule of Law—which, it seems to me, is the shorthand label for Perry's "principled decisions"—is in fact the Rule of Politics. The underclass are the consequence of the scientific-technological revolution, which has managed to create a terminal sense of the loss of work among increasing numbers of people,[252] and which, through improved health measures, keeps more people alive longer than ever before in history. What Veblen foresaw[253] about the turn of the century and what Huxley put in his classic novel, *Brave New World*,[254] is fast becoming reality. The demand is for brain power—for technicians (who are not philosophers or humanists). Only a relative few are needed, and fewer will be needed tomorrow. A technological elite sits on top of the technological society, one dominated by Ellul's *technique;* while at the bottom are growing masses of people to do the menial tasks of society that have not yet been mechanized. There are far too many for even those jobs. The consequence is the creation of a *de facto* class of Huxleyan "proles." The stratified society does not have castes imposed by law, but the accident of birth (including skin color) is making the United States a caste society in fact.

As for the Rule of Politics, little more need be added to what has already been said. Some do not like the notion. For example, Professor Owen Fiss claims to perceive what he calls "a new nihilism, one that doubts the legitimacy of adjudication."[255] He thinks that too many legal scholars are turning their backs on adjudication and beginning "a romance with politics." That is an interesting sentiment, particularly since Fiss maintains that there is such a thing as a "commitment to the rule of law"; and further that what he calls nihilism "threatens our

---

Universities in Crisis (1968).

251. *See* J. Ellul, *supra* note 247, at 291-300; A. Miller, Toward Increased Judicial Activism: The Political Role of the Supreme Court (1982); M. Shapiro, Courts: A Comparative and Political Analysis (1981); Griffith, *The Political Constitution,* 42 Mod. L. Rev. 1 (1979).

252. *Cf.* G. Merritt, World Out of Work (1982); Seabrook, *Unemployment Now and in the 1930s,* 52 Pol. Q. 7 (1981). *See also* Lodge & Glass, *The Desperate Plight of the Underclass,* Harv. Bus. Rev., July-Aug. 1982, at 60.

253. T. Veblen, The Engineers and the Price System (1921).

254. A. Huxley, Brave New World (1932). *See* A. Huxley, Brave New World Revisited (1958).

255. Fiss, *Objectivity and Interpretation,* 34 Stan. L. Rev. 739, 740 (1982).

social existence and the nature of public life in America; and it demeans our lives."[256] That is some charge. Were it accurate and valid, it would deal a telling, even mortal, blow to much of what I have said in this essay. But it is neither accurate nor valid: Fiss is simply wrong. His is a variation on the theme struck by Professor Wechsler's call for "neutral principles."[257] Fiss thinks that adjudication is "interpretation" and that interpretation is neither wholly discretionary nor wholly mechanical. "Viewing adjudication as interpretation helps to stop the slide toward nihilism. It makes law possible."[258] Stopping the new nihilism, he thinks, will help to preserve the fundamental public values of our society. Fiss doesn't like Justice William O. Douglas, but thinks that Chief Justice Earl Warren was a "great judge."[259]

What is one to make of such statements? First, Professor Fiss seems to have a rather odd conception of politics. Second, he seems to deny, but does not actually do so expressly, that the Supreme Court is a political body. This is not the place to discuss his views further; they are mentioned only to indicate that a learned professor at an elite law school (Yale) thinks that exorcism of the devil of "politics" will usher in a terrestrial Nirvana, at least insofar as his ideal of "adjudication" is the sovereign talisman for entry into that state of affairs. Perhaps it would take a Voltaire or a Swift or possibly a Mencken to show the absurdity of Fissian jurisprudence. My talents are only up to the assertion, which surely cannot be gainsaid, that it is one thing to describe the "is"—which I have sought to do in this essay, and quite another to project the "ought"—which Professor Fiss attempts to do. Fiss, of course, has a full first amendment right to publish anything he pleases; but he ought to remember that the amendment merely protects expression and does not require that it be accurate. His is not, as Paul Brest has pointed out.[260]

My final point about societal corporatism is that education generally, and universities particularly, are not only public (governmental)

---

256. *Id.* at 763.

257. Wechsler, *Toward Neutral Principles of Constitutional Law,* 73 HARV. L. REV. 1 (1959).

258. Fiss, *supra* note 255, at 750.

259. *Id.* at 758. Fiss's definition of a "great judge" seems to be a warmed-over version of Wechsler's verbally muddled formulation. It is a striking example of the poverty of adequate intellectual activity about judicial review that Wechsler's demand can have such currency.

260. Brest, *Interpretation and Interest,* 34 STAN. L. REV. 765 (1982). *See also* Brest, *The Substance of Process,* 42 OHIO ST. L.J. 131 (1981). Brest notes that "[i]t is time for those of us who do constitutional law to move on." *Id.* at 142.

A contrary view, badly mistaken in my judgment, is Grano, *Judicial Review and a Written Constitution in a Democratic Society,* 28 WAYNE L. REV. 1 (1981), although Professor Grano does admit that the future should be permitted "to govern itself." *Id.* at 75.

functions but are closely tied in with the groups of society, particularly the corporations. Rather than being disinterested centers of learning, universities all too often exemplify what Julien Benda called, in his classic *La Trahison des Clercs*—"The Treason of the Intellectuals."[261] The word *treason* does not, in Benda's book, mean subversion against the State. Quite the contrary, he laments the adherence of intellectuals ("les clercs") to the ideas of nationalism and to the centers of power generally. "Brain power," says D. N. Chorafas, "is the key to the future."[262] And so it is.

Today's intellectuals are apolitical only in the sense that lawyers are: They will, and do, readily sell their talents to the highest bidder. In recent decades, Peter F. Drucker tells us, knowledge "has become the central capital, the cost center, and the crucial resource of the economy."[263] A knowledge explosion is indeed taking place. However, the holders of knowledge, far from being dispassionate observers dedicated to the pursuit of truth, generally are beholden to those who exercise real power in the nation. Says Professor Victor C. Ferkiss: "The class system of the industrial era remains dominant. The fundamental fact is that legal and political considerations ensure that the technical elite remains secondary to the business elite."[264] It should not be forgotten that, in his famous farewell address warning about the dangers of the "military-industrial complex," President Dwight D. Eisenhower coupled intellectuals into that complex. The classic example of *la trahison des clercs* in modern times is the way in which brilliant scientists and engineers bent their talents to producing not only an atomic bomb but also a thermonuclear bomb.[265] The process continues: "Many industrial social scientists have put themselves on auction. The power elites of America, especially the industrial elite, have bought their services."[266] And it was "the best and the brightest," to use David Halberstam's mordant label,[267] who were largely responsible for getting the United States mired down in the Indo-Chinese "war"—and keeping the nation there long after any possible reason for remaining had vanished. We like to think that universities are centers for the disinterested pursuit of truth. But that is not so: They are service stations for the institutions of American corporatism.

---

261. J. BENDA, THE TREASON OF THE INTELLECTUALS (1927) (R. Adlington trans. 1969).

262. D. CHORAFAS, THE KNOWLEDGE REVOLUTION 13 (1968).

263. P. DRUCKER, THE AGE OF DISCONTINUITY xi (1969).

264. V. FERKISS, TECHNOLOGICAL MAN: THE MYTH AND THE REALITY 140 (1969) (footnote omitted).

265. *See* J. SCHELL, THE FATE OF THE EARTH (1982); S. ZUCKERMAN, NUCLEAR ILLUSION AND REALITY (1982).

266. M. BARITZ, *supra* note 250, at 209.

267. D. HALBERSTAM, THE BEST AND THE BRIGHTEST (1972).

V. Conclusion

There is little to be added to what has been said above. I have tried to indicate that analysis and criticism of judicial review should focus upon all who wield significant power within the American polity, as well as what the Supreme Court has done. Perhaps the late Professor Robert McCloskey had something like that in mind when he maintained:

> American constitutional history has been in large part a spasmodic running debate over the behavior of the Supreme Court, but in a hundred seventy years we have made curiously little progress toward establishing the terms of this war of words, much less toward achieving concord. . . . [T]hese recurring constitutional debates resemble an endless series of rematches between two club-boxers who have long since stopped developing their crafts autonomously and have nothing further to learn from each other. The same generalizations are launched from either side, to be met by the same evasions and parries. Familiar old ambiguities fog the controversy, and the contestants flounder among them for a while until history calls a close and it is time to retire from the arena and await the next installment. In the exchange of assertions and counterassertions no one can be said to have won a decision on the merits, for small attempt has been made to arrive at an understanding of what the merits are.[268]

It will be difficult to shift the nature of the "spasmodic running debate." There is little evidence that McCloskey's counsel is being followed. At a time when the central institutions of normative constitutionalism are under severe and sustained attack, the response, thus far at least, is not up to the mark. Professor Mark Tushnet asserts that legal scholarship has "an intellectual marginality" brought on by "the pressures of professional education."[269] Whether Tushnet is accurate in that assertion I do not say. Surely, however, there is a need for looking at more than the Supreme Court and its opinions when one considers "the" Constitution of the United States.[270]

---

268. M. Perry, *supra* note 1, at 8 (quoting R. McCloskey, The Modern Supreme Court 290-91 (1972) (footnote omitted).

269. Tushnet, *Legal Scholarship: Its Cause and Cure,* 90 Yale L.J. 1205, 1205-06 (1981).

270. I realize that I have larded this preliminary foray into a definition of "the" Constitution with far too many (some might say: too few) footnotes. For that, I apologize. My excuses, such as they are, include: (a) in many respects, this is a work in synthesis, and a decent respect for the tolerance of readers leads me to list the references I have consulted; (b) law review editors seem to like lots of footnotes, perhaps on the theory that there is a correlation between footnotes in plethoric quantity and "sound" scholarship or profundity. That there is no such correlation is self evident. Numerous footnotes may also be an indication of a lack of assurance or confidence in one's idea. In that connection, it is instructive to compare today's scholarly output with such writers as Locke, Hume, Hobbes, Burke, Machiavelli, Plato, Aristotle, among those long dead,

and Isaiah Berlin, among the living; all of those listed are relevant to constitutionalism in America. Law reviews have become examples of an inability to discard much research. That, in itself, is not so bad; after all, one can skim over the text of what is published there, and simply refuse to read the footnotes. But since judges now routinely select law review editors as clerks, and since the judges either want to make their opinions appear to be "scholarly" or kindly include, in their opinions, chunks of the memoranda clerks grind out, or both, then those who do constitutional law—and, indeed, law itself—must face a blizzard of footnotes larding judicial opinions. That, I suggest, is simply too much. It is high time that what is considered to be scholarship be re-examined. I hasten to add that I do not expect that to be done.

CHAPTER **3**

Reason of State and the Emergent Constitution of Control

The Constitution, as written, is noteworthy not only for its express provisions but also for its silences. What was explicitly stated by the framers in 1787 has been so thoroughly discussed that little useful purpose is served by further exposition. The silences are another matter. There is no systematic analysis of what the framers did not say—but what has been filled by subsequent governmental action.

The most important silence, certainly the first important one, was judicial review itself; it was filled by judicial decree aided, so far as the states are concerned, by the Judiciary Act of 1789, enacted by Congress in its first session after the new government was formed. Others are perhaps of somewhat lesser significance. An example is "executive privilege," which did not gain constitutional stature until the 20th century was half over. Not least among the silences is constitutional reason of state (raison d'état), a political theory adhered to by all governments (and perhaps by all collectivities, of whatever type).

Reason of state is basic to the business of ruling. Simply stated, it means that those who are in power can take any action considered necessary to ensure the survival of the state—the collectivity—whether or not the laws permit such action, and, indeed, often contrary to the written law. The state thus follows the laws of necessity, as perceived by the political officers of government. This chapter suggests that American constitutional history exemplifies consistent adherence to reason of state—what John Locke, the "father" of the Constitution, called the prerogative: the executive power to act according to discretion. "There is," said Locke, "a latitude left to the executive power to do many things of choice, which the laws do not prescribe." Presidents beginning with George Washington have not hesitated to act when they considered that the circumstances warranted it. Necessity thus is the mother of constitutional law.

Acting in effect as an arm of the executive, the Supreme Court has gone along with these extraconstitutional measures—best seen in its approval of President Lincoln's actions in the Civil War, but also perceivable in a number of other situations. This chapter is an outline of how that great constitutional silence of reason of state was filled by a combination of government acts; the role of the Court was to legitimize constitutional reason of state.

With the coming of the "national security state" in the post-World War II period, the Court's approval of extraordinary executive actions displays the faint but unmistakable beginnings of the contours of a new constitutional order—herein called the Constitution of Control. This emergent fundamental law exists as a layer on the palimpsest that is the document of 1787. The basic message is that, now as always, the Constitution is relative to circumstances. The chapter concludes with a suggestion that major constitutional change is necessary.

No society in recorded history has ever been able to dispense with political power. This is as true of liberalism as of absolutism, as true of laissez faire as of an interventionist state. No greater disservice has been rendered to political science than the statement that the liberal state was a "weak" state. It was precisely as strong as it needed to be in the circumstances. It acquired substantial colonial empires, waged wars, held down internal disorders, and stabilized itself over long periods of time.

—Franz Neumann[1]

I. INTRODUCTION

This Article is a speculative essay.[2] Its main theme is that the United States is moving, without announcement or fanfare, into government under a *fourth* constitution, a development that can be appropriately labeled the Constitution of Control. Preceding this emerging fourth constitution were three other fundamental laws, two of which still exist: the Articles of Confederation, the 1787 Constitution of Quasi-Limitations (usually misnamed the Constitution of Limitations), and the Constitution of Powers. Currently, few people pay any attention to the first constitution, the Articles of Confederation, although some who fear the power of the State advocate that the Articles be resurrected and put into effect.[3] However desirable that proposal might be in theory, it will not happen. Accordingly, the focus herein will be on the second constitution, the Constitution

---

1. F. NEUMANN, THE DEMOCRATIC AND THE AUTHORITARIAN STATE 8 (1957).

2. My aim is to suggest a way of thinking about the current direction of American constitutional development and to propose a model of the future. The Article is thus an exercise in extrapolation, drawing upon past experience and projecting certain trends as modified by the likely social conditions of the next fifty years. There is, of course, no way *at this time* to prove the validity of the proposed model.

3. *See, e.g.,* W. WILLIAMS, AMERICA CONFRONTS A REVOLUTIONARY WORLD, 1776-1976 (1976).

This chapter was originally published in 64 Minnesota Law Review 585 (1980).

of Quasi-Limitations—the politico-legal palimpsest drafted in 1787 and amended twenty-six times—and its two overlays, the third and fourth constitutions.

The second constitution was predominant from 1789, when the first government was formed, until about 1937. The first overlay, the third constitution, was added when the Supreme Court constitutionalized the New Deal, permitting a government with affirmative obligations. Professor Edward S. Corwin correctly labelled this overlay a "Constitution of Powers in a secular state."[4] When the Employment Act of 1946 was passed,[5] the new posture of government was clearly evident: the Positive State had emerged.[6] Simultaneously, still another layer was developing, in a process that by 1980 has become clear: a fourth constitution, the Constitution of Control, is emerging. This Article outlines that historical development as reflected not only in judicial decisions, but also in other governmental actions. Following the description of the development of the fourth constitution, is a description of the "climacteric"— the coalescence of crises—in which Americans now find themselves. Finally, an extrapolation of these past trends reveals an emerging constitutional troika, a troika which includes the co-existent second, third, and fourth constitutions, but which also indicates that the fourth constitution, the Constitution of Control, is becoming preeminent.

---

4. *See generally* E. CORWIN, A CONSTITUTION OF POWERS IN A SECULAR STATE (1951). Professor Corwin described the replacement of a Constitution of Rights by a Constitution of Powers in these terms: "[T]he Federal System has shifted base in the direction of a consolidated national power, while within the National Government itself an increased flow of power in the direction of the President has ensued." *Id.* at 2. *See also* E. CORWIN, AMERICAN CONSTITUTIONAL HISTORY (1964).

5. Ch. 33, 60 Stat. 23 (1946) (current version at 15 U.S.C. §§ 1021-1025 (1976 & Supp. 1979)).

6. In briefest terms, the Positive State is a label for express acceptance by the federal government—by government generally and thus by the people—of affirmative responsibility to further the economic well-being of all the people. It is a societal undertaking of a duty to attempt to create and maintain minimal conditions within the economy—of economic growth, of employment opportunities, of the basic necessities of life.

A.S. MILLER, THE MODERN CORPORATE STATE: PRIVATE GOVERNMENTS AND THE AMERICAN CONSTITUTION 86-87 (1976) [hereinafter cited as A.S. MILLER, THE MODERN CORPORATE STATE]. For further discussion of the Positive State, see *id.* at 86-112; A.S. MILLER, THE SUPREME COURT AND AMERICAN CAPITALISM 72-132 (1968). For further discussion of the Employment Act of 1946, which declared the federal government's policy and responsibility to be, *inter alia*, "to promote maximum employment, production, and purchasing power," 15 U.S.C. § 1021 (1976), see E. ROSTOW, PLANNING FOR FREEDOM: THE PUBLIC LAW OF AMERICAN CAPITALISM 10-29 (1959).

Constitutional law and government, as Franz Neumann has observed,[7] have always been relative to circumstances. Supposedly constitutional absolutes have a way of being diluted by the crush of the exigencies faced by succeeding generations of Americans. One of the great silences of the fundamental law has thus taken on sufficient substantive content to allow one to assert, with little fear of contradiction, that a concept of "reason of state" (*raison d'état*) is now an integral part of the Constitution. My purpose is to examine the development of this principle (constitutional reason of state) and its implications for the future. To put it another way, the discussion focuses on the extent to which certain Machiavellian principles have become, and will become, part of American constitutional law.

First, however, it is necessary to define the concept of reason of state. Not mentioned in the second constitution, it is "the State's first Law of Motion,"[8] "the doctrine that whatever is required to ensure the survival of the state must be done by the individuals responsible for it, no matter how repugnant such an act may be to them in their private capacity as decent and moral men."[9]

Second, it is necessary also to define the term "State." Again unmentioned by the drafters of the second constitution, there is no shorthand definition for this term. The State is not a "thing"; rather, it is an abstraction—a construct that is not synonymous with either government or society. Government is the apparatus of the State and society is that which is governed—in appearance a collective of individuals, but in reality an aggregate of interacting groups. The Supreme Court has not made that careful distinction; the Justices routinely use the three terms—State, government, and society—synonymously.

---

7. *See* text accompanying note 1 *supra*.

8. F. MEINECKE, MACHIAVELLISM: THE DOCTRINE OF RAISON D'ÉTAT AND ITS PLACE IN MODERN HISTORY 1 (D. Scott trans. 1957) (first published in Germany in 1925 with the title of *Die Idee der Staatsräson in der neueren Geschichte*). Meinecke writes: "Whatever the circumstances the business of ruling is . . . always carried out in accordance with the principles of *raison d'état. Raison d'état* may be deflected or hindered by real or imaginary obstacles, but it is part and parcel of ruling." *Id.* at 25. My purpose in writing this Article is to show that Meinecke's assertion is valid for the United States, even with—perhaps, despite—its written Constitution.

Meinecke's book is indispensable to an understanding of constitutionalism, American or otherwise—Professor Friedrich has expressed the opinion that Meinecke's book "is without doubt one of the most important recent contributions to the history of political ideas." C. FRIEDRICH, CONSTITUTIONAL REASON OF STATE: THE SURVIVAL OF THE CONSTITUTIONAL ORDER 120 (1957).

9. C. FRIEDRICH, *supra* note 8, at 4-5.

The State has no physical existence. Like the business corporation, it is an artificial being, invisible and intangible, existing only in legal and constitutional theory. Even though it cannot be seen, it is nevertheless as real as a natural person. In fact, the State is even more "real," for whenever its will collides with the wills of natural persons, it *always* prevails in any matter considered important by those who wield effective power in the nation. Such a conclusion will become more evident through an examination of several historical episodes. Finally, the State is monistic, in Gierke's sense—it is a "super-group-person" created by the joinder of the *political* government of the nation, states, and localities with the *economic* government of the giant corporations and other social groups.[10] Public government and corporations coexist in a syzygetic system.[11]

II. THE PAST AS PROLOGUE: TWO MORALITIES IN PUBLIC BEHAVIOR

An understanding of the past is necessary in order to gain an understanding of where we are now and where we are likely to be in the future. Although neither the present nor the future are mere extensions of the past, history cannot be escaped; adherence to it, as Holmes said, is not a duty but a necessity. In order to more fully understand the past, an organizing theory is necessary. The thesis of this Article is derived from Machiavelli: "I claim," he said in *The Discourses*, "that republics which, in imminent danger, have recourse neither to a dictatorship, nor to some form of authority analogous to it, will always be ruined when grave misfortune befalls them."[12]

An important caveat, however, must be added to this theory: in the case of the United States, the dangers that have triggered extraordinary responses have not been limited to

---

10. *See* O. Gierke, Natural Law and the Theory of Society 1500 to 1800. (E. Barker trans. 1958); text accompanying notes 108-115 *infra*. *See also* text accompanying notes 151-154 *infra*.

11. Syzygy is a biological term, meaning the joinder of two organisms with each retaining its own identity. For a discussion of the syzygetic system of the United States, see generally A.S. Miller, The Modern Corporate State, *supra* note 6. *See also* M. Kammen, People of Paradox (1972); The Economy as a System of Power (W. Samuels ed. 1979); A New History of Leviathan (R. Radosh & M. Rothbard eds. 1972).

12. N. Machiavelli, The Discourses, I, § 34 [hereinafter cited as The Discourses]. This volume, of greater importance than *The Prince*, was published in 1531. All references to *The Discourses* are to the Pelican paperback edition edited by Professor Bernard Crick and published in 1970.

"grave misfortune."[13] All types of emergencies, *as defined by political officers*, have caused the agents of the State to exercise authority derived from *raison d'état*. Included are wars and rumors of wars (cold wars), internal subversion (actual or supposed), economic depression, labor strife, actions of dissident groups, and natural disasters. Or, as Hannah Arendt said,

> Necessity, since the time of Livy and through the centuries, has meant many things that we today would find quite sufficient to dub a war unjust rather than just. Conquest, expansion, defense of vested interests, conservation of power in view of the rise of new and threatening powers, . . . all these well-known realities of power politics were not only actually the causes of the outbreaks of most wars in history, they were also recognized as 'necessities,' that is, as legitimate motives to invoke a decision by arms.[14]

Arendt and Machiavelli speak of violence, but our canvas is wider and deeper. There are weapons other than violence at the command of those who control the State. The series of historical examples set out below[15] constitute some, but far from all, of the situations in which extraordinary political responses occurred (the use of violence being only an extension of politics). The governing principle is that a given situation must be perceived by the ruling elite or elites to be an emergency before extraordinary action is even contemplated. That action when taken is usually in accord with what can be called the Principle of the Economy of Means. An extraordinary response is employed only to the extent necessary to achieve limited objectives.

The possibility of an extraordinary political response in an emergency demonstrates the fact that two moralities of public behavior have always existed in the United States. One is what government officers do in fact; the other is the ideal epitomized in the concept of constitutionalism.[16] Emergency (or crisis) government is a classic illustration. The Constitution contains no express provision for emergency action. Even so, that silence has never been a barrier to any action deemed desirable by ruling elites.[17] The meaning is clear: a dualism runs

---

13. The triggering dangers extend far beyond those discussed by Professor Clinton Rossiter, who mentions the Civil War, World Wars I and II, and the Great Depression. *See* C. ROSSITER, CONSTITUTIONAL DICTATORSHIP: CRISIS GOVERNMENT IN MODERN DEMOCRACIES. (References in this Article to this seminal work are to the 1963 paperback edition).

14. H. ARENDT, ON REVOLUTION 13 (paperback ed. 1973).

15. *See* pp. 594-612 *infra*.

16. *See* NOMOS XX: CONSTITUTIONALISM *passim* (J. Pennock & J. Chapman eds. 1979).

17. *But see* Youngstown Sheet & Tube Co. v. Sawyer (Steel Seizure), 343 U.S. 579 (1952). The *Steel Seizure* case, in which the Court rejected President

through American constitutional history. The law in books says one thing, while the law in action says another. Orthodox constitutional theory acknowledges only the ideal—stated, for example, by Justice Davis in *Ex parte Milligan*:[18]

> The Constitution of the United States is a law for rulers and people, equally in war and in peace, and covers with the shield of its protection all classes of men, at all times, and under all circumstances. No doctrine involving more pernicious consequences, was ever invented by the wit of man than that any of its provisions can be suspended during any of the great exigencies of government. Such a doctrine leads directly to anarchy or despotism, but the theory of necessity on which it is based is false; for the government, within the Constitution, has all the powers granted to it which are necessary to preserve its existence; as has been happily proved by the result of the great effort to throw off its just authority.[19]

That is a nice sentiment, were it true; but it is not. An "evident piece of arrant hypocrisy,"[20] the statement was an attempt to bring a single truth to the development of American constitutionalism. Justice Davis and others have failed in this effort. An example is the way in which the Supreme Court neatly avoided the rule of *Milligan* in the later case of *Ex parte Quirin*.[21]

In distinguishing the two public moralities, Machiavelli is again relevant. Sir Isaiah Berlin, in his brilliant interpretive essay, "The Originality of Machiavelli,"[22] argues that the Florentine proposed a radical dualism—"two incompatible ideals of life, and therefore two moralities."[23] The first was the morality of the pagan world, whose values were "courage, vigor, fortitude in adversity, public achievement, order, discipline, happiness, strength, justice, and above all the assertion of one's

---

Truman's justifications, based on *raison d'état*, for taking over the steel industry, should be seen as an exception. There can be little question that had Congress and the President been in agreement, the seizure would have been upheld. *See* E. CORWIN, THE PRESIDENT: OFFICE AND POWERS 154-58 (4th rev. ed. 1957).

18. 71 U.S. (4 Wall.) 2 (1866).

19. *Id.* at 120-21.

20. *Ex parte Milligan* was so labelled by Professor Corwin, in E. CORWIN, THE PRESIDENT: OFFICE AND POWERS 165 (2d rev. ed. 1941), *quoted in* C. ROSSITER & R. LONGAKER, THE SUPREME COURT AND THE COMMANDER IN CHIEF 38 (expanded ed. 1976).

21. 317 U.S. 1 (1942). This largely forgotten "case of the Nazi saboteurs" is of considerable importance in any analysis of presidential power. *Compare* F. BIDDLE, IN BRIEF AUTHORITY 325-43 (1962) *with* A. MASON, HARLAN FISKE STONE: PILLAR OF THE LAW 652-59 (1956). Biddle was the Attorney General in 1942, Stone the Chief Justice. Further discussion of the context in which the case arose may be found in C. ROSSITER & R. LONGAKER, *supra* note 20, at 6-7, 112-16.

22. Berlin, *The Originality of Machiavelli*, in STUDIES ON MACHIAVELLI 149 (M. Gilmore ed. 1972).

23. *Id.* at 169.

proper claims and the knowledge and power needed to secure their satisfaction."[24] Machiavelli called this morality *virtù*, not translatable as "virtue" but as "manliness." Much of American history reflects a pursuit of these values. The second morality, of equal importance, is derived from the Judeo-Christian tradition, whose ideals are "charity, mercy, sacrifice, love of God, forgiveness of enemies, contempt for the goods of this world, faith in the life hereafter, belief in the salvation of the individual soul as being of incomparable value—higher, indeed wholly incommensurable with, any social or political or other terrestrial goal, any economic or military or aesthetic consideration."[25]

In shorthand terms, the first (pagan) morality values security, both internal and external, which might be called social order.[26] The second morality involves human dignity, that which Felix Cohen called "the good,"[27] the notion of legally reified decency, which is a distillation of the Bill of Rights and the ideals of American constitutionalism. In *Milligan*, Justice Davis stated a view of American constitutionality that, at least implicitly, adopted Berlin's second morality. Justice Davis did not, of course, employ the language of Judeo-Christian morality. That ideal finds its clearest statement in political speeches and in the underlying assumptions of American constitutionalism.[28] In theory, constitutionalism in the United States not only indi-

---

24. *Id.*

25. *Id.*

26. *Cf.* Dennis v. United States, 341 U.S. 494, 509 (1951) (security is the "ultimate value").

27. *See generally* F. COHEN, ETHICAL SYSTEMS AND LEGAL IDEALS (1933).

28. The second, or Judeo-Christian, morality emphasizes both the value of the individual and limits on the ability of the individual to seek satisfaction of some desires. The individual's salvation and relationship with God is paramount, but the individual is also to act in harmony with a set of materially self-effacing precepts that elevate the worth of others. This is in contrast to the pagan morality, under which the needs of others are necessarily inferior to personal goals.

The Christian tradition was strong among the early settlers of this country and it has remained so; it formed the framework within which American political institutions were created. The formal rules of societal institutions parallel those of Christians. The power of collective society, embodied in government, was under the Constitution to be contained within certain proscriptive rules. The most important of these rules protect the "inalienable" rights of individuals—especially rights to fair treatment and certain basic liberties. Thus, Judeo-Christian emphases on the importance of the individual and on circumscribed prerogatives was embodied in American institutions from the beginning. Nor has our Judeo-Christian heritage been forgotten by those in government. *See* Zorach v. Clauson, 343 U.S. 306, 313 (1952) ("We are a religious people whose institutions presuppose a Supreme Being."). This is not to say that the formal law was, or is, in consonance with the living law.

cates the ideal of the dignity of the individual human being, but is also an articulation of limited government. Due process, broadly defined, is its central core.[29] The principle of limited government, however, is merely the facade of American constitutionalism. The unpleasant reality is that the actions of public officers often comport with the precepts of the pagan morality; indeed, more frequently than many Americans like to think, public action cannot be justified under either morality. Berlin's point is not that one morality is superior to the other (although Machiavelli, of course, adhered to the pagan), but that there are two goals—two ideals—of human endeavor, both used as norms by human beings, that are incompatible with one another.

This dichotomy causes intellectual confusion and a gap between pretense and reality in official behavior. At times, the goals merge in Supreme Court opinions; when they do, the Court usually chooses the pagan over the Judeo-Christian morality. The Court, however, often attempts to rationalize its decisions (as did Justice Davis) in terms of the latter. So, too, do other government officers.

The unavoidable conclusion is that if there is a single morality in American constitutionalism, it is that of the pagan values as delineated by Machiavelli. That is a harsh accusation. Berlin does not make it, his essay being an analysis of Machiavelli, not an application of the Florentine to any nation. Is there evidence sufficient to buttress such a conclusion? The answer, as will be shown, can only be "yes." Machiavelli is relevant to the United States, despite the popular wisdom about him, because he was the first to make the radical dualism in governmental affairs so plain. In his writings (mainly *The Discourses* and *The Prince*) he plunged a sword "into the flank of the body politic of Western humanity, causing it to shriek and rear up."[30] The pain of that sword's thrust is still with us, five centuries after Machiavelli. It is a pain, a contradiction, that has never been directly confronted or reconciled in our constitutional history. The dualism is, of course, disturbing to people,

---

29. *See* NOMOS XVIII: DUE PROCESS *passim* (J. Pennock & J. Chapman eds. 1977); Miller, *An Affirmative Thrust to Due Process of Law?*, in A.S. MILLER, SOCIAL CHANGE AND FUNDAMENTAL LAW: AMERICA'S EVOLVING CONSTITUTION 97 (1979).

30. F. MEINECKE, *supra* note 8, at 49. Professor Crick, in his *Introduction* to THE DISCOURSES, *supra* note 12, at 13, 67, quotes Meinecke's assertion then adds, "The pain is still with us and if we ever cease to feel it, it will not be because the conditions that gave rise to it have miraculously vanished but because our nerves have gone dead."

including judges, who are insistent on finding a single truth, or who otherwise evade such an awkward duality. Not that Machiavelli preferred a prince; despite the belief to the contrary, he recognized that "republics are to be preferred if you can get them."[31] But republics must provide for emergency measures; and even "democracies" act, when their leaders consider it necessary, contrary to the Rule of Law. Few will appreciate the proposition that the primary truth to be distilled from our heritage is that pagan virtues prevail, but it cannot be denied, particularly when it is seen that in the past (even if not in the future) extraordinary actions to meet emergencies were limited in time and space in accordance with the Principle of Economy of Means.

Can one, then, distinguish between the circumstances fit for republican—*i.e.*, democratic—rule and those suited for personal rule? That was Machiavelli's central concern. And that, one would think, should be a fundamental concern of American constitutional scholars in the future. It is *the* crucial question, one that is not yet resolved in theory and seldom even asked.

This Article is a preliminary examination of this question. In what follows, the inevitable conclusion is that there is no middle course between the two moralities. To repeat: one morality—the Judeo-Christian—is the theory of the formal Constitution (it is one way of stating the American Dream);[32] the other (pagan) morality is the guiding principle of the "living" Constitution. The concept of a living Constitution is ambiguous, for it refers to two different phenomena. In its usual sense, it means the way in which specific constitutional terms have evolved through time.[33] Due process, equal protection, and interstate commerce are ready examples. As important as this evolution is, there is another dimension of equal and perhaps greater importance: the Constitution "in operation." Silences of the fundamental law, particularly with respect to executive power, are filled (as in reason of state or executive privilege); "structural" changes in the organization of government occur (as in the system of federalism and separation of powers). The most important aspect of our constitutional law is not what the document says or even what the Supreme Court says; rather, it is what is done by government officers, including the officers of

---

31. Crick, *Introduction* to THE DISCOURSES, *supra* note 12, at 22.

32. *See* R. MILES, AWAKENING FROM THE AMERICAN DREAM: THE SOCIAL AND POLITICAL LIMITS TO GROWTH (1976).

33. *See* W. WILSON, CONGRESSIONAL GOVERNMENT 28-31 (1956) (originally published 1885).

the private governments of the nation. They follow the iron law of necessity—necessity as perceived by the effective holders of power of the nation—even though, as Milton recognized, necessity is the plea of every tyrant.[34] Support for this observation is found in an examination of historical examples from several contexts.

A. USE OF VIOLENCE

One option available to American policy makers is the calculated use of violence. As Professor Abraham Sofaer has shown,[35] presidents since George Washington have employed violence, usually without a declaration of war, when they considered it necessary. The second constitution expressly gives Congress the power to declare war, with the Chief Executive being the commander-in-chief of the armed forces.[36] This language could be interpreted to mean that the President has tactical control of troops once they are committed to war by Congress. But that is only partially true. In a clear example of why the second constitution should be called one of "quasi-limitations," presidents have often tacitly invoked the principle of reason of state to take such violent measures as they considered necessary.

It is not necessary to list all of the instances in which the principle has been invoked. Four illustrative examples will suffice to show the pattern: the Civil War, World War II, Korea, and Vietnam.[37] Each illustrates some of the common elements of American usage of *raison d'état*, including: (a) the President usually takes such action as he deems necessary to meet the threat, whether the threat is actual, as in the case of the Civil War; probable, as in the period prior to World War II; dubious, as during the Korean War; or nonexistent, as during the

---

34. "[A]nd with necessity, [t]he tyrant's plea, excused his devilish deeds." J. MILTON, PARADISE LOST 41 (1894) (bk. iv, line 393).

35. A. SOFAER, WAR, FOREIGN AFFAIRS AND CONSTITUTIONAL POWER: THE ORIGINS (1976).

36. *Compare* U.S. CONST. art. I, § 8, cl. 11 *with id.* art. II, § 2, cl. 1.

37. Another prominent example is the treatment accorded the American Indians under many presidents, both by use of the military and by other means. Until recently, Indians, aggregated into tribes, were "nonpersons" under the Constitution. *See* L. TRIBE, AMERICAN CONSTITUTIONAL LAW § 16—14, at 1014-15 (1978). That enabled them to be driven from their lands, systematically killed, and otherwise brutally dealt with despite the due process clauses. These actions are too well known to need extensive documentation or further discussion. *See generally* D. BROWN, BURY MY HEART AT WOUNDED KNEE (1972). No branch of government protected Indians until long after they had been entirely subdued and penned up on reservations.

American involvement in Vietnam; (b) Congress and the President typically act in concert, with Congress serving largely as a rubber stamp for Executive proposals;[38] (c) the courts, including the Supreme Court, generally do not inhibit whatever actions the political officers wish to take; the judges, in effect, either confess a self-imposed impotence or uphold the political actions; (d) except for relatively few persons, civil liberties are not disturbed; the populace at large is not involved; deprivations are usually economic rather than physical (personal); (e) violence is limited in time and space; and (f) violence is employed only to the extent necessary to achieve postulated goals (with some notable exceptions, such as the use of atomic bombs in 1945 and the scorched-earth policy pursued in Vietnam)—this is the Principle of Economy of Means in the use of violence.

1. *The Civil War*

"Is there in all republics this inherent and fatal weakness? Must a government of necessity be too *strong* for the liberties of its people, or too *weak* to maintain its own existence?" So asked President Lincoln on July 4, 1861.[39] Historically, the answer is clear: a nation—this nation—can fight a successful total war and still remain a "republic." At best, the Constitution was bent in such circumstances; at worst, it was simply ignored.[40]

Lincoln came to office "with little more than an acute understanding of his obligation to see to the due execution of the laws."[41] But he had also sworn to uphold the Constitution, and in his inaugural address he promised that he would preserve the Union. Congress was not in session when fighting began at Fort Sumter. The President proceeded on his own, without regard to law or constitutional processes. Lincoln described his reasons for assuming broad authority:

> It became necessary for us to choose whether, using only the existing means, agencies, and processes which Congress had provided, I should

---

38. *See* C. ROSSITER, *supra* note 13, at 242 (broad delegation of power from Congress to President Wilson during World War I).

39. *See id.* at 1 (quoting a message to Congress by President Lincoln).

40. Nuclear warfare would add a completely different dimension. If such a war occurs, as it might, there can be no question but that a rigid dictatorship would be imposed and kept in power indefinitely. *See* Rossiter, *What of Congress in Atomic War?*, 3 W. POL. Q. 602 (1950); Rossiter, *Constitutional Dictatorship in the Atomic Age*, 11 REV. POL. 395 (1949). *But cf.* C. ROSSITER, *supra* note 13, at 300, 306, 310-11 (proposing strict limitations on the duration of any emergency dictatorship).

41. N. SMALL, SOME PRESIDENTIAL INTERPRETATIONS OF THE PRESIDENCY 31 (1932).

let the Government fall at once into ruin, or whether, availing myself of the broader powers conferred by the Constitution in cases of insurrection, I would make an effort to save it, with all its blessings, for the present age and for posterity.[42]

The flaw in Lincoln's justification is obvious: these "broader powers" he described do not exist as such in the formal Constitution. Lincoln had to draw up Machiavellian principles of *raison d'état* to justify his actions. Interpreting his task as confronting a gigantic mob and dispersing it (the government being faced "by combinations too powerful to be suppressed by the ordinary course of judicial proceedings"),[43] the President took the following actions *before* calling Congress into session: (a) he mobilized 75,000 of the state militia by executive proclamation; (b) he blockaded the ports of the rebellious states, again by proclamations; (c) he added nineteen warships to the navy "for purposes of public defense";[44] (d) he called for 42,000 volunteers and enlarged both the regular army and the navy in an "amazing disregard for the words of the Constitution";[45] (e) he spent public money in disregard of the constitutional requirement that "no Money shall be drawn from the Treasury, but in Consequence of Appropriations made by Law";[46] and (f) he authorized suspension of the writ of habeas corpus, again by proclamation.[47]

When Congress finally convened in July 1861, it speedily ratified President Lincoln's actions. In the leading judicial decision evaluating his authority for such actions, the *Prize Cases*,[48] the Supreme Court held the blockade to be constitutionally warranted, stating:

> Whether the President in fulfilling his duties as Commander-in-chief, in suppressing an insurrection, has met with armed resistance, and a civil war of such alarming proportions as will compel him to accord to them the character of belligerents, is a question to be decided *by him*, and this Court must be governed by the decisions and acts of the politi-

---

42. 6 MESSAGES AND PAPERS OF THE PRESIDENT 78 (J. Richardson ed. 1897) [hereinafter cited as MESSAGES AND PAPERS].

43. The language is that of the Militia Act of 1795, ch. 36, § 2, 1 Stat. 424 (current version at 10 U.S.C. §§ 331-334 (1976)).

44. 6 MESSAGES AND PAPERS, *supra* note 42, at 78.

45. C. ROSSITER, *supra* note 13, at 226.

46. U.S. CONST. art. I, § 9, cl. 7.

47. This is taken from Professor Rossiter's account. *See* C. ROSSITER, *supra* note 13, at 225-28.

48. 67 U.S. (2 Black) 635 (1863). *See also Ex parte* Merryman, 17 Fed. Cas. 144 (1861). In *Merryman*, Chief Justice Taney, sitting alone on circuit, held President Lincoln's suspension of the writ of habeas corpus to be invalid. The President soon defied Taney's decision. For an account of the *Merryman* episode, see J. RANDALL, CONSTITUTIONAL PROBLEMS UNDER LINCOLN 118-39 (rev. ed. 1951).

cal department of the Government to which this was entrusted. . . . He [the President] must determine what degree of force the crisis demands.[49]

The Constitution had thus been neatly amended, and *raison d'état* thereafter became an operative principle of our fundamental law. The "imperial presidency" was born.

2. *World War II*

The precedent set by Lincoln in the Civil War and given a cachet of legitimacy in the *Prize Cases* presaged the acts of President Franklin Roosevelt before and during World War II. In the period before the war, there is little doubt that Roosevelt actually committed the nation to war on the side of Great Britain two years prior to Pearl Harbor[50] and that he probably knew about Japan's plans to attack an American base yet did nothing about it until after the blow was struck.[51] Not only did the President repeatedly give verbal support to the anti-Hitler forces, he pushed the American people to the brink of war through such actions as the call for the Lend-Lease Act, the occupation of Iceland, the Atlantic Charter, the use of convoys, the September 1941 "shoot on sight" order against Nazi U-boats, and the destroyer deal of 1940.[52] William Stevenson's account of that period, *A Man Called Intrepid*, describes Roosevelt's close cooperation with Great Britain, and how he secretly took certain steps that can only be called acts of war.[53]

As for Japan, American policy makers had access to all secret Japanese diplomatic messages after army cryptologists broke the Japanese code in August 1940. It seems clear that Roosevelt knew in late 1941 that an attack was imminent somewhere in the Pacific. Nevertheless, the commanders of the American military bases were not alerted in time,[54] and the Pearl Harbor attack catapulted the United States into war with Japan. That war quickly expanded to Germany, when Hitler declared war on the United States. Perhaps, as many have argued, World War II was a "just" war[55] if ever there was one.

---

49. 67 U.S. (2 Black) at 670. The Supreme Court's deference to the President in times of armed conflict is the norm; the *Prize Cases* are not aberrational. *See generally* C. ROSSITER & R. LONGAKER, *supra* note 20.

50. *See* W. STEVENSON, A MAN CALLED INTREPID (1976).

51. *See* B. BARTLETT, COVER-UP: THE POLITICS OF PEARL HARBOR, 1941-1946 (1979).

52. *See* E. CORWIN, *supra* note 17, at 227-62 (ch. VI) (summary of President Roosevelt's actions).

53. W. STEVENSON, *supra* note 50, *passim*.

54. *See* B. BARTLETT, *supra* note 51.

55. This is not to say that all actions taken by the Allies were "just." Cer-

That, however, is not the point; the relevant fact is that the President followed pagan principles well in advance of a declaration of war. What Lincoln had done soon *after* fighting began at Fort Sumter, Roosevelt did *before* December 7, 1941. The result, for present purposes, is clear: however much judges and others may believe to the contrary, a written constitution is no barrier to the desires of a determined Chief Executive (and a pliable Congress).

Nor was the Constitution a barrier *during* World War II, as evinced—to cite only one example—by Roosevelt's demand that Congress repeal a provision of the Price Control Act of 1942, asserting that if Congress did not do so he, as President, would be left "with an inescapable responsibility to the people of this country to see to it that the war effort is no longer imperiled by threat of economic chaos."[56] That is as clear a statement of *raison d'état* as has ever been uttered by an American President. Other examples of action taken by Roosevelt that evidence *raison d'état* include (a) imposing a nondiscrimination-in-employment clause in all war contracts;[57] (b) forcibly removing and incarcerating more than 100,000 people—including many native-born citizens—of Japanese ancestry;[58] (c) hanging General Yamashita for war crimes even though the evidence showed that Yamashita neither ordered nor knew about the actions of his troops in the Philippines;[59] (d) executing several of the so-called Nazi saboteurs[60] even in the face of *Ex parte Milligan*;[61] and (e) establishing many offices without congressional approval—for example, the Office of War Information.[62] And when President Truman took office, he ordered the use of atomic bombs even though it seemed obvious that Japan was defeated. By the end of the war, presidential action by reason of state had become almost commonplace.

---

tainly the bombing of Dresden was not; nor was the use of atomic weapons against Japan. *See generally* M. WALZER, JUST AND UNJUST WARS (1977).

56. President's Message to Congress on Inflation Control, H.R. DOC. No. 834, 77th Cong., 2d Sess., 88 CONG. REC. 7042, 7044 (1942). *See* E. CORWIN, TOTAL WAR AND THE CONSTITUTION (1946).

57. *See* Miller, *Government Contracts and Social Control: A Preliminary Inquiry*, 41 VA. L. REV. 27 (1955).

58. These actions were litigated and upheld. *See* Hirabayashi v. United States, 320 U.S. 81 (1943); Korematsu v. United States, 323 U.S. 214 (1944). *But see Ex parte* Mitsuye Endo, 323 U.S. 283, 297 (1944) (War Relocation Authority held to have no authority to detain "citizens who are concededly loyal.").

59. *See In re* Yamashita, 327 U.S. 1 (1946).

60. *See Ex Parte* Quirin, 317 U.S. 1 (1942).

61. *See* text accompanying notes 18-21 *supra*.

62. *See* E. CORWIN, *supra* note 17, at 239-50.

3. *Korea and Vietnam*

It is doubtful whether President Roosevelt could have obtained a declaration of war against either Japan or Germany before the attack at Pearl Harbor. It is thus not surprising that the President took extraconstitutional actions to achieve what he probably would have been unable to achieve through more formal constitutional processes. He perceived a need and acted upon it—in accordance with basic Machiavellian principles. Korea and Vietnam were similar in that the decisions to enter those conflicts were largely made by the President, who also supplied the interpretation that American intervention was necessary. President Truman, for example, introduced American troops into Korea on his own authority and without consulting Congress.[63] Despite President Truman's assessment of the need for American entry into Korea, some doubt exists as to the necessity of that involvement.[64] Reason of state again prevailed. For the first time, a major *external* conflict was entered into solely on presidential order, a conflict that did not even remotely threaten American lives or property. Congress, of course, approved the action; appropriations and other supportive statutes were routinely enacted.

The importance of Korea for the development of presidential power cannot be over-emphasized. Previous external forays by American military forces in the absence of declarations of war were far smaller and far more localized. The State Department issued a statement arguing that the President's actions in Korea were fully consonant with his legal authority. Relying principally on "inherent" powers of the Chief Executive, but drawing also on the United Nations Charter and a U.N. Security Council resolution, the State Department asserted that the President has full control over the use of the armed forces. "He also has authority to conduct the foreign relations of the United States. Since the beginning of the United States history, he has, on numerous occasions, utilized these powers in sending armed forces abroad."[65] The State Department ne-

---

63. *See* Longaker, *The Constitution and the Commander in Chief After 1950*, in C. ROSSITER & R. LONGAKER, *supra* note 20, at 135 n.1. *See generally* Lofgren, *Mr. Truman's War: A Debate and Its Aftermath*, 31 REV. POL. 223, 231 (1969); Note, *Congress, the President, and the Power to Commit Forces to Combat*, 81 HARV. L. REV. 1771, 1791-92 (1968).

64. *See* Gittings, *The War Before*, The Guardian (Manchester), June 27, 1975, at 10.

65. *Authority of the President to Repel the Attack in Korea*, 23 DEP'T STATE BULL. 173-74 (1950). The State Department also noted that there was a "tradi-

glected to say, however, that the President had never before used such powers to the extent that they were employed in Korea. The scope of the presidential powers took a quantum leap—his prerogative was completed several months later when Secretary of State Dean Acheson told Congress: "Not only has the President the authority to use the Armed Forces in carrying out the broad foreign policy of the United States and implementing treaties, but it is equally clear that this authority may not be interfered with by Congress in the exercise of powers which it has under the Constitution."[66] That testimony, in sum, is an assertion of reason of state run riot.

At the same time as its activities in Korea, the United States became involved in Indochina—first by recognizing French sovereignty over the area in May 1945,[67] then by providing financial assistance to the French puppet regime beginning in May 1950,[68] later by sending advisers, and finally by committing more than 500,000 troops in what eventually proved to be a futile effort. Presidents Johnson and Nixon maintained that presidential power alone was sufficient to support such activi-

---

tional power of the President to use the Armed Forces of the United States without consulting Congress." *Id.* at 174.

66. SENATE COMM. ON FOREIGN RELATIONS, NATIONAL COMMITMENTS, S. REP. No. 797, 90th Cong., 1st Sess. 17 (1967) [hereinafter cited as S. REP. No. 797].

67. During World War II, President Roosevelt opposed post-war resumption of French sovereignty over Indochina. On March 15, 1945, he indicated that he would agree to a French trusteeship if the French would promise to promote the eventual complete independence of Indochina. Memorandum of Conversation Between President Roosevelt and Charles Taussig, in 1 DEPARTMENT OF STATE, FOREIGN RELATIONS OF THE UNITED STATES, 1945, at 124 (1967), *reprinted in* 1 VIET-NAM CRISIS: A DOCUMENTARY HISTORY 32-33 (W. Cameron ed. 1971) [hereinafter cited as VIET-NAM CRISIS]. *See also* A. WEDEMEYER, WEDEMEYER REPORTS! 340 (1958) (Roosevelt's March 1945 support for independence of French Indochina). Soon after Roosevelt's death on April 12, 1945, the American position seemed to become more passive and was subsequently marked by acquiescence in French exercise of sovereignty, *see* Telegram from Acting Secretary of State Joseph Grew to Ambassador Jefferson Caffery, in 6 DEPARTMENT OF STATE, *supra*, at 307, *reprinted in* 1 VIET-NAM CRISIS, *supra*, at 36 (quoting statement of Secretary of State Edward Stettinius to French Minister for Foreign Affairs Georges Bidault prior to May 9, 1945), refusal to provide active aid, and continued urging of French promotion of Indochinese self-government or independence. *See* 1 THE PENTAGON PAPERS: THE DEFENSE DEPARTMENT HISTORY OF UNITED STATES DECISIONMAKING ON VIETNAM 15-34 (Sen. Gravel ed. 1971) [hereinafter cited as PENTAGON PAPERS].

68. On May 1, 1950, President Truman approved $10 million in military assistance for Indochina. *See* 1 PENTAGON PAPERS, *supra* note 67, at 66. Secretary of State Acheson made a public announcement of economic and military aid to Indochina and France on May 8. *See* Statement by Secretary of State Acheson, United States Aid to the Associated States (May 8, 1950), in 2 DEPARTMENT OF STATE, AMERICAN FOREIGN POLICY 1950-1955: BASIC DOCUMENTS 2365 (1957), *reprinted in* 1 VIET-NAM CRISIS, *supra* note 67, at 148.

ties.[69] It is not the purpose of this Article to assess American involvement in Vietnam. That involvement is too recent to do more than suggest several lessons it illustrates for constitutional government.

One such lesson was described by Justice Robert Jackson in his dissent in the *Korematsu* case: "If the people ever let command of the war power fall into irresponsible and unscrupulous hands, the courts wield no power equal to its restraint. The chief restraint upon those who command the physical forces of the country, in the future as in the past, must be their

---

69. President Johnson, in a news conference on August 18, 1967, claimed that the Gulf of Tonkin resolution was unnecessary: "We stated then, and we repeat now, we did not think the resolution was necessary to do what we did and what we're doing." N.Y. Times, Aug. 19, 1967, at 10, col. 6. *See also* S. REP. NO. 797, *supra* note 66, at 21-23.

President Nixon also took a sweeping view of presidential authority to deploy American combat troops. In November 1973, Congress adopted the War Powers Resolution, Pub. L. No. 93-148, 87 Stat. 555 (1973), over Nixon's veto. *See* 119 CONG. REC. 36202, 36222 (1973). One provision of the Resolution generally requires that the President terminate any use of military forces within sixty days if Congress has not authorized continued use of such forces. War Powers Resolution, Pub. L. No. 93-148, § 5(b), 87 Stat. 555, 556 (1973). In President Nixon's veto message, he asserted that this provision was "clearly unconstitutional" because the powers thus restricted—introducing the United States Armed Forces into hostilities or combat troops into foreign countries—were constitutional powers, "which the President has properly exercised under the Constitution for almost 200 years." Message from President Nixon to the House of Representatives, Oct. 24, 1973, H.R. DOC. NO. 171, 93d Cong., 1st Sess., 119 CONG. REC. 34990. Following the adoption of the resolution over Nixon's veto, the White House refused to state whether it would obey the statute. *See* N.Y. Times, Nov. 8, 1973, at 1, col. 8. In 1976, President Nixon further elaborated his concept of presidential power: "It is quite obvious that there are certain inherently governmental actions which if undertaken by the sovereign in protection of the interest of the nation's security are lawful but which if undertaken by private persons are not. . . . [I]t is naive to attempt to categorize activities a president might authorize as 'legal' or 'illegal' without reference to the circumstances under which he concludes that the activity is necessary." 4 SENATE SELECT COMM. TO STUDY GOVERNMENTAL OPERATIONS WITH RESPECT TO INTELLIGENCE ACTIVITIES, FOREIGN AND MILITARY INTELLIGENCE, S. REP. NO. 755, 94th Cong., 2d Sess. 157 (1976) [hereinafter cited as S. REP. NO. 755].

President Ford's views of the presidential military powers were similar to those of Presidents Johnson and Nixon. He justified the United States Marines' assault on the Cambodian island of Koh Tang and other offensive military action related to the Mayaguez incident as "ordered and conducted pursuant to the President's constitutional Executive power and his authority as Commander-in-Chief." President's Letter to the Speaker of the House and President Pro Tempore of the Senate in Accordance With the War Powers Resolution, 11 WEEKLY COMP. OF PRES. DOC. 515, 516 (May 15, 1975). *See also* A.S. MILLER, PRESIDENTIAL POWER IN A NUTSHELL 192-94 (1977); Paust, *The Seizure and Recovery of the* Mayaguez, 85 YALE L.J. 774 (1976); Note, *The Constitutional Implications of the Mayaguez Incident*, 3 HASTINGS CONST. L.Q. 301 (1976). *See generally* Casper, *Constitutional Constraints on the Conduct of Foreign and Defense Policy: A Nonjudicial Model*, 43 U. CHI. L. REV. 463 (1976).

responsibility to the political judgments of their contemporaries and to the moral judgments of history."[70] I suggest that the war power did indeed fall into irresponsible and unscrupulous hands during the Vietnam "war."[71]

Another lesson was described by Machiavelli: it is "a sound maxim that reprehensible actions may be justified by their effects, and . . . when the effect is good . . . it always justifies the action."[72] In Vietnam, however, the American goal was dominion over Southeast Asia[73]—a goal that was bad under both the pagan and the Judeo-Christian morality. The means employed in Vietnam, therefore, cannot be justified, even under Machiavelli's formula.

The significance of Vietnam for constitutional scholars cannot be overestimated. The fundamental law was neatly amended by presidential fiat; that amendment was approved by a supine Congress and determination of its validity was avoided by a timid judiciary. As Professor Richard P. Longaker has correctly observed, "[T]he presidential position was that while any formal support that Congress might wish to extend in a given instance would be welcomed, the independent power of the executive was sufficient."[74] Such a position means that the Executive Branch considers itself dominant in theory and in fact—not *primus inter pares*,[75] but simply *primus*.

John Locke, in his *Second Treatise of Civil Government*, de-

---

70. Korematsu v. United States, 323 U.S. 214, 248 (1944) (Jackson, J., dissenting).

71. *Compare* M. WALZER, *supra* note 55, *with* W. SHAWCROSS, SIDESHOW: KISSINGER, NIXON AND THE DESTRUCTION OF CAMBODIA (1979). Shawcross demonstrates that the bombing of Cambodia was not a mistake but a crime. Professor Stanley Hoffmann of Harvard University concludes: "Among the casualties of the disaster we must count not only the Cambodians but America's own constitutional order. Shawcross reminds us that the original bombing was not merely concealed but falsified in the official records. Efforts by journalists to 'leak' the truth led to the wiretapping of top officials. Spying and dissimulation between government agencies became routine. Attempts by the staff of the Senate Foreign Relations Committee to investigate in Cambodia were sabotaged. And yet the House Judiciary Committee refused to include Cambodia among the articles of Nixon's impeachment." Hoffmann, *The Crime of Cambodia*, N.Y. Rev. of Books, June 28, 1979, at 3, 4. For arguments in support of the Nixon-Kissinger policy in Indochina, see H. KISSINGER, WHITE HOUSE YEARS (1979), *critically reviewed by* Hoffmann in N.Y. Rev. of Books, Dec. 8, 1979, at 14.

72. THE DISCOURSES, *supra* note 12, bk. I, § 9. The word "justified" might better have been translated as "excused."

73. The oft-announced goal of bringing democracy to that area is sheer nonsense and mere propaganda.

74. Longaker, *supra* note 63, in C. ROSSITER & R. LONGAKER, *supra* note 20, at 137.

75. The first among equals.

fended use of the "prerogative" through the ancient principle *salus populi suprema lex*:[76] "This power to act according to discretion, for the public good, without the prescription of the law, and sometimes even against it, is that which is called the prerogative . . . . There is a latitude left to the executive power, to do many things of choice, which the laws do not prescribe."[77] Well and good, one might say, were it not for two stubborn facts: the Constitution of 1787 contains no provision for such discretion; in Vietnam the essential interests of the American people were not in jeopardy. No crisis existed except one that was manufactured by American policy makers. Although it is unquestionably true that presidents must act in the face of actual crisis, they also labor under the obligation of correctly distinguishing between actual and chimerical crises. Their analyses must be accepted, as Justice Jackson said, both by their contemporaries and by posterity. A president who wishes to avoid serious challenge to the legitimacy of his acts must take care that his acts produce successful results. He labors under the obligation to succeed. Machiavelli maintained that "reprehensible actions" could be justified by "their effects."[78] Presidential actions in Vietnam were thus widely condemned because the consequences of the American involvement were bad by any criterion. It is instructive to compare Vietnam with two other military episodes of dubious propriety: the war against Mexico and the Spanish-American War. Both wars were perceived as successful and, even though many people firmly opposed such imperialistic adventures, they are not currently viewed with great opprobrium.

B. Other Historical Examples

Enough has been said about the use of violence, in declared wars and otherwise, to validate the existence of Berlin's two moralities—one of pretense and the other of action—and to show that at times even the pagan morality is transgressed. Other examples help complete the argument that *raison d'état* is indeed a viable principle of American constitutional law.

---

76. The welfare of the people is the supreme law.

77. J. Locke, The Second Treatise of Civil Government para. 160, at 80 (J. Gough ed. 1946). *See* Hurtgen, *The Case for Presidential Prerogative*, 7 U. Tol. L. Rev. 59 (1975).

78. The Discourses, *supra* note 12, bk. I, § 9.

1. *Economic Depression*

Throughout its history, the United States has experienced cyclical economic fluctuations. The economic system, loosely called capitalism, is based primarily on private ownership and control of production and distribution. For whatever reason, those who control private enterprise have never been able to achieve a stable economy. Destitution has periodically swept the country. Not until the 1930s did the government attempt to systematically remedy the causes of economic distress. In the view of President Roosevelt, the Great Depression called for crisis (warlike) techniques to meet a critical danger to the nation. He proposed "not prudence, but the deliberate assumption of risks in the hope of great gains."[79] Roosevelt pursued such a policy by acting as economic dictator in the early days of his first administration. During that period, he *was* the government of the United States. *Raison d'état* was introduced to economic affairs.

In his first inaugural address, Roosevelt asked for broad emergency powers: "as great as the power that would be given to me if we were in fact invaded by a foreign foe."[80] This was a request for delegated powers. But the President did not wait for Congressional authorization. On March 6, 1933 (two days after his inauguration and three days before Congress was summoned in emergency session), Roosevelt, referring to the existence of a national emergency, ordered a "bank holiday,"[81] forbade the export of gold and silver, and prohibited transactions in foreign exchange. His purported authority was a dubious reading of the Trading with the Enemy Act,[82] a World War I measure aimed at foreign exchange matters. His authority in fact was reason of state. Congress' speedy ratification of these actions (on March 9), which gave the President even greater authority, does not belie the fact that Roosevelt's actions were contrary to the law.

During the famous "Hundred Days" following March 4, 1933, Roosevelt and Congress acted so closely together that Congress appeared to merely rubber-stamp executive actions. Separation of powers was all but forgotten. The chasm be-

---

79. G. JOHNSON, ROOSEVELT: DICTATOR OR DEMOCRAT? 214 (1941).

80. 2 THE PUBLIC PAPERS AND ADDRESSES OF FRANKLIN D. ROOSEVELT 65 (1938).

81. *Id.* at 24-26. *See* Watkins, *The Problem of Constitutional Dictatorship*, in 1 PUBLIC POLICY 324 (C. Friedrich & E. Mason eds. 1940).

82. Ch. 106, 40 Stat. 411 (1917) (current version at 50 U.S.C. App. §§ 1-44 (App. 1976)).

tween the two political branches of government was bridged, but only for a short time. By 1935 there was growing opposition to Roosevelt's policies in Congress, fed by the antagonism of various interest groups. Finally, the Supreme Court began to invalidate New Deal legislation. Prominent among the statutes that were found unconstitutional was the National Recovery Act,[83] which had declared a national emergency and had overtly delegated governing power to industrial groups. As is common knowledge, however, the Court "rewrote" the due process and interstate commerce clauses in 1937,[84] thereby permitting the political branches to freely manage the economy. The abdication of judicial control over the economy, however, is only operative when the President and Congress agree. That is the lesson to be drawn from the *Steel Seizure Case*[85] of 1952, and *AFL-CIO v. Kahn*,[86] a case in which the D.C. Circuit found that Congress had impliedly granted the President power to deny government contracts to companies that do not comply with presidentially promulgated voluntary wage and price standards. When, on July 2, 1979, the Supreme Court denied certiorari in the *Kahn* case,[87] the lesson became even more clear.

2. *Dissident Groups*

The dissident, notwithstanding the mythology to the contrary, has never been easily accepted in the United States. Only when dissent takes innocuous forms—for example, Thoreau at Walden Pond—is the person tolerated. The dissident has usually been controlled through purposive use of law and the legal system. Radicals and deviants, with some exceptions, are seldom shot down, and they are rarely victims of "emergency" legislation. The process is much more subtle: they are enjoined by judges appointed always from among the

83. *See* Schechter Poultry Corp. v. United States, 295 U.S. 495, 529 (1935); Panama Refining Co. v. Ryan, 293 U.S. 388, 414 (1935).

84. *See* West Coast Hotel Co. v. Parrish, 300 U.S. 379 (1937) (due process); NLRB v. Jones & Laughlin Steel Corp., 301 U.S. 1 (1937) (interstate commerce). The history of this constitutional reversal is described in A.S. MILLER, THE SUPREME COURT AND AMERICAN CAPITALISM (1968). *See also* Shapiro, *The Constitution and Economic Rights*, in ESSAYS ON THE CONSTITUTION OF THE UNITED STATES 74 (M. Harmon ed. 1978).

85. Youngstown Sheet & Tube Co. v. Sawyer, 343 U.S. 579 (1952).

86. No. 79-0802 (D.C. Cir. June 22, 1979) (en banc), *cert. denied*, 99 S. Ct. 3107 (1979).

87. AFL-CIO v. Kahn, 99 S. Ct. 3107 (1979). Justices Brennan, White, and Marshall would have granted certiorari. *Id.*

Establishment;[88] congressional and state legislative committees inquire into their actions; and at times they receive an outwardly lawful, but actually political, trial and are convicted of criminal activity. Examples are abundant. In 1920 a man in Connecticut was jailed for six months for saying that "Lenin was 'the brainiest' or 'one of the brainiest' political officers in the world."[89] In North Carolina during the 1970s several civil rights advocates were arrested, convicted on trumped-up charges, and given lengthy prison sentences.[90] "[T]he hidden underbelly of American politics," says Professor Murray Levin, is "[t]he deeply felt intolerance that springs from our intense commitment to Americanism, the irrational and compulsive need to defend the assumptions of John Locke and Adam Smith, the anti-Semitism, the nativism, the antiintellectualism, the vigilantism, the racism, the Xenophobia, the pursuit of self-interest under the guise of superpatriotism, and the profound antiradicalism that can be observed 'in extremis' during the hysteria [of such matters as the Red Scare of 1919-20 and McCarthyism,] have always been and are today the working assumptions of millions of Americans."[91] Repression of dissidents is not an aberration; it is as American as apple pie.

When repression is challenged in court, the result is likely to be similar to the result in *Barenblatt v. United States*.[92] Barenblatt, a witness before the House Un-American Activities Committee, was sentenced to six months in prison for refusal to answer questions about his association with the Communist

---

88. *See* Miller, *The Politics of the American Judiciary*, 49 Pol. Q. 200 (1978). *See also* J. Griffith, The Politics of the Judiciary (1977).

89. M. Levin, Political Hysteria in America 28 (1971). *See* Goldstein, *An American Gulag? Summary Arrest and Emergency Detention of Political Dissidents in the United States*, 10 Colum. Human Rights L. Rev. 541 (1978).

90. This is the case of Rev. Chavis and the civil rights advocates.

91. M. Levin, *supra* note 89, at 9.

92. 360 U.S. 109 (1959). Justice Harlan's opinion for the Court is demonstrably faulty. As Dean Roscoe Pound said: "When it comes to weighing or valuing claims or demands with respect to other claims or demands, we must be careful to compare them on the same plane. If we put one as an individual interest and the other as a social interest we may decide the question in advance in our very way of putting it." Pound, *A Survey of Social Interests*, 57 Harv. L. Rev. 1, 2 (1943). That is precisely what Harlan did in *Barenblatt*: he balanced Barenblatt's interest in remaining silent against a public interest in Congress' knowledge about subversive activities. Correct answers require correct questions. The proper comparison in *Barenblatt* would have been between the common interest in a society free from harassment of individuals because of their associations and a society in which possible subversion is more readily detected.

Party.[93] In his majority opinion, Justice Harlan found that "the balance between the individual and the governmental interests here at stake must be struck in favor of the latter."[94] "In the last analysis," he explained, Congress' power "rests on the right of self-preservation, 'the ultimate value of any society[.]' . . . Justification for its exercise in turn rests on the long and widely accepted view that the tenets of the Communist Party include the ultimate overthrow of the Government of the United States by force and violence, a view which has been given formal expression by the Congress."[95] That is an example of *raison d'état* solidified into constitutional doctrine;[96] moreover, *Barenblatt* and *Dennis v. United States*[97] are forms of officially sanctioned thought control. The aim, no doubt unarticulated, is to purify people's thoughts; or, at the very least, to discourage people from associating with those whose thoughts are considered to be impure.[98] In sum, the Supreme Court is not now, nor has it ever been, a barrier to the use of reason of state against dissidents as determined by the political officers of government.

3. *Alleged Espionage*

Two recent governmental actions involving foreign espionage further illustrate the magnitude of the power exercised by the State. The first example is the District of Columbia Circuit Court of Appeals decision in *Halkin v. Helms*,[99] in which Judge Roger Robb held that the "state secrets" privilege is absolute and, therefore, that American citizens cannot complain to courts about their overseas telephone and telegraph messages

---

93.   360 U.S. at 113-14. Barenblatt refused to rely on his privilege against self-incrimination. *Id*. at 114 & n.3.

94.   *Id*. at 134.

95.   *Id*. at 127-28 (citation omitted).

96.   Justice Harlan, wittingly or not, was adopting a Machiavellian principle: "It is not the well-being of individuals that make cities great, but the well-being of the community." THE DISCOURSES, *supra* note 12, bk. II, § 2. Further: "the common good can be realized in spite of those few who suffer." *Id*. The history of reason of state in the United States is one of a relative few suffering for the putative common good.

97.   341 U.S. 494 (1951). The petitioners in *Dennis* were convicted under the Smith Act, 18 U.S.C. § 2385 (1976), for conspiring to organize the Communist Party to teach the overthrow of the government of the United States by force and violence.

98.   *But see* 341 U.S. at 582-83 (Douglas, J., dissenting); D. WISE, THE AMERICAN POLICE STATE: THE GOVERNMENT AGAINST THE PEOPLE (1976). *See also* A. WOLFE, THE SEAMY SIDE OF DEMOCRACY: REPRESSION IN AMERICA (1973); POLITICAL TRIALS 134-247 (T. Becker ed. 1971).

99.   598 F.2d 1 (D.C. Cir. 1978).

being intercepted and read by American intelligence agencies.[100] The second example is President Carter's Executive Order of January 24, 1978, concerning the intelligence community. "The order contains the most explicit and far reaching claim of an inherent presidential right to intrude without a warrant into areas protected by the Fourth Amendment ever stated by an American President."[101] Section 2-201(b) of the Order reads:

> Activities described in sections 2-202 through 2-205 for which a warrant would be required if undertaken for law enforcement rather than intelligence purposes shall not be undertaken against a United States person without a judicial warrant, unless the President has authorized the type of activity involved and the Attorney General has both approved the particular activity and determined that there is probable cause to believe that the United States person is an agent of a foreign power.[102]

The term "agent of a foreign power" is not defined, and the Executive Order specifically permits implementing directives to be classified "because of the sensitivity of the information and its relation to national security."[103]

Carter's Executive Order has not yet been tested in the courts. The few decisions that have dealt with foreign intelligence, however, have not sustained warrantless searches. If the President prevails here, an exponential jump in executive power will have occurred. The import of *Halkin v. Helms* and the Executive Order is clear: in matters concerning alleged foreign espionage, reason of state prevails. Again, the Constitution will have been neatly amended. The cost, however, is high: individual rights and liberties are diluted. Nevertheless, the incantation of the magic words "national security" has thus far usually been enough to justify these extra-constitutional actions.[104] One can hope, with little expectation that the hope will be fulfilled, that the Supreme Court will cut through this mass of verbiage and enforce the Constitution.

---

100. *Id.* at 8.

101. Halperin, *The Carter Executive Order: A "Foreign Agent" Exception to the Fourth Amendment*, 3 FIRST PRINCIPLES, Feb. 1978, at 1, 3. *Cf.* S. REP. NO. 755, *supra* note 69 (the 1976 views of President Nixon).

102. United States Intelligence Activities, Exec. Order No. 12,036, § 2-201(b), 3 C.F.R. 112, 126 (1979).

103. *Id.* § 4-106, 3 C.F.R. at 133.

104. *See* M. HALPERIN & D. HOFFMAN, FREEDOM VS. NATIONAL SECURITY (1977). *See also* United States v. Ehrlichman, 546 F.2d 910 (D.C. Cir. 1976), *cert. denied*, 429 U.S. 1120 (1977).

4. Evacuation of People

Still another example of *raison d'état* may be seen in the forced evacuation of people. The internment of Japanese-Americans during World War II has been previously noted.[105] Two other instances—the removals of the residents of the islands of Bikini and Diego Garcia—indicate that such activity was not an isolated episode.

When the United States decided in the late 1940s to test atomic weapons, one of the testing sites chosen was the atoll of Bikini, far from American territory. The residents of Bikini were forcibly removed and relocated hundreds of miles away; all this was done under the pretext of national security. To this date, lasting radioactive after-effects prevent these people from returning to their homes.[106] The Diego Garcia incident is less well known. A spit of land in the Indian Ocean, once under British sovereignty, Diego Garcia became a military base for the United States in the 1970s. First, however, the people who lived there had to be evacuated and relocated against their will. Those former residents who are still alive now reside in miserable slums on Mauritius.[107]

---

105. *See* note 58 *supra* and accompanying text. An additional example is the series of forced removals of American Indians, *see* note 37 *supra*. In the 1838 removal of the Cherokee Nation to Oklahoma, 4,000 of 17,000 Cherokees died. *See* L. TRIBE, *supra* note 37, § 16—14 at 1013-14. *See generally* G. FLEISCH-MANN, THE CHEROKEE REMOVAL, 1838 (1971); G. FOREMAN, INDIAN REMOVAL (1932).

106. *See generally* N.Y. Times, Apr. 1, 1979, at 47, col. 1; *id.*, Oct. 17, 1975, at 70, col. 1.

107. Discussion of the Diego Garcia incident may be found in *Diego Garcia, 1975: The Debate Over the Base and the Island's Former Inhabitants: Hearings Before the Special Subcomm. on Investigations of the House Comm. on International Relations*, 94th Cong., 1st Sess. (1975) [hereinafter cited as *1975 Hearings*]. *See also* COMPTROLLER GENERAL OF THE UNITED STATES, REPORT NO. B-184915, FINANCIAL AND LEGAL ASPECTS OF THE AGREEMENT ON THE AVAILABILITY OF CERTAIN INDIAN OCEAN ISLANDS FOR DEFENSE PURPOSES (1976); N.Y. Times, Dec. 25, 1975, at 8, col. 2.

A 1966 agreement between the United States and the United Kingdom made the islands of the British Indian Ocean Territory, including the Chagos Archipelago, available to both countries for defense purposes. *See* Agreement on the Availability of Certain Indian Ocean Islands for Defense Purposes, Dec. 30, 1966, United States-United Kingdom, 18 U.S.T. 28, T.I.A.S. No. 6196. When the United States decided to establish a facility on Diego Garcia, an island of the Archipelago, the British, pursuant to the Agreement, carried out the evacuation that was considered necessary. The inhabitants of the island were contract workers on a coconut plantation, some from families that had resided on the island for generations. In 1964 there were 483 people on the island, about half of whom were considered to be "Ilois"—oriented more towards the Chagos Archipelago than their ancestral Mauritius or Seychelles. *See* U.S. DEP'T OF STATE, REPORT ON THE RESETTLEMENT OF INHABITANTS OF THE CHAGOS ARCHIPELAGO, 121 CONG. REC. 33124, 33124 (1975) [hereinafter cited as STATE DEPART-

The conclusion is clear: when considered desirable, the United States government will remove people against their will in order to further "national security." Again, that is *raison d'état*. Whether it was in fact indispensable to our security to explode atomic weapons at Bikini or confiscate the property of the people on Diego Garcia is doubtful, and does not appear to have been adequately considered by American officials.

5. *Raison de Groupe*

It has been suggested above that the United States is a form of corporate State, a syzygetic order in which corporations and government coexist.[108] If that is indeed so, then *raison d'état* must also encompass a dimension of *raison de groupe*.[109] Several examples illustrate this point.

The involvement of the United Fruit Company (U.F.) in Central America shows that the company was the *de facto* government of several nations for years—with the full knowledge and support of the United States government.[110] U.F. won its

---

MENT REPORT], *reprinted in 1975 Hearings, supra,* at 40-45. The establishment of the base was expected to occupy the land on which the plantation was located, requiring closure of the plantation. *See 1975 Hearings, supra,* at 72 (testimony of George T. Churchill, Director, Office of International Security Operations, Dep't of State). The islanders were thus removed primarily because of their loss of the means of economic support. In addition, the U.S. was concerned about security in the vicinity of a military installation and the possible social problems that might be caused by contact between the military personnel and the natives. *See id.,* at 74 (testimony of George T. Churchill); STATE DEPARTMENT REPORT, 121 CONG. REC. at 33124 (no mention of a need for the plantation's land). The plantation closure made it impossible for the islanders to avoid resettlement and most were removed to Mauritius in 1971. The Mauritian government, at least through 1975, did little to assist the adjustment of the islanders, who were largely untrained for local jobs, and many of whom were forced to live in slum housing. From among the islanders, many of whom resettled in 1973 from the other two Chagos Archipelago islands, about 40 had died by 1975, primarily from influenza and diphtheria. *See* Walker, *Price on Islanders' Birthright,* The Guardian (Manchester & London), Nov. 4, 1975, at 4, col. 2, *reprinted in 1975 Hearings, supra,* at 122-23; Wash. Post, Sept. 9, 1975, at 1, col. 2, *reprinted in 1975 Hearings, supra,* at 102-04.

108. *See* notes 10-11 *supra* and accompanying text.

109. Carl Friedrich speaks of "reason of church," *see* C. FRIEDRICH, *supra* note 8, at 6, and suggests that reason of state need not be limited to the State. *Id.* at 127.

110. *See* T. McCANN, AN AMERICAN COMPANY: THE TRAGEDY OF UNITED FRUIT (1976). *See also* R. HEILBRONER, M. MINTZ, C. McCARTHY, S. UNGAR, K. VANDIVIER, S. FRIEDMAN & J. BOYD, IN THE NAME OF PROFIT (1972); L. SILK & D. VOGEL, ETHICS AND PROFITS (1976). For an account of how Chisso Corporation of Japan poisoned fishing waters but did nothing about it for years, see W. & A. SMITH, MINIMATA (1975). *See also* Dowie, *The Corporate Crime of the Century,* 4 MOTHER JONES, Nov. 1979, at 23; *Developments in the Law—Corporate Crime: Regulating Corporate Behavior Through Criminal Sanctions,* 92 HARV. L. REV. 1227 (1979).

way by force, bribery, and political subversion, all with the acquiescence and often with the cooperation of the State Department and the United States' military forces. In effect, the U.S. and U.F. acted in concert. The Central Intelligence Agency even used U.F. ships in the Bay of Pigs fiasco. Major General Smedley D. Butler (Commander of the Marines) put the situation in colorful terms in 1935:

> I spent thirty-three years and four months in active service as a member of our country's most agile military force—the Marine Corps. . . . And during that period I spent most of my time being a high-class muscle man for Big Business, for Wall Street, and for the bankers. In short, I was a racketeer for capitalism. . . . Thus I helped make Mexico and especially Tampico safe for American oil interests in 1914. I helped make Haiti and Cuba a decent place for the National City Bank boys to collect revenues in. . . . I helped purify Nicaragua for the international banking house of Brown Brothers in 1909-1912. I brought light to the Dominican Republic for American sugar interests in 1916. I helped make Honduras "right" for the American fruit companies in 1903. In China I helped see to it that Standard Oil went its way unmolested.[111]

The bitter fruit of those decades of American intervention on the behalf of totalitarian regimes and their American corporate supporters is now being reaped in Nicaragua and other Latin-American nations.

Domestic industry in the nineteenth century, like international business, grew increasingly powerful and was able to acquire government protection against the rising demands of the working class. Corporate managers, aided by their minions in government, took advantage of an oversupply of labor. At the time, they were able, through both fair and foul methods, to defeat the growing labor movement. One historian, Richard Lester, concluded in 1947: "During the depression from 1873 to 1879, employers sought to eliminate trade unions by a *systematic* policy of lock-outs, blacklists, labor espionage, and legal prosecution. The *widespread* use of blacklists and Pinkerton labor spies caused labor to organize more or less secretly, and undoubtedly helped bring on the violence that characterized labor strife during this period."[112] When labor was able to persuade legislatures to pass minimum wage and maximum hour legislation, most of those laws were promptly struck down by a

---

111. S. LENS, THE FORGING OF THE AMERICAN EMPIRE 270-71 (1971) (quoting an article by Major General Butler in the November 1935 issue of *Common Sense*). Corporations often define the axioms of American foreign policy. It is axiomatic, for example, for government to protect American property abroad. That is what General Butler was doing—protecting the property of American corporations.

112. R. LESTER, ECONOMICS OF LABOR 545 (1947) (emphasis added), *quoted in* 2 THE UNDERSIDE OF AMERICAN HISTORY 13 (T. Frazier ed. 1971).

Supreme Court that operated as "the first authoritative faculty of political economy in the world's history."[113] The Court not only discovered that the corporation was a person under the Constitution, but it also invented the concept of substantive due process.[114]

Since this conduct is familiar enough, it needs no elaboration. The point is simple: Corporations pursued selfish goals and were aided by government. The brutal repression of the Industrial Workers of the World, by both federal and state officials, supplies ample testimony to that point. So, too, does the decision of *In re Debs*,[115] which upheld federal intervention in the Pullman strike.

C. SUMMARY

Machiavellianism has indeed been a consistent part of American public policy since the beginnings of the republic. Franz Neumann was correct; government in the United States has always been as strong as conditions required, conditions that are *perceived by those who wield effective power in the nation*. The conclusion should be clear: (a) the Constitution in the nineteenth century was distinctly *not* one of limitations, despite the popular wisdom to the contrary; (b) it is not hyperbole to apply the term "constitutional dictatorship," or "democratic dictatorship," to the government of the United States during circumstances it perceives as emergencies—within the limits imposed by the Principle of the Economy of Means;[116] (c) two divergent moralities—pagan and "Christian"—have always existed in the United States; (d) when conflicts occur between those two moralities, the pagan usually prevails, making the dualism in constitutional law more apparent than real; (e) some actions are evil under either morality, giving some credence to Lord Acton's comment that "[w]eighed in the scales of Liberalism, the instrument of the Constitution, as it stood, was a monstrous fraud";[117](f) the United States grew powerful and prosperous because extraconstitutional adjustments were made in the second constitution; and (g) people generally do not object to exercises of *raison d'état*; rather, they tend to applaud such activities, thus lending

113.   J. COMMONS, LEGAL FOUNDATIONS OF CAPITALISM 7 (1924).

114.   *See* McCloskey, *Economic Due Process and the Supreme Court: An Exhumation and Reburial*, 1962 SUP. CT. REV. 34.

115.   158 U.S. 564 (1895).

116.   *See* S. WOLIN, POLITICS AND VISION (1960). *See also* p. 589 *supra*.

117.   J. ACTON, LECTURES ON MODERN HISTORY 295 (paperback ed. 1960).

support to the view that the American people favor the pagan morality.

III. THE CLIMACTERIC

Is the United States currently in a crisis or in a climacteric—a coalescence of crises? I suggest that we are in the latter. As a result, the future will not be a calm and ordered existence, and there will be no steady progression toward a better society or group of societies. The idea of progress, born out of the Enlightenment, is dead.[118]

Humans face several vulnerabilities. Energy shortages are currently the most obvious of these. But several others exist, each one of such significance to be a crisis in itself. The vulnerabilities of an industrialized nation such as the United States include, but are not limited to, the following: the threat of thermonuclear warfare, nuclear proliferation, radiation health hazards from widespread employment of nuclear technologies, the population "bomb," food shortages, dependence on nonfuel minerals, terrorism, inflation, unemployment (structural, because of the imminent application of microprocessing), social disruptions,[119] and the psychological problem of a failure of nerve—an inchoate belief that things are in a mess and will not get better. Taken together, as they should be because of their increasing coalescence, these vulnerabilities mark one of the great turning points in human history.

Since we live, as Dr. Harrison Brown put it, "in a largely synthetic ecological system, new in human experience and inadequately understood,"[120] belief systems and behavior patterns that are the products of eons of history must now be employed in wholly novel situations. It is thus not surprising that this is the "me generation," the "age of narcissism,"[121] and that the politics of selfishness are all-pervasive. But it does no good to ask, as some have: "What has posterity done for me?" For because of extraordinarily rapid social change, a recent development, we are our own posterity. It is also not surprising

---

118. *See* L. Brown, The Twenty-Ninth Day (1978); W. Johnson, Muddling Toward Frugality (1978); G. Stent, The Coming of the Golden Age: A View of the End of Progress (1969). A leading neoconservative blames intellectuals for an assault on progress itself. *See* Nisbet, *The Rape of Progress*, 2 Pub. Opinion, June-July 1979, at 2. Nisbet does not identify any specific intellectuals.
119. *See generally* H. Brown, The Human Future Revisited (1978).
120. *Id.* at 227.
121. C. Lasch, The Culture of Narcissism *passim* (1979).

that "Micawberism"[122]—the notion that sooner or later something will turn up to rescue man from his follies—is so prevalent.

In a previous Article, I suggested that this country "has survived and prospered thus far, not because of the Constitution but in spite of it."[123] Rufus E. Miles, Jr., stated the same point in other terms: "The extraordinary affluence of the United States has been produced by a set of fortuitous, nonreplicable, and nonsustainable factors."[124] If that is true, then surely Micawberism is a pathetic fallacy, and the politics of selfishness will lead to disaster. The Constitution, even as a politico-legal palimpsest, is not necessarily able to cope with increasingly evident needs, as the multifarious facets of the climacteric of humankind press harder and harder against American institutions. The obvious requirement is for constitutional change that will both enable people to deal effectively with the burgeoning problems of the human condition and preserve as many of the values of historical constitutionalism as possible.

What those constitutional changes might be is one question; what they should be is another. Neither issue, however, is the subject of this Article. Rather, I should like to suggest that, in the words of Dr. Lester Brown, "[t]here can be little doubt that humanity is on the verge of a profound social transformation, at the edge of a new social frontier,"[125] and that this has immense significance for the Constitution. As a result, Americans are moving into the era of the Constitution of Control.

IV. THE EMERGENT CONSTITUTION OF CONTROL

Any document that exists through time and is still considered to be an authoritative text takes on such a gloss of interpretation, custom, and usage that its modern version has only a tenuous relationship to the original. Exegesis, however, is not confined to theological documents, such as the Bible. The Christian religion has been able to absorb the insights of Co-

---

122. Micawberism, named after the character in Dickens' *David Copperfield*, is particularly evident in those who believe that technological "fixes" can extricate humankind from the climacteric now so evident. *See, e.g.*, H. KAHN, W. BROWN & L. MARTEL, THE NEXT 200 YEARS: A SCENARIO FOR AMERICA AND THE WORLD (1976); Kahn & Phelps, *The Economic Present and Future: A Chartbook for the Decades Ahead*, 13 THE FUTURIST 202 (1979).

123. Miller, *Constitutional Law: Crisis Government Becomes the Norm*, 39 OHIO ST. L.J. 736, 751 (1978).

124. R. MILES, *supra* note 32, at 224.

125. L. BROWN, *supra* note 118, at 324.

pernicus and Darwin and Freud without outward alteration of the ancient language—but with considerable change in its application. In law and politics, even Soviet theoreticians have had to apply a concept of "living Marxism" in order to explain and justify new doctrine.[126] It is not surprising, then, that the second constitution has undergone immense alterations. Specific clauses have been interpreted in different ways at different times; even structural changes have occurred—as in the demise of "dual federalism" and the rise of executive hegemony in government. As noted above, Professor Corwin's label of a "Constitution of Powers," which we have called the third American fundamental law, is a translucent layer of doctrine and practice, which has been developed in the past fifty years.[127] The Constitution of Control—the fourth constitution—exists as still another overlay. More emergent than complete, its contours are becoming obvious. This section outlines its development.

The text for what follows is taken from Justice Holmes's dissenting opinion in *Abrams*. The Constitution, he said, is an experiment, "as all life is an experiment. Every year if not every day we have to wager our salvation upon some prophecy based upon imperfect knowledge."[128] A comprehensive discussion of the theory of the Constitution of Control is not within the scope of this Article. Instead, some of its more prominent features are discussed, with reference to some of the relevant literature.

A. LAW AS A MEMORANDUM

Law, including constitutional law, is not *a priori*. Rather, it is a reflection of the society in which it operates: *a posteriori*. Or, as Emerson said, law is "only a memorandum."[129] But of what is law a memorandum?

We are living in the Technological Age, an obvious fact, but

---

126. *See* Kolakowski, *Permanent and Transitory Aspects of Marxism*, in THE BROKEN MIRROR 157, 158-59. (P. Mayewski ed. 1958), *quoted in* C. FRANKEL, THE DEMOCRATIC PROSPECT 189 (1962); V. LENIN, MARX, ENGELS, MARXISM 385-86 (4th English ed. 1951) ("[T]he incontestable truth is that a Marxist must take cognizance of actual events, of the precise facts of reality, and must not cling to a theory of yesterday, which, like all theories, at best only outlines the main and general, and only approximates to an inclusive grasp of the complexities of life."). *See also* A.S. MILLER, SOCIAL CHANGE AND FUNDAMENTAL LAW: AMERICA'S EVOLVING CONSTITUTION 343, 382 (1979) (reprinting Lenin's quote).

127. *See* notes 4-6 *supra* and accompanying text.

128. Abrams v. United States, 250 U.S. 616, 630 (1919) (Holmes, J., dissenting).

129. R.W. Emerson, *Politics*, in THE COMPLETE ESSAYS AND OTHER WRITINGS OF RALPH WALDO EMERSON 423 (Atkinson ed. 1940) (Modern Library edition).

one too little considered in legal thought. Humankind is in the midst of the greatest environmental changes in its history. "There is little of importance in the world which does not depend in some measure on technology, even in its most restricted sense as man's mechanical means to his ends."[130] Our interest in technology lies not in what is accomplished in the laboratory or production plant, although what happens there is significant. Rather, we are interested in what effect the technological revolution has on politico-legal mechanisms—on law, on constitutions, and on economic systems. Thus, attention must be given to the following aspects of advanced technology:

1. The art of invention has itself been invented;
2. What is technologically possible will be done, sooner or later;
3. Technology works toward the consolidation of political power; it is centripetal, not centrifugal;
4. Technology has accelerated time;
5. Change is a social constant; and
6. A variety of techniques of control over human beings now exist and are being used.

These self-evident factors should be common knowledge, part of the "given" of ordinary discourse. Unfortunately, however, this is not so. Even though the United States is the technological society *par excellence*, Americans, generally speaking, unthinkingly accept the benefits (and suffer the detriments) of technology without noticing technology's subtle effects on the quality of life; nor do they perceive the effects of technology on the nature of the constitutional order. In briefly examining some conclusions drawn from the impact of technology, two of the above factors will be emphasized. First, as Franz Neumann said, "[t]he higher the state of technological development, the greater the concentration of political power."[131] And, second, technology now permits mass control measures to be employed.

The first point requires little discussion. No doubt exists that political and legal power in the United States has tended to be consolidated almost from the beginnings of the Republic. Chief Justice John Marshall's "nationalizing" decisions laid the early groundwork for that development. Later, in the period after the Civil War, the influences of economics and technology

---

130. Watson-Watt, *Technology in the Modern Worlds*, in THE TECHNOLOGICAL ORDER 1, 7 (C. Stover ed. 1963).

131. F. NEUMANN, *supra* note 1, at 10.

combined to create, in Galbraith's terms, "the new industrial state."[132] A national economic system of giant corporations was superimposed on a decentralized political system with nexuses in each of the several states. Something had to give— and it did. That "something" was traditional federalism, which changed from "dual" to "cooperative" with the arrival of the New Deal.[133] The giant corporations began to supplant the states in the federal system—their role became as important as, or even more important than, that of the allegedly sovereign states in providing a counterbalance to the power of Washington. Simultaneously, growth in the number and complexity of the tasks of government led to the dominance of the Executive (including the bureaucracy) within the tripartite division of powers in the national government. Each branch might have been, in Chief Justice Roger Taney's terms, "equal in origin and equal in title,"[134] but the Constitution of Powers meant that the Executive Branch was, and will remain, preeminent.

At about the same time, something important happened in the jurisprudence of the Supreme Court of the United States. Rather than pursuing a "principled," conceptualistic approach to decisionmaking, the Court overtly began to adopt a pragmatic methodology of "interest-balancing"; in the resulting balances, the State's interest was always weighty. This had one important consequence: the interests of the State became avowedly dominant at precisely the time that government (the apparatus of the State) began an exponential growth. The individual was submerged in a congeries of bureaucracies, public and private.

The rise of the bureaucratic State means that the balancing system developed by the drafters of the Constitution of 1787 has gone awry. Far from "keeping power within tolerable boundaries, the American system has encouraged power to go underground."[135] The surface is one thing; there the formal institutions of public life block each other. The reality, however, is different: beneath the surface are the "subgovernments" of Washington,[136] the informal methods by which important governmental decisions are in fact reached. Political power is becoming increasingly centralized in the executive bureaucracies,

---

132. J. GALBRAITH, ECONOMICS AND THE PUBLIC PURPOSE (1973); J. GALBRAITH, THE NEW INDUSTRIAL STATE (1967).
133. Corwin, *The Passing of Dual Federalism*, 36 VA. L. REV. 1 (1950).
134. Gordon v. United States, 117 U.S. 697, 701 (1864) (published 1885).
135. R. KRAEMER, AMERICAN DEMOCRACY: THE THIRD CENTURY 492 (1978).
136. *See* D. CATER, POWER IN WASHINGTON (1964).

independent fiefdoms, which operate within the Executive Branch but which have close connections with industries that they ostensibly regulate and with influential members of Congress. There can be no doubt that power centralization exists. The rise of the bureaucracy to power has made the agencies, as Justice Jackson said in 1952, "a veritable fourth branch of the Government, which has deranged our three-branch legal theories much as the concept of a fourth dimension unsettles our three-dimensional thinking."[137]

A second, and quite different, consequence of technology is the control of humans through ostensibly benign measures. There can be little doubt that such control is already taking place. In 1978, Peter Schrag observed:

> In the past generation, there has been a fundamental shift in the way government and other organizations control the lives and behavior of individuals. No single method and no single phrase adequately describe it—it is both too subtle and too pervasive—but it represents a radical change in the way people are treated and in the relationship between the citizen, his employer, the state, and the state's institutions. In general, it is a shift from direct to indirect methods of control, from the punitive to the therapeutic, from the moralistic to the mechanistic, from the hortatory to the manipulative. More specifically, it is reflected in the replacement of overt and sometimes crude techniques—threat, punishment, or incarceration—with relatively "smooth" methods: psychotropic drugs; Skinnerian behavior modification; aversive conditioning; electronic surveillance; and the collection, processing, and use of personal information to institutionalize people outside the walls of institutions.[138]

The ideologist for this development is B.F. Skinner.[139] The goal is "predictable" man—a person who conceives of freedom in Hegelian terms: doing what one is supposed to do.

My point, again, is not to document extensively such assertions, but merely to indicate that the means of technological control of people are not only present but they are being used, and further, that there is a considerable body of respectable thought that believes that those means *should* be used. Schrag tells us that they *are* being used, thus exemplifying the notion that whatever is technologically possible will be done.

The meaning for law and constitutions should be obvious. Science and technology are slowly, subtly, and "humanely" re-

---

137. Federal Trade Comm'n v. Ruberoid Co., 343 U.S. 470, 487 (1952) (Jackson, J., dissenting).

138. P. SCHRAG, MIND CONTROL xi (1978). *See* A. SCHEFLIN & E. OPTON, THE MIND MANIPULATORS (1978). *See also* C. LASCH, *supra* note 121, at 154-86.

139. *See, e.g.*, B. SKINNER, BEYOND FREEDOM AND DIGNITY (1971).

pealing the Constitution.[140] Millions of Americans are being subjected to behavior modification and control through the use of law and the legal process for the newly emergent highest good: the welfare of society.

An example is the use of computer technology to quietly encroach upon fundamental rights such as privacy.[141] Recently, the "third industrial revolution"[142] of microprocessing—the "silicon chip revolution"—has enhanced the potential of computers to be used as a means by which the behavior of people can be monitored and controlled. Modern society is the "information society";[143] he who controls the data controls society. Privacy, no matter how much it may be desired, is becoming a wasting asset and is disappearing in the new era of microelectronics.[144]

Microprocessing will provide cheaper, smaller computers. As a result, the use of computers in modern society will greatly accelerate, simultaneously accelerating the danger to personal freedoms inherent in a widespread capacity for interchangeable data storage and retrieval. Increasingly, a person's record follows him closely throughout life. In a large, continentally sized nation such as the United States, developments such as the National Crime Information Center and computerized criminal history files[145] can have many social benefits. But the cost is high: use of such information systems leads to loss of privacy and, of more importance, diminution of human dignity.

The question for constitutional lawyers in the Age of Tech-

---

140. *See* P. SCHRAG, *supra* note 138, at 252-55. Aldous Huxley put the matter in pungent terms:

We have had religious revolutions, we have had political, economic, and nationalistic revolutions. All of them, as our descendants will discover, were but ripples in an ocean of conservatism—trivial by comparison with the psychological revolution toward which we are so rapidly moving. *That* will really be a revolution. When it is over, the human race will give no further trouble.

A. SCHEFLIN & E. OPTON, *supra* note 138, at 10 (quoting Aldous Huxley).

141. In his opinion for the Court in Griswold v. Connecticut, 381 U.S. 479 (1965), Justice Douglas described privacy as a penumbral constitutional right, implicitly emanating from the Bill of Rights. *Id.* at 484-85.

142. *See* C. JENKINS & B. SHERMAN, THE COLLAPSE OF WORK (1979).

143. *See, e.g.,* I. BARRON & R. CURNOW, THE FUTURE WITH ELECTRONICS (1979); ELECTRONICS: THE CONTINUING REVOLUTION (P. Abelson & A. Hammon eds. 1977); Branscomb, *Information: The Ultimate Frontier*, 203 SCIENCE 143 (1979).

144. To a great extent, a person's name has become a number—his social security number.

145. The Office of Technology Assessment, which services Congress, is conducting a systematic and comprehensive analysis of the National Crime Information Center (NCIC) and computerized criminal histories (CCH).

nology is whether the values of constitutionalism can be preserved. On this question, the jury is still out, but the *means* for
control of people are available and if it is true that what is technologically possible will be done, then we will move into a
Skinnerian world, one in which Americans "will no longer
know, or care, whether they are being served or controlled,
treated or punished, or whether they are volunteers or conscripts. The distinctions will have vanished."[146] This is a grim
scenario, to be sure, but one toward which technological imperatives are taking the nation and, indeed, people everywhere. If,
in sum, law is a reflection of society, then it cannot escape being vitally affected by the scientific-technological revolution
even more than it has been in the past.

B. THE STATE AS "GROUP-PERSON"

The major prophet for the emergent Constitution of Control is Thomas Hobbes, who in his classic *Leviathan* both gave
a name to the modern State and set forth its philosophy. Those
who would understand the United States under the Constitution of Control must first understand Hobbes, who was surely
as influential as Locke and Montesquieu were upon those who
wrote the Constitution of 1787. The framers were well aware of
the dark side of man. "[T]he theme of man's irrationality," Arthur O. Lovejoy maintained, "and especially of his *inner* corruption was no longer [during the seventeenth and eighteenth
centuries] a specialty of divines; it became for a time one of the
favorite topics of secular literature."[147] European and American political theorists came to emphasize the dangers rather
than the advantages of government. If a man was depraved
and antisocial, then he required control; but those who controlled, themselves human beings, would mercilessly exploit
their subjects unless there was some way to limit their power.
In the words of James Madison: "If men were angels, no government would be necessary. If angels were to govern men,
neither external nor internal controls on government would be
necessary. In framing a government which is to be administered by men over men, the great difficulty lies in this: *you
must first enable the government to control the governed, and in
the next place oblige it to control itself.*"[148] Control over the

---

146. P. SCHRAG, *supra* note 138, at 255. *See also* W. OPHULS, ECOLOGY AND
THE POLITICS OF SCARCITY: PROLOGUE TO A POLITICAL THEORY OF THE STEADY
STATE (1977); W. THOMPSON, EVIL AND WORLD ORDER (1976).

147. A. LOVEJOY, REFLECTIONS ON HUMAN NATURE 15 (1961).

148. THE FEDERALIST No. 51 (J. Madison) (emphasis added).

governed is well established; but will government control itself? The answer is fast becoming "no." As it has been shown, it was also "no" in the past, but only when certain extraordinary situations obtruded, situations in which political officers considered it necessary to draw upon the reserve powers of the State.[149]

"Leviathan," says William Ophuls, "may be mitigated, but not evaded."[150] Hobbes advocated complete domination by the State to prevent internal disorder and to protect against external threats. Today, the Hobbesian world is fast emerging: Leviathan is being created—in Gierkian terms, a "super-group-person" with drives and interests of its own that transcend the sum of the private interests of the nation.[151]

Little attention has been accorded the nature of "the State" in the literature on American constitutionalism.[152] Judges and commentators alike have slid over analysis of the concept, often blithely, but erroneously, equating the State with government or with society. The terms are not synonymous, and should not be considered as equivalents. Constitutional scholarship is flawed by the failure to probe deeply into the meaning of the three terms—how they are used, by whom, and for what purposes. The question, to be sure, is one of political theory, but that should not inhibit legal analysis because it is widely conceded that the Supreme Court, in its constitutional decisions, articulates juristic theories of politics.

It has earlier been suggested that the United States has become a "corporate State."[153] The overarching social reality in this nation is the State, an anthropomorphic group-person with drives and interests of its own—an "organism," as Holmes said.[154] Of course, the State cannot be seen; it is a method, not

---

149. One of those reserve powers, of course, is reason of state. Another reserve power is the degree of presidential confidentiality recognized in United States v. Nixon, 418 U.S. 683, 708 (1974).

150. W. OPHULS, *supra* note 146, at 163.

151. See the discussion in A.S. MILLER, THE MODERN CORPORATE STATE, *supra* note 6. *See also* note 154 *infra*.

152. One has to turn to political theorists or to sociologists for discussions of "the State." *See, e.g.*, E. CASSIRER, THE MYTH OF THE STATE (1946); A. D'ENTREVES, THE MODERN NOTION OF THE STATE (1946); H. KELSEN, GENERAL THEORY OF LAW AND STATE (A. Wedberg trans. 1945); G. POGGI, THE DEVELOPMENT OF THE MODERN STATE: A SOCIOLOGICAL INTRODUCTION (1978). A colleague and I have essayed a few preliminary thoughts about the nature of the State in modern separation of powers litigation. *See* Miller & Bowman, *Presidential Attacks on the Constitutionality of Federal Statutes: A New Separation of Powers Problem*, 40 OHIO ST. L.J. 51, 60-74 (1979).

153. *See* A.S. MILLER, THE MODERN CORPORATE STATE, *supra* note 6.

154. Missouri v. Holland, 252 U.S. 416, 433 (1920). Judge Learned Hand once

a thing. Like the business corporation, in law an artificial person, the State exists in constitutional theory even though it has "no anatomical parts to be kicked or consigned to the calaboose; no soul for whose salvation the parson may struggle; no body to be roasted in hell or purged for celestial enjoyment."[155] The State, a legal fiction, does no act, thinks no thought, speaks no word, but exists both to the extent that those who wield the power in government speak for it and to the extent that men may die and property may be seized in its name.

A little-noted, but important, court of appeals decision in 1978 illustrates this point. In *Halkin v. Helms*,[156] opponents of the Vietnam "war" filed suit against several officials of the intelligence community, alleging that the National Security Agency (NSA) conducted warrantless interceptions of their international wire, cable, and telephone communications. Judge Roger Robb, speaking for the panel, framed the issue in these terms: "[S]hould the NSA be ordered to disclose whether international communications of the plaintiffs have been acquired by the NSA and disseminated to other federal agencies?"[157] NSA services the intelligence community by electronically monitoring overseas communications. "Watchlists"—words and phrases identifying communications of intelligence interest—are employed to isolate communications of

said that judges "called upon to pass on a question of constitutional law . . . must be aware of the changing social tensions in every society which [make] it an organism." Hand, *Sources of Tolerance*, 79 U. PA. L. REV. 1, 12-13 (1930). Such an organismic conception of the State (often with the word used synonymously with government or society) is fundamental to an understanding of American constitutional law. Compare these statements: "[G]overnment is not a machine, but a living thing. It falls, not under the theory of the universe, but under the theory of organic life. It is accountable to Darwin, not to Newton. It is modified by its environment, necessitated by its tasks, shaped to its functions by the sheer pressure of life." W. WILSON, CONSTITUTIONAL GOVERNMENT IN THE UNITED STATES 56 (1908); President John F. Kennedy, in answering a question about a "public interest" in collective bargaining negotiations: "These companies are free and the unions are free. All we [the Executive] can try to do is indicate to them the public interest which is there. After all, the public interest is the sum of the private interests, or perhaps it's even sometimes a little more. *In fact, it is a little more*." N.Y. Times, Mar. 8, 1962, at 14, col. 5 (emphasis added).

155. W. Hamilton, *On the Composition of the Corporate Veil* (1946), *quoted in* R. EELLS & C. WALTON, CONCEPTUAL FOUNDATIONS OF BUSINESS 132-33 (1961). Hamilton was speaking about the corporation, but surely his remarks are also applicable to the State.

156. 598 F.2d 1 (D.C. Cir. 1978). *See In re* Halkin, 598 F.2d 176 (D.C. Cir. 1978). *See also* Hayden v. National Security Agency, No. 78-1728 (D.C. Cir. Oct. 29, 1979) (NSA does not have to give public detailed explanation for refusal to disclose documents sought under the Freedom of Information Act.).

157. 598 F.2d at 3.

specific intelligence interest from the enormous numbers of foreign communications. Thus, in actuality, *everyone*'s overseas wire, cable, and telephone messages are monitored by the NSA. Copies of all cables are sent to NSA by Western Union, RCA, and ITT.

One would think that message interceptions of all "communications having at least one foreign terminal" and watch-lists of "approximately 1200 Americans"[158] would present an obvious instance of police-state tactics wholly inimical to the American system of government. After all, the Supreme Court has never authorized warrantless wiretaps, even for foreign intelligence purposes, and lower federal courts that have dealt with the question are split. The panel of judges in *Halkin* saw it otherwise. In the words of Judge Robb:

> A ranking of the various privileges in our courts would be a delicate undertaking at best, but it is quite clear that the privilege to protect state secrets must head the list. The state secrets privilege is absolute. However helpful to the court the informed advocacy of the plaintiffs' counsel may be, we must be especially careful not to order any dissemination of information *asserted* to be privileged state secrets.[159]

The court accepted the untested assertion of the Secretary of Defense that "[c]ivil discovery or a responsive pleading . . . would severely jeopardize the intelligence collection mission of NSA by identifying present communications collection and analysis capabilities."[160] Not even *in camera* proceedings are to be permitted. Paying "utmost deference" to the Executive,[161] the court found that the interests of the State overrode any interest of the individual. Even though "the" United States,[162] as such, was not a party to the lawsuit, it nonetheless was able to prevail. When *Halkin* is added to President Carter's executive order authorizing sweeping presidential use of warrantless wiretaps,[163] it becomes clear that an organismic conception of the State is being reified by a series of official actions.[164]

This conclusion is buttressed by Judge Warren's prior-restraint injunction in *United States v. The Progressive, Inc.*[165] There, for the first time in American history, a judge enjoined

---

158. *Id.* at 4.
159. *Id.* at 7 (emphasis added).
160. *Id.* at 4-5.
161. *Id.* at 9.
162. *See* Miller & Bowman, *supra* note 152.
163. *See* note 102 *supra* and accompanying text.
164. *See also* Halperin v. Kissinger, No. 77-2014 (D.C. Cir. July 12, 1979); Smith v. Nixon, No. 78-1526, (D.C. Cir. July 12, 1979).
165. 467 F. Supp. 990 (W.D. Wis. 1979).

the publication of an article for reasons of national security. Judge Warren swept aside prior law in order to reach the decision. In addition, he did not require the government to produce evidence sufficient to fulfill the very heavy burden that any attempt at prior restraint must meet. And to cap it off in Kafkaesque style, Judge Warren's opinion was kept secret.[166]

Two lessons may be drawn from the *Progressive* case: first, the mere assertion of "national security" is enough to make some judges run for cover; and second, Judge Warren saw the State's asserted interests as preeminent and simply refused to enforce the plain language of the first amendment and first amendment case law that has existed since *Near v. Minnesota*.[167] Judge Warren apparently did not even attempt to balance the interests involved; or if he did, he incorrectly identified the interests of the defendants. In the *Progressive* case, the publishers, editors, and writers posed an issue beyond that of a tiny (40,000 circulation) magazine; what was involved is not merely *their* interests, as important as they are, but the interests of the entire nation—all of the people, who fall within the ambit of the first amendment. The magazine in this litigation was a surrogate for all Americans. The government speaks for the State, not for the disparate congeries of individuals and groups that make up "society." Once that fact is understood, a federal district judge should be able to discern that censorship of a magazine article, the contents of which were taken from the public record, cannot comport with the Constitution.

These illustrations are merely present-day instances of what has long been true but has seldom been asserted: the State wins in constitutional litigation in all cases in which it—the State, speaking through government—considers its interests to be in jeopardy. In other words, the State is a group-person with drives and interests of its own, which do not necessarily coincide with the interests of Americans, either as

---

166. *See* 5 MEDIA L. REP. (BNA) at page opposite 1113 (June 26, 1979) (On June 15, Judge Warren continued his earlier preliminary injunction against publication and issued a one-sentence public statement and a seven-page secret opinion in support of his action.). *The Progressive* appealed to the Seventh Circuit, but, in September, the government dropped its efforts to enjoin publication after the sensitive information (relating to construction of nuclear devices) was published elsewhere. *See id.* at page opposite 1545 (Sept. 25, 1979). The Seventh Circuit then vacated the injunction and remanded all unresolved issues to Judge Warren. *The Progressive* is still seeking to have the opinion and *in camera* district court proceedings declassified. Telephone interview with Erwin Knoll, Editor of *The Progressive* (Feb. 1, 1980).

167. 283 U.S. 697 (1931). For recent discussion, see J. BARRON & C. DIENES, HANDBOOK OF FREE SPEECH AND FREE PRESS ch. 2 (1979).

individuals or in their collective capacity as society—the arithmetical sum of the private interests of the nation.[168] As the Constitution of Control slowly emerges from its chrysalis, this conclusion will become more evident. The greatest good in this dangerous situation is defined as the survival of the collectivity known as the United States. Machiavelli probably would have approved; that is, the Machiavelli who wrote *The Prince* rather than Machiavelli the statesman of *The Discourses*. "Many," he said in *The Prince*, "have dreamed up republics and principalities which have never in truth been known to exist; the gulf between how one should live and how one does live is so wide that a man who neglects what is actually done for what should be done learns the way to self-destruction rather than self-preservation. The fact is that a man who wants to act virtuously in every way necessarily comes to grief among so many who are not virtuous. *Therefore if a prince wants to maintain his rule he must learn how not to be virtuous, and to make use of this or not according to need.*"[169] Substitute "a State" for "a prince," and much of American constitutional history unfolds—particularly the history of recent vintage. The teachings of *The Prince* may be repulsive, but the harsh fact is that most people, including politicians, follow those teachings in practice.

Machiavelli frankly admitted that in practice those who govern (formally or tacitly) are always willing to act ruthlessly to achieve their ends. He knew that a ruler should be both loved and feared, but he also saw that if it appears to be difficult to have both, then "it is far better to be feared than loved."[170] But, he cautioned, a ruler should escape being hated, not because of moral scruples, but because it is in his best interests (*vide* Batista of Cuba, the Shah of Iran, and Samoza of Nicaragua). Finally, so long as the ruler "does not rob the great majority of their property or their honor, they remain content. He then has to contend only with the restlessness of a few, and

---

168. President Kennedy's statement, *see* note 154 *supra*, evidenced (perhaps unwittingly) pure Machiavellianism. What the President called "the public interest" may be equated with the State. *See also* Barcelo v. Brown, 478 F. Supp. 646 (D.P.R. 1979). In *Barcelo*, Judge Torruella denied an injunction against the Secretary of Defense and the Navy, even though defendants admittedly were in violation of two federal statutes and an executive order. This case is a clear example of how national defense considerations can override even the letter of the law, an example of "judicially recognized Reason of State."

169. N. MACHIAVELLI, THE PRINCE, ch. XV (G. Bull trans. paperback ed. 1961) (emphasis added).

170. *Id*. ch. XVII.

that can be dealt with easily and in a variety of ways."[171] Thus, so long as the confrontations in *Halkin v. Helms* and *United States v. The Progressive* are perceived as being between a few discrete individuals and the State, such "restlessness . . . can be dealt with easily."

C.   INSTRUMENTALISM IN LAW

Despite outward appearances to the contrary, a decline in *interdictory* constitutional law is fast becoming apparent. When the third Constitution (of Powers) edged aside and overlapped the second Constitution (of Quasi-Limitations), a process began in which the actions of government were limited less by prohibitory rules of law than by technical considerations and the political system. Thus, the question for policy makers today is not: Do the rules permit the proposed action? Instead, it is: Is the action physically and politically possible? The limitations promulgated in 1787, 1791, and 1868 still exist, to be sure, but they are applied as limitations only in situations in which the State has no overriding interest. Neither the fundamental law nor the Supreme Court will stop the drift of public policy from the direction in which political officers want it to go. Constitutional law, in sum, has become *instrumental*.

This important jurisprudential development did not spring forth full-blown, like Aphrodite, in the past few decades. The beginnings of the development may be seen in early American history. What Professor Morton Horwitz has concluded about the common law is equally true for constitutional law:

> By 1820 the legal landscape in America bore only the faintest resemblance to what existed forty years earlier. While the words were often the same, the structure of thought had dramatically changed and with it the theory of law. Law was no longer conceived of as an eternal set of principles expressed in custom and derived from natural law. Nor was it regarded primarily as a body of rules designed to achieve justice only in the individual case. Instead, judges came to think of the common law as equally responsible with legislation for governing society and promoting socially desirable conduct. The emphasis on law as an instrument of policy encouraged innovation and allowed judges to formulate legal doctrine with the self-conscious goal of bringing about social change.[172]

This statement reads remarkably like what the Supreme Court and other courts have been overtly doing for at least a generation, an action for which they have been severely criti-

---

171.   *Id.* ch. XIX.
172.   M. HORWITZ, THE TRANSFORMATION OF AMERICAN LAW, 1780-1860, at 30 (1977). *See* Robinson, *The Routinization of Crisis Government*, 63 YALE REV. 161 (1973).

cized.[173] Since as early as the time of *Cooper v. Aaron*,[174] the Court has occasionally, but not always, viewed a lawsuit as more than a dispute to be decided "by a body of rules designed to achieve justice only in the individual case."[175] The Court has issued norms of "general applicability."[176] Indeed, it does have "the self-conscious goal of bringing about social change." Consider, in this connection, the valedictory of Chief Justice Earl Warren, in which he said: "We, of course, venerate the past, but our focus is on the problems of the day and of the future as far as we can foresee it."[177] He went on to say that in one sense the Court was similar to the President, for it had the awesome responsibility of at times speaking the last word "in great governmental affairs"[178] and of speaking for the public generally. "It is a responsibility," he continued, "that is made more difficult in this Court because we have no constituency. We serve no majority. We serve no minority. *We serve only the public interest as we see it, guided only by the Constitution and our own consciences.*"[179]

That remarkable burst of candor merits careful attention. It acknowledges that the Court follows an instrumentalist concept of their function. Twenty years ago, a colleague and I suggested that the time had come for an avowedly teleological jurisprudence, "one purposive in nature."[180] Enough has occurred since then to conclude that our suggestion should not have been a *call* for teleological jurisprudence but a *description* of what the Supreme Court and other courts were already

---

173. *See, e.g.*, R. BERGER, GOVERNMENT BY JUDICIARY (1977); Glazer, *Towards an Imperial Judiciary?*, 41 PUB. INTEREST 104 (1975). *But see* Miller, *Judicial Activism and American Constitutionalism: Some Notes and Reflections*, in NOMOS XX: CONSTITUTIONALISM, *supra* note 16, at 333; Miller, *The Case for Judicial Activism*, in S. HALPERN & C. LAMB, SUPREME COURT ACTIVISM AND RESTRAINT (to be published in 1980); Tribe, *Seven Pluralist Fallacies: In Defense of the Adversary Process—A Reply to Justice Rehnquist*, 33 U. MIAMI L. REV. 43 (1978).

174. 358 U.S. 1 (1958). This was the Little Rock school desegregation case.

175. *See* text accompanying note 172 *supra*.

176. These are "legislative" norms that purport to state law for the entire nation. Little attention has been accorded this development in scholarly circles. *But see* P. KURLAND, POLITICS, THE CONSTITUTION, AND THE WARREN COURT 170-206 (1970); Miller & Barron, *The Supreme Court, the Adversary System, and the Flow of Information to the Justices: A Preliminary Inquiry*, 61 VA. L. REV. 1187 (1975), *reprinted in* A.S. MILLER, THE SUPREME COURT: MYTH AND REALITY 253 (1978) (ch. 8).

177. 395 U.S. viii, x (1969).

178. *Id.* at xi.

179. *Id.* (emphasis added).

180. Miller & Howell, *The Myth of Neutrality in Constitutional Adjudication*, 27 U. CHI. L. REV. 661, 684 (1960).

doing and a *prediction* of what they would continue to do. We are now witnessing "the growth of systematic participation of the judiciary . . . in the travail of society."[181] There can be no doubt that law is instrumental under the Constitution of Control.

D. SOME SPECIFIC DOCTRINES

The generalized statements about the Constitution of Control set forth above can be supplemented with a brief enumeration of specific doctrines. These observations will be stated as conclusions, with little documentation. Each, however, can easily be verified by readily accessible literature. The citations to the statements below are merely illustrative.

1. *Presidential government has come to stay.* Despite the popular wisdom to the contrary, Watergate and its aftermath have created only the appearance of a renascent Congress.[182]

2. Despite the recent Supreme Court decisions in support of states' rights,[183] *federalism as it has been known is fast becoming moribund.* A national income tax, technological imperatives, immersion of the nation in world affairs—these and other factors mean that the several states are political anachronisms.[184]

3. *Overt economic planning has come to stay.*[185] Although some primitive forms of planning have always existed in the United States, the steady and inexorable trend since the 1930s has been toward more and more governmental planning. Taxing and spending powers are now used to further economic planning objectives. The result, in Professor Kenneth Dam's terminology, is the creation of "the fiscal constitution."[186]

4. The commerce clause has been broadly interpreted to permit extensive exercise of powers at the national level; for example, it provides constitutional warrant for economic plan-

---

181. A. PEKELIS, LAW AND SOCIAL ACTION: SELECTED ESSAYS 39 (M. Konvitz ed. 1950).

182. *Cf.* R. PIOUS, THE AMERICAN PRESIDENCY 419-20 (1979) ("The only certain forecast about the presidency is that no forecast is certain.").

183. *See, e.g.,* National League of Cities v. Usery, 426 U.S. 833, 840-52 (1976).

184. Currently, a national economic system is superimposed on a decentralized political order. Politics and law tend to follow economics; the inexorable result is that the states will become even less important in the future. *See* A.S. MILLER, SOCIAL CHANGE AND FUNDAMENTAL LAW, *supra* note 126, at 43-95 (1979) (ch. 3, "The Constitutional Law of the 'Security State'").

185. *See* N. CHAMBERLAIN, PRIVATE AND PUBLIC PLANNING (1965); G. SOULE, PLANNING: U.S.A. (1967). *See also* F. ALLVINE & F. TARPLEY, THE NEW STATE OF THE ECONOMY (1977).

186. Dam, *The American Fiscal Constitution*, 44 U. CHI. L. REV. 271 (1977).

ning. Of equal importance, *federal power over interstate commerce is the constitutional justification for a growing number of social regulations.*[187]

5. *Freedoms of speech and the press are receiving less protection.*[188]

6. *Paradoxically, certain liberties not considered to be inimical to the State now receive the highest degree of protection ever enjoyed by Americans.*[189]

7. *When the State's fisc is threatened, the fourth amendment gives way.*[190]

8. *The constitutional command of equal protection of the laws is more fantasy than fact.* Concentration upon what judges *say* about equal protection, rather than upon what other governmental officials *do*, hides a harsh reality.[191]

9. *The Nixon Court is chipping away at the protections of*

---

187. The Civil Rights Act of 1964, 42 U.S.C. §§ 2000e to 2000e-17 (1976), is the most prominent example of this justification. *See* Katzenbach v. McClung, 379 U.S. 294, 300-05 (1964); Heart of Atlanta Motel, Inc. v. United States, 379 U.S. 241, 249-62 (1964).

188. *See, e.g.,* United States v. O'Brien, 391 U.S. 367, 375-77 (1968) (speech); Gannett Co. v. DePasquale, 99 S. Ct. 2898 (1979) (press).

189. *E.g.,* Stanley v. Georgia, 394 U.S. 557, 559 (1969) (private possession of obscene matter). The idea is proffered in Miller, *Constitutional Law, supra* note 123, at 748-50.

190. *See, e.g.,* Wyman v. James, 400 U.S. 309, 318-19 (1971).

191. Granted, equal protection law has advanced significantly since Holmes attacked it as the usual last resort of constitutional arguments. Buck v. Bell, 274 U.S. 200, 208 (1927) (upholding compulsory sterilization of an allegedly mentally defective person). Indeed, the civil rights movement of the 1960s was, in large part, a by-product of judicial willingness to reinterpret the equal protection clause. My point, however, is that although the formal law has greatly changed, the same is not true of law as applied to individuals. The law in action—how people are actually treated by public officials, including judges (as in sentencing)—fails to measure up to the promise of the formal, positive law. *See, e.g.,* W. WILSON, *supra* note 33, *passim*; Miller, *Brown's 25th: A Silver Lining Tarnished with Time*, 3 DIST. LAW., April-May 1979, at 22 (Journal of the District of Columbia Bar). In other words, the teaching of Yick Wo v. Hopkins, 118 U.S. 356, 373-74 (1886), should be the basic standard for all legal analysis. What matters is not what officials, including legislators and judges, *say*, but what they *do*. *See* J. AUERBACH, UNEQUAL JUSTICE 79-80 (1976).

Legal educators have forgotten the teachings of Underhill Moore and others, who, forty to fifty years ago, sought to determine how legal precepts were in fact applied. Most law professors still consider the appellate court opinion to be the *ne plus ultra* of scholarship—a sad commentary on legal education. But even appellate opinions are given only cursory scrutiny. Little or nothing is said, for example, about how judges inform themselves, about their predilections, and about how they weigh (if they do) the societal impacts of their decisions. Thus, the adversary system is never subjected to rigorous examination. *See generally* A.S. MILLER, THE SUPREME COURT: MYTH AND REALITY (1978); Miller, *Reductionism in the Law Schools, or, Why the Blather About the Motivation of Legislators?*, 16 SAN DIEGO L. REV. 891 (1979); Miller, *Legal Education as a Form of Brain Damage* (forthcoming).

Miranda and other decisions.[192]

10. *Ours is emphatically a government of men, not of laws.*[193] In the "administrative State," discretion is the norm, and judicial review of public administration is largely ineffectual.

E. SUMMARY

It is dubious, at best, whether institutions created prior to 1790—despite nearly two centuries of adaptation—are adequate to meet the needs of the present and the emergent future. The Constitution of Control has arisen to strengthen a government faced by continuing crises. "There is no escape from politics. As a consequence of ecological scarcity, major ethical, political, economic and social changes are inevitable whatever we do."[194] Legal education and constitutional law as formulated by lawyers reveal little or no appreciation of that dialectic. Public dialogue should focus on the precipitant question of whether Americans will be able to escape the impact of Arnold Toynbee's doleful forecast: "In all developed countries," he was quoted in 1975 as saying, "a new way of life—a severely regimented way—will have to be imposed by a ruthless authoritarian government."[195]

The outlines of the Constitution of Control are becoming clearly visible, a process that will accelerate as fast-moving technological and economic changes press ever harder on ancient political institutions. I do not, however, wish to unduly accentuate the transition. The fourth fundamental law coexists with the second and third: We still have *some* limitations on government. Moreover, the Constitution of Control is simply a radical version of the Constitution of Powers. The effective exercise of burgeoning governmental powers necessarily implies increasing limitations on personal freedoms and liberties.[196] Those liberties that remain may be likened to Aldous Huxley's

---

192. Early analysis may be found in L. LEVY, AGAINST THE LAW: THE NIXON COURT AND CRIMINAL JUSTICE (1974). *See* R. FUNSTON, CONSTITUTIONAL COUNTERREVOLUTION? 330-32 (1977); Shapiro, *Mr. Justice Rehnquist: A Preliminary View,* 90 HARV. L. REV. 293 (1976).

193. *See* HORSKY, THE WASHINGTON LAWYER (1952); Gramm, *Industrial Capitalism and Breakdown of the Liberal Rule of Law,* 7 J. ECON. ISSUES 577 (1973).

194. W. OPHULS, *supra* note 146, at 161-62.

195. Christian Science Monitor, Feb. 10, 1975, at 5, col. 7 (quoting Arnold Toynbee).

196. *See generally* W. OPHULS, *supra* note 146.

"soma" pills—a means by which discontent can be siphoned off.[197]

V. CONCLUSION

This Article, a speculative essay, is intended to raise questions rather than to proffer answers. If I am correct—and I think that at least a prima facie case can be made for the new fundamental law, thus shifting the burden of proof to those who dispute the thesis—then a challenge to constitutional scholarship is both obvious and unmet. That challenge is to determine whether politico-legal (constitutional) changes will enable Americans (and others) to escape from the ecological trap.

Such an inquiry must have at least two facets. First, it must encompass an analysis of the extent to which law, however and by whomever articulated, can be an instrument of social change. The ancient wisdom, per Sumner, is that "stateways" cannot change "folkways."[198] I have suggested elsewhere, in an as yet unpublished paper, that the Supreme Court can and indeed does help promulgate national goals.[199] Acting as an "oracle in the Marble Palace," the Court tries to operate as a modern version of Plato's philosopher-king. In making such a statement, I do not mean to suggest that "the universe will obey the judicial decree."[200] I agree with Brooks Adams, who observed that "[n]o delusion could be profounder and none, perhaps, more dangerous."[201] Constitutional change comes not only by amendment and judicial decision but also by certain acts of Congress and the President.[202] The parts of the system interact. Judges have some, but not much, direct political power. Their greatest influence comes through stating standards toward which Americans can aspire; they can alter the "mix" in political debates. Although our reach, as in all things, may exceed our grasp, a carefully chosen group of judges who realize that decisions can, at times, be logically arbitrary and at the same time sociologically nonarbitrary can help in the endless pursuit of justice—of what Felix Cohen called "the good."[203] Of course, judges are far from omnipotent; they are,

---

197. *See* A. HUXLEY, BRAVE NEW WORLD 70-71, 121-23 (1932).
198. *See* W. SUMNER, FOLKWAYS (1906).
199. Miller, *The Case for Judicial Activism, supra* note 173.
200. B. ADAMS, THE THEORY OF SOCIAL REVOLUTIONS 219 (1913), *quoted in* A. MASON, SECURITY THROUGH FREEDOM 149 (1955).
201. *Id.*
202. *See* A.S. MILLER, SOCIAL CHANGE AND FUNDAMENTAL LAW, *supra* note 126.
203. *See* F. COHEN, *supra* note 27.

however, best suited not only to make other governmental officials take a sober second thought before implementing decisions, but also to assist in the establishment of national values. The Constitution, in itself, is not a self-defining instrument that sets forth such values. Only as a patina of interpretation is added do those values emerge.[204]

The second facet of the constitutional reexamination must be to redraft our constitutional text. The ancient words of 1787 need substantial alteration. Built-in roadblocks frustrate efficiency in government and do not prevent despotism. The orthodoxy tells us, usually quoting Brandeis and at times Warren, that separation of powers was designed not to promote efficiency but to prevent the misuse of power.[205] That, however, is only a half-truth. The framers in 1787 wanted to separate the executive from Congress in order to have a more effective government.[206] The institutions have worked for nearly two hundred years largely because of extra-constitutional techniques devised to supplement what the framers created and, as we have said above, because the silences of the original document were filled by principles (except for judicial review) common to all governments.

Constitutional revision by custom and usage, however, is no longer adequate to meet the manifest needs of the nation. Americans are now hampered by the terms of a written instrument drafted for different times and conditions. Among possible constitutional changes, at least the following require serious consideration: (a) pluralizing the presidency; (b) making Congress a unicameral body of not more than 100 members; (c) making the entire bureaucracy responsible to the President and to Congress; (d) eliminating the fifty states and creating not more than ten to twelve regional governments; (e) constitutionalizing the giant corporations[207] and other pluralistic social

204. *See* Murphy, *The Art of Constitutional Interpretation: A Preliminary Showing*, in Essays on the Constitution of the United States 130, 147-55 (M. Harmon ed. 1978).

205. *See* United States v. Brown, 381 U.S. 437 (1965) (Warren, C.J.); Myers v. United States, 272 U.S. 52, 240 (1926) (Brandeis, J., dissenting).

206. *See, e.g.*, L. Fisher, President and Congress: Power and Policy 1-27 (1972). Dr. Fisher has been the leader in modern reinterpretation of separation of powers. He asserts that it was because Congressional government under the Articles of Confederation was ineffectual that a separate executive—the President—was created. In other words, the founding fathers wanted to prevent despotism *and* promote efficiency in government.

207. *See* Miller, *A Modest Proposal for Helping to Tame the Corporate Beast*, 8 Hofstra L. Rev. (1979); Miller, *Toward "Constitutionalizing" the Corporation: A Speculative Essay*, 80 W. Va. L. Rev. 187 (1978).

groups; (f) allowing the Supreme Court to issue advisory opinions at the request of other organs of government and standards of national purpose as well; (g) constitutionalizing the political party; (h) establishing a "devil's advocate" within government; (i) requiring a social audit of all governmental programs; (j) enlarging the environmental impact statement requirement to mandate "social impact statements" for all proposed governmental actions; and (k) establishing an ecological planning unit in the federal government.

The listing of such changes points up the staggering dimensions of the constitutional crisis in which Americans are now deeply immersed. Whether such fundamental alterations can help achieve a good society is an unanswered question. However glorious the past may have been, stolid adherence to concepts developed by people long dead—the Founding Fathers—will not serve the pressing needs of the modern era. Those people—the saints in America's hagiology—should not be ignored. Indeed, they cannot be. But *their* answer for the climacteric of humankind may be simply stated: solve your own problems. The drafters of the Constitution of 1787 left it up to each generation of Americans to write its own fundamental law. That has been done in the past by making the written Constitution in large part an unwritten one. Such an approach, however, is no longer adequate.

Finally, those who think about American constitutionalism should begin with Machiavelli. As Sir Isaiah Berlin puts it: "In the famous fifteenth chapter of *The Prince* he [Machiavelli] says that liberality, mercy, honour, humanity, frankness, chastity, religion, and so forth, are indeed virtues, and a life lived in the exercise of these virtues would be successful 'if men were all good.' But they are not; and it is idle to hope that they will become so. We must take men as we find them, and seek to improve them along possible, not impossible, lines. . . . [H]uman societies in fact stand in need of leadership, and cannot become what they should be, save by the effective pursuit of power, of stability, *virtù*, greatness."[208] Anyone who wishes to think seriously about constitutionalism in the United States today must come to terms with the challenges laid down by Machiavelli nearly five centuries ago.

---

208. Berlin, *supra* note 22, at 175-76 (footnote omitted).

CHAPTER 4

Interstate Equal Protection

(Co-author: JEFFREY H. BOWMAN)

Although the Declaration of Independence asserted that "all men are created equal," the commitment to equality was dropped when the Constitution was drafted. Not until 1868, after the sanguinary Civil War, did it reappear—this time in the Fourteenth Amendment. Promulgated to aid the freed slaves, the amendment reads in part: No state shall "deny to any person within its jurisdiction the equal protection of the laws." Even then, the paper promise of the Constitution proved to be ephemeral for many Americans—most of all the former slaves. Black Americans had neither the consolations of formal equality nor the practice of protection from discrimination. In 1896, the Supreme Court determined through an intuition known only to the Justices that the formula of "separate-but-equal" satisfied the command of equal protection. As is well known, blacks were then, and continued to be, both separate and unequal. Equal protection was in large part a dead letter, so much so that Justice Oliver Wendell Holmes could sneer in 1927 that it was "the usual last resort" of constitutional arguments.

For reasons that have not yet been fully studied or understood, that judicial attitude changed in the 1940s. For at least a generation, egalitarianism was the pole star of much of the Supreme Court's jurisprudence. The judicial drive has been somewhat abated in recent years, but the demand for equality continues unchanged. This chapter suggests that the next logical step that interpretation of the equal protection clause should take is to define the word "laws" expansively. Rather than looking only to the laws of one state (one jurisdiction), it is argued that courts should establish a national standard and that all states should adhere to that standard. Centering on the right to vote as an example, it is maintained that the standards for voting should be the same the country over, and that the equal protection clause can be construed, without undue strain, to attain that end. A nation that asserts, often quite vehemently, that it is a democracy requires, at a minimum, that the fundamental rights of the citizenry—such as voting—be governed by uniform standards. Otherwise, the largest single group of voters—those who call themselves independents—are often effectively disenfranchised.

Today, the fourteenth amendment embodies much of what has become our natural-law Constitution. After a century, the amendment stands as both a symbol of national unity and a practical guarantee of nationally established rights.
—Kenneth L. Karst*

I. INTRODUCTION

"During the twentieth century, the United States became a united state. Given the world and national history of our troubled century, that was probably inevitable, and there is surely no turning back . . . ."[1] That comment by Professor Theodore Lowi is the basic theme of this essay, which suggests that the time has come for our constitutional law to recognize that we are indeed a "united state." The immediate focus will be upon equal protection of the laws, an express limitation on the states only, but a concept that is at times "incorporated" into the fifth amendment's due process limitation on the federal government. We argue for a national—an *interstate*—standard for equal protection, predicated on the basic position that the term, "the laws," in the fourteenth amendment should be interpreted to mean more than those of one state or one jurisdiction only.

That, to be sure, cuts against the grain of orthodox equal protection doctrine. But it is the next logical step for equal protection interpretation to take. In a well-known sentence, Archibald Cox maintained that "[o]nce loosed, the idea of equality is

---

* Karst, *Not One Law at Rome and Another at Athens: The Fourteenth Amendment in Nationwide Application*, 1972 WASH. U.L.Q. 383, 404.

1. T. LOWI, THE END OF LIBERALISM 295 (2d ed. 1979).

"Interstate Equal Protection" was originally published under the title of "Toward an Interstate Standard of Equal Protection of the Laws: A Speculative Essay" in 1981 Brigham Young University Law Review 275. It is reproduced here with permission of the Brigham Young University Law Review, and with the permission of Jeffrey H. Bowman.

not easily cabined."[2] Surely that is accurate. A little over a half-century ago, Justice Holmes, in an opinion his idolators would like to forget, called equal protection the usual last resort of constitutional arguments—and brusquely dismissed Carrie Buck's plea that she should not be involuntarily sterilized.[3] Since then the idea of equal protection has indeed been loosed so that commentators routinely talk about the "new" or "substantive" equal protection.

That familiar learning will not be retraced here. Nor is this essay an exhaustive delineation of all of the nuances and permutations of interstate equal protection; rather, it is a speculative essay, designed more to stimulate debate than to answer all of the questions of such a doctrinal extension. We recognize that it will take a considerable mental leap into the dark future for others to grasp and agree with our net conclusion. The discussion below begins with an examination of the "new" jurisprudence of the Supreme Court, which cannot be traced beyond *Cooper v. Aaron*[4] in 1958, and then proceeds to set forth the arguments, pro and con, for interstate equal protection. The resurrection of substantive due process with its significant elements of equal protection, in conjunction with the concept of "reverse incorporation" and the potential meaning of "national citizenship," suggests that the growth of equal protection is far from over.

II. THE HISTORICAL AND SOCIAL CONTEXT OF EQUAL PROTECTION

The nation began in 1789 without an equality principle in the Constitution, it having been dropped after enunciation in the Declaration of Independence. Only when the Civil War produced the fourteenth amendment did one appear—as a limitation on the states alone, not on the federal government. Only in this century—and, then, mostly since 1954—has the principle been applied to the federal government.[5] This essay does not trace that development, for Professor Karst's recent discussion of the congruence between the equality protections of the four-

---

2. Cox, *The Supreme Court, 1965 Term-Foreword: Constitutional Adjudication and the Promotion of Human Rights*, 80 HARV L. REV. 91 (1966).

3. Buck v. Bell, 274 U.S. 200 (1927).

4. 358 U.S. 1 (1958).

5. *See* Bolling v. Sharpe, 347 U.S. 497 (1954); Karst, *The Fifth Amendment's Guarantee of Equal Protection*, 55 N.C.L. REV. 541 (1977).

teenth and fifth amendments ably sets out the several considerations therein.[6]

Historically, equal protection provides a classic illustration of one aspect of the "living" or "operative" Constitution. The words in the document remain the same, but their content continues to change through time. That disturbs some commentators, who believe that we have an "imperial judiciary" or "government by judiciary."[7] Those accusations are hardly accurate, even though their basis—that the Supreme Court has read new meaning into ancient clauses—is correct. There should be no surprise that a further extension of equal protection is recommended. Cardozo once maintained that there were fields in the "domain of law where fundamental conceptions have been developed to their uttermost conclusions by the organon of logic."[8] He was not then talking about the Constitution; and it is by no means clear that he was correct. The genius of American law, including the area of "constitutional common law,"[9] is that principles have a way of being ameliorated in a sort of Hegelian synthesis, or of striking some type of Aristotelian golden mean, rather than being extended to the outermost limits of their logic. To cite but one relevant example, *Shelley v. Kramer*[10] could have revolutionized private law; but it has not. The principle has scarcely been extended since 1948. Nevertheless, as de Tocqueville noted a century and a half ago, there seems to be a marked tendency toward egalitarianism in the United States.[11] That, according to the late Professor Alexander Bickel,[12] has been one of the drummers to which the Supreme Court has marched in recent decades. The history of Supreme Court lawmaking since *Buck v. Bell* evidences the accuracy of Bickel's observation.

It is not that the actual social structure in the United States has been altered substantially—as Bickel implied—because it has not. No massive redistribution of wealth has occurred, although members of the working class have been able to catch at

6. Karst, *supra* note ***.

7. *E.g.*, R. BERGER, GOVERNMENT BY JUDICIARY (1977); L. GRAGLIA, DISASTER BY DECREE (1976); Glazer, *Towards an Imperial Judiciary?*, 41 PUB. INTEREST 104 (1975).

8. SELECTED WRITINGS OF BENJAMIN NATHAN CARDOZO 294 (M. Hall ed. 1947).

9. *See* Monaghan, *The Supreme Court, 1974 Term-Foreward: Constitutional Common Law*, 89 HARV. L. REV. 1 (1975).

10. 334 U.S. 1 (1948).

11. A. DE TOCQUEVILLE, DEMOCRACY IN AMERICA (F. Borren ed. 1864).

12. A. BICKEL, THE SUPREME COURT AND THE IDEA OF PROGRESS 103 (1970).

least some crumbs from the groaning table of economic opulence that is the United States. The expansion of equal protection law occurred almost entirely during America's true "golden age"—that time from about 1945 to 1970 when the dollar was king and American military might supreme, when commentators could seriously talk about a *Pax Americana,* and when economic growth within the United States seemed to know no bounds.[13] However, in the last ten years recognition of "the limits to growth" and the coming of a steady-state economy has so altered the social milieu[14] in which constitutional norms are applied that one must recognize that discussions of constitutional issues outside of the social context in which they arise tend, more and more, to be mere sterile exercises in doctrinal exegesis—helpful perhaps to lawyers but not at all helpful to the lawyer-judges who sit upon the High Bench.[15] The point is obvious. At least, it should be obvious; but it is little acknowledged in the law journals and elsewhere in the legal profession. "Legalism"—the notion that law is *there,* separate and apart from the warp and woof of society—still is the prevailing ideology of lawyers.[16] That is a pathetic fallacy, but one routinely purveyed to thousands of law students.

A full contextual analysis is not possible within the scope of this essay. Suffice it merely to draw attention to Professor Lester C. Thurow's insightful book, *The Zero-Sum Society.*[17] He maintains that the political (for which, read constitutional) order is in disarray, unable to deal effectively with the consequences of burgeoning and coalescing economic problems such as inflation, unemployment, slow growth, low productivity, environmental decay, economic discrimination, and inequality, because massive distributional actions must be taken. "In the past," Thurow says, "political and economic power was distributed in such a way that substantial economic losses could be imposed on parts of the population . . . . Economic losses were allocated to particular powerless groups rather than spread across the population. These groups are no longer willing to accept losses and are

13. *See* A. MILLER, DEMOCRATIC DICTATORSHIP: THE EMERGENT CONSTITUTION OF CONTROL (1981).

14. *See* W. OPHULS, ECOLOGY AND THE POLITICS OF SCARCITY (1976).

15. For examples, see almost any issue of the Supreme Court Review and any of the Harvard Law Review's annual summaries of Supreme Court activities.

16. *See* J. SHKLAR, LEGALISM (1964).

17. L. THUROW, THE ZERO-SUM SOCIETY (1980).

able to raise substantially the costs for those who wish to impose losses upon them."[18]

The meaning in political or constitutional terms is paradoxical: pluralism as a political order is breaking down *simply because it has been successful.*[19] Thurow ends his important discussion of "the zero-sum society" with these ominous words:

> As we head into the 1980s, it is well to remember that there is really only one important question in political economy. If elected, whose income do you and your party propose to cut in the process of solving the economic problems facing us? Our economy and the solutions to its problems have a substantial zero-sum element. Our economic life would be easier if this were not true, but we are going to have to learn to play a zero-sum economic game. If we cannot learn, or prefer to pretend that the zero-sum problem does not exist, we are simply going to fail.[20]

Law, including constitutional law, is a reflection of economics. A number of zero-sum Supreme Court decisions on equal protection have been rendered in recent years—*Bakke,*[21] *Weber,*[22] *Rodriguez,*[23] and *Fullilove*[24] are perhaps the outstanding examples. The Justices are playing a zero-sum economics game while using lawyers' language—an example of how economists and lawyers can be talking about the same thing but using different word symbols, and thus not communicating at all (as John R. Commons observed in 1950).[25]

In sum, then, equal protection law and its analysis by courts and commentators alike should be seen in the context of the zero-sum society. That society is, as Lowi says, a "united state." The thesis of this essay is that it is both feasible and desirable to think of equal protection as a national standard, one that recognizes "the claims of equal national citizenship" in a "national community,"[26] with that standard being interstate, not intra-

---

18. *Id.* at 12.

19. *See* A. Miller, Oracle in the Marble Palace: Politics and the Supreme Court (manuscript in possession of author); T. Lowi, *supra* note 1. *See also* H. Kariel, The Decline of American Pluralism (1961).

20. L. Thurow, *supra* note 17, at 214.

21. Regents of the University of California v. Bakke, 438 U.S. 265 (1978).

22. United Steel Workers v. Weber, 443 U.S. 193 (1979).

23. San Antonio Independent School Dist. v. Rodriguez, 411 U.S. 1 (1973).

24. Fullilove v. Klutznick, 448 U.S. 448 (1980).

25. J. Commons, The Economics of Collective Action 309-14 (1950).

26. Karst, *The Supreme Court, 1976 Term-Foreword: Equal Citizenship Under the*

state. The fourteenth amendment, of course, speaks in terms of *no state* denying to any *person* within its jurisdiction the *equal protection* of the *laws*. That delphic command is far from clear, as dozens of cases illustrate. But those decisions revolve around two basic questions—what is state action? and what is equal protection?—and one important, but seldom discussed, question: what is a person? It is familiar learning that state action has been an evolving concept whose development is not yet over, and that equal protection is determined by different standards according to the factual contexts in which issues arise. As for the problem of who or what is a person, a tribunal that without argument conceded that the disembodied entities called corporations are constitutional persons[27] almost a century later refused that status to a fetus.[28]

The meaning of the word, "laws," in the fourteenth amendment has not been subjected to rigorous analysis by scholars. Historically, of course, it meant the laws of a given state or of a given jurisdiction within one state. At most, the Court, as in *Yick Wo v. Hopkins*,[29] has been willing at times to penetrate the thicket of administration and determine how given statutes or ordinances are administered; or it has made, as in *Palmer*[30] and *Davis*,[31] the motivation of legislators the determining criterion. In *San Antonio School District v. Rodriguez*,[32] a Court majority rejected disparities of financing between school districts, finding no equal protection violation.

If one takes an antiquarian view of constitutional interpretation, resting primarily on *stare decisis* and ultimately on the intentions of those who wrote the fourteenth amendment, then the answer to the question—should there be an interstate standard of equal protection?—is easy: No. But the Justices, save when they wished, and that is seldom, have never been circumscribed by such a rigid view of interpretation. Those who acknowledge, in Professor Ray Forrester's language, "truth in judging,"[33] readily concede that the Justices make up the law as they go along—always have, as Justice White said in *Miranda v.*

Fourteenth Amendment, 91 Harv. L. Rev. 1 (1977).

27. Santa Clara County v. Southern Pac. Ry., 118 U.S. 394 (1886).
28. Roe v. Wade, 410 U.S. 113 (1973).
29. 118 U.S. 356 (1886).
30. 403 U.S. 217 (1971).
31. 426 U.S. 229 (1976).
32. 411 U.S. 1 (1973).
33. Forrester, *Are We Ready for Truth in Judging?*, 63 A.B.A.J. 1212 (1977).

Arizona[34]—and no doubt will continue to do so as long as the Court functions. Indeed, as Justice Brennan flatly stated in *Richmond Newspapers v. Virginia*,[35] "Under our system, judges are not mere umpires, but, in their own sphere, lawmakers—a coordinate branch of government."[36] The road, thus, is open for new vistas to be seen in equal protection law—and it is one of those vistas that we advocate: Equal protection, to repeat, should include discriminations among states, with "laws" meaning the laws of other states as well, whenever fundamental rights are at issue. A tribunal that can swallow, without difficulty, the notion that an artificial economic collectivity is a person, and even extend freedom of speech to it,[37] surely should be able to read the word "laws" more expansively.

III. THE NEW JURISPRUDENCE OF THE SUPREME COURT

That there is a sociological basis for the United States being a united state admits of no doubt. Americans are far more closely knit together today, because of scientific and technological developments in transportation, communications, and other economic activities, than were their predecessors in 1787, 1800, 1850, or even 1900. There have been more changes in the human condition in the little more than a century since the fourteenth amendment was placed in the Constitution than in known human history before 1868. We are in the midst today of a *third* industrial revolution, one which bids fair to alter the environment in which *Homo sapiens* exist more than either the first or second,[38] and one which can only be compared to the agricultural revolution that occurred eons ago. There should, therefore, be little wonder that ancient constitutional mechanisms and institutions are being adapted to new social conditions. The scrutiny here is on one of those institutions—the Supreme Court of the United States and its "new" jurisprudence of the past quarter-century.

Our account, necessarily brief, begins with *Cooper v.*

---

34. 384 U.S. 436, 531 (1966) (White, J., dissenting).

35. 448 U.S. 555 (1980).

36. *Id.* at 595 (Brennan, J., concurring).

37. First Nat'l Bank of Boston v. Bellotti, 435 U.S. 765 (1978). *See* Miller, *On Politics, Democracy, and the First Amendment: A Commentary on* First National Bank v. Bellotti, __WASH. & LEE L. REV. __ (1981).

38. *See, e.g.,* P. LARGE, THE MICRO REVOLUTION (1980); A. BURKITT & E. WILLIAMS, THE SILICON CIVILIZATION (1980).

Aaron,[39] the Little Rock school desegregation decision of 1958. There, in a unique opinion individually signed by all nine Justices, the Court unanimously held that defiance of the principle of *Brown v. Board of Education* (I & II)[40] could not be tolerated, and that a Supreme Court decision was "the law of the land."[41] As such, the Court said, it was, under the theory of article VI's principle of federal supremacy, superior to and overriding of any inconsistent state law or policy. In the words of Professor Philip Kurland, "the Court seemed to assume the same scope for its decision as the statute [the 1964 Civil Rights Act] could claim."[42] Kurland goes on to assert that "[a] Supreme Court opinion, whatever its merits, cannot seriously be treated as the equivalent of a statute for purposes of the Supremacy Clause. Nor have they been so treated, however highly the Supreme Court itself may regard some of them."[43]

On the latter point, Professor Kurland is technically correct. But on the larger matter he surely can be faulted. Decisions of the Supreme Court, whether liked or not, *are* considered to be "the law of the land" and thus to be the "equivalent of a statute for purposes of the Supremacy Clause." Not only laymen but members of the legal profession view those decisions as establishing a norm of conduct not unlike a statute. The meaning for present purposes is clear: a decision on equal protection in, say, a case coming from New York is the law of the land. That means that law enforcement personnel in all other states are similarly bound even though they could not be held in contempt for refusing to adhere to the decision. That, at least, is the inescapable inference to be drawn from such decisions as *Shapiro v. Thompson.*[44] There should not be, as Professor Karst has said in quoting Cicero, "one law at Rome and another at Athens."[45]

Although it is logically impossible to infer a general principle from a particular one, that is precisely what is being done. Law is far from the logical endeavor that some think it is. Justice Felix Frankfurter said it well in 1954:

---

39. 358 U.S. 1 (1958).
40. 347 U.S. 483 (1954); 349 U.S. 294 (1955).
41. 358 U.S. at 18.
42. P. KURLAND, POLITICS, THE CONSTITUTION AND THE WARREN COURT 185 (1970).
43. *Id.* at 186.
44. 394 U.S. 618 (1969).
45. Karst, *Not One Law at Rome and Another at Athens: The Fourteenth Amendment in Nationwide Application,* 1972 WASH. U.L.Q. 383, 404 (1972).

Human society keeps changing. Needs emerge, first vaguely felt and unexpressed, imperceptibly gathering strength, steadily becoming more and more exigent, generating a force which, if left unheeded and denied response so as to satisfy the impulse behind it at least in part, may burst forth with an intensity that exacts more than reasonable satisfaction. Law as the response to those needs is not merely a system of logical deduction, though considerations of logic are far from irrelevant. *Law presupposes sociological wisdom as well as logical unfolding.*[46]

One of the considerations of logic that distinctly is not relevant is the plain and simple proposition that a Supreme Court decision in a *single case* (even though not a class action) is the statement of a *general norm*. Some language of Chief Justice Fred Vinson is apposite: "[Y]ou are," he told the American Bar Association, "in a sense, prosecuting or defending class actions; . . . you represent not only your clients, but tremendously important principles, upon which are based the plans, hopes, and aspirations of a great many people throughout the country."[47] In other words, cases are chosen not in the interests of the litigants but in the interests of the development of the law—the development of general principles. The Court rules not only for the parties at the bar, but for generations yet unborn. The "class actions" that are constitutional cases are, to be sure, "backdoor" or de facto class actions, for often, perhaps usually, litigation is solely between the parties before the Court. (They can also validly be called "backdoor" advisory opinions.)[48] However, once the Justices have decided a dispute on the merits the result has the practical, but not the technical, effect of binding everyone similarly situated throughout the nation. The meaning should be clear: the Court has assumed "the role of a third legislative chamber."[49] Some decry that,[50] but most do not deny it. For better or for worse, something akin to, but not exactly the same as,

---

46. F. Frankfurter, Of Law and Men 35 (1956) (emphasis added).

47. Address by Chief Justice Vinson to the American Bar Association (Sept. 7, 1949), *reprinted in* 69 S. Ct. v, vi (1949). *See* Miller, *Constitutional Decisions as De Facto Class Actions,* __ U. Det. J. Urb. L. __ (1981).

48. *See* Miller & Barron, *The Supreme Court, the Adversary System, and the Flow of Information to the Justices: A Preliminary Inquiry,* in A. Miller, The Supreme Court 261 (1978).

49. L. Hand, The Bill of Rights 55 (1958).

50. *See, e.g.,* Leedes, *The Supreme Court Mess,* 57 Tex. L. Rev. 1361 (1979); Bridwell, *The Scope of Judicial Review: A Dirge for the Theorists of Majority Rule?,* 31 S.C.L. Rev. 617 (1980).

what the Framers refused to put into the Constitution when drafted in 1787—a Council of Revision[51]—has been created by judicial assertion and public acquiescence.

That means, however, merely that a single Supreme Court decision can have a statute-like effect. As with Congress, the Justices feel free to "repeal" previous decisions and to "enact" others, for as Justice William O. Douglas said in *Glidden v. Zdanok,* constitutional questions are "always open."[52] There is another, more portentious development in the new jurisprudence, heralded by *Cooper v. Aaron*—the propensity of the Court at times, but far from always, to set forth its rulings in deliberate general language. *Cooper* started it, but the process has not ended. The decisions are not many, but they are significant. They include, but are not limited to *Reynolds v. Sims*[53] (one person/one vote); *Miranda v. Arizona*[54] (on what police officers should do with criminal suspects); *Green v. School Board*[55] (in which an "affirmative duty" was imposed upon school boards to integrate public schools); the abortion cases[56] (setting forth when a woman may voluntarily have an abortion based on a trimester system); and *United States v. Snepp*[57] (where a contractual agreement was held to override first amendment rights). The point is that in these illustrative cases, the Justices openly and outwardly used statutory-like language and wrote opinions couched in general terms (for the entire nation) and with little regard for the actual litigants. Clarence Gideon, to take another example, was of little importance *as an individual* to the Court; his significance was that the facts of his incarceration by Florida provided a looked-for stimulus to make a general rule about the availability of counsel in noncapital criminal cases.[58] Support for the point being made may be found in *Pickering v. School Board,*[59] where Justice Marshall expressly refused to extend the "rule of the case" beyond the specific facts of the *Pickering*

---

51. Under Randolph's proposed Council of Revision, every law passed by the legislature automatically would have been previewed by the judiciary before taking effect. *See* United States v. Richardson, 418 U.S. 166, 189 (1974) (Powell, J., concurring).

52. 370 U.S. 530, 592 (1962) (Douglas, J., dissenting).

53. 377 U.S. 533 (1964).

54. 384 U.S. 436 (1966).

55. 391 U.S. 430 (1968).

56. Roe v. Wade, 410 U.S. 113 (1973); Doe v. Bolton, 410 U.S. 179 (1973).

57. 444 U.S. 507 (1980), *rehearing denied,* 100 S. Ct. 1668 (1980).

58. Gideon v. Wainwright, 372 U.S. 335 (1963).

59. 391 U.S. 563 (1968).

litigation.

This is not the time to discuss the matter further. Suffice it to conclude that the time-honored result of the adversary system—the production of the "law of the case"—is slowly being changed to mean the "law of the land."[60] From that may be derived the proposition that the "laws" covered by equal protection should have an interstate dimension in those areas considered to be "fundamental rights." That is the ultimate meaning of *Cooper v. Aaron.* Our discussion now narrows to a case study on voting, which will be used as an example for the larger principle.

IV. ENFRANCHISING THE INDEPENDENT VOTER

In 1980 some 35 states held a presidential primary, determining over 65 percent of each convention's votes. Yet voters in sixteen of these states, who did not wish to be publicly affiliated with a political party, were statutorily barred from voting in their state's primary. These states selected a total of 1,324 delegates to the Democratic and 735 delegates to the Republican National Conventions. Statutes there prescribe a "closed primary," by which voting is restricted to those who, in some manner and at some time prior to voting, publicly declare their affiliation with a political party and have that affiliation recorded. The consequence is a gross disenfranchisement of millions of Americans that raises serious questions about the most significant voting bloc in the country, the independent voters.[61] Is

---

60. *Compare* Cooper v. Aaron, 358 U.S. 1 (1958), *with* President Lincoln's views: Judicial decisions "must be binding in any case upon the parties to a suit as to the object of the suit," and "while they are also entitled to very high respect and consideration in all parallel cases by all other departments of the Government," nonetheless,

> if the policy of the Government is to be irrevocably fixed by decisions of the Supreme Court, the instant they are made in ordinary litigation between parties in personal actions the people will have ceased to be their own rulers, having to that extent practically assigned their Government into the hands of that eminent tribunal.

Quoted in J. CHOPER, JUDICIAL REVIEW AND THE NATIONAL POLITICAL PROCESS 213 (1980). *See also* R. JACKSON, THE STRUGGLE FOR JUDICIAL SUPREMACY 96-104 (1941) (discussing how national monetary policy was set by the Supreme Court in a lawsuit between private parties involving the sum of $15.60).

61. There is a growing movement away from the two major political parties. A recent Gallup Poll, conducted from November 1980 to February 1981, indicates that 31% of the American voters consider themselves to be "independents." (42% were Democrats and 29% were Republicans). N.Y. Times, Mar. 8, 1981, at 30, col. 2. Moreover, it is likely that this figure will continue to grow in future elections since 45% of the voters under 30 classify themselves as independents. N. NIE, S. VERBA, & J. PETROCIK, THE CHANGING

their fundamental right to vote fatally diluted? And, if so, are they being accorded equal protection of the laws?

Political parties have existed in this nation for over 175 years and today dominate the presidential nominating process. In most elections, participation in the political party nominating process is the *sine qua non* to meaningful participation in the electoral process. As the impetus for increased popular participation in the nominating process has grown from the progressive movement of the early twentieth century,[62] the traditional party caucus has been replaced by popularly elected nominating conventions and by the increased use of direct primaries.[63] Justice Pitney's oft-quoted statement in *Newberry v. United States*[64] that "every voter comes to the polls on the day of the general election confined in his choice to those few candidates who have received party nominations"[65] evidences early judicial recognition of the important role political parties and primary elections play in the electoral process.

Beginning with Wendell Wilkie's attempt to use the 1944 Wisconsin presidential primary as a vehicle for demonstrating his popular support within the Republican Party, primary competition has become a feature of every presidential election.[66] Primaries played an especially important role in the campaigns for the Republican nominations in 1948 (Stassen, Dewey, and

---

AMERICAN VOTER 64 (1976).

62. States that have passed primary election laws have done so because "[c]onventions were thought to be susceptible to manipulation by party leaders and a wide-spread faith existed that more popular participation would have a cleansing effect on politics." V. KEY, JR., POLITICS, PARTIES AND PRESSURE GROUPS 409 (5th ed. 1964). Similarly, Robert M. LaFollette, Sr., called for the adoption of the primary, arguing,

> No longer . . . will there stand between the voter and the official a political machine with a complicated system of caucuses and conventions, by the easy manipulation of which it thwarts the will of the voter and rules of official conduct . . . . If the voter is competent to cast his ballot at the general election for the official of his choice, he is equally competent to vote directly at the primary election for the nomination of the candidates of his choice.

Speech by Robert M. LaFollette, Sr., accepting nomination for governor, August 8, 1900. Interestingly, this speech was not quoted in TORRELLE, LAFOLLETTE'S POLITICAL PHILOSOPHY 36-37 (1920), as reported in LaFollette v. Democratic Party, 93 Wis. 2d 473, 492-93, 287 N.W.2d 519, 527 (1980).

63. C. MERIAM & R. OVERACKER, PRIMARY ELECTIONS 60-67 (1928).

64. 256 U.S. 232 (1921).

65. *Id.* at 286 (Pitney, J., dissenting).

66. Presidential primaries, of course, have been on the American political scene longer than this. Their effect on the party nominating process, however, was questionable. In 1912, for example, Theodore Roosevelt won 9 out of 12 primaries yet lost his race against President William Howard Taft for the Republican Party nomination.

Taft), 1952 (Eisenhower and Taft), 1964 (Goldwater and Rocke-feller), 1976 (Ford and Reagan), and 1980 (Reagan and Bush); and the Democratic nominations in 1952 (Kefauver,[67] Russell, and Truman—supported favorite sons), 1956 (Stevenson and Kefauver), 1960 (Kennedy and Humphrey), 1968 (McCarthy, Kennedy, and Johnson—supported favorite sons), 1972 (Mc-Govern, Humphrey, Muskie, Wallace and Jackson), 1976 (Carter and Udall) and 1980 (Carter and Kennedy).[68]

Moreover, it is clear that the winners of the Democratic and Republican Party nominations are historically the only viable candidates for election to the presidency.[69] Professor R. A. Dahl, writing in 1964, noted the dominance of the two-party system with respect to both the executive and legislative branches:

> Since 1860 every presidential election has been won by ei-ther a Democrat or a Republican; in only four presidential elections during that period has a third party ever carried a single state. . . . Since 1862 one of the two parties has always had a clear majority of seats in the House; in the Senate, in-dependents or third party members have prevented a clear ma-jority during a total of ten years. The number of seats held by third party members is almost always extremely low.[70]

Nomination by a recognized party substantially reduces the scope of a citizen's real choice in the general election. Today, the nomination process is controlled by voting in the primary elec-tions (and caucuses). Theodore H. White has appraised the im-

---

67. In 1952, Senator Kefauver won 12 of the 16 presidential primaries, yet the nomi-nation went to Senator Adlai E. Stevenson, who had entered no primaries.

68. For the official primary returns from 1948-1972, see CONGRESSIONAL QUARTERLY, GUIDE TO U.S. ELECTIONS 332-49 (1975). For the 1976 primary returns, see CONGRES-SIONAL QUARTERLY, POLITICS IN AMERICA 142-47 (1979).

69. Indeed, the District of Columbia Circuit recently recognized this phenomenon: Regular presidential contests between the Republican and Democratic parties began in 1852. However, the present Democratic Party can trace its origins to the Democratic Republican Party which Thomas Jefferson began to assemble even before the end of Washington's first term. H. BONE, AMERICAN POLITICS AND THE PARTY SYSTEM, 28-30 (1971). A case can likewise be made that Hamil-ton's Federalists and subsequently the Whig Party were the predecessors of the present Republican Party. E. SAIT, AMERICAN PARTIES AND ELECTIONS 205 (1927). If so, then the only Presidents who may plausibly claim not to be the products of the two-party rivalry are James Monroe and John Quincy Adams, who served during a sort of party "interregnum" after the decline of the Feder-alists and before the rise of the Whigs. See Bone, supra, at 28.
Ripon Society v. National Republican Party, 525 F.2d 567, 581, n.37 (D.C. Cir. 1975) (en banc), cert. denied, 424 U.S. 933 (1976).

70. R. DAHL, PLURALIST DEMOCRACY IN THE UNITED STATES 214 (1967).

portance of the primary election this way:

> Primaries had already thus become, by 1972, one of the great drive engines of American politics—for a primary is a deed. All else in politics, except money, is words—comment, rhetoric, analysis, polls. But a primary is a fact. There is a hardness to such a fact, especially if the victory is a contested one. With the lift of such an event, a candidate can compel attention, build votes, change minds. It is the underdog's classic route to power in America.[71]

Presidential primaries should be viewed for what they actually are, integral parts of the general election, controlling the choices of those who have the right to vote. Because of this determinative role, primary outcomes should be truly representative of all the voters, not merely of avowed party members. A recent but single United States Supreme Court case interferes with this position.

A.   The LaFollette Case

In *Democratic Party of the United States v. LaFollette,*[72] the Supreme Court considered a challenge by the National Democratic Party to Wisconsin's open primary law.[73] The Wisconsin law permits all qualified voters to cast ballots in the presidential preference primary regardless of their party affiliation. Wisconsin delegates to the national convention are selected by party members at statewide party caucuses, but they are bound by state statute to vote in accordance with the preferences expressed in the primary. However, this open primary approach conflicts with the rules of the Democratic Party which decree that only those persons who openly and publicly declare their adherence to the principles of the Democratic Party may participate in the party's presidential preference primary. The National Party argued that as a result of Wisconsin's failure to restrict its Democratic primary to publicly declared party members, the popularity of various candidates within the party was distorted. The Party further argued that the binding open

---

71. T. White, The Making of the President 1972 at 71 (1973).

72. 101 S. Ct. 1010 (1981).

73. The "open primary" is so named because the "voter is not required to declare publicly a party preference or to have that preference publicly recorded. Each voter makes a choice of party in the privacy of the voting booth." 93 Wis. 2d at 485, 287 N.W.2d at 523.

primary would "infringe severely on the Democratic Party's effort to conduct its affairs."[74]

A divided Court, speaking through Justice Stewart, ruled that Wisconsin could not bind the Democratic Party to honor the results of the open primary at its national convention. Justice Stewart found that the "issue is whether the state may compel the National Party to seat a delegation chosen in a way that violates the rules of the Party."[75] He asserted that resolution of this issue was controlled by the Court's decision in *Cousins v. Wigoda*.[76] There, the Court held that the 1972 Democratic National Convention had the right to refuse to seat an Illinois delegation that was chosen in accordance with state law but that violated party rules regarding participation of minorities, women and young people. In *LaFollette,* the Court found that "the members of the National Party, speaking through their rules, chose to define their associational rights by limiting those who could participate in the processes leading to the selection of delegates to the National Convention."[77] Because of this the Court concluded that "a State, or a court, may not constitutionally substitute its judgment for that of the Party."[78]

The Court's analysis is seriously defective on two counts. First, the emphasis placed on *Cousins* is inappropriate. Indeed, as Justice Powell recognized in dissent, "[T]he facts of this case present issues that differ considerably from those we dealt with in *Cousins*."[79] In *Cousins* the Court was concerned that the delegates who vote on party rules and procedure, adopt a party platform, and vote for party officers be party members chosen in accordance with party rules and not a court order. There, "suffrage was exercised at the primary election to elect delegates to a National Party Convention."[80] In *LaFollette* the selection of individual delegates to the National Convention was not at issue because the delegate selection process was under the exclusive control of the Democratic Party. Wisconsin law provides that

---

74. Brief for Appellants at 33, Democratic Party of the United States v. LaFollette, 101 S. Ct. 1010 (1981).

75. Democratic Party of the United States v. LaFollette, 101 S. Ct. at 1018.

76. 419 U.S. 477 (1975).

77. 101 S. Ct. at 1019.

78. *Id.* at 1020. Justice Stewart merely restated the question at issue, and then used the question as a "reason." A conclusion is not a reason, even when uttered by a Supreme Court Justice.

79. *Id.* at 1022. (Powell, J., dissenting).

80. 419 U.S. 477, 489 (1975).

the "method of selecting the delegates or alternates [is] determined by the state party organization."[81] No delegates are selected by the voter in Wisconsin. Once a delegate is elected, through whatever manner or process, Wisconsin law requires only that the delegate "vote in accord with the results of the open primary election."[82] As Justice Powell noted, "While this regulation affecting participation in the primary is hardly insignificant, it differs substantially from the direct state interference in delegate selection at issue in *Cousins*."[83]

Secondly, in an opinion which exalts form over substance, Justice Stewart, under the guise of associational rights, has given the two major parties a blank check to make rules for themselves and for all others affected by the parties' rules. In finding that "a State or a court may not constitutionally substitute its own judgment for that of a party,"[84] the Court has gone much too far in protecting the right of association. It has in practical effect, permitted those who control the major parties to make rules for all Americans. When the actions of any association have such a profound and far-reaching effect, not only on the group itself, but upon a state (as in *LaFollette*) and, indeed, upon the nation as a whole, members of the association should be held to have duties beyond that of looking out for their own protected rights. The National Democratic Party performs a significant public[85] function every four years when it selects one of the two major candidates for President of the United States.

---

81. Wis. Stat. Ann. § 8.12(3)(b) (West Supp. 1980).

82. Democratic Party of the United States v. LaFollette, 101 S. Ct. 1010, 1014 (1981).

83. *Id.* at 1023. (Powell, J., dissenting) (emphasis added).

84. *Id.* at 1020. Justice Stewart offers no authority in support of this contention. He further states: "A political party's choice among the various ways of determining the make-up of a State's delegation to the party's national convention is protected by the Constitution." *Id.* Again, Stewart fails to cite authority for support or on point. Instead, he refers to Ripon Society v. National Republican Party, 525 F.2d 567, 585 (D.C. Cir. 1975) (en banc), *cert. denied,* 424 U.S. 933 (1976). That is hardly dispositive, particularly since Stewart designated it as a "*cf.*"

85. The *public* nature of the primary is the extent to which public money is used in the primary process. The Presidential Primary Matching Payment Account Act, 26 U.S.C. §§ 9031-9042 (1976), provides limited public financing of presidential primary elections by authorizing federal matching payments for certain contributions to eligible candidates. The Act establishes a separate account within the United States Treasury known as the Presidential Primary Matching Payment Account from which the Secretary of the Treasury transfers funds to candidates whom the Federal Election Commission certifies are eligible to receive such funds. As of February 26, 1981, a total of $31,309,062.16 had been certified to ten presidential candidates eligible to receive federal primary matching funds.

The Democratic Party is not a mere "private club"[86] primarily concerned, like the NAACP, with the associational rights of its members. When, as has become obvious, early presidential primaries (as in New Hampshire) and even party caucuses (as in Iowa) can have significant national ramifications—mainly, it seems, because of the mass media—then the privateness of the "political associations" should give way to clear recognition of their public, indeed national, status. This is what Justice Stewart in his majority opinion failed to perceive,[87] and what, therefore, makes his opinion and the decision faulty.[88]

Voting is the first duty of democracy. Indeed, the Founding

---

86. 93 Wis. 2d at 515, 287 N.W.2d at 538.

87. Justice White, as a result of his association with the 1960 campaign of President Kennedy, and Chief Justice Burger, as a result of his association with the 1948 presidential campaign of Harold Stassen, are the only members of the current Court with even minimal national political experience. It has been suggested that

[i]n matters of political structure and process, . . . judges properly give deference to legislators whose work requires them to be in the thick of active political engagement. For when judges, particularly those appointed for life, come to questions of political process, they almost by definition do not have the benefit of current experience.

Leventhal, *Courts and Political Thickets,* 77 COLUM. L. REV. 345, 380 (1977). To illustrate the point, Judge Leventhal noted,

In 1916, Felix Frankfurter observed that Charles Evans Hughes, although a former governor, was waging a commonplace political campaign that was utterly lacking in distinction, a condition that he thought was in part due to the different nature of the intervening assignment on the Supreme Court where he had served with distinction.

Id.

88. *LaFollette* also presents the interesting question of whether the associational rights of the National Party transcend those of the State Party. As Justice Powell pointed out: "It is significant that the Democratic Party of Wisconsin, which represents those citizens of Wisconsin willing to take part publicly in party affairs, is here *defending* the state law." 101 S. Ct. 1010, 1024 (Powell, J., dissenting). The State Party, originally named in the action as respondent with the National Party, responded by agreeing that the state law may be validly applied against it and the National Party. The State Party then cross-claimed against the National Party and asked the court to recognize its delegation selected in accord with Wisconsin law. The State Party also filed papers in support of the Wisconsin law with the Supreme Court.

The Wisconsin law also had the support of the Democratic controlled state legislature. On September 5, 1979, by a unanimous vote of the state senate and a 92-1 vote of its assembly, the Wisconsin legislature by joint resolution supported the "firm and enduring commitment of the people of Wisconsin to the open presidential preference primary law as an integral element of Wisconsin's proud tradition of direct and effective participatory democracy." Democratic Party v. LaFollette, Docket No. 79-1631 (February 25, 1981) (Joint Appendix at 75-78). Moreover, on September 14, 1979, a bill intended to create a modified closed primary was firmly rejected in committee. 93 Wis. 2d at 490 n.14, 287 N.W.2d at 526 n.14.

Fathers[89] recognized that "[a] fundamental principle of our representative democracy is," in Alexander Hamilton's words, "'that the people should choose whom they please to govern them.'"[90] As stated by James Madison:

> As each representative will be chosen by a greater number of citizens in the large than in the small republic, it will be more difficult for unworthy candidates to practice with success the vicious arts by which elections are too often carried; and the suffrage of the people being more free will be more likely to centre in men who possess the most attractive merit and the most diffusive and established characters.[91]

Not only does the Court's approach in *LaFollette,* with its emphasis on the associational rights of party members, seemingly ignore the importance of the vote in a democracy, but it runs counter to the Court's traditionally vigilant interest in protecting the right of the voting franchise against state or party abridgment. One hundred years ago in *Ex parte Siebold,*[92] the Supreme Court held that Congress may enact statutes which protect every citizen against state interference with the right to vote. In *Yick Wo v. Hopkins,*[93] the Court recognized that "the political franchise of voting" was a "fundamental political right,"[94] preservative of all other individual rights. During the past two decades the Supreme Court has repeatedly emphasized the significance of a citizen's right to vote and has vigorously protected it against infringement in any form. In 1964 in *Reynolds v. Sims,*[95] the Court stated,

> Undoubtedly, the right of suffrage is a fundamental matter in a free and democratic society. Especially since the right to exer-

---

89. The wisdom and expectations of the drafters of the Constitution have served as a foundation for the continued expansion of popular suffrage. Thus, six of the last twelve amendments to the Constitution have extended the elective franchise by restricting limitations thereon and expanding the ambit of protected participation. Amendment XV (race, color and previous condition of servitude); Amendment XVII (senatorial elections); Amendment XIX (women's suffrage); Amendment XXIII (District of Columbia); Amendment XXIV (abolition of the poll tax); Amendment XXVI (18 year-old right to vote).

90. Powell v. McCormack, 395 U.S. 486, 547 (1969) (quoting Alexander Hamilton, from 2 DEBATES ON THE FEDERAL CONSTITUTION 257 (J. Elliot ed. 1876)).

91. THE FEDERALIST No. 10 (J. Madison), at 58 (H. Lodge ed. 1888).

92. 100 U.S. 371 (1880).

93. 118 U.S. 356 (1886).

94. *Id.* at 370.

95. 377 U.S. 533, 562 (1964). Although technically dicta, subsequent citation has made the Court's language an accurate statement of law.

cise the franchise in a free and unimpaired manner is preservative of other basic civil and political rights, any alleged infringement of the right of citizens to vote must be carefully
and meticulously scrutinized.[96]

The Court decided *Wesberry v. Sanders*[97] that same year and
observed that "[n]o right is more precious in a free country than
that of having a voice in the election of those who make the laws
under which, as good citizens, we must live. Other rights, even
the most basic, are illusory if the right to vote is undermined."[98]

Two years later, in *Harper v. Virginia Board of Elections*,[99]
the Court declared the right to vote to be one of the fundamental rights protected by the equal protection clause of the fourteenth amendment, and concluded that "classifications which
might invade or restrain them must be closely scrutinized and
carefully confined."[100] Subsequent cases have amplified and considerably broadened these holdings in applying them to specific
circumstances.[101] Moreover, it is no longer open to serious question that the right to vote in a primary election is as protected
against state encroachment as is the right to vote in the general
election.

The early attitude of the Supreme Court toward
of primary elections may be gleaned from *Newberry v. United
States*.[102] There the Court found that

> [primaries] are in no sense elections for an office, but merely
> methods by which party adherents agree upon candidates
> whom they intend to offer and support for ultimate choice by
> all qualified electors. General provisions touching elections in
> constitutions or statutes are not necessarily applicable to
> primaries—the two things are radically different.[103]

The Court held that article I, section 4 of the Constitution, giving Congress power to regulate the manner of holding elections
for the House of Representatives and the Senate, did not em-

---

96. *Id.* at 561-62 (1964).
97. 376 U.S. 1 (1964).
98. *Id.* at 17.
99. 383 U.S. 663 (1966).
100. *Id.* at 670.
101. *See, e.g.,* Dunn v. Blumstein, 405 U.S. 330 (1972) (durational residence requirement for voting found unconstitutional); Kramer v. Union Free School Dist. No. 15, 395
U.S. 621 (1969) (a state may not deny the right to vote to a citizen because he does not
own or lease taxable realty).
102. 256 U.S. 232 (1921).
103. *Id.* at 250.

power Congress to limit expenditures of candidates in senatorial primaries.[104]

As late as 1935 primaries were considered, in the absense of state regulation, to be functions of the political parties, which were recognized as private associations. In *Grovey v. Townsend*,[105] the Court held that the decision of the Convention of the Texas Democratic Party to exclude all blacks from participating in the Democratic primary did not constitute state action and therefore was not prohibited by either the fourteenth or the fifteenth amendments. This ruling came despite the Court's earlier decisions in *Nixon v. Herndon*[106] and *Nixon v. Condon*.[107] In *Herndon* a Texas law declaring blacks ineligible to vote in the Democratic primary was held to violate the fourteenth amendment. In *Condon* a subsequent Texas statute which likewise excluded blacks by allowing the Democratic Party executive committee to determine its voting membership was also found to violate the equal protection clause. In neither *Herndon* nor *Condon*, however, did the Court define "primary" as part of the electoral process.

The judicial view represented by *Grovey* underwent a radical change beginning with *United States v. Classic*.[108] The Court there overruled its decisions in *Newberry* and *Grovey* and held that the right to vote in a primary election was entitled to the same amount of protection from state abridgement as the right to vote in a general election:

> Where the state law has made the primary an integral part of the procedure of choice, or where in fact the primary effectively controls the choice, the right of the elector to have his ballot counted at the primary, is likewise included in the right protected by Article I, § 2. And this right of participation is protected just as is the right to vote at the election, where the primary is by law made an integral part of the election machinery, whether the voter exercises his right in a party primary

---

104. Substantial disagreement with this point was expressed by the concurring Justices. Four Justices would have held that Congress had the power to regulate primary elections selecting senatorial nominees. *Id.* at 267-68 (White, C.J., concurring in part); *Id.* at 291 (Pitney, J., concurring in part, joined by Brandeis and Clarke, J.J.). One Justice reserved the question. *Id.* at 258 (McKenna, J., concurring, but reserving the question of Congress' power under the seventeenth amendment).

105. 295 U.S. 45 (1935).

106. 273 U.S. 536 (1927).

107. 286 U.S. 73 (1932).

108. 313 U.S. 299 (1941).

which invariably, sometimes or never determines the ultimate choice of the representative.[109]

Three years later in *Smith v. Allwright*[110] (the third of the quartet of cases commonly referred to as the "White Primary" cases),[111] the Supreme Court recognized the significance of the primary and the interest of each voter in effective political participation at this decisive stage of the electoral process. In *Smith* the Court held that the exclusion of blacks from the Texas Democratic primaries was state action in violation of the fifteenth amendment. Specifically overruling *Grovey*, the Court finally concluded that "the right to vote in . . . a primary for the nomination of candidates without discrimination by the State, like the right to vote in a general election, is a right secured by the Constitution."[112] The Court later extended constitutional protections to voters in "unofficial" primaries. In *Terry v. Adams*[113] the Court scrutinized an association of qualified white Democratic voters which selected candidates who would then run for nomination in the official Democratic primary in Texas. The Court held that exclusion of blacks was invalid under the fifteenth amendment because they were not permitted to participate in a significant stage of the electoral process[114] —"the sole stage of the electoral process where the bargaining and interplay of rival political forces would make [the blacks' vote] count." Although *Smith* and *Terry* were not fourteenth amendment cases, the principle is clear. Our argument herein merely takes the *Terry* principle one step further. Just as the exclusion from the primary election stage, where effective formation and compromise take place, denied the blacks their fifteenth amendment rights, we suggest that closed primary systems (such as Florida's) operate to exclude unaffiliated voters from the determinative "primary" stage of the electoral process,[115] and thus in-

---

109. *Id.* at 318.

110. 321 U.S. 649 (1944).

111. Terry v. Adams, 345 U.S. 461 (1953); Smith v. Allwright, 321 U.S. 649 (1944); Nixon v. Condon, 286 U.S. 73 (1932); Nixon v. Herndon, 273 U.S. 536 (1927).

112. Smith v. Allwright, 321 U.S. at 661-62.

113. 345 U.S. 461 (1953).

114. *Id.* at 484 (plurality opinion of Clark, J., concurring, joined by Vinson, C.J., Reed and Jackson, J.J.).

115. Although to our knowledge no data exist, if it could be shown that a significant number of independent voters are either black or members of other minority groups, the extension of equal protection analysis to the rights of independents to vote in primary elections could be seen merely as the application of the standard adopted by the Court

volve an equal protection dimension.

The essence of the White Primary decisions is the premise that determination of who *can* be voted for in the general election is as important, or more important, as who *will* be voted for in that election. As Justice Pitney has stated, "The likelihood of a candidate succeeding in an election without a party nomination is practically negligible . . . . As a practical matter, the ultimate choice of the mass of voters is predetermined when the nominations have been made."[116] Indeed, the Supreme Court has recently noted the winnowing process inherent in primary elections and its importance in a full election cycle. In *Storer v. Brown*,[117] the Court upheld the state's move to guarantee that the primary election process reduce the number of candidates in the general election. Sustaining a state law that refused to permit defeated primary election candidates to get on the general election ballot via a third party candidacy, the Court reasoned,

> The direct party primary in California is not merely an exercise or warm-up for the general election but an integral part of the entire election process, the initial stage in a two-stage process by which the people choose their public officers. It functions to winnow out and finally reject all but the chosen candidates.[118]

The right of citizens to vote in primaries was aptly described by the Third Circuit in *Lynch v. Torquato:*[119]

> [T]he citizen's constitutional right to equality as an elector . . . applies to the choice of those who shall be his elected representatives in the conduct of government, not in the internal management of political party. It is true that this right extends to state regulated and party conducted primaries. However, this is because the function of primaries is to select nominees for governmental office even though, not because, they are party enterprises. The people, when engaged in primary and general elections for the selection of their representatives in government, may rationally be viewed as the 'state' in action, with the consequence that the organization and regulation of these enterprises must be such as accord each elector equal

---

in the "White Primary" cases.

116. Newberry v. United States, 256 U.S. 232, 286 (1921) (Pitney, J., concurring in part).

117. 415 U.S. 724 (1974).

118. *Id.* at 735. *See also* Lubin v. Panish, 415 U.S. 709, 715-16 (1974).

119. 343 F.2d 370 (3d Cir. 1965).

protection of the laws.[120]

Although most of the cases in this series[121] dealt with black voting rights, the underlying principle is that the same set of rules which govern the conduct of the general election should also operate in the regulation of the nomination process. That means that the spirit of the fifteenth amendment should be read into the equal protection clause and be applied generally. It is valid to maintain that the Court has at least tacitly recognized that the right to vote may be rendered meaningless in the absence of a correlative right to participate in the nominating process by which candidates are selected.

It is clear that the presidential primary is far more than a mere warm-up for the general election. It is an integral part of the entire selection process—the beginning of a two stage process. It functions to winnow out and finally reject all but the chosen candidates for the November election. But this is done in the closed primary states without allowing all voters to participate. Voters who choose to remain unaffiliated are barred from the most important ballot box, rendering their opportunity in the general election, as in November 1980, an empty charade. The question is whether that is desirable and also whether it jibes with the Constitution. The answer on both counts should be in the negative, both for purposes of policy and, for constitutional reasons. The right to vote can only mean the right to cast a meaningful ballot—something not now possible in Florida and other closed primary states, and something wrongfully limited by *LaFollette*.

B. Reasons for Enfranchisement

Three important arguments stand out in favor of opening primaries to all eligible voters, regardless of their willingness to declare party affiliation. The first, a practical observation, arises from an increasing political independence in this nation. The second finds root in considerations of our right to privacy. The third   is   that   closed   primary   systems   are   unjustifiably

120. *Id.* at 372.
121. In addition to the judicial decisions discussed above, Congress enacted two pieces of legislation which had the effect of removing restrictions on the franchise: the Voting Rights Act of 1965, Pub. L. No. 89-110, 79 Stat. 437 (codified in 42 U.S.C. §§ 1971 to 1973bb-1 (1976)), and the Voting Rights Act Amendments of 1970, Pub. L. No. 91-285, 84 Stat. 314 (amending 42 U.S.C. §§ 1973b, 1973c, 1973aa to 1973bb-4 (1970) (amended and repealed in part, 1975)).

discriminatory.

1. Increasing political independence. Many Americans are "issue-oriented," and for that reason are not party followers.[122] Since John F. Kennedy's success in 1960, the personality and "media image" of political candidates dominate over political party labels. Presidential candidates are marketed through television by advertising specialists. As political analyst David Broder observed in 1972, "Television and radio enable well-financed candidates to go directly into the homes of voters far more effectively than even the most well-organized political machine."[123] There is strong evidence that the parties are weakening.[124] Indeed, recent polls have indicated a steady rise in the number of voters who consider themselves independent.[125] Fewer than fifty percent of the eligible voters voted for either Ronald Reagan or Jimmy Carter in 1980. Moreover, the national party-affiliated voters increasingly split tickets in general elections—a sign of weakened party loyalty and increased voter independence. This trend is documented in an electoral study which illustrates "defection rates" for those who profess affiliation with a political party.[126] Justice Powell, in his dissenting

---

122. D. BRODER, THE PARTY'S OVER (1972). "Seen as not relevant, parties are bypassed with the voters making their choices on the basis of their own issue preferences and those of the candidates." G. POMPER, VOTERS' CHOICE 183 (1975). *See also* E. LADD, JR. & C. HADLEY, TRANSFORMATIONS OF THE AMERICAN PARTY SYSTEM 301 (1975) (parties are perceived as less than needed by the contemporary electorate). Many voters go beyond merely viewing political parties as irrelevant, but actually distrust them. *See* A. RANNEY, CURING THE MISCHIEFS OF FACTION 56 (1973); G. POMPER, VOTER'S CHOICE 183 (1975).

123. D. BRODER, THE PARTY'S OVER 239-40 (1972). The Supreme Court in *Buckley* recognized the "electorate's increasing dependence on television, radio, and other mass media for news and information." Buckley v. Valeo, 424 U.S. at 19.

124. *See* Branti v. Finkel, 445 U.S. 507, 531-32, n.18 (1980) (Powell, J., dissenting) (citing Burnham, *The 1976 Election: Has the Crisis Been Adjourned* in AMERICAN POLITICS AND PUBLIC POLICY 19-22 (W. Burnham & W. Weinberg eds. 1976); D. BRODER, THE PARTY'S OVER 239-40 (1972); Herbers, *The Party's Over for the Political Parties,* N.Y. Times, Dec. 9, 1979, § 6 (Magazine), at 159; Pomper, *The Decline of the Party in American Elections,* 92 POL. SOC. Q. 21, 40-41 (1977)).

125. Perhaps this is also caused by the lack of discernible differences in ideology between the major parties. "Political parties in this country traditionally have been characterized by a fluidity and overlap of philosophy and membership." Rosario v. Rockefeller, 410 U.S. 752, 769 (1973) (Powell, J., dissenting). Three Justices joined Powell in the dissent.

126. N. NIE, S. VERBA, & J. PETROCIK, THE CHANGING AMERICAN VOTER 52 (1976). Similarly, a 1952 survey reported 74% of the electorate as party regulars in voting for state and local offices. By 1974, however, that percentage had dropped to 42%. E. LADD, JR. & C. HADLEY, TRANSFORMATION OF THE AMERICAN PARTY SYSTEM 293-96 (1975).

opinion in *Rosario v. Rockefeller*,[127] recognized the trend toward greater voter independence: "Partisan political activities do not constantly engage the attention of large numbers of Americans, especially as party labels and loyalties tend to be less persuasive than issues and qualities of individual candidates."[128] In sum, the voter evaluates candidates on the basis of information and impressions conveyed by the mass media, and "acts as an individual, not a member of collectivity."[129]

   2. *Right to privacy.* Another important reason for abolishing the closed primary system is that it violates the constitutional right to privacy[130] and secrecy of the ballot by forcing voters to declare publicly their party preferences. It is clear that

> [o]ne simple recognition of privacy's importance to self-governance is the curtain on the voting booth. But the shelter of privacy is needed for more than the casting of the formal vote, both because there are other ways of registering self-governing choices and because the process of reaching a decision does not take place only at the moment of formal choice registering; it is a continuous process which extends from the receipt of each item of information from a speaker to each choice, formal or informal, which the citizen registers. He who performs his listening and deciding functions in a glass house is coerced by public opinion, whether anyone is actually looking in or not. If every magazine he reads, every rally he attends, every person he speaks to might somehow become a matter of public knowledge, he would feel inhibiting pressure. The pressure is the same as that felt by a member of the NAACP in Alabama when he fears that the fact of his membership will be publicized.[131]

Yet, in a closed primary system, the names of publicly declared

---

127. 410 U.S. 752 (1973). In *Rosario* the Court merely held that a state *may* establish a public declaration of party affiliation as a prerequisite to voting in a party primary in order to prevent raiding.

128. *Id.* at 771 (Powell, J., dissenting).

129. Note, *The Constitutionality of Non-Member Voting*, in *Political Primary Elections*, 14 WILLAMETTE L.J. 259, 289 (1978), (citing N. NIE, S. VERBA, J. PETROCIK, THE CHANGING AMERICAN VOTER 347 (1976)).

130. *See, e.g.*, West Va. Bd. of Educ. v. Barnette, 319 U.S. 624 (1943) (declaring that a state statute compelling each public school student to pledge allegiance to the flag violated the first amendment). The Court stated, "[I]f there is any fixed star in our constitutional constellation, it is that no official, high or petty, can prescribe what shall be orthodox in politics, nationalism, religion, or other matters of opinion or force citizens to confess by word or act their faith therein." *Id.* at 642.

131. Note, *Privacy in the First Amendment*, 82 YALE L.J. 1466-67 (1973).

voters appear on a "poll list" of a particular political party. These poll lists are public documents and as such, are available both for public inspection and sale.[132] It is not surprising that many people are unwilling to declare party preference because of fear of undue pressure or harassment from employers, business associates, social acquaintances or opposing party members.[133]

In the few states, including Wisconsin, where the legislatures have adopted an open primary system, voters are not required to state publicly a party preference. Each voter makes a choice of party in the privacy of the voting booth. It is this important essence of the system, rather than its particular form, that characterizes the open primary. As the Wisconsin Supreme Court recognized, "It is . . . the 'private declaration' of party preference in the voting booth, as compared with a public, recorded declaration, that characterizes the Wisconsin presidential preference vote as an open primary."[134]

In guaranteeing a private primary ballot, the open primary law serves an interest fundamental to democracy—privacy of political preferences and convictions.[135] Indeed, this right of privacy was recently reaffirmed by the Supreme Court in *Buckley*

---

132. At least one court has observed that compiling lists of supporters and nonsupporters for campaigning, polling, patronage and other uses may be very helpful to a political organization. Nader v. Schaffer, 417 F. Supp. 837, 848 (D. Conn. 1976), *aff'd mem.*, 424 U.S. 989 (1976). *See also* C. MERRIAM & H. GOSNELL, THE AMERICAN PARTY SYSTEM 288 (1940).

For a good discussion of compelled disclosure through poll lists, see Skornicka, *State Action in Presidential Candidate Selection*, 1976 U. WIS. L. REV. 1269, 1296-97.

133. In *LaFollette* two independent voters filed an amici curiae brief with the United States Supreme Court. James MacDonald and Elliott Maraniss presented the "interests of independent voters who wish to participate in presidential primaries, but who decline to affiliate with an organized party." Brief of Amici Curiae James MacDonald and Elliott Maraniss Urging Affirmance at 2, Democratic Party v. LaFollette, Docket No. 79-1631 (February 25, 1981). Both Mr. MacDonald and Mr. Maraniss have been independent voters for nearly twenty years. Neither can wholeheartedly support the goals of either major party. As a journalist wishing to maintain impartiality, the interest of Mr. Maraniss in not publicly affiliating with a major party is particularly compelling.

134. LaFollette v. Democratic Party, 93 Wis. 2d 473, 485, 287 N.W.2d 519, 523 (1980).

For a discussion of this and a detailed analysis of the open primary, see Comment, *The Constitutionality of Non-Member Voting in Political Primary Elections*, 14 WILLAMETTE L.J. 259 (1978); Comment, *Open Versus Closed Primaries: A Dilemma in the Illinois Election Process*, 1977 S. ILL. L.J. 210.

135. The Court has long held fundamental the right of privacy of association and beliefs. *See, e.g.*, Buckley v. Valeo, 424 U.S. 1 (1976); Griswold v. Connecticut, 381 U.S. 479 (1965); NAACP v. Button, 371 U.S. 415 (1963); Shelton v. Tucker, 364 U.S. 479 (1960).

v. Valeo.[136] There, the Court found this right to be "fundamental in a free society," and the advent of the secret ballot to be "one of the great political reforms."[137] The *Buckley* Court, in discussing the disclosure requirements of the Federal Election Campaign Act of 1971,[138] recognized that compelled disclosure "can seriously infringe on privacy of association and belief guaranteed by the First Amendment."[139] Drawing from a long line of cases invalidating various disclosure requirements,[140] the Court established a balancing test between the infringement of first amendment rights and the governmental interest asserted. As applied here, the burden that compelled disclosure imposes on the independent primary voter must be balanced against the associational interests of the national party and its members or the general interests of the state.

What societal interest does a closed primary further? It is by no means clear that any such group interest, as opposed to associational interest, is served by the closed primary. Since primary elections are an integral part of the electoral process, they must be held to a standard of serving the large interest of all people rather than a small group of people who call themselves Democrats or Republicans.

Even though advocates of a closed primary would argue that an open primary permits non-party members to have a significant effect on the selection of a Democrat or Republican presidential candidate[141] and that the open primary therefore violates

---

136. 424 U.S. 1 (1976).

137. Buckley v. Valeo, 424 U.S. 1, 237 (1976) (Burger, C.J., concurring in part and dissenting in part).

138. The Federal Election Campaign Act of 1971, Pub. L. No. 92-225, 86 Stat. 3 (1972), has been amended as follows: Federal Election Campaign Act Amendments of 1974, Pub. L. No. 93-443, 88 Stat. 1263 (1974); Federal Election Campaign Act Amendments of 1976, Pub. L. No. 94-283, 90 Stat. 475; Federal Election Campaign Act Amendments of 1977, Pub. L. No. 95-216, 91 Stat. 1655; Federal Election Campaign Act Amendments of 1979, Pub. L. No. 96-187, 93 Stat. 1339 (1980). The Act is codified as amended beginning at 2 U.S.C. § 431.

139. Buckley v. Valeo, 424 U.S. 1, 64 (1976).

140. *See, e.g.,* Gibson v. Florida Legislative Comm., 372 U.S. 539 (1963); NAACP v. Button, 371 U.S. 415 (1963); Shelton v. Tucker, 364 U.S. 479 (1960); Bates v. Little Rock, 361 U.S. 516 (1960); and NAACP v. Alabama, 357 U.S. 449 (1958).

141. One writer states that a political party may advance its own and its supporters' ideology through the nomination of a candidate and that this freedom would be meaningless if parties could not determine that ideology. Note, *Presidential Nominating Conventions: Party Rules, State Law and the Constitution,* 62 Geo. L.J. 1621, 1626-27 (1974). Another commentator argues that because a major aspect of the primary is the furtherance of associational interest, the primary election should express the party members' consensus. Note, *Primary Elections: The Real Party in Interest,* 27 Rutgers L.

the constitutionally guaranteed freedom to associate for political purposes, that is not the critical point. It is true that in *Cousins v. Wigoda*,[142] Justice Brennan described the protected right of a major party and its adherents this way:

> [I]ts adherents enjoy a constitutionally protected right of political association. "There can no longer be any doubt that freedom to associate with others for the common advancement of political beliefs and ideas is a form of 'orderly group activity' protected by the First and Fourteenth Amendments. . . . The right to associate with the political party of one's choice is an integral part of this basic constitutional freedom."[143]

The national political party is thus interested in protecting the integrity of the primary as a party function protecting its associational interests "from intrusion by those with adverse political principles."[144] The Constitution and the electoral process it protects speak, however, in terms of the individual's rights as a unit of what Professor Karst calls a "national citizenship." Permitting all voters to participate in party primaries does not dilute the right of association one iota. The exact contrary is more accurate. No person, as in *Terry v. Adams,* is being denied the right to act collectively with others. All that would be done is to prevent the collectivity—the party—from discriminating against those who choose to march alone to the ballot box.

The argument that a contemporaneous, publicly recorded statement of party preferences is necessary to maintain the integrity of associational rights is therefore specious. The Wisconsin Supreme Court correctly observed that this objection is dependent upon two unsupported assumptions: "[F]irst, that voters who do not have a commonality of interest with the party will attempt to vote on the party ballot in sufficient numbers to jeopardize the primary's integrity; and second, that a contemporaneous declaration of party preference is a necessary and effective way of preventing this result."[145] It should be noted that a national party has the burden of persuading the court that a

---

Rev. 298, 306 (1974). Parties, however, are "mere vague electoral alliances." L. Thurow, The Zero-Sum Society 212 (1980).

142. 419 U.S. 477 (1975).

143. *Id.* at 487. *See also* the concurring opinion of Justices Rehnquist, Stewart, and Chief Justice Burger at 491.

144. Ray v. Blair, 343 U.S. 214, 221-22 (1952).

145. LaFollette v. Democratic Party, 93 Wis. 2d 473, 495, 287 N.W.2d 519, 533 (1980).

particular state statute infringes upon a national party's associational rights.[146] Analysis of the closed primary indicates that such a system cannot support a compelling societal interest, and, on the other hand, the open primary system protects vital individual interests.

There are three categories of voters who may be charged as not having a commonality of interest with a national party. One such category is made up of "raiders." "Raiding" has been defined by the Supreme Court as "the practice whereby voters in sympathy with one party vote in another's primary in order to distort that primary's results."[147] Raiding, when it occurs, presents a serious problem because it "is an act hostile to the party; it amounts to a fraud on the party. It deprives the party and its members of the purpose of their association."[148] Yet, documented instances of raiding are relatively rare[149] and are not a significant problem or serious threat to party integrity. Indeed, the National Democratic Party has acknowledged that there is no real evidence to show the existence of raiding.[150]

---

146. Marchioro v. Chaney, 442 U.S. 191, 195 (1979). *See also* American Party of Texas v. White, 415 U.S. 767, 790 (1974).

147. Kusper v. Pontikes, 414 U.S. 51, 59 (1973).

148. 93 Wis. 2d at 506, 287 N.W.2d at 532. In 1910 the Wisconsin Supreme Court, upholding its open primary law, commented on raiding: "That any considerable following of one political creed will deliberately desert their own party at the primary to foist an unworthy set of candidates on a rival party presupposes a degree of moral turpitude that we cannot presume to exist." Van Alstine v. Frear, 125 N.W. 961, 969 (Wis. 1910).

149. *Developments in the Law—Elections*, 88 HARV. L. REV. 1111, 1173 (1975) ("Although there are documented cases of organized raiding [citing no cases after 1950], the recent decline of party machines capable of inducing their members to raid and the absence of durational requirements in many states suggest that the likelihood of raiding may be overstated.")

Indeed, raiding is not a serious threat. *See* Skornicka, *State Action in Presidential Candidate Selection*, 1976 WIS. L. REV. 1269, 1301-03; Democratic Party of the United States v. LaFollette, 101 S. Ct. 1010, 1026 (1981) (Powell, J., dissenting). *See also* LaFollette v. Democratic Party, 93 Wis. 2d 473, 495 n.32, 287 N.W.2d 519, 533 n.32, (1980), *citing* Note, *The Constitutionality of Non-Member Voting in Primary Elections*, 14 WILLAMETTE L.J. 259, 282-86 (1978); Adamany, *Communication: Cross-Over Voting and the Democratic Party's Reform Rules*, 70 AM. POL. SCI. REV. 536, 538 (1976); Note, *Primary Elections: The Real Party in Interest*, 27 RUTGERS L. REV. 298, 307 n.74 (1974); *Developments in the Law—Elections*, 88 HARV. L. REV. 1111, 1172-73 (1975); Note, *Constitutional Issues in Durational Party Affiliation Requirements*, 25 MAINE L. REV. 147, 154 (1973).

150. REPORT OF THE COMMISSION ON PRESIDENTIAL NOMINATION AND PARTY STRUCTURE, OPENNESS, PARTICIPATION AND PARTY BUILDING: REFORMS FOR A STRONGER DEMOCRATIC PARTY 68 (1978) (Winograd Commission) ("Some have argued the Republicans 'raid' Democratic primaries. However, the existence of 'raiding' has never been conclusively proven by survey research.").

A second category of voters presumably not possessing a commonality of interest with a party are adherents to the alternative national party or other parties. These are the "crossover" voters. Theoretically, the closed primary prevents members of one political party from voting on the rival party's ballot—a not uncommon occurrence and allegedly harmful under the open primary system. Thus, the Democratic Party opposes open primaries because of a concern that that delegation allocated according to the primary results would not fairly reflect the division of preferences among "Democratic identifiers in the electorate."[151] Yet, as the Wisconsin Supreme Court concluded in analyzing data submitted by the Democratic Party, "Wisconsin's open primary produces an electorate which is as representative (or as unrepresentative) of 'Democratic identifiers in the electorate' as is the electorate produced by closed primaries and caucuses which are acceptable to the National Party."[152]

Additionally, it seems clear from the Wisconsin experience that when a member of one party decides to cross over and vote in another party's primary, the vote is cast out of a desire to express principled support for a particular presidential candidate. In 1968, for example, Wisconsin Republicans voted for Senator Eugene McCarthy in the Democratic primary. Political scientist Austin Ranney described the crossover voters this way:

> [They] deserted their party to register their special approval of a candidate, or policy associated with a candidate, available only in the other party. [Eugene] McCarthy's Republican supporters clearly did not vote for him because they thought he would be the easiest Democrat for Nixon to beat in November; they did so because they liked him and his opposition to the Vietnam War.[153]

---

151. LaFollette v. Democratic Party, 93 Wis. 2d at 508, 287 N.W.2d at 534.

152. *Id.* The court's conclusion is also supported by past experience in the Wisconsin primary. In 1968 Senator Eugene McCarthy won the Wisconsin Democratic primary. In 1972 Senator George McGovern won the Wisconsin primary and went on to win the Democratic nomination on the first ballot. Similarly, in 1976 and 1980, Jimmy Carter won the Wisconsin Democratic primary and the nomination of the Democratic primary.

On the Republican side, Richard Nixon won both the Wisconsin primary and the Republican nomination in 1968 and 1972. Similarly, both Gerald Ford in 1976, and Ronald Reagan in 1980 won the Wisconsin primary and the Republican nomination.

In short, the winners of the Wisconsin open primary seem to be reflective of the views of their respective political parties as confirmed by the national nominating conventions and are not some sort of aberrant.

153. Ranney, *Turnout and Representation in Presidential Primary Elections*, 66 Am. Pol. Sci. Rev. 35 (1972).

Studies of the Wisconsin open primary indicate that a small percentage of the total primary voters were persons who chose to vote in the other party's primary.[154] Moreover, the studies demonstrate that the statewide result of the primary election was not affected by Republican crossover voting, even though the vote was admittedly diluted.[155] Justice Powell, dissenting in *Rosario v. Rockefeller*,[156] summed up the reasons for voting in the other party's primary when he wrote:

> Citizens generally declare or alter party affiliation for reasons quite unconnected with any premeditated intention to disrupt or frustrate the plans of a party with which they are not in sympathy. Citizens customarily choose a party and vote in [the] primary simply because it presents candidates and issues more responsive to their immediate concerns and aspirations.[157]

A third possible category of voters who do not have a commonality of interest are the "independents."[158] The declaration of preference required by a closed primary appears to be no more effective than the open primary in deterring the participation of independent voters. Indeed, some studies suggest that in closed primary systems, some voters who consider themselves independent enroll or register as party members to vote in the primary of their choice.[159] It seems clear that voters who do not share a commonality of interest with a political party will not vote on that party's ballot in sufficient numbers to jeopardize the primary's integrity. Even if this were to occur, however, the closed primary is an unnecessary and ineffective way of preventing this result.

In Rule 2A of its Delegate Selection Rules for the 1980 Convention, the Democratic Party regulates participation in the delegate selection process by defining Democratic voters as those persons "who publicly declare their party preference Democratic and have that preference publicly recorded."[160] By implication

---

154. Hedlund, *Cross-Over Voting in a 1976 Open Presidential Primary*, 41 PUB. OPIN. Q. 498, 502, 513 (1979).

155. *Id.* at 502-03.

156. 410 U.S. 752 (1973).

157. *Id.* at 769-70 (Powell, J., dissenting).

158. Those not affiliated or registered with any political party.

159. Note, *The Constitutionality of Non-Member Voting in Primary Elections*, 14 WILLAMETTE L.J. 259, 277 n.103, 288 (1978); Hedlund, *Cross-Over Voting in a 1976 Open Presidential Primary*, 41 PUB. OPIN. Q. 498, 502, 513 (1979).

160. Delegate Selection Rules for the 1980 Democratic National Convention, Rule 2.

the party is saying that it does not want independents to participate because they do not share a common interest with voters
who have publicly affiliated themselves with the party.

Yet, under Rule 2A, voters are Democratic voters simply if
they think they are and say they are, even if only for the purpose of voting in one primary election. Indeed, the Wisconsin
Supreme Court noted that "the [Democratic] Party does not set
forth any objective standards against which a voter may test his
or her self-designation. Nor does the National Party set forth
any subjective standards to guide voters in determining their
party preference."[161] Under Rule 2A any person of any political
party or persuasion would be eligible to vote in a Democratic
primary if that person would be willing to affiliate with the
Democratic Party for that one primary election. It is difficult to
perceive the increased benefits of associational rights under this
system as opposed to the Wisconsin "open primary" system.[162]

"Defining who is and who is not a Republican or Democrat,
defining the commonality of interest which binds Democrats or
Republicans, or defining the Republican's or Democrat's commitment to the party are key issues which have not been resolved by the parties."[163] The significance of the declaration of
party preference is far from clear. Indeed, it is uncertain exactly
what membership in a political party signals. Contrary to the
experience of many European democracies and the fears of the
Founding Fathers,[164] the formation of political parties in the
United States has not exerted a fragmenting effect upon our political life. The reason for this is that pluralism within parties,
rather than pluralism among parties has been a hallmark of
American politics.

---

161. LaFollette v. Democratic Party, 93 Wis. 2d at 505, 287 N.W.2d at 531.

162. Justice Powell keenly points out:

   The Wisconsin statute states that "[i]n each year in which electors for
   president and vice-president are to be elected, the voters of this state shall be
   given an opportunity to express their preference for the person to be the presidential candidate *of their party.*" Wis. Stat. § 8.12(1) (emphasis added). Thus
   the act of voting in the Democratic primary fairly can be described as an act of
   affiliation with the Democratic Party. The real issue in this case is whether the
   party has the right to decide that only *publicly* affiliated voters may
   participate.

Democratic Party of the United States v. LaFollette, 101 S. Ct. 1010, 1023 n.2 (1981)
(Powell, J., dissenting).

163. 93 Wis. 2d at 505, 287 N.W.2d at 531.

164. *See* L. EPSTEIN, POLITICAL PARTIES IN WESTERN DEMOCRACIES (1967); R. DAHL,
PLURALIST DEMOCRACY IN THE UNITED STATES (1967).

Political parties have been viewed not as ideological refuges for "true believers," but as groupings of diverse interests joined together in a coalition for the purpose of achieving shared political goals. Only under such a pragmatic view could men of such diverse ideologies as George Wallace and the late Allard Lowenstein in the Democratic Party, and Ronald Reagan and Pete McCloskey in the Republican Party, share the same party affiliation.[165] Given such a non-ideological tradition in party politics, it is not surprising that interparty mobility has been a facet of American political life. The two major parties with rather nebulous and informal criteria for party membership have, in the United States, created parties broadly composed of "persons from all walks of life" and of "all shades of economic and political opinion."[166] Thus, it seems that the chief characteristic of parties is not the commonality of aims among its membership to be advanced by candidates, but rather, as one court stated, it is "the direction and control of the struggle for political power among men who may have contradictory interests and often mutually exclusive hopes of securing them. This the parties do by institutionalizing the struggle and emphasizing positive measures to create a strong and general agreement on policies."[167] Indeed, the intellectual nature of a political party has been characterized this way:

> It is not concerned with matters of fact, or doctrine, or even principle, except as they bear upon the great cause for existence: success at the polls. Such organizations contain not only men of divergent views; they must also appeal to voters of differing opinions, prejudices and loyalties. It is folly to talk of finding an actual basis [for political parties] in any set of principles relating to public welfare.[168]

The closed primary's contemporaneous declaration of party preference is an "unnecessary and ineffective way to prevent raiders, members of an alternative national party, adherents of

---

165. It is little wonder that the Supreme Court has noted, "Major parties encompass candidates of great diversity. In many situations the label 'Republican' or 'Democrat' tells the voter little." Buckley v. Valeo, 424 U.S. 1, 70 (1976).

166. H. Bone, American Politics and the Party System 284 (1955).

167. *Compare* Irish v. Democratic-Farmer-Labor Party, 287 F. Supp. 794, 805 (D. Minn. 1968) *with* Bendinger v. Oglivie, 335 F. Supp. 572, 575 (N.D. Ill. 1971).

168. Alexander v. Todman, 337 F.2d 962, 973 (3d Cir. 1964) (citing Robinson, *The Place of Party in the Political History of the United States*, Annual Reports of the American Historical Association for the Years 1927 and 1928 at 202 (1929)).

other parties and independents from voting in a national party primary ballot."[169] Indeed, there seems to be little difference in effect between the closed and open primary systems:

> [T]he essence of the legal definitions of party membership in the United States will surely continue to be self-designation. The fact remains that today even in Illinois, New York, or any other closed primary state you are a Democrat if you say you are; no one can effectively say you are not; and you can become a Republican any time the spirit moves you simply by saying that you have become one. You accept no obligations by such a declaration; you receive only a privilege—the privilege of taking an equal part in the making of a party's most important decision, the nomination of its candidates for public office. The only remaining restriction is that in some states, such as California, you may have to let the registrar of voters know that you have changed parties, and you may even have to do so several weeks or even months before your new party's next primary. But in many closed primary states you do not even have to do that, and in Wisconsin and other open primary states you are not allowed to make an official declaration of your party membership . . . . One can only conclude that the so-called 'closed' primaries are just a hair more closed than the so-called 'open' primaries.[170]

The significant difference between the open and closed primary is that voters "resent being prohibited from voting if they refuse to [make] a party declaration and having their affiliation a matter of public record for fear of losing their jobs or risking other penalties."[171] The difference between the open and closed primary is not, as advocates of the closed primary would assert, that the open primary permits large numbers of Republicans, independents, and other party adherents to vote, for example, on the Democratic Party ballot. Rather, the difference is that the open primary permits more people to vote for the candidate and issues of their choice by allowing a private declaration of party preference. Publicly stating a party preference can be a dilemma for the independent voter who does not understand the significance of such a public declaration or is unwilling to do so because of a fear of undue pressure or harassment. The question thus becomes which is worse, the alleged dangers of "crossover"

---

169. 93 Wis. 2d at 497, 287 N.W.2d at 535.
170. A. RANNEY, CURING THE MISCHIEFS OF FACTION 166-67 (1975).
171. W. GOODMAN, THE TWO-PARTY SYSTEM IN THE UNITED STATES 207-08 (1964).

voting or the disenfranchisement of independent voters unwilling to record publicly a party preference. It is our contention that the closed primary system, in light of the *Buckley* test, cannot support a sufficient governmental interest to justify compelled disclosure of party affiliation.

Conversely, the open primary serves a significant state interest of encouraging voters to participate in selecting the candidates of political parties which, in turn, fosters democratic government.[172] As the Supreme Court has pointed out, "Preservation of the democratic process is certainly an interest protection of which may in some instances justify limitations on First Amendment freedoms."[173] Historically, the primary was intended to enlarge citizen participation in the political process and remove from political bosses the process of selecting candidates. Presumably, the legislatures of open primary states believe democracy is best served by stimulating political activity and that "facilitat[ing] and enlarg[ing] public discussion and participation in the electoral process [are] goals vital to a self-governing people."[174]

It is "ironic," as Justice Powell forcefully pointed out in *La-Follette*, that Rule 2A has the "effect of calling into question a state law that was intended itself to open up participation in the nominating process and minimize the influence of 'party bosses.' "[175] The *LaFollette* decision, with its deference to national party rules allows the political bosses to wrest control of the nominational process from the hands of the primary voters. As David Broder commented, "The justices clearly signaled the Democrats that the way is open for them to begin repair of their own distorted nominating process by curbing the number of delegates chosen in primaries."[176]

---

172. The National Democratic Party in fact replaced the Wisconsin open primary with a closed caucus system in 1980. A similar displacement was made in Michigan, which had an open primary system. Only 15,000 people in the state of Michigan participated in the Democratic closed caucus. *See* N.Y. Times, April 27, 1980, at p. 1, col. 2. By comparison, 625,185 people voted in the Wisconsin Democratic primary and 897,464 voted in the Republican primary. 38 Cong. Q. W. Rpts. 901 (April 5, 1980). Wisconsin had the second highest percentage of voter age turnout in its 1976 primary of the 24 states conducting primaries. A. Ranney, Participation in American Presidential Nominations 25 (1977).

173. Elrod v. Burns, 427 U.S. 347, 368 (1976).

174. Buckley v. Valeo, 424 U.S. 1, 92-93 (1976).

175. Democratic Party of the United States v. LaFollette, 101 S. Ct. 1010, 1022 (1981) (Powell, J., dissenting).

176. Broder, *But Will They Change Those Rules*, Wash. Post, March 1, 1981, § C,

It has been clear since the NAACP cases were decided,[177] that "freedom to associate with others for the common advancement of political beliefs and ideas is . . . protected by the First and Fourteenth Amendments."[178] A close corollary to the right of association is the right to be free of unwanted association.[179] Even though the Court has traditionally tended to limit the right of nonparticipation to cases involving personal convictions so deeply held as to be considered matters of conscience,[180] in recent years it has extended the right to include situations where an individual has been required to support a political or ideological cause with which the individual simply disagrees.[181] The Court, in *Elrod v. Burns*,[182] held that state officials could not condition retention of public employment on the affiliation with a particular political party. Similarly, in *Abood v. Detroit Board of Education*,[183] the Court held that the first amendment prevents the government from requiring objecting public employees to contribute to union political or ideological activities not germane to collective bargaining.[184] Recently, in *Branti v. Finkel*,[185] the Court likewise upheld the right of public defenders to be free from coerced political affiliation as a condition of employment. This trilogy of cases marks the emergence of a distinctive first amendment right to resist coerced participation in or support of political or ideological activity. Indeed, the Court in *Abood* said that such a right was "at the heart of the First Amendment."[186] Similarly, the independent voter should not be

at 7, col. 2.

177. Gibson v. Florida Legislative Investigation Comm., 372 U.S. 539 (1963); NAACP v. Button, 371 U.S. 415 (1963); Gremillion v. NAACP, 366 U.S. 293 (1961); Shelton v. Tucker, 364 U.S. 479 (1960); Bates v. City of Little Rock, 361 U.S. 516 (1960); and NAACP v. Alabama, 357 U.S. 449 (1958).

178. Cousins v. Wigoda, 419 U.S. 477, 487 (1975) (citing Kusper v. Pontikes, 414 U.S. 51, 56-57 (1973)).

179. One commentator notes that "[t]his right has most often been asserted in a labor law context. *See, e.g.*, Brotherhood of Railway Clerks v. Allen, 373 U.S. 113 (1963); International Ass'n. of Machinists v. Street, 367 U.S. 740 (1961); Railway Employees Dep't v. Hanson, 351 U.S. 225 (1956). *See also* Lathrop v. Donohue, 367 U.S. 820 (1961) (attack on the dues requirement under an integrated bar system)." Skornicka, *State Action in Presidential Candidate Selection*, 1976 U. Wis. L. Rev. 1269, 1296-97.

180. *See, e.g.*, Board of Educ. v. Barnette, 319 U.S. 624 (1943).

181. For a thorough treatment of this subject area, see Comment, *The Right of Ideological Nonassociation*, 66 Cal. L. Rev. 767 (1978).

182. 427 U.S. 347 (1976).

183. 431 U.S. 290 (1977).

184. *Id.* at 235.

185. 445 U.S. 507 (1980).

186. 431 U.S. at 234-35.

coerced into joining one of the major parties in order to exercise the right to vote in a primary.

3. *Unjustified discrimination.* The third reason for enfranchising the independent voter is that the closed primary also ignores the right of all persons to vote once the state has decided to make the right available to some. Membership in either the Democratic or Republican parties should not be an admission ticket to the primary ballot box. This is especially so, as the Supreme Court said in *United States v. Classic*,[187] "[w]here the state law has made the primary an integral part of the procedure of choice, or where in fact the primary effectively controls the choice."[188] After all, political parties are not mentioned, directly or indirectly, in the United States Constitution.[189] The drafters of the Constitution did not foresee the modern importance of political parties in the United States. They were non-party—even anti-party—independents. Thus on October 2, 1780, John Adams, writing to a friend about the new constitution for Massachusetts, said: "There is nothing which I dread so much as a division of the republic into two great parties, each arranged under its leader, and concerting measures in opposition to each other. This in my humble apprehension, is to be dreaded as the greatest political evil under our constitution."[190] The view that the rise of political parties was an evil, tending to foment strife and discord in the body politic, was widespread. George Washington similarly warned his countrymen "in the most solemn manner against the baneful effects of the spirit of party,"[191] and James Madison thought it the principal task of the new Constitution to hold the "mischiefs of faction"[192] in check.

The meaning is clear: the independent voter in a closed primary state is being denied a fundamental right.[193] That in turn

---

187. 345 U.S. 461 (1953).

188. *Id.* at 467.

189. "Partisan politics bear the imprimatur only of tradition, not the Constitution." Elrod v. Burns, 427 U.S. 347, 369 n.22 (1976).

190. 9 J. ADAMS, THE WORKS OF JOHN ADAMS 511 (1854).

191. G. WASHINGTON, *Farewell Address, reprinted in* DOCUMENTS OF AMERICAN HISTORY 169, 172 (H. Commager ed. 1946).

192. THE FEDERALIST No. 10 (J. Madison) at 52 (H. Lodge ed. 1888). Indeed, in the early 1790's "most Americans did not want parties." J. BURNS, THE DEADLOCK OF DEMOCRACY 27 (1967).

193. Ideally, of course, the primary should not only be open, but also have delegates allocated in accordance with its results. Although it might be argued, as Justice Powell suggests with regard to the Vermont primary, Democratic Party v. LaFollette, 101 S. Ct. 1010, 1025 n.11 (1981) (Powell, J., dissenting), that a nonbinding primary is but an idle

can only mean that he is being denied equal protection. But, if
the Supreme Court so held, a major expansion of equal protection could occur—to make the Constitutional standard national
or interstate rather than intrastate. The time has come for such
a development. After all, the fourteenth amendment speaks of
"equal protection of the laws"—but does not define "laws." Arguably the Justices would not have to embrace a concept of interstate equal protection. They could rule that an independent
voter in a closed primary state was being denied his fourteenth
amendment rights vis-a-vis other voters in that same state. But
under the "new" jurisprudence of the Court, even such a limited
decision would have a general effect.

Ours is a national citizenship.[194] Justice Bradley, addressing
the issue of equality in the Slaughter-House Cases, judicially expressed the view of such a citizenship:

> A citizen of the United States has a perfect constitutional
> right to go and reside in any state he chooses, and to claim
> citizenship therein, and an equality of rights with every other
> citizen . . . . He is not bound to cringe to any superior, or to
> pray for any act of grace, as a means of enjoying all the rights
> and privileges enjoyed by other citizens . . . . If a man be de-
> nied full equality before the law, he is denied one of the essen-
> tial rights of citizenship as a citizen of the United States.[195]

Although Justice Bradley spoke in dissent, his words capture
nicely the concept of a national citizenship and a "united state."

---

gesture; nevertheless, the intense attention of the media and the perception of the people
in the other states is to the contrary. In his famed August 1974 memorandum outlining
President Carter's successful 1976 strategy, Hamilton Jordan wrote:

> The press shows an exaggerated interest in the early primaries as they
> represent the first confrontation between candidates . . . We would do well to
> understand the very special and powerful role the press plays in interpreting
> the primary results for the rest of the nation. What is actually accomplished in
> the New Hampshire primary is less important than how the press interprets it
> for the rest of the nation.

J. WITCOVER, MARATHON 144 (1978). The primary process is important not only as a
delegate selection process, but also, in this "media age," as a means of creating and
maintaining the impression of an electable presidential candidate. The independent
voter in Florida, unlike the independent voter in Wisconsin, is cut out of that process.

194. *See* Karst, *The Fifth Amendment's Guarantee of Equal Protection*, 55 N.C.L.
REV. 541, 550-51 (1977).

195. Slaughter-House Cases, 83 U.S. (16 Wall. 1872) 36, 112-13 (Bradley, J., dissenting). Professor Karst notes constitutional support for the idea of equal national citizenship, *e.g.*, the prohibition against the granting of titles of nobility by the United States,
U.S. CONST., art. I, § 9, cl. 8; the prohibition against direct federal taxes that are not
proportional to population, *id.* § 9, cl. 4. Karst, *supra* note 194, at 550 n.53.

As Professor Karst wrote a century later, "The substantive core of the amendment, and of the equal protection clause in particular, is a principle of equal citizenship, which presumptively guarantees to each individual the right to be treated by the organized society as a respected, responsible, and participating member."[196]

Professor Karst maintains that if, after the Civil War, there could be any doubt that we are all citizens of the United States, that doubt was removed by the fourteenth amendment's explicit declaration: "All persons born or naturalized in the United States, and subject to the jurisdiction thereof, are citizens of the United States and of the State wherein they reside."[197] Indeed, absent that specific command, Karst believes that a spirit of national citizenship would prevail, such that we would think of ourselves primarily as citizens of the nation, and only secondarily of the several states, for "[w]e are all part of one economy; we are highly mobile, both in capacity and in inclination; a national system of communication hands us the same news and the same entertainment; we look to the national government as the chief arena for the interplay of political forces."[198] It is clear that these aspects of our nationhood demand a generous view of the powers of the national government.[199] "And as those expanded powers have been exercised, we [Americans] have come to perceive the obligations of citizenship as running primarily to the national polity."[200] The principle of equal national citizenship means more than the correction of abuses by the state; the heart of the principle is that citizens have the right to equal treatment by the government. Equality in the electoral process is a crucial affirmation of the equal worth of citizens.[201]

Some may object that such a concept of equal protection would strike a body blow at federalism and state sovereignty. Yet, despite recent Supreme Court decisions in support of

---

196. Karst, *The Supreme Court, 1976 Term—Foreword: Equal Citizenship Under the Fourteenth Amendment*, 91 HARV. L. REV. 1, 4 (1977).

197. U.S. CONST. amend. XIV.

198. Karst, *supra* note 194, at 550-51.

199. Stern, *The Commerce Clause and the National Economy, 1933-46*, 59 HARV. L. REV. 645, 883 (1946).

200. Karst, *supra* note 194, at 551.

201. "To the extent that a citizen's right to vote is debased, he is that much less a citizen." Reynolds v. Sims, 377 U.S. 533, 567 (1964), *cited in* Karst, *supra* note 196, at 29.

states' rights, federalism as it was once known is dead.[202] Among other factors, a national income tax, technological imperatives, and immersion of the nation in world affairs point to a conclusion that the several states are political anachronisms.[203] If people truly believed in federalism, there would be no New York City going to the federal government to avoid bankruptcy, no Chrysler seeking a similar financial bailout, and no state and local governments receiving enormous grants-in-aid from the federal government. The death knell for federalism occurred long ago; it should be recognized and accepted.

Moreover, the decline of federalism is apparent in the electoral process. Uniform, nationwide standards for electoral practices and voting rights have increasingly supplanted diverse election laws.[204] This result runs contrary to a long history of state control in conducting elections and defining the scope of the franchise. One need only look at four developments in the last twenty-five years to understand how this transfer of power away from the states has occurred: constitutional amendments;[205] Supreme Court decisionmaking;[206] congressional legislation;[207] and the Federal Election Commission.[208]

202. Strong national unity was recognized by Justice Holmes:
I do not think the United States would come to an end if we lost the power to declare an Act of Congress void. I do think the union would be imperiled if we could not make the declaration as to the laws of the several states.
J. BARRON & C. DIENES, CONSTITUTIONAL LAW 36 (1975).

203. Currently, a national economic system is superimposed on a decentralized political order. Politics and law tend to follow economics; the inexorable result is that the states will become even less important in the future. *See* A. MILLER, SOCIAL CHANGE AND FUNDAMENTAL LAW 43-95 (1979); Miller, *Reason of State and the Emergent Constitution of Control,* 64 MINN. L. REV. 585 (1980).

204. For a complete discussion of this subject, see Claude, *Nationalizing Electoral Process Standards: Is an Obituary for State's Rights Premature?* 13 IDAHO L. REV. 373 (1977).

205. *See* note 89 *supra.*

206. *E.g.,* Buckley v. Valeo, 424 U.S. 1 (1976); Bullock v. Carter, 405 U.S. 134 (1972); Williams v. Rhodes, 393 U.S. 23 (1968); Reynolds v. Sims, 377 U.S. 533 (1964).

207. *E.g.,* the Federal Election Campaign Act of 1971, Pub. L. No. 92-225, 86 Stat. 3 (1972), as amended, Pub. L. No. 93-443. Voting Rights Act Amendment of 1970, Pub. L. No. 91-285, 84 Stat. 314 (1970) (amended and repealed in part in 1975); Civil Rights Act of 1965, Pub. L. No. 89-110, 79 Stat. 437 (1965).

208. The Commission is the independent agency of the United States government charged with primary and exclusive jurisdiction to implement civil enforcement of the federal election laws. 2 U.S.C. § 437c(b)(1) (1976). The laws over which the Commission has civil enforcement jurisdiction are the Federal Election Campaign Act of 1971, as amended, *supra* note 139; the Presidential Election Campaign Fund Act, 26 U.S.C. §§ 9001-9013 (1976); and the Presidential Primary Matching Payment Account Act, 26 U.S.C. §§ 9031-9042 (1976).

The federalism argument also ignores that the nomination of a presidential candidate is not a regional or state function but rather a national function of the national parties. It is clear that the National Democratic and Republican Parties are no more than loose federations of state parties. The nomination of a presidential candidate once every four years is perhaps the only national organizational effort undertaken by the national parties. The procedure used by both the major parties is clearly a nationwide process. Political science studies have noted that the "argument for recognition of state sovereignty in a national political convention is specious."[209] Moreover, to analogize between a state whose sovereignty in the electoral college is constitutionally established, and the state political party to the national political party is inappropriate. It has been concluded that "[a] national political party has its federal aspects, such as its dependence on state victories to give it the electoral votes necessary for winning a presidential election. But in its national convention its chief business, the nomination and election of a President, is an operation more national than federal."[210]

V. Conclusion

Enough has been said to show that voting is indeed a fundamental right, and that voting in primaries should be included in that right. As long as the two-party system continues, which may not be more than a few years, a further point can be made: all voters should be able to cast a ballot in primaries for one of the candidates in each party. There is no logical reason why even the Wisconsin system should not be expanded that far. We, however, do no more than mention the point here; and do not argue for it at this time. Our net conclusion is that there are solid legal and policy grounds for fully enfranchising the independent voters in America.

That need not take a constitutional amendment. The Supreme Court can do it in an appropriate case brought, say, by an independent voter in Florida. What external standards of judgment should the Justices apply should such a case eventuate? We suggest that the Wisconsin system be enunciated as the constitutional minimum. And, as suggested above, that part of the

---

209. P. David, R. Goldman, & R. Bain, The Politics of National Party Conventions 177 (1960).

210. *Id.*

Wisconsin system which allows delegate selection by caucus, without regard to the primary, violates fundamental principles of fairness. In short, "interstate equal protection" should be the law, by giving to the word "laws" in the fourteenth amendment an expansive reading. Whether that is a "neutral principle," as some people who should know better plump for,[211] we do not say. The point is that a nation that calls itself democratic, that has a commitment to equality, and that seeks to be a model for nations elsewhere can no longer suffer the actual disenfranchisement of what is perhaps the largest—certainly the fastest growing—group of voters. There is nothing sacrosanct in the two-party system; or, indeed, in parties themselves.

In saying all of this, in advocating an interstate standard for equal protection, we recognize, with Jeremy Bentham, that "[t]he establishment of perfect equality is a chimera; all we can do is to diminish inequality."[212] Interstate equal protection is one way to do that. Americans living in the zero-sum society deserve no less. Surely, it is the logical extension of the Court's pronouncement in *Cooper v. Aaron* that its decisions are "the law of the land." Equal protection is an area where a fundamental conception should be developed, in Cardozo's words, "to their uttermost conclusions."[213]

A further point deserves mention. There is no need at this time to suggest all possible human rights that might be considered to be so fundamental as to fall under the rubric of interstate equal protection. Once the principle is established, as it can be with the right to vote, then the other areas of concern can be analyzed with an eye toward determining whether they too should receive nationwide protection. The concept of national citizenship in a "united state" that is the United States requires precisely that.

Some may argue that if regulation of political parties comes it should be by statute, not be judicial decision. If the elected representatives of the people in Congress can be persuaded to enact a comprehensive voting rights law that would go not only

---

211. *See, e.g.,* Greenwalt, *The Enduring Significance of Neutral Principles,* 78 COLUM. L. REV. 983 (1978), which is a latter-day celebration of Weschler, *Toward Neutral Principles of Constitutional Law,* 73 HARV. L. REV. 1 (1959) (rightly called "verbally muddled" by Anthony R. Blackshield of the Faculty of Law, University of Sydney). *See* A. MILLER, SOCIAL CHANGE AND FUNDAMENTAL LAW 170 (1979).

212. J. BENTHAM, THE THEORY OF LEGISLATION 120 (1931).

213. SELECTED WRITINGS OF BENJAMIN NATHAN CARDOZO 294 (M. Hall ed. 1947).

to the right to cast a ballot (as in the Voting Rights Act of 1965) but also to the ways in which candidates are selected, then there would be no need for the Court to intervene.[214] Absent such a statute (and the likelihood of one being enacted is remote at best) the Court is the only avenue open to those who are disenfranchised by the present system. The Supreme Court has already involved itself in the election process, principally in the White Primary and Legislative Reapportionment Cases; hence, there is no good reason why it should not enter this "political thicket."[215] The essential argument here is not so much over what should be done, but over how it can be effected. Those who argue for a quietistic role for the Supreme Court will, of course, abhor interstate equal protection and call for a legislative resolution;[216] but those who see a larger role for the Court, such as Professor John Hart Ely with his "representation-reinforcing" theory of judicial review,[217] just might accept the basic conclusions of this article.

---

214. The extreme deference the *LaFollette* Court showed to the political party system poses the question of who, if anyone, can control these private governments. Could, for example, Congress legislate a national or regional primary system? Arthur Schlesinger Jr. suggests that such a measure "might well administer the coup de grace" to the political parties and, would almost certainly be opposed by the major parties. Arthur S. Schlesinger, *Crisis of the Party System: II*, Wall St. J., May 14, 1979, at 14, col. 4. If so, would the principle of *LaFollette* ("a State, or a court, may not constitutionally substitute its own judgment for that of a party") prohibit or foreclose Congress from doing that?

215. Baker v. Carr, 369 U.S. 186, 266 (1961) (Frankfurter, J., dissenting).

216. A. BICKEL, THE SUPREME COURT AND THE IDEA OF PROGRESS (1970); A. BICKEL, THE MORALITY OF CONSENT (1975).

217. J. ELY, DEMOCRACY AND DISTRUST (1980).

CHAPTER 5

Social Justice and the Warren Court

Beginning about 1950, civil rights and civil liberties received comprehensive attention and protection. When Earl Warren became Chief Justice in 1953, the movement accelerated. The Supreme Court began to advance the cause of social justice.

What was the underlying purpose of the many decisions that furthered human rights since the early 1950s? This is the question that is asked and given at least a tentative answer in Chapter 5. It is suggested that all social activities, including Supreme Court decisions, have two types of beneficiaries—the manifest and the latent. During the sixteen years of the Warren Court, the manifest beneficiaries were those obviously helped by the Court's rulings—blacks, urban voters, criminal suspects, among others. For the first time in American history, they received the consolations of at least formal protection under the law. The second class of beneficiary, however, was perhaps of more importance: They are the ones who have always profited, as a class, from the workings of the constitutional order—those Alexander Hamilton called the "rich and the well-born" in the 1787 constitutional convention. Decisions aiding the manifest beneficiaries, it is hypothesized, had the sociological function of siphoning off discontent among the disadvantaged, and thus helped to preserve the relative positions of power, wealth, and prestige of the upper and middle classes.

All of this occurred during what should be viewed as the true "golden age" of the United States—the post-1945 period when American military might was supreme, the dollar was king among foreign currencies, and, for a time at least, a period of Pax Americana seemed to characterize world affairs. The economic pie was growing larger, and permitted some of the former "have-nots" to share in the groaning table of opulence that is the American economy.

The "activist" decisions of the Warren Court, therefore, are best seen as being profoundly conservative in nature, conservative in the sense of helping to maintain the status quo insofar as the comparative positions of America's social classes are concerned. Small, and at times token or cosmetic, gains were attained by the manifest beneficiaries, but nothing substantial was altered in the social structure. Chapter 5 began as an extended review of a recent biography of Chief Justice Warren, but became an article.

Whether courts should attempt to advance social justice is a much debated topic in American jurisprudence. The conventional wisdom about the judicial process is to the contrary. In this article, Professor Arthur S. Miller suggests that the Supreme Court's innovative civil rights and civil liberties decisions during Chief Justice Earl Warren's tenure had the ultimate effect of helping to preserve the status quo of the social order. Its decisions, coming at a time of economic abundance, were a means of siphoning off discontent from disadvantaged groups at minimum social cost to the established order. The "activist" decisions under Warren were thus of a profoundly conservative nature. Using a recent biography of Chief Justice Warren as a point of departure, Professor Miller's analysis is a provocative examination of the Supreme Court's work during the years of 1953 to 1969.

I. Introduction: The Essence of Constitutional Decision-Making

"Judicial power," Chief Justice John Marshall once asserted, "is never exercised for the purpose of giving effect to the will of the judge; always for the purpose of giving effect to the will of the Legislature; or, in other words, to the will of the law."[1] That, of course, was the conventional wisdom of the day, stated in classic terms by Blackstone: the judge is "sworn to determine, not according to his own private judgment, but according to the known laws and customs of the land; not delegated to pronounce a new

---

1. Osborn v. Bank of the United States, 22 U.S. (9 Wheat.) 738, 866 (1824). For a well-known judge's reaction to that statement, see B. Cardozo, The Nature of the Judicial Process 169-70 (1921).

This chapter was originally published under the title of "Social Justice and the Warren Court: A Preliminary Examination" in 11 Pepperdine Law Review 473 (1984).

law, but to maintain and expound the old one."[2] Marshall's and Blackstone's "wisdom"—it was hardly that—still abides, as witness almost any coursebook used in law school and certainly any of the standard constitutional law coursebooks. The editors routinely proceed on the assumption that the ancient "wisdom" is the norm, and construct tortuous edifices of legal doctrine to show to their satisfaction that there is something other than "the will of the judge" in constitutional decisions. In this, they are aided by commentators who parse Supreme Court decisions with an intensity similar to that of Scholastics arguing over the meaning of the ancient texts of Aristotle and Plato. Judges, too, contribute to the intellectual confusion—possibly because they want to make their opinions look scholarly or because they want to write in the language with which lawyers are familiar or because they have law clerks mint-fresh from law school and law review training who follow the paths of judicial elucidation honored by time but little else.

All of this is quite well known and is, indeed, one of the commonplaces of the day. But the ancient practices continue. Why they do so is an important question. Some commentators, such as Professor Paul Mishkin, argue that even sophisticated laymen are too naive to understand the truth about the process of judging.[3] It is entirely all right, in this view, for law professors and even law students to know more than the Marshall/Blackstone version of judging. But, they assert, the dirty little secrets about judging should be kept within the confines of the profession.

I think there is another reason: the vested interest that those who edit coursebooks and write textbooks have in the existing system. Upon admitting that Marshall and Blackstone were wrong, Pandora's Box would spring open; the books would have to be completely rewritten. Furthermore, there is the vested interest that law professors have in the "case method" of instruction. Cut below the surface of judicial decisions, however, and the professoriate will quickly find themselves adrift without a rudder or a compass. The case method is probably the worst possible means of transmitting information. Its employment is based on the supposition that engaging in the verbal jousts that travel under the banner of the Socratic method helps legal neophytes "to think like lawyers."[4]

---

2. 1 W. BLACKSTONE, COMMENTARIES 69.

3. *See* Mishkin, *Foreword: The High Court, The Great Writ, and the Due Process of Time and Law,* 79 HARV. L. REV. 56, 62 (1965). *See also* M. SHAPIRO, LAW AND POLITICS IN THE SUPREME COURT c.1 (1964).

4. *See generally* Levinson, *Taking Law Seriously: Reflections on "Thinking Like a Lawyer,"* 30 STAN. L. REV. 1071 (1978).

Thinking like lawyers is, I suggest, a form of brain damage. It is a means of addressing the very real problems of very real people in an intellectual vacuum. High-level abstractions take the place of thorough analyses of those problems. A "principled" opinion becomes the *ne plus ultra* of the judicial process. The never adequate and seldom defined notion of sovereign "reason" should rule, so we are told, and many commentators wax apoplectic about what they consider to be the failure of judges to follow the dictates of principle or of reason. Granted, this ideal should be considered a desirable means of deciding cases. But the spotted actuality is to the contrary. Although Chief Justice Marshall in 1803 could assert that "[t]he government of the United States has been emphatically termed a government of laws, and not of men,"[5] no thoughtful person realistically believes that today. Indeed, said the *London Economist,* "in 1960-80 America became a government of laws instead of men. The country had previously thrived by being exactly the opposite, although its lawyers wrote books pretending it wasn't. In the castrated great society after about 1966, appeals and decisions about everything began to meander right up to the political or bureaucratic top."[6]

The *Economist* was only partially correct: despite appearances to the contrary, American government—the constitutional order—still remains a government of men. Law in its interdictory sense constrains or restrains governmental officials only slightly, especially those at the higher levels. All too often, the rule of law becomes the rule of discretion; in other words, the rule of politics. In such a situation, reason or principle, whatever the *jurisprudence publique* may say, gives way to a form of *jurisprudence confidentielle.*[7]

Yves Simon once asserted that in a democratic state "deliberation is about means and presupposes that the problem of ends has been settled."[8] People can agree that their rights and liberties can be affected or dealt with by the state when they also agree on the aims that their collective endeavor should attain.

---

5. Marbury v. Madison, 5 U.S. (1 Cranch) 137, 163 (1803).

6. Macrae, *President Reagan's Inheritance,* 277 THE ECONOMIST No. 7165, at 13, 22 (Dec. 27, 1980).

7. W. REISMAN, FOLDED LIES: BRIBERY, CRUSADES, AND REFORMS 12-13 & *passim* (1979) (drawing upon N. LEITES, THE OPERATIONAL CODE OF THE POLITBURO (1951)). For a well-known state judge's application of Reisman's methodology, see R. NEELY, HOW COURTS GOVERN AMERICA (1981).

8. Y. SIMON, PHILOSOPHY OF DEMOCRATIC GOVERNMENT 123 (1951).

That is true of all forms of dispute settlement and resolution, whether it is the give-and-take of routine face-to-face dealings, the operation of the political system, or the invocation of the courts to settle constitutional controversies. (The latter are always the "pathological" disputes, those that cannot otherwise be settled by other means of social control.) "Democracy implies . . . that the *way* in which men adjust or resolve their differences is of crucial importance, that conflicts of opinion as to what constitutes the right moral and political ends are not to be resolved arbitrarily— (e.g.), by fiat of a stronger or allegedly superior group—but are to be mediated and temporarily adjusted through a political process that builds on the free exchange of opposing ideas. . . ."[9]

Put another way, the fundamental constitutional principle is procedural due process. But that assumes a common acceptance of "the right moral and political ends." By assuming no dispute about the *goals* of social action, people within a nation that calls itself democratic can afford to allow the *tactics* to be decided through the political process or through resort to official organs. The central spirit that underlies the entire scheme is that of compromise, of a willingness to give up some immediate gain (or suffer some loss) because the system is perceived as fair and the greater (common) good is thereby realized. A corollary is that once the ritual has been followed—once "due procedure" has been allowed to run its course—there will be a general willingness to abide by the results.

That, I think, is a fair description of such "process-oriented" commentators upon the Supreme Court as the late Alexander Bickel[10] and Dean John Ely.[11] It is, as has been said, the accepted view of most Supreme Court-watchers. Little by little, however, the intellectual underpinnings of that conventional position are perceived as being built on shifting sands. Consider, in this respect, the position of black Americans in American society. Accorded, at long last, formal equality under the law (under the *jurisprudence publique*), it is beyond question that for most blacks, that is at best an empty promise. Many white Americans, obviously with exceptions, simply are not willing to assimilate people of color into the mainstream of society. The result is a *de facto* caste system, with the majority of blacks becoming ever more a permanent segment of the underclass in America. The point is, that the *ends,* the goals of identified social action, are in

---

9. D. Spitz, Democracy and the Challenge of Power 106 (1958) (emphasis in original).

10. A. Bickel, The Morality of Consent (1975).

11. J. Ely, Democracy and Distrust (1980).

disagreement with the private reality of too many citizens. Under the *jurisprudence confidentielle* of the constitutional order, therefore, the law permits massive actual discriminations against the eleven to twelve percent of Americans who were born with black skins.

The result, for present purposes, is that adherence to "reason" or to "principle" in Supreme Court adjudication is, or should be, a futile quest. As Nobel Laureate Herbert A. Simon recently asserted: "Reason, taken by itself, is instrumental. It can't select our final goals, nor can it mediate for us in pure conflicts over what final goal to pursue—we have to settle these issues in some other way. All reason can do is help us reach agreed-on goals more efficiently."[12] Accepting Professor Simon's assertion to be correct, the question becomes one of determining (and enforcing) those "agreed-on goals." That is the essence of constitutional decision-making.

II. THE JUSTICES MAKE UP THE LAW AS THEY GO ALONG

That "essence of constitutional decision-making" brings up the data now at hand in Bernard Schwartz's recently published book *Super Chief,* a biography of Chief Justice Earl Warren.[13] *Super Chief* ranks with Mason's biography of Chief Justice Harlan Fiske Stone[14] as a documented study of what transpired behind the velvet curtain during the sixteen years that Earl Warren occupied the center seat of the Supreme Court. When Schwartz's book is added to such others as Woodford Howard's biography of Justice Frank Murphy,[15] Walter Murphy's *Elements of Judicial Strategy,*[16] and even Woodward and Armstrong's keyhole look into the High Bench,[17] we now have readily at hand data that illuminate the judicial process in action since Stone became a Justice in

---

12. H. SIMON, REASON IN HUMAN AFFAIRS 106 (1983).

13. B. SCHWARTZ, SUPER CHIEF: EARL WARREN AND HIS SUPREME COURT—A JUDICIAL BIOGRAPHY (1983).

14. A. MASON, HARLAN FISKE STONE: PILLAR OF THE LAW (1956) (describing the two decades up to 1946).

15. J. HOWARD, MR. JUSTICE MURPHY (1968) (helping to fill the gap between 1946 and 1953, when Warren succeeded Fred Vinson as Chief Justice).

16. W. MURPHY, ELEMENTS OF JUDICIAL STRATEGY (1964).

17. B. WOODWARD & S. ARMSTRONG, THE BRETHREN (1979) (providing information about the post-Warren period). I do not, of course, suggest that this exhausts the literature. *See* for example, Miller & Bowman, *"Slow Dance on the Killing Ground": The Willie Francis Case Revisited,* 32 DE PAUL L. REV. 1 (1982).

1925. The lesson, illustrated by Professor Schwartz's effort, is clear and unmistakable: no longer can constitutional scholars parse Supreme Court decisions as the main, and usually sole, focus of attention in trying to understand what the Court decides. What Professor Schwartz documents in plethoric detail may be simply stated: the Justices make up the law as they go along.

This revelation, in and of itself, is no flashing insight. It has long been known by Court-watchers (but, as has been mentioned, no one wants to blurt out the fact that the Emperor has no clothes). Even some of the present-day Justices—notably Byron White and William Brennan, both of whom were weaned on the heady milk of the Legal Realist movement—have acknowledged as much in opinions.[18] Chief Justice John Marshall, of course, pretended otherwise, but that was probably for the purpose of staving off mounting criticisms of some of his rulings. *Cohens v. Virginia*[19] is one such example where Judge Spencer Roane of Virginia called it "[a] most monstrous and unexampled decision" that "can only be accounted for from that love of power which all history informs us infects and corrupts all who possess it, and from which the upright and eminent Judges are not exempt."[20]

It is worth at least passing mention that Marshall himself was uneasy about Supreme Court lawmaking. Soon after the attempted impeachment of Justice Samuel Chase in 1805, Marshall wrote an astonishing letter to Chase proposing to forgo the whole pretension to judicial supremacy in the meaning of the Constitution. "I think," Marshall stated, "the modern doctrine of impeachment should yield to an appellate jurisdiction in the legislature. A reversal of those judicial decisions deemed unsound by the legislature would certainly better comport with the mildness of our character than [would] a removal of the judge who has rendered them unknowing of his fault."[21] That was in the early nineteenth century, fifteen years before the *Cohens* decision that so enraged Spencer Roane. By 1821, Marshall's Supreme Court had managed to construct the formal legal edifice for federal as well as judicial supremacy.

A century and a half after John Marshall, the Supreme Court's position in the governing order is as solid, and perhaps even more solid, than it has ever been. Even those who bitterly criticize some of its decisions do not dispute the legitimacy of the High

---

18. Richmond Newspapers, Inc. v. Virginia, 448 U.S. 555, 595-96 (1980) (Brennan, J., concurring); Miranda v. Arizona, 384 U.S. 436, 531 (1966) (White, J., dissenting).
19. 19 U.S. (6 Wheat.) 264 (1821).
20. 2 C. WARREN, THE SUPREME COURT IN UNITED STATES HISTORY 15-16 (1922).
21. *Quoted in* R. JACKSON, THE STRUGGLE FOR JUDICIAL SUPREMACY 28 (1941).

Bench's exercise of governmental power. Raoul Berger, a leading spokesman in this area, maintains in a series of tendentious books and articles that the Supreme Court has in some instances acted unconstitutionally.[22] Berger demands that the Justices adhere to the intentions of the framers as the *sine qua non* of proper judicial action. That they have seldom done so does not deter him. For example, even as far back as the *Dartmouth College Case,*[23] Marshall conceded that the framers had not contemplated the issue before the Court. Additionally, when Chief Justice Roger Taney did follow the intentions of the framers, in the dreadful *Dred Scott*[24] case, the Court suffered what Charles Evans Hughes later called "self-inflicted wounds" that badly harmed it.[25]

In recent years, the Justices have made an exponential jump in their self-assumed powers by stating, and getting away with it in *Cooper v. Aaron,*[26] that the Court's rulings are general norms binding the nation. They do not always do so; at times the Justices take pains to limit the scope of their rulings. But following the usual reasoning, constitutional decisions are *de facto* class actions, with the "class" being the nation at large. In my judgment, *Cooper* set the pattern because it was the Warren Court's most important decision (although Schwartz does not say that),[27] and it has become sufficiently routine so that the logically impossible is now commonly accepted: a general principle may be inferred from one particular decision. That, of course, makes the Justices a third branch of the national legislature and, indeed, the highest branch.[28]

22. *See, e.g.,* R. BERGER, GOVERNMENT BY JUDICIARY (1977) (criticizing the Supreme Court's interpretation and application of the fourteenth amendment).

23. Dartmouth College v. Woodward, 17 U.S. (4 Wheat.) 518 (1819).

24. Scott v. Sandford, 60 U.S. (19 How.) 393 (1857).

25. C. HUGHES, THE SUPREME COURT OF THE UNITED STATES 50-54 (1928). Other "wounds" Hughes mentioned were the Legal Tender Cases and the Income Tax Cases.

26. 358 U.S. 1, 18 (1958) (citing Marbury v. Madison, 5 U.S. (1 Cranch) at 177).

27. *See* Miller, *Constitutional Decisions as De Facto Class Actions: A Comment on the Implications of Cooper v. Aaron,* 58 U. DET. J. URB. L. 573 (1981).

Chief Justice Warren thought that *Baker v. Carr*, the Tennessee reapportionment case, "was the most important case of [his] tenure on the Court." SCHWARTZ, *supra* note 13, at 410. That, however, can hardly be correct. The combination of *Cooper v. Aaron* and *Brown v. Board of Educ.* far overshadowed *Baker v. Carr* and every other case decided during Warren's tenure.

28. The concept that a Supreme Court decision is "the law of the land" rather than merely "the law of the case" has, of course, its detractors. *See, e.g.,* Ely, *The*

The concept that the Supreme Court deems itself the highest branch has become familiar learning and need not be reworked here. I do not propose in what follows to delineate what Professor Schwartz has to say either on this notion in particular or his book in general, with one exception. Schwartz does set forth an inside view of the Supreme Court that is replete with numerous anecdotes drawn from interviews with colleagues of Warren and with his law clerks. All of this is supplemented by an exhaustive search of the collected papers of many of the Justices plus other bibliographical sources. It is a tremendous job. Yet Schwartz errs in exactly the same place as is his strength by emptying his file cabinets and card catalogs, with the result that he strings together in a journalistic style what took place during Warren's tenure as Chief Justice. There is no analysis of the meaning of what Warren did, nor is there an attempt to explicate why he did it.

In some respects, such a product may be considered to be quite enough. I take it that Professor Schwartz assumes that the facts as he has determined them speak for themselves. Accordingly, there is no need to delve deeper. But Schwartz does not ask what seems to be the important and demanding questions: *Why* did the civil rights/civil liberties revolution characteristic of the Warren Court come at that point in history? After all, the Bill of Rights had been in the formal Constitution for a century and a half, and the fourteenth amendment was formal law for almost 100 years. Second, what, if any, sociological function did that revolution serve? Obviously, neither question is easily answered. And equally obviously, the answers overlap or at least complement each other, especially when viewed in connection with the concept of social justice.

III. JUDICIAL PRESUMPTIONS, RESULT-ORIENTATION, AND THE
PRINCIPLE OF REASON-DIRECTED SOCIETAL SELF-
INTEREST

It is axiomatic, to begin with, that there is no such thing as unbiased knowledge or impartial judging. Everyone, including judges, carries his "can't-helps" around with him, as in the statement "I can't help believing such-and-such." We must, accordingly, "reject the ideal model of an empty mind passively contemplating pure data presented to pure awareness. . . ."[29]

Wages of Crying Wolf—A Comment on Roe v. Wade, 82 YALE L.J. 920 (1973), in which Professor Ely asserts—incorrectly in my judgment—that the *Roe* ruling "is *not* constitutional law." (Ely should tell that to Chief Justice Burger.) The idea, enunciated expressly for the first time in *Cooper v. Aaron,* is what makes the Supreme Court's rulings so important.

29. P. RHINELANDER, IS MAN INCOMPREHENSIBLE TO MAN? 98 (1973).

That is the tacit assumption of coursebook editors, and other commentators, who believe that such an ideal model should not only be striven for but is humanly possible to achieve. But that is not the case, as Schwartz exhaustively documents. "The ideal of a knowledge embodied in strictly impersonal statements," Michael Polanyi maintained, "now appears self-contradictory, meaningless, a fit subject for ridicule. We must learn to accept as our ideal a knowledge that is manifestly personal."[30]

There is no need to labor the point. I take it as one of the givens of human, including judicial, activity. The problem is what to do about it. Gunnar Myrdal believes that the most that can be done is for a writer to "face his valuations,"[31] to state as best he can where he comes from when he comments upon the human condition—or, indeed, when he is chosen to judge his fellow humans. The need is for candid disclosure of one's biases or, perhaps better, one's personal philosophy. "The decisions of the courts on economic and social questions depend on their economic and social philosophy . . ." asserted Theodore Roosevelt.[32] The same may be said about commentators: their opinions about judicial decisions depend on their "economic and social philosophies." Thus I begin this analysis of the work of the Warren Court with the admission that I find most of the decisions of that Court entirely desirable. When one views in retrospect what the Justices did during Warren's sixteen years, it is difficult to understand why there was any controversy about many of their rulings.

---

30. M. POLANYI, THE STUDY OF MAN 27 (1958). *See also* P. BRIDGMAN, THE WAY THINGS ARE 308-09 (1959); M. POLANYI, PERSONAL KNOWLEDGE (1958); K. MANNHEIM, IDEOLOGY AND UTOPIA: AN INTRODUCTION TO THE SOCIOLOGY OF KNOWLEDGE (1951). Mannheim states: "The juristic administrative mentality constructs only closed static systems of thought, and is always faced with the paradoxical task of having to incorporate into its system new laws, which arise out of the unsystematized interaction of living forces as if they were only a further elaboration of the original system." *Id.* at 105. *See also* Miller & Howell, *The Myth of Neutrality in Constitutional Adjudication,* 27 U. CHI. L. REV. 661 (1960), *reprinted in* A. MILLER, THE SUPREME COURT: MYTH AND REALITY 51 (1978).

31. *See* G. MYRDAL, VALUE IN SOCIAL THEORY: A SELECTION OF ESSAYS ON METHODOLOGY (Streeten ed. 1958). See also *id.* at ix, xxxiv-xxxvi, 54, and 155 for interesting insights.

32. 43 CONG. REC. 21 (1908) (annual message to Congress), more completely stated as: "The chief lawmakers in our country may be and often are, the judges, because they are the final seat of authority. Every time they interpret contract, property, vested rights, due process of law, liberty, they necessarily enact into law parts of a system of social philosophy; and as such interpretation is fundamental, they give direction to all law-making. The decisions of the courts on economic and social questions depend upon their economic and social philosophy, . . ."

Some I disagree with—*Ginzburg,*[33] *O'Brien,*[34] *Williams v. Georgia,*[35] and *Naim v. Naim*[36] are four which I think were unfortunate. I also have trouble with *Barenblatt.*[37] But those are exceptions. Warren is no hero of mine, but compared with some of the others who served with him on the Court, he fully deserves the accolade of Justice William J. Brennan: "For those who served with him, Earl Warren will always be the Super Chief."[38]

Second, after more than 200 years as a nation-state, with a judiciary that ever increasingly is important in the governing process, there is no settled, widely-accepted conception of how judges *should* operate. The myth system erects an impossible standard for judges to attain. That mythology, plus the pervasive secrecy that surrounds all courts, means that there is precious little knowledge about how they *do* operate. Professor Schwartz, and the others mentioned above, have helped to sweep aside the curtain of secrecy, but much more needs to be known before comprehensive knowledge about the appellate process (to say nothing about trial courts) will become available. Most lawyers, as Chief Justice Roger Traynor of the California Supreme Court suggested some years ago, have only the haziest knowledge about the nature of the appellate judicial process.[39]

Third, it follows from the first point made above, that what is important to know about the Supreme Court Justices is why they adhere to certain often-unarticulated major premises when they approach decisions in specific cases. As Justice Oliver Wendell Holmes said in 1905, a constitutional decision depends "on a judgment or intuition more subtle than any articulate major premise."[40] That sentiment was echoed by Dean Eugene Rostow in 1962: "there is an inescapable Bergsonian element of intuition in the judges' work—in their ordering of 'facts,' in their choice of premises, in their formulation of the postulates we call 'rules' or 'principles,' in their sense of the policy or policies which animate the trend, or change it."[41] If that is true, as surely it is, then what price reason or rationality or the call for principled decisions? Holmes said it well in 1899, in language reminiscent of Professor

---

33. Ginzburg v. United States, 383 U.S. 463 (1966).

34. United States v. O'Brien, 391 U.S. 367 (1968).

35. Williams v. Georgia, 349 U.S. 375 (1955).

36. Naim v. Naim, 350 U.S. 891 (1955).

37. Barenblatt v. United States, 360 U.S. 109 (1959).

38. SCHWARTZ, *supra* note 13, at vii.

39. Traynor, *Badlands in an Appellate Judge's Realm of Reason,* 7 UTAH L. REV. 157, 158 (1960).

40. Lochner v. New York, 198 U.S. 45, 76 (1905) (Holmes, J., dissenting).

41. Rostow, *American Legal Realism and the Sense of the Profession,* 34 ROCKY MTN. L. REV. 123, 144 (1962).

Simon's observation, quoted above: "I sometimes tell students that the law schools pursue an inspirational combined with a logical method, that is, the postulates are taken for granted upon authority without inquiry into their worth, and then logic is used as the only tool to develop the results."[42]

There is a corollary to this proposition. If, as Cardozo once asserted, "the thing that counts chiefly is the nature of the premises,"[43] the important matter to perceive is that the relevant or apposite premises in constitutional cases tend to be multiple rather than single. Schwartz amply documents the point. In litigation, at least two conflicting major premises can always be formulated, one embodying one set of interests and the other embodying the other. The adversary system of litigation at the appellate level can be justified on no other basis. It is a poor lawyer indeed who cannot find some authority for the result his client desires once a human dispute has gone beyond informal settlement, and certainly beyond the trial court. Put another way, constitutional cases, those the Supreme Court decides on the merits, tend to be "trouble" or "hospital" cases. They represent the pathological instances in society. The parties call upon the courts because they cannot settle their disputes extra-judicially.

The importance of premises in constitutional adjudication is displayed in *Kennedy v. Mendoza-Martinez,*[44] which is discussed by Schwartz insofar as the internal dynamics of the Supreme Court were concerned, but not as to the specific point about premises. In a classically clear example of how premises are both taken for granted without inquiry into their worth, *pace* Holmes, and tend to travel in pairs of opposites, the decision merits careful study. As Justice Potter Stewart said in dissent:

> The Court's opinion is lengthy, but its thesis is simple: (1) The withdrawal of citizenship which these statutes provide is "punishment." (2) Punishment cannot constitutionally be imposed except after a criminal trial and conviction. (3) The statutes are therefore unconstitutional. As with all syllogisms, the conclusion is inescapable if the premises are correct. But I cannot agree with the Court's major premises—that the divestiture of citizenship . . . is punishment in the constitutional sense of that term.[45]

Which, then, is the "correct" premise—Stewart's or that of Justice Arthur Goldberg, who wrote for the majority? Neither of the

42. O. HOLMES, COLLECTED LEGAL PAPERS 238 (1920).
43. B. CARDOZO, THE GROWTH OF THE LAW 62 (1924).
44. 372 U.S. 144 (1963).
45. *Id.* at 201-02 (Stewart, J., dissenting).

learned judges vouchsafed an explanation as to why his premise was correct or, for that matter, why he chose it in the first place. We were left without guidance or insight into those questions. What Stewart made explicit in his dissent is characteristic of all constitutional decisions (and, as mentioned, documented in exhaustive detail by Schwartz). To a great extent, these unanswered questions regarding premises make the call for reason or principled decisions a bootless quest.

Fourth, it is beyond argument that all judges are "result-oriented," as, indeed, are all commentators on the judiciary. The term apparently is one of Justice Felix Frankfurter's neologisms.[46] He used it, as Schwartz notes, to castigate some of his colleagues on the High Bench, particularly Chief Justice Warren and Justices Hugo Black, William Brennan, and William Douglas. It has since been used by the coterie of commentators who are votaries in the cult of Frankfurter worship. Their principal stance is that of judicial self-restraint, supposedly the hallmark of Frankfurter's jurisprudence. Accordingly, this group of Frankfurter worshippers sneer, in one way or another, at those judges who are more "activist" and who believe that attention should be paid to the consequences of decisions. That Frankfurter and his acolytes are basically in error on the level of *description*, to say nothing about *prescription*, almost goes without saying. Frankfurter himself was far from the non-activist that he liked to say. Chief Justice Warren so believed:

> Warren also thought that Frankfurter's vote and opinion in the 1957 case of Rowoldt v. Perfecto showed that Frankfurter's restraint doctrine was often a facade to mask the fact that the Justice could be as human in his decision process as any of the Brethren. . . . When Warren met his law clerks after the *Rowoldt* conference, he told them that Frankfurter had provided the vote for the bare majority to reverse. The clerks expressed surprise because Frankfurter's action was so inconsistent with his previous decisions [dealing with deportation because of Communist affiliations]. At this, the Chief said, "Well, you know, I think Frankfurter is capable of a human instinct now and then. Frankfurter really obviously just felt sorry for this poor old immigrant." . . .
>
> Warren used to express irritation at Frankfurter's constant lecturing of the Justices that they were nothing but a group of "result-oriented judges," who did not have the courage to vote for a decision that was mandated by precedent, where they felt it was not the right decision. To Warren, a case such as *Rowoldt* demonstrated that Frankfurter could be as "result-oriented" as any of the Brethren.[47]

Indeed, he could. One searches in vain for any time, save perhaps the *Steel Seizure Case*,[48] when Frankfurter voted *against*

---

46. *See, e.g.,* SCHWARTZ, *supra* note 13, at 267.

47. *Id.* at 266-67. For further evidence of Frankfurter's result-orientation, see Miller & Bowman, *supra* note 17, *passim*.

48. Youngstown Sheet & Tube Co. v. Sawyer, 343 U.S. 579 (1952) (Frankfurter, J., concurring). The *Steel* case is really not apposite, for it was essentially not so

what the federal government wanted to do in an important case. An "intense patriot,"[49] Frankfurter was also a close advisor of President Franklin Roosevelt, both before and after he became a judge. He usually found ways to sustain federal governmental action, even in *Korematsu v. United States*.[50] In that and other wartime cases, the Court, including Frankfurter, came perilously close to becoming a part of the "executive juggernaut."[51] Result-orientation, pure and simple. The same may be said for Frankfurter's actions in *Louisiana ex rel. Francis v. Resweber*,[52] where he, while stoutly maintaining that he was exercising judicial self-restraint and deferring to state authorities in a capital punishment case, obviously pursued a set of his own personal values.

Some judges have been more candid than Frankfurter and have admitted that result-orientation is inevitable. Two examples will suffice: Judge Braxton Craven of the Fourth Circuit Court of Appeals and Judge J. Skelly Wright of the District of Columbia Court of Appeals. In a little noted but important article, Craven flatly stated that all judges are result-oriented, the difference between them being mainly that some know it and some do not.[53] As for Wright, he wrote this in 1963:

> I also agree with you that criticism of court decisions because they have not been "reasoned" or because they fail to expound the principles on which they rely and show how the principles lead to the result should be answered. In my judgment, a court opinion is not a mechanical thing producible by computer. *Intellectual honesty requires an admission that most opinions are result-oriented—initially, at least, visceral reactions to a given set of facts. Whether the initial reaction becomes the final result depends on a subsequent check of the legal authorities which support it. And if the initial reaction is strong enough, it will tend to overcome precedents which stand in the way.*[54]

Sixteen years later Judge Wright reiterated in other words his earlier candid admission:

> [I] think the key . . . is doing justice within the law. You have to stay

---

much a question of governmental power as a dispute between the President and Congress, as Justice Black's opinion for the Court made clear.

49. *See* H. HIRSCH, THE ENIGMA OF FELIX FRANKFURTER *passim* (1981).

50. Korematsu v. United States, 323 U.S. 214 (1944).

51. A. MASON, *supra* note 14, at 666.

52. 329 U.S. 459 (1947). For a discussion, see Miller & Bowman, *supra* note 17.

53. Craven, *Paean To Pragmatism*, 50 N.C.L. REV. 977 (1972).

54. Letter from Judge Wright to Arthur S. Miller, Oct. 9, 1963 (emphasis added) (used with permission). I asked him in 1982 if he still adhered to that position, and he replied in the affirmative. For discussion, see A. MILLER, A "CAPACITY FOR OUTRAGE": THE JUDICIAL ODYSSEY OF J. SKELLY WRIGHT c.9 & *passim* (forthcoming in 1984, to be published by Greenwood Press).

within the law, but you can press against the law in all directions to do what you perceive to be justice. . . . I think it's justified to do what's right. I know that sounds like gobbledegook . . . but there're certain things that remain pretty accepted as what the law is, and it's just a question of how vigorously, how enthusiastically you embrace these things, particularly in the civil rights area.

I guess I am an activist, but I want to do what's right. When I get a case, I look at it and the first thing I think of automatically is what's right, what should be done—and then you look at the law to see whether or not you can do it. That might invert the process of how you should arrive at a decision, of whether you should look at the law first. . . . I am less patient than other judges with law that won't permit what I conceive to be fair. Now, there's a legitimate criticism of that, because what's fair and just to X may not be fair and just to Y—in perfect good faith on both sides. But if you don't take it to extremes, I think that it's good to come out with a fair and just result and then look for law to support it.[55]

Judges Craven and Wright—and, indeed, Chief Justice Warren, as Schwartz documents—openly concede the fact of judicial result-orientation. They are not aberrational: to the extent that we know anything about the nature of the judicial process, all judges so operate. That appears to be the clear lesson from the massive detail delineated in *Super Chief*.

Finally, if the foregoing is true, then the question becomes: what results? What is "right" and "fair" to Judge Skelly Wright? What was "fair" to Chief Justice Warren? The question brings up the concept of *social justice*. While this is not the time or place to do more than adumbrate some of the essentials of social justice, my basic point is that during Earl Warren's tenure as Chief Justice, the Supreme Court generally—when, that is, he could command a majority—followed the idea that the Court's task was to try to help America realize social justice. In that, Warren and his principal cohorts—Douglas, Brennan, Goldberg, Fortas, and (at times but not always, especially in his later years) Black—believed that there was much more to judging than a purely procedural approach, as so many advocate. They adhered to Professor William A. Galston's view, not overtly, to be sure, but tacitly:

[T]he quest for a purely institutional or procedural solution to the practical problem of obtaining justice is futile. Every community, whether democratic or not, must rely on a rudimentary sense of fairness and equity among its members. This sense is not innate, but must rather be fostered through some system of education. The traditional American penchant for political engineering or institutional tinkering is thus profoundly one-sided; democratic procedures are almost vacuous in the absence of collectively held moral convictions.[56]

The Warren Court, insofar as it followed the views of the Chief Justice, was a part of a national system of education. The Jus-

---

55. *Quoted in* J. Bass, Unlikely Heroes 115-16 (1981).
56. W. Galston, Justice and the Human Good 279 (1980). In the quoted statement, Professor Galston notes his agreement with J. Rawls, A Theory of Justice (1971).

tices, in the words of Judge Wright, were the "conscience of a sovereign people."[57]

What, then, is social justice? It is basically a form of distributive justice, concerned with the ways in which benefits are distributed in society through its major institutions: how wealth is allocated; personal rights are protected; and other positive benefits are divided among the populace. Dr. David Miller maintains that the "most valuable general definition of justice is that which brings out its distributive character most plainly: justice is *suum cuique,* to each his due."[58] Furthermore, "[t]he just state of affairs is that in which each individual has exactly those benefits and burdens which are due to him by virtue of his personal characteristics and circumstances."[59] Implicit in that definition is the idea that "equals should be treated equally."

How can it be determined what a person's "due" actually means? Dr. Miller carefully distinguishes "conservative" from "ideal" justice:

> For, from one point of view, we are disposed to think that the *customary* distribution of rights, goods, and privileges, as well as burdens and pains, is natural and just, and that this ought to be maintained by law, as it usually is: while, from another point of view, we seem to recognize an ideal system of rules of distribution which ought to exist, but perhaps have never yet existed, and we consider laws to be just in proportion as they conform to this ideal.[60]

Similarly, D.D. Raphael has contrasted "conservative" and "prosthetic" justice. The former has the object of preserving "an existing order of rights and possessions, or to restore it when any breaches have been made," while the latter aims at "modifying the *status quo*."[61] In essence, the Warren Court balanced the ideal of justice as rights against the instinctive belief in justice in an ideal or prosthetic sense. The Constitution of 1787 is basically one of rights, but in the sense of "vested" rather than "civil" rights. Rights, Dr. Miller believes,

> generally derive from publicly acknowledged rules, established practices, or past transactions: they do not depend upon a person's current beha-

---

57. Wright, *The Role of the Courts: Conscience of a Sovereign People,* 26 THE REPORTER No. 5, at 27 (Sept. 26, 1963). See also A. MILLER, *supra* note 54, at c.1 for further discussion.

58. D. MILLER, SOCIAL JUSTICE 20 (1976) (emphasis in original).

59. *Id.*

60. *Id.* at 25 (quoting H. SIDGWICK, THE METHODS OF ETHICS 273 (1907) (emphasis in original)).

61. Raphael, *Conservative and Prosthetic Justice,* 12 POL. STUD. 149, 154-55 (1964) (emphasis in original).

viour or other individual qualities. For this reason it is appropriate to describe this conception of justice as "conservative." It is concerned with
the continuity of a social order over time, and with ensuring that men's
expectations of one another are not disappointed.[62]

Social justice as rights requires judges to protect the "is" (the status quo) in society. Judges generally do so, including members of
the Warren Court. Where Warren and his activist colleagues di-
verged was in discerning, however intuitively, that the "is" that is
to be protected at times necessitates more than blindly and stub-
bornly following precedent.

The task of the judiciary in any modern industrial society is to
be part of governmental order and thereby to underpin the stability of the system and protect the system by resisting truly serious
attempts to alter it.[63] No one becomes a judge in the United
States who is not either a member of that nebulous but nonetheless existent group called the Establishment or has views similar
to that group. The legal profession is rights oriented. The basic
doctrine of constitutional law has long been that of "vested
rights." Those rights revolve principally around the concept of
property, the protection of which, John Locke maintained, was
the first duty of government.[64] Litigation is spawned when those
rights, or perceived rights, come into conflict with other perceived
rights, or human needs. The tensions emanating from those conflicts are reconciled in courts presided over by an Establishment
judge that seeks to protect rights, and is often guided by application of what will later be called the Principle of Reason-Directed
Societal Self-Interest.

Rights do not exhaust the concept of social justice; needs must
also be considered. James C. Davies has accurately maintained
that no one can expect humans to participate in politics (which is
what constitutions are all about) until certain basic human needs
are fulfilled.[65] Human needs theory is not only a means of explaining certain political behavior but also a basis for judging politics and political institutions.[66] Indeed, one can validly argue that
reasonably adequate satisfaction of human needs is the ultimate
purpose of politics, and thus of constitutions. The Warren Court
often focused on human needs in making decisions. The essential

---

62. D. MILLER, *supra* note 58, at 26.

63. *See* Miller, *The Politics of the American Judiciary,* 49 POL. Q. 200 (1978); J.
GRIFFITH, THE POLITICS OF THE JUDICIARY (1977).

64. *Quoted in* Gramm, *Industrial Capitalism and the Breakdown of the Liberal
Rule of Law,* 7 J. ECON. ISSUES 577, 599 n.17 (1973). For further discussion, see
Miller, *Toward a Definition of "The" Constitution,* 8 U. DAYTON L. REV. 633, 671-91
(1983).

65. Davies, *The Development of Individuals and the Development of Politics,* in
HUMAN NEEDS AND POLITICS 74 (R. Fitzgerald ed. 1977).

66. *See* the several essays in HUMAN NEEDS AND POLITICS *supra* note 65.

point, however, is that in so doing, the Justices—usually, but not always, less than all of them—also protected vested rights.

The Justices perceived the problem of satisfaction of human needs as basic to social stability. They were concerned with the continuity of social order over time. Stability and continuity are conservative virtues which, paradoxically, were furthered by the liberal, activist decisions of the Warren Court. Put another way, the Justices were fully aware that people today live in a time of extremely rapid social change and bent their efforts to help preserve the fundamental values of an open society. They knew that as society changes, so too must the law, subject of course to the notion that there are certain basic rights that are immutable and that should be protected—protected in the sense of making them applicable to the citizenry at large. Whereas the Supreme Court before Warren was mainly concerned with the protection of the established property interests, under Warren, the High Bench, by moving to protect many of the poor and disadvantaged, also helped those highest in the social pecking order. I do not contend that this thought was foremost in their minds, or even that they thought about it at all. What I do assert, however, is that it is a necessary inference that should be drawn from a survey of their many decisions.

But what are *human needs?* Only a brief statement is necessary or possible at this time. Perhaps best known is Abraham Maslow's hierarchy: "physiological, safety, love, esteem, and self-actualization."[67] Professor William A. Galston argues that the concept of need has a "threefold classification: natural need, social need, and luxury."[68] Natural needs are "the means required to secure, not only existence, but also the development of existence."[69] Developmental needs include adequate nurturance, adequate education, institutions that permit the exercise of a wide range of capacities, and a variety of friendships and social relations.[70] Luxury, of course, needs no special explanation. According to Dr. David Miller, "[h]arm, for any given individual, is

---

67. Maslow, *A Theory of Human Motivation,* 50 PSYCHOLOGICAL REV. 370, 394 (1943). While that formulation need not be accepted, as Professor Christian Bay has commented, it should be used until a more useful alternative model is provided. Bay, *Needs, Wants, and Political Legitimacy,* 1 CAN. J. POL. SCI. 241, 247 (Sept. 1968).

68. W. GALSTON, *supra* note 56, at 164.

69. *Id.* at 164.

70. *Id.* at 164-65.

whatever interferes directly or indirectly with the activities essential to his plan of life; and correspondingly, his needs must be understood to comprise whatever is necessary to allow those activities to be carried out."[71]

Obviously, the concept of human needs as a philosophical and jurisprudential construct is complex and controversial. It calls for reorientation of orthodox thinking about the law and legal institutions. To analyze the judicial process generally and the Warren Court's work specifically, employing a dichotomous model of rights and needs, is to tread upon legal *terra incognita*. Yet when one deals with language that is part of a constitutive act (i.e., the Constitution of the United States), much more than purely legal phenomena must be considered. H.J. McCloskey has explained that needs are things which ought, where possible, to be available, not withheld or prevented, and indeed, be supplied where necessary. Where needs cannot be met, society or the world ought to be reordered so that they are capable of being met, or obtained by the person with the need, provided that greater goods are not thereby jeopardized. Finally, a discussion respecting human needs and needs of particular persons involves reference to natures, the perfection, development, and nonimpairment of which are good.[72]

To an indeterminate extent, and not always consistently, Chief Justice Warren and his colleagues were interested in reordering society to lend help to those in need. They perceived their goal as a moral imperative and as a means by which the fundamental values of constitutionalism could be preserved. That way of thinking leads to a fundamental dualism, one overt and the other tacit, that comes together in the Principle of Reason-Directed Societal Self-Interest.

Consider, for example, the principle of equality. Although Professor Peter Westen has recently attempted to show that it is an "empty idea,"[73] it was far from that for members of the Warren Court. For the first time in American history, the Court put substantive content into a concept that Americans have—under the myth system—struggled to fulfill since the commitment to equality contained in the Declaration of Independence. Not that the myth comported with bleak reality, as indentured servants, slaves, Indians, women, and others, knew and know all too well.

---

71. D. MILLER, *supra* note 58, at 134.

72. McCloskey, *Human Needs, Rights and Political Values*, 13 AM. PHIL. Q. 1 (1976).

73. *See, e.g.*, Westen, *The Empty Idea of Equality*, 95 HARV. L. REV. 537 (1982). *Compare* Greenawalt, *How Empty Is the Idea of Equality?*, 83 COLUM. L. REV. 1167 (1983).

The Declaration's commitment to equality was dropped in the Constitution of 1787. Not until 1868, when after the sanguinary Civil War the fourteenth amendment was added, did "equal protection" become an express constitutional command. Even then, the hard fact was that what the paper promises quickly proved to be ephemeral for many Americans. Black Americans, as J.R. Pole has remarked, did not have "the consolations of equality or the practice of protection."[74]

For a great many years, the Supreme Court did not enforce the equal protection clause. In *Hall v. DeCuir*,[75] for example, it struck down a Louisiana statute requiring similar accommodations for all travelers and expressly forbidding discrimination on the basis of color. "[E]quality does not mean identity," intoned Justice Nathan Clifford for the Court,[76] in what was to become a famous aphorism—and thereby helped to commit the freed slaves to a *de facto* caste system. That system was further constitutionalized in 1896 when the Court determined through an intuition known only to the majority Justices that equal protection meant "separate but equal."[77] Pole asserts that "white racial prejudice was profound and resilient, as the history of Reconstruction shows. The Court chose to settle [the problem of racial antagonism] not in accordance with its authority under the Fourteenth Amendment . . . but in accordance with the actual distribution of social and political power in Southern States."[78] To conclude that in so doing the Justices were major contributors to development of a boiling reservoir of social discontent is not a difficult step.

The Supreme Court Justices were, of course, quite aware of the *de facto* caste system in America. Where they differed was not in their perception but in what to do about it; or more precisely, what they as judges could or should do about it. Not until 1938, in the *Missouri Law School Case*,[79] did a majority of the Justices see fit to begin undermining the wall of separation between the castes. That development began a series of judicial and executive decisions that culminated in 1954 in *Brown v. Board of Educa-*

---

74. J. POLE, THE PURSUIT OF EQUALITY IN AMERICAN HISTORY 193 (1978).

75. 95 U.S. 485 (1878).

76. *Id.* at 503.

77. Plessy v. Ferguson, 163 U.S. 537, 543 (1896).

78. J. POLE, *supra* note 74, at 193.

79. Missouri *ex rel.* Gaines v. Canada, 305 U.S. 337 (1938).

tion.[80] Interestingly, the key decision may well have been executive rather than judicial. When President Roosevelt was dragooned into signing an executive order in 1942 calling for nondiscrimination in employment in war industries,[81] black Americans began to increase their pressure group tactics, but mainly against the courts. Neither the caste system nor the Supreme Court has been the same since; although it must still be noted that the change in legal status for black Americans has come more in the formal positive law than in the living operational code of the nation.

During Warren's tenure on the Supreme Court, equality became a major theme of governmental policy. The lead often came from federal judges, including the Supreme Court. Few scholars have asked why the judicial explosion in civil rights and liberties, both revolving around the equality concept, came when it did. In 1927, Justice Holmes sneered that equal protection—the Constitution's reification of equality—was "the usual last resort" of constitutional arguments, and summarily dismissed Carrie Buck's plea that she should not be involuntarily sterilized by the state of Virginia.[82] Within a generation that judicial attitude had altered. The question is why.

I have suggested above that the Court under Warren, by helping to protect the poor and the disadvantaged, also aided those highest in established society. Briefly, two factors seem to be significant in developing an answer to the civil rights/civil liberties revolution and its cause. First, in the post-World War II period the United States entered its true Golden Age.[83] Beginning in 1945 the economic pie seemed to be getting larger and larger; an economy of abundance was being created. It therefore became possible to carve slices out of that pie for the theretofore "have-nots" but without diminishing the material well-being of the "haves."[84]

Second, the Warren Court's egalitarian decisions were a means of siphoning off discontent from the disadvantaged. Blacks, for

---

80. 347 U.S. 483 (1954). There was a follow-up decision the next year: Brown v. Board of Educ., 349 U.S. 294 (1955).

81. *See* L. RUCHAMES, RACE, JOBS, AND POLITICS (1953). *See also* Miller, *Government Contracts and Social Control: A Preliminary Inquiry,* 41 VA. L. REV. 27 (1955).

82. Buck v. Bell, 274 U.S. 200, 208 (1927).

83. That Golden Age has now run its course, and with it has come an economy of scarcity—and the apparent end of the Second Reconstruction.

84. One other factor is worth noting and study: blacks and others among the underclass were forced to fight and at times to die in World War II, Korea, and Vietnam. My hypothesis is that governmental programs promoting equality are a part of the trade-off, the payment, made for that sacrifice.

example, were at least extended gains under the *formal* Constitution. In other words, the equality decisions should be seen as part of the development of a permissive society, one that also provided the economic basis of material betterment for more and more people. The consequence is that the bulk of the populace is relatively docile, although how long that will continue is by no means certain.

By no means is it suggested that this analysis was uppermost in the minds of the Supreme Court during Warren's tenure. To the extent, however, that the analysis is accurate, it may be said that not only the disadvantaged profited from the Warren Court's decisions. They were of course the obvious or manifest beneficiaries. But it also seems correct to say that those who have always benefited under the law and the Constitution, the moneyed and the propertied, were also served as hidden or latent beneficiaries. That some of the latter class have not been perceptive enough to realize that token satisfaction for the demands of the underclass helped to protect them does not belie the point.

Earl Warren and those who identified with him acted on the assumption that the person, particularly members of disadvantaged groups, was a free-standing individual struggling to retain or to gain a measure of personal identity and security in an increasingly bureaucratized society. Knowing that one's personhood or identity comes from being able to stand tall in the community, Warren sought to enhance the status of some on the lower rungs of our *de facto* class society, both because they deserved it as persons and because of larger community interests. Dr. David Miller remarks that "[j]ustice as respect for established rights, without regard to how those rights are distributed among persons, is intelligible when it is seen as the principle which restrains men from destructive greed."[85] It is intelligible when those who are favored by fortune have the good sense—the common sense, that most uncommon of all the senses—to perceive that it is in *their* interest to help the less favored.

It is on this basis that the Warren Court can and should be evaluated. If we acknowledge that people will act from self-interest, it then becomes a task of any society to enunciate policies that will establish a social milieu in which self-interest has reason to be enlightened. As Professor Herbert A. Simon has remarked:

---

85. D. MILLER, *supra* note 58, at 175.

> Success depends on our ability to broaden human horizons so that people will take into account, in deciding what is to their interest, a wider range of consequences. It depends on whether all of us come to recognize that our fate is bound up with the fate of the whole world, that there is no enlightened or even viable self-interest that does not look to our living in a harmonious way with our total environment.[86]

Warren's focus was not as broad as that of Simon, but nonetheless the point is accurate. Warren sought to help Americans answer George Orwell's question about Great Britain: "Whether the British ruling class are wicked or merely stupid is one of the most difficult questions of our time, and at certain moments a very important question."[87] Are America's rulers "wicked or merely stupid"? The question demands an answer. It is the essential question presented by the human rights revolution of the Warren Court.

The point is that Warren, as Chief Justice, intuitively realized the importance of satisfying human needs in order to attain and retain the collective values of stability and vested rights. He did not outwardly or consciously adhere to the Principle of Reason-Directed Societal Self-Interest; but his decisions, taken together, are an invitation to those on top of the social totem pole to use *their* reason to perceive that it is in *their* self-interest for the needs of the less favored to be reasonably satisfied—within ecological restraints, of course. In so doing, Warren followed his instincts: hard-headed compassion; knowing what was fair and decent under the circumstances; and translating those instincts for helping the "great unwashed" into an implicit signal for those who rule to make the requisite adjustments so that all can benefit. He used his reason to determine, as best he could, where the self-interest of society reposed in any given circumstance. At times, to be sure, he may well have been wrong; and at times, furthermore, he flatly refused to follow his instinct for fairness to its logical conclusion. But his record, on the whole, displayed an understanding that, as Professor Ronald Dworkin said in a different context, "[o]ur constitutional system rests on a particular moral theory, namely, that men have moral rights against the state."[88] Warren knew that those moral rights required an "activist" Supreme Court, and did not hesitate to use his full powers in that direction. Rather than being targeted for impeachment by some misguided people, he should have been applauded for doing the necessary: for making decisions that helped to knit the fabric of society closer together.

---

86. H. SIMON, *supra* note 12, at 107.

87. *Quoted in* Hitchens, *Anthony Wedgwood Benn: Can He Put England Together Again?,* Mother Jones, Nov. 1981, at 14.

88. R. DWORKIN, TAKING RIGHTS SERIOUSLY 147 (1977).

The Principle of Reason-Directed Societal Self-Interest is by no means a new technique of governance. Alexis de Tocqueville noted 150 years ago that the United States had an ingrained drive toward equality. "Equality," he wrote, "every day gives every man a multitude of little delights. The charms of equality are felt every hour and are within everyone's reach: the noblest hearts are not insensitive to them and the commonest souls delight in them. The passion to which equality gives birth must thus be at once energetic and general."[89] So it must, although America's ruling class has not been quick to perceive the point. Tocqueville knew that: "I am of the opinion, on the whole, that the manufacturing aristocracy which is growing up under our eyes is one of the harshest which ever existed in the world."[90]

In many respects, the Progressive movement, *circa* the turn of the century, was an acknowledgment that that harshness should be ameliorated, not necessarily in the interests of the working class but to bleed off social discontent. The policies that emanated from Progressivism were, in some observers' eyes, designed to do just that.[91] Those policies gave the appearance of regulation without much internal content; they were tokens rather than substantial changes, symbolic gestures toward reform. Only when the Great Depression hit the nation in the 1930's was there even a grudging concession by the "manufacturing aristocracy" that New Deal programs designed to alleviate economic distress were desirable. The New Deal—with social security, unemployment compensation, labor relations, and agricultural adjustment statutes as the most important measures—was a social safety valve which helped to diminish discontent among those who were being denied any real chance of fulfillment of the American Dream. It was a means by which the system of corporate capitalism could be saved at a minimum cost. The worst aspects of poverty and economic distress were dealt with. But clearly the central dedication of the Franklin Roosevelt administration was to business recov-

---

89. A. DE TOCQUEVILLE, DEMOCRACY IN AMERICA (quoted in J. POLE, *supra* note 74, at 131).

90. *Quoted in* L. BERG, H. HAHN & J. SCHMIDHAUSER, CORRUPTION IN THE AMERICAN POLITICAL SYSTEM 11 (1976).

91. *See, e.g.,* G. KOLKO, THE TRIUMPH OF CONSERVATISM: A REINTERPRETATION OF AMERICAN HISTORY, 1900-1916 5-6 & *passim* (1963). *Compare* R. LUSTIG, CORPORATE LIBERALISM: THE ORIGINS OF MODERN AMERICAN POLITICAL THEORY, 1890-1920 (1982).

ery, rather than to social reform.[92] Nonetheless, "the sheer need of governments to allay working-class discontents that were dangerous to the stability of the state"[93] was obviously central to the New Deal ethos. After all, it was Bismarck, the conservative chancellor of Germany and no admirer of democracy, who pioneered the welfare state in the late nineteenth century, and for precisely the purpose of dampening working-class discontent.

The revolution wrought by the Warren Court came about because it became possible for the first time in history to satisfy some of the pent-up economic demands of the underclass. That revolution's function was to allay the populace, insofar as law could do it, by giving at least the appearance and at times the reality of equality, of "equal justice under law." It served as a safety valve. But it should be realized that the judicial revolution, and thus the change in the formal law of the Constitution, was merely one part of a more profound social revolution. A cultural change has taken place during the past few decades. A permissive society, at times helped by the Court, has come into being: a drug culture has blossomed; the most flagrant pornography is no longer outlawed; alcohol consumption has escalated; abortions have become routine; and freedom of expression receives the highest degree of protection in American history. At the very time that additional controls are being placed upon human activity, some personal freedoms are not only permitted, they are encouraged.[94]

The basic function of all of this, it seems to me, should be determined. All political and social phenomena have definite functions; they facilitate the adaptation of a system or regime to changing conditions. Judicial decisions are political epiphenomena, and courts are instruments of politics both in their law-making proclivities and in the fact that they often are the targets of interest groups. The judiciary's main function is to produce decisions that are not only system-maintaining but system-develop-

---

92. Bernstein, *The New Deal: The Conservative Achievements of Liberal Reform,* in Towards A New Past 264-65 (B. Bernstein ed. 1963).

93. C. Macpherson, The Real World of Democracy 14 (1966).

94. One is hard pressed to find *any* Supreme Court decision upholding personal freedoms when *important* societal matters are at issue. In other words, freedoms are honored under the constitutional order when their exercise makes little or no difference. The *locus classicus* for that proposition is perhaps United States v. O'Brien, 391 U.S. 367 (1968) (upholding the conviction of a man for publicly burning his draft card as a protest against the Vietnam war). *See* Schwartz, *supra* note 13, at 683-85, 728. I have suggested elsewhere that, in Auguste Comte's phrase, the United States is moving toward a condition of "popular dictatorship with freedom of expression." *See* A. Miller, Democratic Dictatorship: The Emergent Constitution of Control 7 & *passim* (1981) (citing A. Comte, System of Positive Policy (1851)).

ing. Any political order requires both stability and a process of orderly change.

Judges facilitate both elements. They buttress the constitutional order—the "system"—by making incremental changes to reflect societal conditions. Earl Warren was, first and foremost, a member of the Establishment. But he was one who saw more clearly than others that there must be some play in the constitutional (and thus, the social) joints if the system is to endure. To repeat the example noted earlier, by 1953, when Warren became Chief Justice, the assault against the caste system of the United States that separated people by skin color had become a moral imperative of the Constitution. Thus, by aiding black Americans insofar as the Court could, benefits accrued not only to blacks but to the nation as a whole.

IV. CONCLUSION

There is much more, of course, to the concept of social justice, and there is much more to be said in analyzing the work of the Warren Court. This, however, is only a preliminary paper. Professor Schwartz has given us a remarkable amount of data to further our understanding of the High Bench, and he has pointed in the direction of even greater understanding by his numerous interviews and his perusal of the collected papers of some of the Justices.

In many respects his very propensity for detail, accompanied by his failure to erect an organizing principle or set of principles for the "Super Chief," dulls and blurs his effort. By treating the Warren Court chronologically rather than by substantive areas of concern (first amendment, national security, and the like), Schwartz's revelations about the internal dynamics of the Court become, through sheer repetition, boring. We know something about what happened regarding a number of the cases, but has he told the complete story? That is doubtful, simply because no one can really learn everything that took place in the resolution of any given case that the Court decided.

Schwartz's findings, furthermore, will occasion no surprise in any experienced Court-watcher. Only the incurably idealistic or naive person will find anything in *Super Chief* that shocks or unduly disturbs. His book will not change the minds, the attitudes, or the habits of those who edit coursebooks in constitutional law or write textbooks, either about the entire subject or a segment thereof. Those worthies will continue their solemn ways, following the "wisdom" of Marshall and Blackstone set forth at the beginning of this essay, which ultimately means that "constitutional theory, including the theory of judicial review, has come to a dead end."[95] The great merit of Schwartz's *Super Chief* is that it, with several other studies, can provide the factual basis for a new theory, of which, unfortunately, there is presently little evidence of serious thought.

---

95. A. MILLER, TOWARD INCREASED JUDICIAL ACTIVISM: THE POLITICAL ROLE OF THE SUPREME COURT *xi* (1982).

CHAPTER **6**

The Constitutional Challenge of Nuclear Weapons

What is the legal status of nuclear weapons? What should it be? Is their use unlawful? The questions have seldom been asked. In recent years, however, a number of international lawyers have begun a dialogue that features some of them contending that the ultimate weapon is unlawful under the tenets of international law.

But what of American constitutional law? Is there lurking somewhere in the interstices of the Constitution principles or concepts that are relevant in answering that question? Chapter 6 is a preliminary (pioneering) analysis of that question. In it, I argue that the very existence of nuclear weapons poses a clear and present danger to time-honored constitutional values, so much so that they should be considered to be unlawful. At the very least, their existence imposes a duty on the responsible officers of American government to take action designed to eliminate all nuclear weapons throughout the world. The essay is emphatically not a plea for unilateral disarmament. Rather, it is an argument that the new social milieu created by the advent of nuclear weaponry created a situation where established rules of warfare no longer are relevant—and where constitutional principles must be reexamined in the light of the ultimate peril.

The basic argument is a logical extension of due process principles: The American people are so threatened in their lives, liberty, and property that the very existence (and ever more probable use) of nuclear weapons constitutes an "anticipatory breach" of the due process clause of the Fifth Amendment. Anticipatory breach is a new theory of constitutional interpretation, but is is less a sharp break with the past than a necessary addition to past due process doctrine. Reason of state (see Chapter 3), therefore, can no longer be a viable principle of governance when there is any possibility of the employment of nuclear weapons. When the fate of the earth literally hangs in the balance when decisions are made about nuclear weapons systems and their use, ancient ideas of governance must be rethought and applied to new situations. No more portentous constitutional question exists today.

I. INTRODUCTION

"The doctrines which best repay critical examination," Alfred North Whitehead once observed, "are those which for the longest period have remained unquestioned."[1] Since the first relatively primitive atomic bombs all but obliterated Hiroshima and Nagasaki in August 1945, almost no lawyer — and to my knowledge no constitutional lawyer — has questioned the "doctrine" that a nation-state may employ such weapons, in its absolute discretion in warfare. That doctrine is applicable even to the exponentially more powerful hydrogen bombs. The time has come — indeed, it is long past — to examine that doctrine critically, not only under the precepts of international law — the focus of other contributions in this symposium — but under the command of the United States Constitution. These comments are a tentative probe in that direction. My principal conclusion is that the very existence of thermo-nuclear weapons in ever-increasing numbers poses such a threat to the life, liberty and property of everyone in the United States, that it should be considered a violation of the Constitution.

This article, then, is a probe into legal *terra incognita*, predicated on the belief that Einstein was wholly correct when he maintained that the existence of nuclear weapons must cause humans to change their "modes of thinking."[2] In briefest terms, I argue herein for development of a concept of "anticipatory taking" or "anticipatory deprivation," analogous to, but of course not the same as, anticipatory breach in contract law; and I argue that nuclear weapons present a clear and present danger to dem-

---

1. A. WHITEHEAD, ADVENTURES OF IDEAS (1933), *quoted in* Miller, *A Note on the Criticism of Supreme Court Decisions*, 10 J. PUB. L. 139 (1961).
2. J. SCHELL, THE FATE OF THE EARTH (1982) [hereinafter cited as SCHELL].

This chapter was originally published under the title of "The Constitutional Challenge of Nuclear Weapons: A Note on the Obligation to Ward Off Extinction" in 9 Brooklyn Journal of International Law 317 (1983).

ocratic society and the constitutional objective.[3]

What follows has three main parts: (a) a summary of additional constitutional arguments about nuclear weapons published elsewhere;[4] (b) the concept of "anticipatory taking" or "deprivation" contrary to the fifth amendment; and (c) an argument that the existence of the "National Security State," which has nuclear weapons high on the list of available means of contesting an enemy nation-state, so undermines the premises of democracy that democracy is seriously threatened. In sum, I maintain that it is far from foolish to say that law and lawyers have something useful to contribute to the growing debate over nuclear war.[5]

I do not, of course, expect ready agreement on either my specific arguments, herein and elsewhere, or the general view that basic principles of American constitutionalism are seriously endangered by the existence of 50,000 nuclear warheads throughout the world and their possible, indeed increasingly probable, use. Lawyers usually fly backwards to see where they have been, in an effort to locate an applicable precedent or analogy, and do little or nothing to anticipate the future. Nothing is a problem for the lawyer until it exists in fact and can be dealt with pragmatically. Nuclear bombs call for a change in the way that lawyers think: parsing past decisions of courts or trying to plumb the minds of the Founding Fathers simply will not do. There are no precedents and those who wrote the Constitution, in effect, told succeeding generations of Americans to solve their own problems.[6]

There is, furthermore, a danger in referring to the Constitution of the United States only. After all, other nations — principally the U.S.S.R. — also have enormous stockpiles of nuclear weapons. As a totalitarian nation, the U.S.S.R. is not subjected

---

3. The concept of constitutionalism, as distinguished from the Constitution as a legal document, has been little explored by the legal profession. *See,* however, essays collected in NOMOS XX: CONSTITUTIONALISM (J. Pennock & J. Chapman eds. 1979), particularly Grey, *Constitutionalism: An Analytical Framework, id.* at 189. *See also* the works cited in notes 77-78 *infra.*

4. Miller, *Nuclear Weapons and Constitutional Law,* 7 NOVA L.J. 21 (1982).

5. A. Whitehead has stated: "[A]lmost all really new ideas have a certain aspect of foolishness when they are first presented." A. BRECHT, POLITICAL THEORY: THE FOUNDATIONS OF TWENTIETH-CENTURY POLITICAL THOUGHT 262 (1959).

6. I have explored this proposition in TOWARD INCREASED JUDICIAL ACTIVISM: THE POLITICAL ROLE OF THE SUPREME COURT (1982) [hereinafter cited as MILLER, JUDICIAL ACTIVISM].

to the type of internal criticism that the United States routinely receives. I emphasize, therefore, that this paper is not a plea for unilateral disarmament. I believe that *all* nuclear weapons should be destroyed, but that can only come on a multilateral basis. Multilateralism merely complicates the problem; it does not eliminate it. Consistent with George Kennan, my purpose is to assert that people the world over are growing "increasingly exasperated" at their governmental leaders' inability and unwillingness to take measures adequate to deal with the nuclear threat.[7] There are, moreover, limits to law as a principle of social order. No one can validly believe that law, however and by whomever enunciated, is the sole means of social control; it probably is not even the principal such means. Law must take its place among other techniques.[8] That, however, does not mean that law is useless. My position is that it is incumbent upon people everywhere, and especially those in the legal profession, to help mankind from dropping into the abyss of extinction.

A few final words by way of introduction: (a) even though it has faults, Jonathan Schell's *The Fate of the Earth,*[9] is a book that should be pondered by all who care about the fate of *Homo sapiens* (and only saints and fools do not); (b) there is no such thing as a "limited" nuclear war, for sooner or later it will escalate into an all-out conflict; (c) the living will envy the dead should a nuclear war break out; (d) so-called "conventional" weapons have become so horrific that their employment, in World Wars I and II and since 1945, clearly indicates that they, too, are major problems — less than nuclear weaponry only because, contrary to H-bombs, they threaten limited areas and can be confined in space and time; and (e) some of the present concern about the nuclear threat appears to come from people who in ordinary or conventional wars would be immune, or almost so, from danger. In this connection, I make specific reference to the "born-again" opponents of a nuclear first strike, McGeorge Bundy, George Kennan, Gerard Smith, and Robert McNamara; these worthies have published a widely publicized article in *Foreign Affairs* calling upon the United States to renounce a "first

---

7. Kennan, *On Nuclear War*, N.Y. Rev., Jan. 21, 1982, at 8 [hereinafter cited as Kennan].

8. For further discussion, see I. JENKINS, SOCIAL ORDER AND THE LIMITS OF LAW (1980).

9. SCHELL, *supra* note 2.

strike" use of nuclear weapons.[10] At the same time, these Eminent Members of the Establishment (EMEs) advocate beefing up our conventional weapons. Now, what is to be made of that? First, all should welcome the born-again opponents of nuclear war. Second, the EMEs, at least two of whom were among the architects of disaster in Vietnam and all of whom have had a part in the development of American nuclear policy,[11] make one think that it is only when *their* oxen are gored that they care about spending the treasure and blood of others. I am reminded of how the opposition to Vietnam escalated when the manpower pool of the poor and disadvantaged had been almost depleted and the military services were beginning to think in terms of drafting middle-class American youths. The EMEs know that nuclear war will in all likelihood be in *their* own backyards — and that, as Samuel Johnson said in a different but analogous context, does tend powerfully to concentrate a person's mind.

II.   THE RELEVANCE OF THE CONSTITUTION

As mentioned above, I have argued elsewhere that the Constitution is relevant to the nuclear problem. This section summarizes those arguments.

To analyze the concept that nuclear weapons are unlawful under constitutional law, and perhaps under international law, one is required to start with the knowledge that law has always been "instrumental"; it is telocratic, rather than nomocratic.[12] Rather than a body of fixed pre-existing immutable principles, it is goal-seeking, purposive, a type of human activity that exists for identifiable ends. Furthermore, constitutional law is always relative to circumstances and thus constantly in a state of "becoming."[13] Law helps to achieve internal order and external security.

Nuclear weapons endanger both national survival and democratic values. Senator J.W. Fulbright, then chairman of the

---

10. Bundy, Kennan, McNamara & Smith, *Nuclear Weapons and the Atlantic Alliance,* 60 FOR. AFF. 753 (1982).

11. Bundy was a national security advisor to Presidents Kennedy and Johnson, McNamara was Secretary of Defense. Both had a leading role in the Vietnam disaster.

12. For a discussion of law as an instrumental concept, *see* M. HORWITZ, THE TRANSFORMATION OF AMERICAN LAW, 1780-1860 (1977).

13. On constitutional relativity, *see* A. MILLER, DEMOCRATIC DICTATORSHIP: THE EMERGENT CONSTITUTION OF CONTROL (1981) [hereinafter cited as MILLER, DEMOCRATIC DICTATORSHIP]; Miller, *Reason of State and the Emergent Constitution of Control,* 64 MINN. L. REV. 585 (1980) [hereinafter cited as Miller, *Reason of State*].

Senate Foreign Relations Committee, stated in 1967:

> [B]y acquiring the authority to commit the country to war, [the President] now exercises something approaching absolute power over the life or death of every American — to say nothing of millions of other people all over the world. . . . No human being or group [is] wise and competent enough to be entrusted with such vast power. Plenary powers in the hand of any man or group *threaten all* other men with *tyranny* or *disaster*.[14]

So it does — whether the power resides in the Kremlin or the White House. Karl von Clausewitz's oft-quoted statement about war being diplomacy carried on by other means[15] may well have been accurate when made early in the nineteenth century. Unleashing the atom has invalidated it, and presents the challenge to law and lawyers.

The texts discussed in this section come from Justice Felix Frankfurter, who maintained in 1949 that "[i]t is of the very nature of a free society to advance in its standards of what is reasonable and right";[16] and from Leon Duguit: "Any system of public law can be vital only so far as it is based on a given sanction to the following rules: First, the holders of power cannot do certain things; second, there are certain things they must do."[17] I contend that it is "reasonable and right" to hold governmental officers to a constitutional duty to eliminate nuclear weapons; they "cannot" continue the madness of the present arms program and they "must" take steps to achieve complete nuclear disarmament. International law merges with constitutional law to proscribe use of nuclear weapons. Once that is seen, then it goes without saying that their manufacture and deployment are also outlawed. In essence, my argument is that the existence of nuclear weapons places a duty upon those who wield both formal authority and effective control in America to ensure that multilateral action is taken to stop production of and to destroy existing nuclear arsenals. That duty is of constitutional dimension; it is one to initiate and carry through negotiations with other nuclear powers to eradicate the growing threat.

---

14. NATIONAL COMMITMENTS, S. REP. No. 797, 90th Cong., 1st Sess. 26 (1967), *noted in* Fried, *War-Exclusive and War-Inclusive Style in International Conduct*, 11 TEXAS INT'L L.J. 26 (1967).

15. K. VON CLAUSEWITZ, 1 ON WAR 23 (1966).

16. Wolf v. Colorado, 338 U.S. 25, 27 (1949).

17. L. DUGUIT, LAW IN THE MODERN STATE 26 (H. Laski trans. 1919).

Certainly those who drafted the Constitution did not intend that government officers have the power *in their own discretion* to make human life itself extinct. They wrote a document designed, as Chief Justice John Marshall said in 1819, "to endure for ages to come and, consequently, to be adapted to the various crises of human affairs."[18] The ultimate "crisis of human affairs" is now hard upon us: the editors of the *Bulletin of Atomic Scientists* recently moved their "doomsday clock" from seven minutes to midnight to four minutes to midnight — three minutes closer, that is, to nuclear holocaust.[19]

The Constitution's purpose is set forth in its preamble: "to form a more perfect union, establish justice, ensure democratic tranquility, provide for the common defense, promote the general welfare, and secure the blessings of liberty to ourselves and our posterity."[20] Nuclear weapons jeopardize each of these goals; and nuclear war would eliminate them. Surely the Framers could not have contemplated such a result either for themselves or their posterity. We are that posterity. The preamble has never before been given substantive content, to be sure, but the time has come to do so. Posterity has its claims under the Constitution. Furthermore, since today's extremely rapid rate of social change, produced by science and technology, means that most people alive today are their own posterity, the preamble's importance readily becomes evident. Those who ask: "What has posterity done for me?" would do well to remember that they are their own posterity.

In 1810 Chief Justice Marshall invoked the first "principles of natural justice and social policy" to invalidate a Georgia statute, maintaining that Georgia was restrained "either by general principles which are common to our free institutions, or by the particular provisions of the Constitution."[21] The shorthand label for those principles is "natural law," a theory that has greatest currency among Roman Catholic jurists.[22] The Supreme Court has never been reluctant to employ natural-law principles, al-

---

18. McCulloch v. Maryland, 17 U.S. (4 Wheat.) 316, 415 (1819). *See also* E. CORWIN, THE CONSTITUTION AND WHAT IT MEANS TODAY, 2 (H. Chase & C. Ducat rev. 13th ed. 1973), "[The Constitution] should be interpreted in the light of present conditions and with a view to meeting present problems."

19. BULL. ATOMIC SCIENTISTS, Jan. 1982.

20. U.S. CONST. preamble.

21. Fletcher v. Peck, 10 U.S. (6 Cranch) 87 (1810).

22. On the relation between natural law and legal ideology, *see* J. SHKLAR, LEGALISM 64-88 (1964) [hereinafter cited as SHKLAR].

though the Justices uniformly have clothed their decisions in language more palatable to lawyers.[23] The Court has shoehorned "natural law" into Marshall's "particular provisions of the Constitution" — in the Georgia case, the obligation-of-contracts clause.

One need not rely on only the preamble of the Constitution to conclude that nuclear weaponry should be considered a constitutional violation. Several other arguments support this conclusion. First, by delegating, tacitly or expressly, warmaking powers to the president, Congress has given up one of its greatest powers. Even though presidents since George Washington have employed violence without congressional approval,[24] each instance, even including the Civil War and the Vietnam conflict, was for a limited goal. Certainly the Framers did not want the blood and wealth of the nation to be committed to one person. Elbridge Gerry observed during the 1787 Convention that he "never expected to hear in a republic a motion to empower the Executive alone to declare war."[25] In constitutional terms, that is an invalid delegation of congressional power to the president. Saying this does not mean that presidents cannot and should not *respond* to attack without resort to Congress. At the very least, however, it requires that first-strike use of nuclear weapons be forsworn.

Second, the Bill of Rights was an effort to place restrictions on government and to "oblige" it, in Madison's terminology, to "control itself."[26] The Bill was a recognition that "reasons of freedom and personal security" were on par with, or perhaps superior to, "reasons of state."[27] The men who wrote the Constitution were not naive; they knew history and they knew the dark side of man.[28] The point is that today there can be no true *personal* security and no real *national* security as long as nuclear

---

23. *See, e.g.*, Griswold v. Connecticut, 381 U.S. 479, 486 (1965) (Goldberg, J., concurring).

24. For a discussion of separation of powers in the context of United States foreign policy, *see* A. SOFAER, WAR, FOREIGN AFFAIRS AND CONSTITUTIONAL POWER: THE ORIGINS (1976) [hereinafter cited as SOFAER]; Scigliano, *The War Powers Resolution and the War Powers*, in THE PRESIDENCY IN THE CONSTITUTIONAL ORDER 115 (J. Bessette & J. Tullis eds. 1981). An example of express delegation of such powers is found in the War Powers Resolution of 1973, 87 Stat. 555, Pub. L. No. 93-148, 93d Cong. (H.R. Res. 542, adopted over a presidential veto on Nov. 7, 1973).

25. SOFAER, *supra* note 24, at 31.

26. THE FEDERALIST No. 51 (J. Madison) (C. Beard ed. 1948).

27. *See* MILLER, DEMOCRATIC DICTATORSHIP, *supra* note 13.

28. *See* A. LOVEJOY, REFLECTIONS ON HUMAN NATURE 15 (1961).

weapons exist and proliferate.

Third, Congress should not be permitted to refuse or neglect to exercise any of its powers. War-making has already been mentioned. Another is the authority — the duty — to punish offenses against "the law of nations."[29] International law proscribes nuclear weaponry;[30] and Congress has a constitutional duty to implement that legal norm.[31] It is, for example, generally agreed — although of course not entirely adhered to — that nuclear testing on the high seas is illegal.[32] No nation has a right to pollute the seas or the air.[33] That points out the lunacy of the present situation: it is unlawful to pollute, but political officers maintain that it is lawful to obliterate cities, and even civilizations. In 1887, the Supreme Court ruled that international law places a duty on every government to prevent a wrong from being done within its own jurisdiction to another nation, or to the people thereof, with which it is at peace.[34] No doubt this one case is scant precedent, as lawyers understand precedent, to conclude that Congress is duty-bound to determine and enforce international law concerning nuclear weapons. Nevertheless, Congress cannot escape the hard fact that, as some international lawyers maintain, "any threat or contemplated use of nuclear weapons is contrary to the dictates of international law and constitutes a crime of state."[35] Or, as the United Nations has repeatedly said, the threat or use of nuclear weapons is a "crime against mankind and civilization."[36]

Fourth, the president, too, has a constitutional duty — an

---

29. RESTATEMENT (TENT. DRAFT NO. 2) OF FOREIGN RELATIONS LAW OF THE UNITED STATES § 404 (1980).

30. Falk, Meyrowitz & Sanderson, *Nuclear Weapons and International Law* 78 (1981) Occasional Paper No. 10, World Order Studies Program, Center of International Studies, Princeton University [hereinafter cited as Falk, Meyrowitz & Sanderson].

31. The Paquete Habana, 175 U.S. 677, 700 (1900) ("International law is part of our law").

32. Tiewul, *International Law and Nuclear Test Explosions on the High Seas*, 8 CORNELL INT'L L.J. 45 (1974).

33. *Id.*

34. United States v. Arjona, 120 U.S. 479, 484 (1887). There is nothing in The Antelope, 23 U.S. 66 (1825) to the contrary. That the *Arjona* principle is not a dead-letter may be seen in its employment by the Supreme Court in *Ex parte* Quirin, 317 U.S. 1 (1942) and *In Re* Yamashita, 327 U.S. 1 (1946).

35. Falk, Meyrowitz & Sanderson, *supra* note 30. *See also* Fried, *Law and Nuclear War*, BULL. ATOMIC SCIENTISTS, June/July 1982, p. 67; Meyrowitz, *Nuclear Weapons are Illegal*, 2 CALIF. LAW. at 12 (April 1982); *Law Panel Sees Atom Arms as Illegal*, N.Y. Times June 7, 1982, § 2 at 2, col. 1.

36. *See* Falk, Meyrowitz & Sanderson, *supra* note 30.

express duty — to execute the laws faithfully.[37] Surely those laws include more than congressional statutes. Arguably, the judge-made laws of the Supreme Court and, of greater present significance, international laws, must also be faithfully executed.[38] And to "execute" them, as Senator Sam Ervin often reminded executive officials, means to implement, not kill, them. Furthermore, the president should not be permitted to delegate his war-making power — even if it is invalid, as suggested above — to subordinates in the military services and even, as has been horrifyingly all too true on a number of occasions, to the vagaries of computers interpreting radar messages.

Fifth, the Constitution protects individuals against deprivation of life, liberty and property without due process of law.[39] Historically, due process meant due procedure, but in the late nineteenth century, a substantive dimension was found by the Supreme Court. Emergent today is a third dimension to due process: *affirmative* due process.[40] As Chief Justice Charles Evans Hughes opined in 1937, the liberty safeguarded by the Constitution is "liberty in a social organization which requires the protection of law against the evils which menace the health, safety, morals and welfare of the people."[41] The meaning of that pregnant statement is clear: due process can be construed to *require* government action, affirmative government action, to protect the people. Protection, at a time when all thoughtful people concede that nuclear war cannot be won, means positive action to diminish or eliminate the likelihood of war.

My suggestion in this section, in sum, is that the Constitution imposes duties as well as confers powers upon government officers. I do not say that the Supreme Court will leap to confront the challenge of pending nuclear doom. Judges, in general,

---

37. U.S. CONST. art. 1, § 3. That the President is selective in enforcement is common knowledge. Congress may propose but the Executive disposes; when the President or an executive officer does not do something, there is little that anyone can do. *But see* National Treasury Employees Union v. Nixon, 492 F.2d 587 (D.C. Cir. 1974). Recent Presidents even go to the extent of contesting in court the constitutionality of federal statutes. For a discussion of these challenges, *see* Miller & Bowman, *Presidential Attacks on the Constitutionality of Federal Statutes: A New Separation of Powers Problem*, 40 OHIO STATE L.J. 51 (1979).

38. *Cf.* MILLER, JUDICIAL ACTIVISM, *supra* note 6, at ch. 5.

39. U.S. CONST. amends. V & XIV.

40. *See* Miller, *An Affirmative Thrust to Due Process of Law?*, 30 GEO. WASH. L. REV. 399 (1962).

41. West Coast Hotel Corp. v. Parrish, 300 U.S. 379, 391 (1937), *discussed in* Miller, *Toward a Concept of Constitutional Duty*, 1968 SUP. CT. REV. 199.

are timorous officers of government, looking upon opportunities to go beyond the familiar and the expected as frightful occasions.[42]

Judges, however, are not the only guardians of the Constitution. So are all governmental officials, including attorneys. As for lawyers, who take pride in being "officers of the court" — having, that is, quasi-governmental status — the need is obvious. They should, indeed, they must, help devise means by which the world can peacefully settle issues that historically were determined by war. Failure to do so would be the ultimate folly. A freeze or an elimination of nuclear weapons must be accomplished by a simultaneous unfreezing of the rigidity of the governments of the world so that they can begin to deal rationally with human survival.

III. ANTICIPATORY BREACH OF THE FIFTH AMENDMENT

Extraordinary conditions call for extraordinary actions. We cannot escape the past, but today's future is not merely an extension of what has transpired before. The production and proliferation of nuclear weapons has led not only all Americans but all of humankind into a "fearful trap."[43] In this section I propose to explore a new concept — that of anticipatory breach of the fifth amendment's due process[44] and taking clauses.[45] As with the arguments set forth in Section II above, this is a suggestion for the direction that constitutional law should take, rather than a statement of what the present law is.

We have become accustomed in recent years to "inverse condemnation," a constitutional violation which refers, in general, to government-placed restrictions on the use of one's property that denies him its value. To remedy that constitutional violation, one must be compensated.[46] I propose to take that concept one step further and argue that the danger created by

---

42. SHKLAR, *supra* note 22, at 101-02.

43. Kennan, *supra* note 7.

44. The due process clause of the fifth amendment requires that no person "be deprived of life, liberty, or property, without due process of law . . . ." U.S. CONST. amend. V, cl. 4.

45. The taking clause of the fifth amendment mandates: "[N]or shall private property be taken for public use, without just compensation." U.S. CONST. amend. V, cl. 5.

46. Inverse condemnation is "a shorthand description of the manner in which a landowner receives just compensation for taking of his property when condemnation proceedings have not been instituted [by the government]." Agins v. Tiburon, 477 U.S. 255, 258 n.2, *quoting* United States v. Clarke, 445 U.S. 253, 257 (1980).

nuclear weapons is so gross and so debilitating to the welfare of all Americans that it deprives individuals of their personal rights and psychological well-being. This danger refers to their lives and their liberties, as well as their property. There is a "taking" of the right set forth in the Declaration of Independence,[47] but omitted from the Constitution of 1787, to the "pursuit of happiness." I realize that this adds a new dimension to due process of law and the law of eminent domain; I also fully realize that the "pursuit of happiness" has never been given substantive content by the Supreme Court, although the term is mentioned repeatedly in the *United States Reports.*[48] To employ the words of Chief Justice Hughes, just as liberty "requires the protection of law against the evils which menace the health, safety, morals and welfare of the people,"[49] so too it requires the recognition that the government violates the fifth amendment when it carries out its policy of pursuing an endless arms "race." In 1950, Justice Felix Frankfurter remarked:

> It is now settled doctrine that the that the Due Process Clause embodies a system of rights based on moral principles so deeply embedded in the traditions and feelings of our people as to be deemed fundamental to a civilized society as conceived by our whole history. Due Process is that which comports with the deepest notions of what is fair and right and just.[50]

Although Frankfurter's notions of what is "fair and right and just" were not always in accord with those of his colleagues,[51] his statement cannot be faulted as a general proposition. Justice Holmes' assertion in *Lochner v. New York,*[52] established that "[g]eneral propositions do not decide concrete cases."[53] However, there can be no meaningful thought without general ideas. "[W]ithout the use of concepts and general principles we can have no science, or intelligible systematic account, of the law or

---

47. Declaration of Independence, para. 1 (U.S. 1776).

48. According to a recent Juris search, "pursuit of happiness" is mentioned 65 times in 51 decisions.

49. West Coast Hotel Co. v. Parrish, 300 U.S. 379, 391 (1937).

50. Solesbee v. Balkcom, 339 U.S. 9, 16 (1950) (Frankfurter, J., dissenting). Frankfurter chose not to divulge how he ascertained those "deepest notions of what is fair and right and just." *Compare* his concurring opinion in Louisiana *ex rel.* Francis v. Resweber, 329 U.S. 459 (1947) (Frankfurter, J., concurring).

51. *Compare* Frankfurter's dissenting opinion in *Solesbee,* 339 U.S. 9, 16 (1950), with the majority opinion therein, 339 U.S. at 9-14.

52. 198 U.S. 45 (1905) (Holmes, J., dissenting).

53. *Id.* at 76.

of any other field. And the demand for system in the law is urgent not only on theoretical but also on practical grounds. Without general ideas, human experience is dumb as well as blind."[54]

The "moral principle" involved in the existence and probable use of nuclear weapons is this: American citizens — and indeed, people the world over — have a right to be free from both the *immediate* and *potential* effects of nuclear weaponry upon the body politic.[55] I take that classification from *Carolina Environmental Study Group, Inc. v. United States Atomic Energy Commission*,[56] a decision which, although overruled by the Supreme Court, nonetheless enumerates the immediate and potential effects of nuclear power better than any other decision. True enough, the question there was the validity of the so-called Price-Anderson Act,[57] which limits liability for explosions in nuclear power plants. I should like to adapt Judge McMillan's opinion to the question of nuclear weaponry.[58] Once done, it will be seen that the combination of the immediate and potential effect of such weapons constitutes a deprivation of due process of law.

As for the immediate effects, it can surely be said that the storage of bombs and nuclear waste has posed insoluble problems of safety. This is particularly true with regard to waste material with which no one really knows what to do. However, the danger posed is not limited to the present problem of nuclear waste. It is the future that is far more grim. There is mounting evidence, from qualified experts, of the growing likelihood of nuclear war. Jonathan Schell has detailed that evidence in *The Fate of the Earth*.[59] And should a nuclear war erupt, there is no possible way that civilization, as we know it, can survive. It can, for example, be forecast with precision that American health systems simply could not cope with nuclear casualties.[60]

---

54. M. Cohen, Reason and Law 63 (1950).

55. For some of the immediate effects, *see infra* text accompanying notes 75-96.

56. 431 F. Supp. 203 (W.D.N.C. 1977), *rev'd sub nom.* Duke Power Co. v. Carolina Environmental Study Group, Inc., 438 U.S. 59 (1978).

57. *Id.* at 204-06.

58. *See infra* notes 62-64 and accompanying text.

59. Schell, *supra* note 2.

60. There is an increasing amount of literature on the medical aspects of nuclear weaponry. *E.g.,* Kerzner, *The Last Epidemic,* Miami Herald, Mar. 6, 1982, at E1: "Nuclear war could be the last epidemic our civilization will know. Hundreds of millions of people would be killed or injured, and the economic, ecological and social fabric on which

This is not the time nor the place to repeat what has been published elsewhere at great length. My point is strictly legal. The following conclusions seem to be inescapable:

First, either by design or by accident, there is a high probability of nuclear war.

Second, there is no escape from the impact of nuclear war.

Third, there is no possible way that civil defense measures can protect the residents of any city in the United States.

Fourth, the risks involved in the use of the nuclear weaponry are not those which a responsible government places upon its citizens.

Once these conclusions are accepted — as they have been by a growing number of people, probably by a majority — then it can clearly be seen that, to use Judge McMillan's language, the existence of nuclear weapons violates the due process clause because it facilitates "the destruction of the property or the lives of those affected by nuclear catastrophe without reasonable certainty that the victims will be justly compensated."[61] In short, there is an anticipatory taking of life, liberty and property, an anticipatory breach of the due process clause.

I hasten to add the obvious: the Supreme Court, in its infinite wisdom, unanimously reversed Judge McMillan's decision.[62] Where then, does that leave us? I think that we are left precisely where the plaintiffs were left on March 31, 1977, when Judge McMillan issued his opinion. The Supreme Court's reversal should not and cannot be extended to the issue of nuclear weapons. Chief Justice Warren Burger, in his opinion for the Court, employed a limited standard of review — in determining whether, as an economic regulation, the Price-Anderson Act was arbitrary or irrational — and he had no difficulty in holding that the Act "passes constitutional muster."[63] Burger also relied heavily upon "an explicit congressional commitment to take further action to aid victims of a nuclear accident in the event that the $560 million ceiling on liability [was] exceeded."[64] Under no

---

human life depends would be shattered." *See also* A. KATZ, LIFE AFTER NUCLEAR WAR: THE ECONOMIC AND SOCIAL IMPACTS OF NUCLEAR ATTACKS ON THE UNITED STATES (1982).

61. Carolina Environmental Study Group v. United States Atomic Energy Commission, 431 F. Supp. at 222.

62. Duke Power Co. v. Carolina Environmental Study Group, Inc., 438 U.S. 59 (1978).

63. *Id.* at 84.

64. *Id.* at 93.

conceivable set of circumstances can Burger's "reasoning" be extended to apply, not to accidents at nuclear power plants, but to nuclear war itself. The differences between these two factual circumstances are far more than ones of degree; they are ones of type. The American people have a constitutional right to be free from the ultimate peril of nuclear devastation.

Can there, however, be a legal norm — a right — absent a means of enforcement? That is the jurisprudential question posed by the assertion that there is a constitutional right to be free from nuclear war. On one level, of course, there can be no right without a remedy.[65] That, however, cannot stop the inquiry into the applicability of constitutional precepts to the nuclear weapons question. Recall, in this regard, what Chief Justice Marshall said in *Marbury v. Madison*:[66] he admitted that Marbury had a right to his position as a justice of the peace but then went on to deny him a remedy — not because of any fault of Marbury, but because Congress had unconstitutionally tried to enlarge the original jurisdiction of the Supreme Court. The answer, thus, is that some rights do exist without remedies. Witness, furthermore, the recent decisions of the Supreme Court which recognized a right of privacy as protected by the Constitution,[67] a right to travel,[68] a right to be free from invidious racial discrimination,[69] a right to have one's vote count as much as anyone else's in a given jurisdiction,[70] a right of corporations to speak on non-business-related electoral questions,[71] not to mention the blinding flash of revelation in 1886 that led a unanimous Court to call a corporation a person within the meaning of the fourteenth amendment[72] and to create the area of substan-

---

65. The very essence of civil liberty certainly consists in the right of every individual to claim the protection of the laws, whenever he receives an injury. One of the first duties of government is to afford that protection. . . . The government of the United States has been emphatically termed a government of laws, and not of men. It will certainly cease to deserve this high appellation, if the laws furnish no remedy for the violation of a vested legal right.
Marbury v. Madison, 5 U.S. 1 (Cranch) 137, 163 (1803).

66. *Id.* at 175-80.

67. Roe v. Wade, 410 U.S. 113 (1973).

68. United States v. Guest, 383 U.S. 745 (1966).

69. Brown v. Board of Education, 347 U.S. 483 (1954); Bolling v. Sharpe, 346 U.S. 497 (1954).

70. Reynolds v. Sims, 377 U.S. 533 (1964).

71. First National Bank of Boston v. Bellotti, 435 U.S. 765 (1978).

72. Santa Clara County v. Southern Pacific Railroad Co., 118 U.S. 394 (1886). *See also* Miller, *The American Economic Constitution*, THE CENTER MAGAZINE, Vol. XV, No. 4, at 18 (1982).

tive due process.[73] The list is not endless, but it is substantial; certain rights have emerged and have been recognized by the Supreme Court which in many instances do not have a textual connection to the Constitution. "Behind the words of the constitutional provisions are postulates which limit and control."[74] One postulate underlying the Bill of Rights, and particularly the fifth amendment, is the moral principle of freedom from nuclear disaster.

IV. DEMOCRACY UNDERMINED

I do not wish to be placed in the position of using constitutional arguments as "desperate legal acrobatics."[75] Rather, my wish is to pose the constitutional question about nuclear weaponry, and to stimulate a debate — that is, to change "our modes of thinking" about law and war. The difficulties are fully realized. The question will not go away if we simply deny its existence. In this final section, I will advance the proposition that nuclear weapons threaten the very essence of constitutionalism as it has been known in the United States.

I begin with this assumption: since 1944, the United States has been waging an undeclared war — one that can validly be called World War III — against the Soviet Union. That condition has been papered over with the euphemism of "Cold War."[76] The meaning of this "war" for the United States is that

---

73. For a discussion of the advent of due process, *see* E. CORWIN, LIBERTY AGAINST GOVERNMENT (1948).

74. Principality of Monaco v. Mississippi, 292 U.S. 313, 322 (1934).

75. Levinson, Book Review, *Self-Evident Truths in the Declaration of Independence,* 57 TEX. L. REV. 847, 848 (1979). *See also* Tushnet, *Truth, Justice and the American Way: An Interpretation of Public Law Scholarship in the Seventies,* 57 TEX. L. REV. 1307 (1979).

76. *See* Kenworthy, *Reagan Rediscovers Monroe,* 2 DEMOCRACY No. 3, at 80 (July 1982), *quoting* The Committee of Santa Fe, "A New Inter-American Policy for the Eighties," (Washington, D.C. Council for Inter-American Security, 1980), to the effect that we are in the "third phase of World War III." *Id.* at 81. Without at all agreeing with that Committee's analysis of what should be done, I think it is clear beyond doubt that the U.S.-U.S.S.R. confrontation began as soon as it became clear that Hitler was defeated. Of course, the Cold War is not merely a shooting war between the two principal adversaries; it is waged on other grounds (economic, social, etc.). And when shooting starts, thus far at least, surrogates are the combatants for the U.S.S.R. (as in Korea and Vietnam). *See also* Dugger, *On to World War IV?,* THE PROGRESSIVE, June 1982, at 20.

The Cold War lasted five years, from the end of World War II to the outbreak of the Korean War. Applied to events later than mid-1950, the Cold War is a misnomer that has misled the world's population about the realities for the sporadic but very hot worldwide war — World War III — that has continued

a National Security State has been created, one in which national security is the ultimate value — a State that has statutory grounding in the National Security Act of 1947.[77] A further meaning is that nuclear war, when and if it comes, will be World War IV.

Constitutionalism in America has always been normative. As Friedrich Hayek has put it:

> [C]onstitutionalism means that all power rests on the understanding that it will be exercised according to commonly accepted principles, that the persons on whom power is conferred are selected because it is thought they are most likely to do what is right, not in order that whatever they do should be right.[78]

More tersely, Charles Howard McIlwain tells us that "[C]onstitutionalism has one essential quality; it is a legal limitation on government."[79] The fundamental value protected is "human dignity."[80] The meaning should be clear; constitutionalism in America is more than a process — more that procedure alone — it has substantive, normative content looking toward the responsibility of government to the governed. Madison said this in classic terms in *The Federalist No. 51:* "In framing a government which is to be administered by men over men, the great difficulty lies in this: you must first enable the government to control the governed; and in the next place oblige it to control itself."[81] The Constitution was framed with precisely this principle in mind. Whether the government established by the Constitution is correctly termed a "democracy" or a "republic"[82] is not

---

now for nearly a third of this century. . . . The peculiar character of World War III — battles that appear to be local — is caused by nuclear weapons. That is the only way World War III can be fought without destroying at least half the species. Even so, on a number of occasions the war could have become nuclear.

Id. at 26. (Dugger's article is an excerpt from his book entitled THE POLITICIAN: THE LIFE AND TIMES OF LYNDON JOHNSON (1982)).

77. For discussion, *see* Raskin, *Democracy versus the National Security State,* 40 LAW & CONTEMP. PROBS. 189 (1976).

78. F. HAYEK, THE CONSTITUTION OF LIBERTY 181 (1960).

79. C. MCILWAIN, CONSTITUTIONALISM: ANCIENT AND MODERN (1940). McIlwain also said: "All constitutional government is by definition limited government." *Id.* at 23.

80. Murphy, *An Ordering of Constitutional Values,* 53 S. CAL. L. REV. 703, 708 (1980).

81. THE FEDERALIST No. 51, at 225 (J. Madison) (C. Beard ed. 1948).

82. On the distinction between a democracy and a republic, *see* Koch, *Introduction to* NOTES OF DEBATES IN THE FEDERAL CONVENTION OF 1787 REPORTED BY JAMES MADISON

the point. Whatever the label, there is a definite responsibility flowing from those in political power to the electorate at large.

That there is an irreconcilable conflict between basic principles of democracy, constitutionalism and the existence of war, whether "hot" or "cold", is a proposition that needs no support. This is so even in the absence of nuclear weapons. There is a label for this, one little used in America but having wide currency in Europe: *raison d'etat* — or in English translation, *constitutional reason of state*. What is reason of state? It is "the State's first Law of motion,"[83] "the doctrine that whatever is required to insure the survival of the state must be done by the individuals responsible for it, no matter how repugnant such an act may be to them in their private capacity as decent and moral men."[84] In sum, it is the application of Machiavellian principles to the constitutional order.

I have written elsewhere that, notwithstanding the myth to the contrary, the United States has consistently followed basic Machiavellian principles.[85] Ethics are subordinated to considerations of state power. Andre Glucksmann has pointed out that reciprocal terror characterized Western culture long before the thought of nuclear weapons.[86] Surely that was true for World War II, particularly in the massive air bombardments by both the Axis and Allied Powers. Since 1945, the technological improvements in so-called conventional weapons have made them far more deadly. Reason of state is still an operative principle of the Constitution, the actual fundamental law as distinguished from the Constitution of the books.

That reason of state should no longer be, at least insofar as nuclear weapons are concerned, is the message of this section. Should nuclear war break out, political leaders simply cannot "insure the survival of the state," to say nothing of the American people themselves. These weapons, therefore, are no longer a viable option, even though American politicians still cling stub-

---

vii-xxiii (1966) (1969 paperback ed.).

83. F. Meinecke, Machiavellism: The Doctrine of Raison d'Etat and Its Place in Modern History 1 (D. Scott trans. 1957).

84. C. Friedrich, Constitutional Reason of State 4-5 (1957).

85. *See* Miller, *Reason of State, supra* note 13; A. Miller, Democratic Dictatorship, *supra* note 13.

86. A. Glucksmann, The Master Thinkers 151 (B. Pearce trans. 1980). *See* Falk, Nuclear Weapons and the End of Democracy, IFDA Dossier No. 28, at 56 (March/April 1982) (publication of the International Foundation for Development Alternatives, Nyon, Switzerland) [hereinafter cited as Falk].

bornly to the option of "first strike."

The point is that "survival of the state" is significant only if democratic values are also preserved. The problem with nuclear weapons is that their very existence "interferes with democratic government in fundamental ways."[87] We are already beginning to pay the price of a decline of the democratic principle. That a National Security State has evolved since 1947 is positive proof that democratic values are in a marasmic state. Witness, for example, the firestorm of disapproval that burst out when *The Progressive* planned to publish an article on the alleged secret of the H-bomb, using data taken entirely from the public record.[88] First amendment proscriptions were swept aside by a federal judge who ordered the censorship of the article, issuing an opinion that is still kept secret. Witness also the practice of the National Security Agency, as revealed in *Halkin v. Helms*,[89] of intercepting *everyone's* overseas telephonic and cable messages — upheld by the Court of Appeals for the District of Columbia because a "state secrets" privilege was involved.[90] One need not be deluged with examples of this phenomenon to be able to conclude that when the Supreme Court balances considerations of national security against human rights and liberties, the government *always* wins in any important matter.[91]

We delude ourselves if we think that courts are other than as described by Professor Martin Shapiro:

> No regime is likely to allow significant political power to be wielded by an isolated judicial corps free of political restraints. To the extent that courts make law, judges will be incorporated into the governing coalition, the ruling elite, the responsible representatives of the people, or however else the political regime may be expressed.[92]

---

87. *Id.* at 57.

88. The *Progressive* case in discussed in Cheh, *The Progressive and the Atomic Energy Act: Waking to the Dangers of Government Information Controls*, 48 GEO. WASH. L. REV. 163 (1980). *See also* Knoll, *National Security: The Ultimate Threat to the First Amendment*, 66 MINN. L. REV. 161 (1981).

89. 598 F.2d 1 (D.C. Cir. 1978).

90. *Id.* at 5.

91. Not even Youngstown Sheet & Tube Co. v. Sawyer, 343 U.S. 579 (1952), in which President Truman's seizure of the steel mills during the Korean War was invalidated, is to the contrary. The battle there, as Justice Black opined, was really one of separation of powers — between President and Congress — and not one of government authority to commandeer the steel mills.

92. M. SHAPIRO, COURTS: A COMPARATIVE AND POLITICAL ANALYSIS 34 (1981).

We may live under a constitution — a written constitution — which often is, as is frequently remarked, what the judges say it is; but the real point is that what the judges say is reflective of the values of the ruling elites. For those elites, democracy has become ungovernable.[93] Constitutionalism in its normative sense is dying.[94] It is a casualty of the nuclear age, although other reasons exist for its death.[95]

Democratic forms of government persist, but will increasingly be seen as an empty shell. If we wish to regain even the semblance of representative democracy, then the nuclear threat must be eliminated. That is the ultimate constitutional challenge of nuclear weapons.

V. Conclusion

There is little to be said by way of conclusion. This essay is a preliminary discussion of whether constitutional law and constitutionalism are relevant to the nuclear debate. I maintain that they are. But I must hasten to add that other factors threaten the structure of American constitutionalism.[96] What is unique about nuclear weapons is their awful and awesome power to extinguish life itself, or if not all life, then at least civilization as we know it. There is an obligation on everyone, and particularly on lawyers, to help ward off this mode of extinction.

---

93. *See* Huntington, *The United States,* in M. Crozier, S. Huntington & J. Watanuki, The Crisis of Democracy 59-118 (1975).

94. *See* Miller, *Toward a Definition of "The Constitution"* (forthcoming in the U. Dayton L. Rev.). *See also* Levinson, *"The Constitution" in American Civil Religion,* 1979 Sup. Ct. Rev. 123.

95. For example, the pressure of population on resources and the inability of the economy to stabilize itself at low inflation, high employment, improved productivity, and sustained economic growth. For discussion, *see* A. Miller, Getting There From Here: Constitutional Changes for a Sustainable Society (in progress); A. Miller, Democratic Dictatorship, *supra* note 13. *See also* Falk, *supra* note 86.

96. *See* works cited in note 95, *supra.*

CHAPTER 7

The Iranian Hostages Case:
A Political Decision
by a Political Court

When in November 1979 the United States embassy was seized by Iranian terrorists, a number of Americans were taken hostage. To counter that action, President Jimmy Carter immediately froze Iranian assets in the United States. Among them were some contracts that American companies had with the government of Iran. One of the companies, Dames & Moore, filed suit in December 1979 to be reimbursed for its losses. Before the lawsuit could be litigated, the President concluded an executive agreement with Iran for return of the hostages; as a part of that agreement (in January 1981), the Iranian assets were transferred to a special claims tribunal to arbitrate all of the monetary claims that arose from the episode. Dames & Moore promptly filed another suit, alleging that its property (its contract rights) had been taken without just compensation. The Supreme Court declined to review, saying that the case was not yet "ripe" for judicial review but also upholding the validity of the executive agreement.

"Ripeness" is a self-imposed limitation on judicial review. The decision is significant because, as Chapter 7 demonstrates, it illustrates the high degree of deference the Supreme Court accords to the President in foreign policy matters. In national security matters, the Justices in effect operate as a de facto arm of the executive. They are part of the governing coalition of the nation, never far out of phase with the avowedly political branches of government. In practical effect, this is a variation on the theme of reason of state (discussed in Chapter 3), and it bears out Alexander Hamilton's comments in Federalist No. 31: "As the duties of superintending the national defense and of securing the public peace against foreign or domestic violence involve a provision for casualties and dangers to which no possible limits can be assigned, the power of making that provision ought to know no other bounds than the exigencies of the nation and the resources of the community."

The larger meaning is that the rule of politics, not the rule of law, as the myth would have it (see Chapter 1), is controlling in constitutional adjudications. This chapter discusses a facet of this fundamental, but little recognized, principle of American governance. Although Alexis de Tocqueville could observe in 1832 that "scarcely any question arises in the United States that does not become, sooner or later, a subject of judicial debate," the point is that the Supreme Court decides those debates in accordance with the dictates of configurations of political power.

One of the central tasks of modern government is to make wise balancing choices among courses of action that pursue one or more of our many conflicting and competing objectives. —Lloyd N. Cutler[1]

INTRODUCTION

To understand the Supreme Court's decision in *Dames & Moore v. Regan,*[2] one should perceive at the outset that it is basically a compromise between harsh international reality and abstract constitutional norms. Although crafted in familiar lawyers' language, Justice William H. Rehnquist's opinion for the Court reeks with the odor of compromise forced by necessity. Principle, as usual, gave way to *realpolitik.* The Justices had, in the last analysis, no choice save to sustain the validity of President Carter's hurried deal for the release of the hostages. Invalidation of the executive agreement would have placed the prospective conduct of American foreign policy in an intolerable position. The decision, therefore, exemplifies Professor Martin Shapiro's recent comment: "No regime is likely to allow significant political power to be wielded by an isolated judicial corps free of political restraints."[3] The key word is "isolated." My suggestion is not that the Court does not wield political power, but rather that its power is employed as a constituent part of the governing coalition— in fact though not in theory an often necessary arm of the avowedly political branches of government. To paraphrase one of

---

1. Cutler, *To Form A Government,* 59 FOREIGN AFF. 126, 133 (1980).
2. 453 U.S. 654 (1981).
3. M. SHAPIRO, COURTS: A COMPARATIVE AND POLITICAL ANALYSIS 34 (1981).

This chapter was originally published under the title of "*Dames & Moore v. Regan*: A Political Decision by a Political Court" in 29 UCLA Law Review 1104 (1982).

Machiavelli's principles ("A republic or a prince should ostensibly do out of generosity what necessity constrains them to do")[4], a republic—the United States—should purport to do under the law what political necessity requires that it do. Phrased even more bluntly, *Dames & Moore* is a pure example of a political Hobson's Choice: the Justices not only had to take the first horse in Mr. Hobson's livery stable, it was the only horse there. Thus, *Dames & Moore* was also, *pace* Lloyd Cutler, a "wise" decision.

The two-pronged result, of course, is not the first—nor will it be the last—time when the realities of politics collide with seemingly clear constitutional precepts. In such instances, a form of domestic *realpolitik* almost invariably prevails.[5] The Constitution, despite contrary theory, is relative to circumstances. Government in the United States has always been precisely as strong as conditions necessitated; as perceived by those who wield effective power in the nation; surely this is the clear lesson of American history. Whether government will remain so, however, or whether it already displays definite signs of senility, is a large and important question that is beyond the scope of this Essay. Suffice it to say that Lloyd Cutler is not the first to suggest that the theory of separated powers in the national government requires re-examination and alteration.[6] My purpose in this Essay is to invite attention to what should be, but is not, obvious to all who follow and seek to understand the nuances of Supreme Court lawmaking: "the judiciary in any modern industrial society . . . is an essential part of the system of government"; its function is to underpin "the stability of that system" and to protect it by resisting "attempts to change it."[7] In slightly different terms, judges in the United States, particularly the Justices of the Supreme Court, protect the existing political order against undue change and thus shelter those who control and benefit most from it. In making that state-

---

4. N. MACHIAVELLI, THE DISCOURSES 234 (B. Crick ed. 1981). Although Machiavelli is one of the most maligned—wrongfully, in my judgment—men in Western political thought, his teachings are essential to an understanding of the development of American constitutional law. I have discussed that point in A. MILLER, DEMOCRATIC DICTATORSHIP: THE EMERGENT CONSTITUTION OF CONTROL (1981). *See also* Crick, *Introduction* to THE DISCOURSES, *supra*; Berlin, *The Originality of Machiavelli,* in STUDIES ON MACHIAVELLI 149 (M. Gilmore ed. 1972); F. MEINECKE, MACHIAVELLISM: THE DOCTRINE OF RAISON D'ETAT AND ITS PLACE IN MODERN HISTORY (D. Scott trans. 1957).

5. For discussion, see A. MILLER, *supra* note 4; Miller, *Reason of State and the Emergent Constitution of Control,* 64 MINN. L. REV. 585 (1980).

6. *See, e.g.,* A. MILLER, PRESIDENTIAL POWER IN A NUTSHELL 314-23 (1977); Phillips, *An American Parliament,* HARPER'S MAGAZINE, Nov. 1980, at 14; Phillips, *Our Obsolete System,* NEWSWEEK, Apr. 23, 1973, at 13. *Cf.* L. FISHER, THE POLITICS OF SHARED POWER: CONGRESS AND THE EXECUTIVE (1981); Levi, *Some Aspects of Separation of Powers,* 76 COLUM. L. REV. 371 (1976).

7. J. GRIFFITH, THE POLITICS OF THE JUDICIARY 213 (1977).

ment, I am of course repudiating as unrealistic and unrealizable the dogma of popular sovereignty. Since at least the first sovereign immunity decision, and probably before, that dogma has been a facade behind which the levers of power are operated by those with effective control of the nation. From this perspective, *Dames & Moore* is a decision that at once shores up the political status quo and seemingly enhances presidential power. Those two ideas are really not inconsistent, once one perceives that Congress not only does not govern, it does not want to govern.[8]

All human institutions, including the Supreme Court, have definite, ascertainable sociological functions.[9] Institutional functions are both manifest and latent.[10] The manifest function of the Court, so theory goes, is to protect individual rights and liberties against the overweening power of the State—in short, to protect the values of constitutionalism. Beneficiaries of judicial decisions are the persons, natural and artificial, who receive succor from what many assert is an undemocratic body—a "deviant" institution, as Alexander Bickel put it.[11] Those beneficiaries, particularly the ones advantaged by the civil rights/civil liberties "revolution" of the Warren Court, should be considered to be the outward or ostensible winners. Did not those well-known decisions have a much more important latent function, however, one serving hidden (or actual) beneficiaries? The answer must be "yes": succinctly, they were those who have always benefited from the "system"—the moneyed and the propertied. The civil rights/civil liberties decisions illustrate the role of the Court as a social safety-valve, bleeding off discontent by extending at least

---

8. I speak here of Congress *as an institution,* rather than of individual members who are part of the subgovernments of Washington. *See* J. SUNDQUIST, THE DECLINE AND RESURGENCE OF CONGRESS (1981) (stating that historically Congress has lacked "a will to govern."). *See also* Miller, *An Inquiry into the Relevance of the Intentions of the Founding Fathers, With Special Emphasis Upon the Doctrine of Separation of Powers,* 27 ARK. L. REV. 583 (1973). On subgovernments, *compare* D. CATER, POWER IN WASHINGTON (1964) *with* Heclo, *Issue Networks and the Executive Establishment,* in THE NEW AMERICAN POLITICAL SYSTEM 87 (A. King ed. 1978) *and* A PANEL OF THE NATIONAL ACADEMY OF PUBLIC ADMINISTRATION, A PRESIDENCY FOR THE 1980S: A REPORT ON PRESIDENTIAL MANAGEMENT (1980).

9. Their purposes are both open and obscured. The gap that exists between the formal Constitution, as interpreted by the Court, and the living or operative fundamental law illustrates how legal norms promulgated by government can often be altered by the social habits of the people—the populace's resistance even to ordered changes in the status quo. (Ordered change is not necessarily orderly; nor are official orders always followed.) There are, in sum, limits to effective legal action. *Cf.* I. JENKINS, SOCIAL ORDER AND THE LIMITS OF LAW: A THEORETICAL ESSAY (1980); R. POUND, SOCIAL CONTROL THROUGH LAW (1942).

10. This classification is taken from R. MERTON, SOCIAL THEORY AND SOCIAL STRUCTURE 115-21 (rev. ed. 1968).

11. A. BICKEL, THE LEAST DANGEROUS BRANCH 18 (1962). *See also* A. BICKEL, THE MORALITY OF CONSENT (1975).

symbolic and perhaps even concrete victories to complainants while protecting the system itself from jeopardy.[12]

Let me be very clear about this. I am saying, first, that Supreme Court decisions should be analyzed by asking and answering the question: *cui bono?,* who benefits from them?[13] Second, there are usually, perhaps always, two classes of beneficiaries—the manifest and the latent. Finally, the latent beneficiaries of civil rights/civil liberties decisions are those who profit most from the stability of the system. I am not saying that some manifest beneficiaries are not in fact advantaged by at times becoming members of the class that has always wielded effective control over the political order. Nor am I saying that the consequence labeled as a latent benefit is the product of a dark conspiracy by a hidden power elite. What I am saying is that this briefly-described system is an indubitable fact of American governance.

I.   *A POLITICAL DECISION BY A POLITICAL COURT*

Dames & Moore should be read in light of this history and analysis. Governance in the United States has been and is essentially a series of compromises forced by external circumstances, whether domestic stresses (such as economic depressions) or constraints from abroad (wars and the like). The one consistent principle of American constitutional history is Hamiltonian republicanism, Alexander Hamilton being by far the most influential of all of the Founding Fathers. Disputed matters of public policy have been settled not by rigid adherence to what at times seem to be absolute constitutional provisions, but by ad hoc political adjustments.[14] The storied Rule of Law thus in reality often is the Rule of Barter Economics.

Who benefited from the decision in *Dames & Moore?* Quite obviously, the manifest beneficiaries were the hostages and their families. But equally obviously, there were latent beneficiaries. Two points are important. First, the atmosphere of patriotic fervor accompanying the return of the hostages was caused by a palpable manipulation of mass public opinion, whipped up with the ready cooperation of the media. This signaled the beginning of the end of disquietude over the Vietnam adventure, and thus paved the way for attempts to recreate the American "empire."[15]

---

12. This point is discussed in my book, A. MILLER, TOWARD INCREASED JUDICIAL ACTIVISM: THE POLITICAL ROLE OF THE SUPREME COURT (1982).

13. This is the theme of my forthcoming book. *Id.*

14. Justice Richard Neely of the West Virginia Supreme Court of Appeals concedes this point in his recent book. R. NEELY, HOW COURTS GOVERN AMERICA (1981).

15. For discussion of the American "empire," see W. WILLIAMS, EMPIRE AS A WAY OF LIFE (1980). In final analysis, the hostages were important as propaganda

To the extent that such attempts are successful, the latent beneficiaries are those who profit most from that "empire." This leads to the second point: the decision helps those who define the axiomatic in American foreign policy. The decision means that the government, and thus the nation, stands ready to protect American lives when American property abroad is in danger. Whether the lives of the American hostages were the first priority has been doubted. The decision to freeze "was not a desire to punish Iran for taking the hostages, but fear that a sudden withdrawal of those assets might set off a major currency and banking crisis for the United States."[16] Private banks, such as Citibank and Chase, "stood to lose a lot of money if Iran repudiated its debt."[17] In sum, the hostages were mere pawns in a game of high finance and government policy. The freeze was in effect a bailout of bankers who had overextended themselves.[18] Property protection has always been axiomatic, and *Dames & Moore* reaffirms the principle. The fact that the company ostensibly lost is wholly overshadowed by the fact, left unstated by Justice Rehnquist, that the Executive (and Congress too) stands ready to serve the needs of American business abroad. That "loss," in the long run, is more likely to be a gain.

The accuracy of this analysis is attested to by the fact that the decision, although outwardly a defeat for American business interests, provoked no negative outcry. *Dames & Moore* has been accepted with equanimity. To analogize to the Sherlock Holmes tale: why didn't the dog bark?[19] Quite simply, because the American business community perceives the decision to be in both its long- and short-term interests. Not even the "crazies" from the far right (for example, those who complained bitterly about the Panama Canal "giveaway") deplore the result. The Supreme Court tapped a vein in the *zeitgeist*.[20]

In more conventional terms, *Dames & Moore* is, as Justice Rehnquist said, merely "one more episode"[21] in a process of pragmatic accommodation between the President and Congress (and the people), an episode played out in the Marble Palace because

tools for the government and for those who had extended too much credit to Iran. The fears of both public and private officials were essentially *economic* rather than *personal.* Lissakers, *Money and Manipulation,* 44 FOREIGN POLICY 107, 110 (1981).

16. *See* Lissakers, *supra* note 15, at 107.

17. *Id.* at 114.

18. *See id.* at 126.

19. A. DOYLE, *The Adventure of Silver Blaze,* in THE COMPLETE ADVENTURES AND MEMOIRS OF SHERLOCK HOLMES 172, 183-84 (1975).

20. The Court cannot stay out of phase with the dominant elements in society except on a sporadic basis. *See* M. PARENTI, DEMOCRACY FOR THE FEW 295-313 (3d ed. 1980); M. SHAPIRO, *supra* note 3.

21. Dames & Moore v. Regan, 453 U.S. at 662.

so many political problems are brought to the Justices for resolution. The meaning, of course, is that the "some sort of system of checks and balances"[22] that Rehnquist recognized is, in the final analysis, a matter of high politics larded with crude bargaining. Lawyers have a name for this: "interest balancing." Although Rehnquist did not use the expression in his opinion, he nonetheless engaged in that mental exercise, seeming to balance the interests of the United States in having only one voice in foreign affairs against a major constitutional silence—the President's discretionary power to enter into executive agreements on his own authority. Rehnquist, however, came down squarely for the protection of property.[23] From this view there could have been only one result: sustaining President Carter's authority—and also, the authority of President Reagan, who, shortly after taking office, "ratified" the actions of his predecessor.

With no precedent directly on point, the best analogy to *Dames & Moore* in Supreme Court history was neither the *Steel Seizure Case*[24] nor *United States v. Pink*[25] (both cited by Rehnquist), but *Wilson v. Girard,*[26] a decision controversial when made but now largely forgotten. *Wilson v. Girard* upheld the power of the Executive to permit through executive agreement the trial and punishment of American servicemen by foreign courts for crimes committed abroad. A brief discussion of the cases is in order.

In the well-known *Steel Seizure Case,* the Court invalidated President Truman's takeover of the nation's steel mills, an action premised on grounds of national emergency during the Korean War. Writing for the Court, Justice Hugo L. Black refused to acknowledge that a true emergency existed, saying that the seizure had to be authorized by Congress. Why that was so Black really did not explain; his opinion reads like a draft of a dissenting opinion that suddenly became the voice of the Court's majority.[27] In sum, congressional silence (on seizure) was held to mean an absence of authority in the President.

Dames & Moore is directly contrary. Congressional silence, through a tortured construction of the International Emergency

---

22. *Id.*

23. This is consistent with Rehnquist's judicial philosophy. *Compare* Shapiro, *Mr. Justice Rehnquist: A Preliminary View,* 90 HARV. L. REV. 293 (1976) *with* Fiss & Krauthammer, *The Rehnquist Court,* THE NEW REPUBLIC, Mar. 10, 1982, at 14. Fiss & Krauthammer maintain that "Rehnquist . . . uses state autonomy less to promote liberty than to promote property." *Id.* at 21.

24. Youngstown Sheet & Tube Co. v. Sawyer, 343 U.S. 579 (1952).

25. 315 U.S. 203 (1942).

26. 354 U.S. 524 (1957).

27. Several concurring opinions were filed, the best being one by Justice Robert H. Jackson, for whom Rehnquist clerked at the time.

Economic Powers Act (IEEPA)[28] and the Trading with the Enemy Act (TWEA),[29] was held to signify that the President could free and transfer frozen assets. It would take a pre-Bentham common law pleader or a Jesuit casuist to reconcile these two divergent views. They are consistent only when viewed politically: in 1952, the Court simply refused to believe that an actual emergency existed, whereas in 1981 anyone could plainly see that return of the hostages and access to Iranian assets were in the national interest. As exemplified by the Civil War *Prize Cases,*[30] the Justices do not hesitate to sustain Executive actions that appear to be in the interests of the nation at large. They have readily constitutionalized and thus legitimized instances of Executive fiat.[31] As Secretary of State Charles Evans Hughes once put it: "Foreign policies are not built upon abstractions. They are the result of practical conceptions of national interest arising from some immediate exigency or standing out vividly in historical perspective."[32] To the extent that Dames & Moore has suffered, as perhaps it has, its interests gave way to a judicially recognized practical conception of the national interest. There is, however, no real likelihood that Dames & Moore will suffer in the long run, for, if it gets no satisfaction from the international tribunal it seems clear that the United States can still be sued. The guiding principle of the national interest comes not only from Machiavelli, but also from John Locke.[33]

Justice Rehnquist answered the first question he addressed— could the President nullify the attachments on frozen Iranian assets and transfer them to the jurisdiction of an ad hoc international tribunal?—on statutory grounds. Nevertheless, there are overtones of larger constitutional questions. Rehnquist emphasized the character of the assets as a negotiations "bargaining chip."[34] He disagreed with the argument that the President was

---

28. 50 U.S.C. §§ 1702-1706 (Supp. IV 1980).

29. 50 U.S.C. App. §§ 1-44 (1976 & Supp. IV 1980).

30. 67 U.S. (2 Black) 635 (1862).

31. *See* C. ROSSITER, CONSTITUTIONAL DICTATORSHIP 230 (1948).

32. C. BEARD, THE IDEA OF NATIONAL INTEREST 1 (1934) (quoting 111 ANNALS OF THE AMERICAN ACADEMY OF POLITICAL AND SOCIAL SCIENCES 7 (Supp. 1924)).

33. Machiavelli wrote, "It is not the well-being of individuals that make cities great, but the well-being of the community," and "the common good can be realized in spite of those few who suffer." N. MACHIAVELLI, THE DISCOURSES, *supra* note 4, at 2. John Locke stated the principle differently:

> This power to act according to discretion, for the public good, without the prescription of the law, and sometimes even against it, is that which is called the prerogative. . . . There is a latitute left to the executive power, to do many things of choice, which the laws do not prescribe.

J. LOCKE, THE SECOND TREATISE OF CIVIL GOVERNMENT 160 (J. Gough ed. 1966). *See also* Hurtgen, *The Case for Presidential Prerogative,* 7 U. TOL. L. REV. 59 (1975).

34. Dames & Moore v. Regan, 453 U.S. at 673.

limited to authority " 'only to continue the freeze or to discontinue controls,' "[35] for agreement would have meant that individual claimants in the United States could completely nullify that "chip." The larger meaning is that individual rights, and possibly, but not probably, even property rights, must sometimes give way to State interests. Rehnquist thus assumed the crucial question at issue. He was not prepared to say that "the Federal Government as a whole lacked the power exercised by the President."[36] Nor was he prepared to state any theory or principle for validating Executive control over the frozen assets. His opinion is largely a conclusion without valid reasons.

As a matter of abstract constitutional theory, where does Congress, or Congress and the President acting together, derive such a power? Why, furthermore, should the presidential action, when taken with express or implied authorization from Congress, be held to be "supported by the strongest of presumptions and the widest latitude of judicial interpretation"?[37] The answer appears when *Dames & Moore* is viewed as a political epiphenomenon, the product of a highly sophisticated political process operated in part by nine men whose personal antennas were finely tuned to the fundamental requirements of that process. Justice Rehnquist fudged the question of the derivation of constitutional power to freeze, unfreeze, and transfer assets. In other words, he found President Carter's action valid because Carter had received delegated power from Congress—by inference from the statutes—but simply refused to ask and answer the ultimate and crucial question of the source of Congress's power. Thus, he had to assume that Congress by itself could have accomplished the freezing and unfreezing of the assets. That assumption fails, however, if for no other reason than that Congress as a collectivity cannot engage in international bargaining; it is not institutionally equipped to do so. The conduct of foreign relations is indubitably executive, notwithstanding interventions into the area such as possible legislative vetoes over specific presidential foreign policy decisions (for example, the attempt to veto the sale of AWACS aircraft to Saudi Arabia). Of much more importance, however, is the total absence of an express or implied constitutional peg validating such action by Congress, save if one assumes a "taking" of property for which, as Justice Lewis Powell said in dissent, the government "must pay just compensation."[38] One is forced to return, accordingly, to Jus-

---

35. *Id.* at 672 (quoting Brief for Petitioner at 32).

36. *Id.* at 674.

37. *Id.* at 668 (quoting Youngstown Sheet & Tube Co. v. Sawyer, 343 U.S. 579, 637 (1952)).

38. 453 U.S. at 691 (Powell, J., concurring and dissenting in part).

tice Sutherland's rationale in *United States v. Curtiss-Wright Export Corp.*[39]—that the United States government has all the powers of any sovereign in the conduct of foreign affairs. If that means that the Constitution is subtly suspended during times of acknowledged crisis, or is badly bent even absent a crisis when important foreign policy matters are concerned, that should occasion no surprise. A conception of the "national interest," rather than the words of a document drafted in 1787, guides the course of American foreign relations. The national interest is a political rather than a legal concept, and any attempt to reduce it to a legal code, such as the *Restatement of Foreign Relations Law,* is futile.

The political nature of *Dames & Moore* becomes even clearer in the answer to the second question, which is whether the President could suspend claims pending in American courts. Justice Rehnquist refused to rewrite the relevant statutes: the IEEPA[40] and the "Hostage Act" (Act of July 27, 1868).[41] Exhibiting tunnel vision, he called the lawsuits *"in personam,"*[42] and could not find "specific authorization"[43] under the IEEPA for the President's action. He similarly concluded that the Hostage Act did not constitute "specific authorization."[44]

Having shown adeptness in the fine art of casuistical statutory construction—construing congressional silence and considering ambiguity in diametrically opposed ways—Rehnquist then went on to use both the IEEPA and the Hostage Act as a "looser"[45] indication of "congressional acceptance of a broad scope for executive action in circumstances such as those presented"[46] in *Dames & Moore.* This is a prime example of a judge having it both ways. The extraordinary result, a matter of political principle forced by circumstance, became possible because of some prior decisions that could be cited for authority for the President to interfere with litigation pending in American courts. Drawing upon *Haig v. Agee*[47] for the notion that congressional silence, " 'especially . . . in the areas of foreign policy and national security,' "[48] does not imply congressional disapproval, Rehnquist found lurking somewhere in the interstices of the two statutes an invitation[49] for the

---

39. 299 U.S. 304, 317-18 (1936).
40. 50 U.S.C. §§ 1701-1706 (Supp. IV 1980).
41. 22 U.S.C. § 1732 (1976).
42. Dames & Moore v. Regan, 453 U.S. 654, 675 (1981).
43. *Id.*
44. *Id.* at 676.
45. *Id.*
46. *Id.*
47. 453 U.S. 280 (1981).
48. Dames & Moore v. Regan, 453 U.S. 654, 678 (1981) (quoting Haig v. Agee, 453 U.S. 280, 291 (1981)).
49. 453 U.S. at 678.

President to act on his " 'independent presidential responsibility.' "[50] That bit of judicial hocus-pocus was buttressed by citation of *United States v. Pink,*[51] the well-known decision involving settlement of claims arising from American recognition of the Soviet Union. That case, however, is not really on point, and could easily have been distinguished as a matter of black-letter law. When *Pink* is seen as a political decision by a political court, it is readily obvious that there was little else that the Justices could have done other than go along with the terms of the Litvinov Assignment. Once again the President's conception of the national interest prevailed over the interests of individuals or corporations.

It could scarcely be otherwise. No nation, of whatever stripe, can allow the details of its foreign relations to rest upon the happenstance of litigation, particularly when the results of lawsuits are so idiosyncratic. Add the well-known lengthy delays in the litigation process and the answer comes through loudly and clearly: uphold the President. That may be law, constitutional law, as lawyers understand the nature of law, but it is also political law enunciated by a political Court. Congress, true enough, has at least inferentially accepted the President's authority to settle international claims by executive agreement. The legislative history of the Case-Zablocki Act[52] validates that conclusion. But surely Congress, too, cannot do what the Constitution forbids. This is a foreign relations issue that never has received definitive examination and resolution. How can a type of *private* property—the claims of Dames & Moore—be transmuted, at least temporarily, into some sort of *public* property (the "bargaining chip")? *Pink* and *United States v. Belmont*[53] are not really relevant, despite Rehnquist's reliance on *Pink* (and thus on *Belmont*). Those cases, moreover, dealt with a federalism question; *Dames & Moore* does not. The law enunciated in *Pink* and *Belmont* has thus been extended. It is worth at least passing mention that *Seery v. United States*[54] was largely but not entirely ignored by the litigants and wholly ignored by the Supreme Court. In *Seery* the Court of

---

50. *Id.* (quoting Youngstown Sheet & Tube Co. v. Sawyer, 343 U.S. 579, 673 (1952)).

51. 315 U.S. 203 (1942). For discussion of this case, see L. HENKIN, FOREIGN AFFAIRS AND THE CONSTITUTION 59, 61, 185, 187 (1972).

52. International Agreements—Transmission to Congress Act, Pub. L. No. 92-403, 86 Stat. 619 (1972) (current version at 1 U.S.C. § 112(b) (Supp. IV 1980)). *See* L. FISHER, THE CONSTITUTION BETWEEN FRIENDS 192-213 (1978).

53. 301 U.S. 324 (1937).

54. 127 F. Supp. 601 (Ct. Cl. 1955), *cert. denied,* 359 U.S. 943 (1959). Does the failure of the Solicitor General to cite the *Seery* case in his brief raise an ethical problem? In other words, do lawyers have an ethical responsibility to inform the Court about precedents adverse to their argument? On this point, see Leventhal, *What the Court Expects of the Federal Lawyer,* 27 FED. B.J. 1, 3-4 (1967).

Claims rejected an argument that an executive agreement between the United States and Austria could extinguish a plaintiff's right to sue in American courts for damages to property in Austria: "It would be indeed incongruous if the Executive Department alone, without even the limited participation by Congress . . . could not only nullify the Act of Congress consenting to suit on Constitutional claims, but, by nullifying that Act of Congress, destroy the Constitutional right of a citizen."[55]

Why Justice Rehnquist did not mention *Wilson v. Girard*[56] is a minor, unexplained mystery. Certainly that case would have buttressed his conclusion about the Executive's power to conclude agreements that have the consequence of transgressing on the rights of persons. *Girard* upheld the Status of Forces Agreement between the United States and Japan after World War II that involved in part the governance of American servicemen stationed in Japan. Girard killed a Japanese woman; the issue was whether he was amenable to trial in Japanese courts for an admitted homicide. The administrative agreement provided for such trials. When the matter reached the Supreme Court, it was in the midst of a hubbub, mainly initiated by American super-patriots. The case was heard and quickly decided. In a *per curiam* opinion notable for its circular reasoning, the Court sustained the agreement—and thus the trial of Girard in a Japanese court. He was tried, convicted, and given a suspended sentence, after which he was quickly returned to the United States and discharged. Thus the principle was established, although the culprit went free. Again, a decision forced by political necessity, rendered by a Court attentive to international reality.

True, the executive agreement in *Girard* was in furtherance of a treaty approved by the Senate; but it is difficult to perceive how that, by itself, could validate the agreement. Nevertheless, the Court sustained the agreement. At about the same time the Court flip-flopped in *Reid v. Covert,*[57] which held that a female dependent of an American serviceman in England could not, even though a trial was authorized by another Status of Forces Agreement, be subject to military court martial for the murder of her husband on an American airbase. Again, only a mind able to construct sharp quillets of the law could reconcile *Girard* and *Covert* under one principle of law. Also at issue in *Covert* was a section of the Uniform Code of Military Justice, but why that would

---

55. Seery v. United States, 127 F. Supp. 601, 607 (Ct. Cl. 1955), *cert. denied,* 359 U.S. 943 (1959).

56. 354 U.S. 524 (1957).

57. 354 U.S. 1 (1957). The case was decided on rehearing, the Court reversing its previous position. *See* 351 U.S. 487, *reh'g granted,* 352 U.S. 901 (1956).

make a difference is difficult to see. It is also true that in both cases the agreements acknowledged the sovereignty of the host countries, and thus are not on all fours with *Dames & Moore*. But the following statement from the Court's opinion in *Girard* looks suspiciously like a carte blanche for the avowedly political branches of government, mainly the Executive, to trench upon constitutional rights:

> In the light of the Senate's ratification [*sic*] of the Security Treaty after consideration of the Administrative Agreement, which had already been signed, and its subsequent ratification [*sic*] of the NATO Agreement, with knowledge of the commitment to Japan under the Administrative Agreement, we are satisfied that the approval of Article III of the Security Treaty authorized the making of the Administrative Agreement and the subsequent Protocol embodying the NATO Agreement provisions governing jurisdiction to try criminal offenses.[58]

If, however, *Girard* and *Covert* are seen as political decisions,[59] they fit nicely into a pattern of political law. They were decisions made by a political Court, decisions forced by the constraints of the political process, foreign and domestic.

II.   Some Implications of the Rehnquist Opinion

What can be inferred from these several decisions, including *Dames & Moore*? Several conclusions seem possible.

First: The Supreme Court in such cases reads its own notions into the Constitution of how best to conduct the government. As the Court said in *Pink,*

> Power to remove such obstacles to full recognition as settlement of claims of our nationals . . . certainly is a modest implied power of the President . . . . No such obstacle can be placed in the way of rehabilitation of relations between this country and another nation, unless the historic conception of the powers and responsibilities of the President . . . is to be drastically revised.[60]

Just why that is so was not explained by Justice William O. Douglas, who wrote for the Court. We are left to infer that the gloss of history outweighs express constitutional terms—that, in other words, a constitutional silence can be more important than a constitutional precept. The written Constitution, therefore, receives

---

58. Wilson v. Girard, 354 U.S. at 528-29. Ratification, it should be noted, is a function of the Executive, not the Senate as the Court says. The Senate consents to ratification, which can still be withheld by the President if he so desires.

59. *Covert* was decided in an effort to help stave off the so-called "Bricker Amendment." The Bricker Amendment was an attempt in the early 1950s to curtail the agreement-making power of the President; it of course failed. *See* G. Gunther, Cases and Materials on Constitutional Law 252-53 (10th ed. 1980).

60. United States v. Pink, 315 U.S. 203, 229-30 (1942).

only ostensible obeisance. If that be so, then Professor Louis Henkin was plainly wrong when he maintained in 1972 that "[n]othing in the Constitution suggests that the rights of individuals in respect of foreign affairs are different from what they are in relation to other exercises of governmental power."[61]

The meaning of *Dames & Moore* plus *Pink* is quite important: the interests of "society," i.e., the collectivity known as the nation-state, prevail over those of the individual. This is an example of pure Machiavellianism. Machiavelli placed the well-being of the State over that of individuals; to him it was the *summum bonum.*[62] (Parenthetically, it is meet to note that such a conclusion is not confined to foreign affairs; it is accurate to say that this has always been the case, internally as well as externally. In that sense Professor Henkin is accurate.)

Second: The basic principle is "constitutional reason of State." Reason of State is one of the several great silences of the formal Constitution. It exists, though it is seldom acknowledged in the standard constitutional law textbooks and teaching materials. It has a long history, running at least as far back as Thucydides,[63] but modern thinking about the principle is largely exegesis upon Niccolo Machiavelli's *The Discourses* and *The Prince.*[64]

I have suggested elsewhere[65] that an understanding of the Florentine is necessary for a complete understanding of the course and direction of American constitutional law, and I do not wish to repeat myself. It is enough to maintain that Machiavelli's theory of the State was and is a frontal assault on orthodox American constitutional theory; Machiavelli's theory was, as Friedrich Meinecke put it, "a dagger plunged into the flesh of the body politic of Western humanity, causing it to cry out and struggle with itself."[66] If for "Western humanity" one reads "American democracy," the basic point—the fundamental challenge of Machiavelli—is made.

A republic, said the Florentine, must make provision for

---

61. L. HENKIN, *supra* note 51, at 252.

62. *See* N. MACHIAVELLI, THE PRINCE (G. Bull trans. 1981); N. MACHIAVELLI, THE DISCOURSES, *supra* note 4, *passim.*

63. THUCYDIDES, HISTORY OF THE PELOPONNESIAN WAR (R. Warner trans. 1954).

64. *See, e.g.,* Boyle, *The Law of Power Politics,* 1980 U. ILL. L.F. 901.

65. A. MILLER, *supra* note 4.

66. This version of Meinecke comes from Crick, *supra* note 4, at 67. Scott's translation, as published in the United States, reads as follows: "Machiavelli's theory was a sword plunged into the flank of the body politic of Western humanity, causing it to shriek and rear up." F. MEINECKE, *supra* note 4, at 49. Professor Crick states: "The pain [of that sword's thrust] is still with us and if ever we cease to feel it, it will not be because the conditions that give rise to it have miraculously vanished but because our nerves have gone dead." Crick, *supra* note 4, at 67.

emergency action; it must be able to govern as does a prince.[67] That is also an important teaching of *Dames & Moore* and one that has significant consequences. It means that the storied notion of a "government of laws, not of men," so often repeated without thought, is at best a wistful dream, an ideal never realized, an ideal that has little or no relevance in the conduct of American foreign relations. As I have said elsewhere:

> Reason of State, or as it is often put, the interests of "society," [have] become paramount—the overriding criterion of public policy. In foreign relations the State not only may but *must* use any stratagem, employ any mendacity, or resort to whatever degree of violence is required for its survival *and* the success of [its] policies. In domestic matters it can resort to any type of oppression, repression, lawlessness, or individual injustice thought necessary to avert its own destruction or to suppress undue internal disorder.[68]

I do not say that *Dames & Moore* is of that order of significance, but I do suggest that the decision points in that way and that way only. Dames & Moore, a partnership, has definite, ascertainable interests, but they must apparently give way to a conception of the national interest (the common good)[69] determined by the President and sustained by the Supreme Court.

But how can a democratic nation, a society predicated on the great and enduring principle of "equal justice under law," be preserved by committing what could be considered to be injustice? After *Dames & Moore,* litigants are forced to resort to an international tribunal for relief. Although access to United States courts was not cut off entirely, a long period of litigation is certain to ensue. That result appears to create a lawyers' paradise,[70] but does it serve the interests of the litigants or of the abstract values of constitutionalism? Is Dames & Moore being treated justly? This question is a paradox that lies at the core of the political order called the nation-state, and is the ultimate question presented in *Dames & Moore.* Its answer involves playing a zero-sum game, one in which for every winner there must be a loser. The choice of the winner can be by no means "principled"; it is

---

67. N. MACHIAVELLI, THE DISCOURSES, *supra* note 4, at 193-96.

68. A. MILLER, *supra* note 4, at 51.

69. I do not suggest that either the national interest or the common good are concepts that have definite, ascertainable meanings. But I do say that the Court in *Dames & Moore* is stating what it considers to be the national interest, agreeing, of course, with the President. *Cf.* Vagts, *Introduction* to C. BEARD, *supra* note 32, at xxii ("there is in the American system of government and politics no fixed or final arbiter on the question of what constitutes national interest.") Beard's book, although almost fifty years old, merits close and continuing attention of those who would think seriously about the Constitution in the area of foreign affairs.

70. *See* Tell, *Assets Going, but Suits Remain,* NAT'L L.J., July 20, 1981, at 3.

arbitrary. *Dames & Moore* is an example of judicial fiat, not unlike some well-known equal protection decisions—*Regents of the University of California v. Bakke, United Steel Workers v. Weber* and *Fullilove v. Klutznick*.[71] Saying this is not to denigrate the Court or disagree with those decisions; I merely wish to underscore the obvious—that it is the will of the judge, not as Chief Justice John Marshall once asserted,[72] the will of the law, that determines the results in such cases. I would go even further and agree with Professor Ray Forrester and Justices Byron White and William Brennan that all of the Supreme Court's constitutional decisions fall into that category.[73]

Reason of State may be deduced from the very nature of State organization; it is inherent in any government. Throughout American history, every national crisis and many minor ones have produced outwardly irreconcilable conflicts between "reasons of State" and "reasons of freedom," between claims of "liberty" and the claims of "national interest." It is difficult to see how such a power can in logic (or as a matter of practical politics) be denied to the State speaking through its apparatus of government. No one has yet developed a convincing rebuttal to reason of State, except by ceding sovereignty to some higher order—either the moral law to which philosophers have appealed (and which no political order has ever followed) or a world government (in which event the principle would merely be transferred to that government). Until such a rationalization is produced, the paradox to be faced is that a nation will at times be forced to maleficent means in the interests of the greater value of national security or of the good of the collectivity. That is the teaching of Machiavelli; it has not been refuted. Reason of State, exemplified by *Dames & Moore,* has been little acknowledged in any area, let alone that of presidential authority to nullify attachments and transfer assets by means of executive agreement.

Third: By assuming a posture of exaggerated deference to the Executive in such cases, the Supreme Court becomes in fact an arm of the Executive. The theory—the myth—of course is quite

---

71. Respectively, 438 U.S. 265 (1978); 443 U.S. 198 (1979); 448 U.S. 448 (1980). These well-known decisions concern "affirmative action" plans. I happen to agree with the results in each of them; but my point is that none was principled in the way that some commentators wish. *Cf.* Saphire, *The Search for Legitimacy in Constitutional Theory: What Price Purity?*, 42 OHIO ST. L.J. 335 (1981), *and* authorities cited therein.

72. Osborn v. Bank of the United States, 22 U.S. (9 Wheat.) 738, 866 (1824). *See* B. CARDOZO, THE NATURE OF THE JUDICIAL PROCESS 169-70 (1921).

73. *See* Richmond Newspapers, Inc. v. Virginia, 448 U.S. 555, 595-96 (1980) (Brennan, J., concurring); Miranda v. Arizona, 384 U.S. 436, 531 (1966) (White, J., dissenting); Forrester, *Are We Ready for Truth in Judging?*, 63 A.B.A. J. 1212 (1977). I have expanded on the theme of judicial freedom in A. MILLER, *supra* note 12.

different. The Court functions in such instances to bring the "myth system" and the "operational code" into consonance.[74] This the Justices do by writing opinions couched in language familiar to lawyers. Justice Rehnquist's opinion in *Dames & Moore* appears to be reasoned, and that is enough to satisfy the rules of the game. It is fairly apparent, however, that he started with the result he wanted and then found ways to justify it. I do not suggest that this differs in any significant way from the manner in which Supreme Court Justices have always written opinions.[75]

Fourth: During crises, of whatever order, politics rule. Interdictory rules of law play little or no part. During such times, constitutional proscriptions on the power of the national government are, however subtly, shelved. According to Chief Justice Hughes, emergency provides only the condition for the exercise of already existing powers:

> Emergency does not create power. Emergency does not increase granted power or remove or diminish the restrictions imposed upon power granted or reserved. The Constitution was adopted in a period of grave emergency. Its grants of power to the Federal Government . . . were determined in the light of emergency and they are not altered by emergency.[76]

Taken literally, this can hardly be correct. The very power Hughes sustained (could Minnesota under the obligation-of-contracts clause change the remedy of existing contracts?) was a creature of the Great Depression. By no means would it have been upheld a few years before, for example, in 1925. Hughes' statement poses more questions than it answers, although the decision in which it appears should be considered to be a clear example of domestic crisis overriding plain constitutional terms, as Justice Sutherland pointed out in dissent. Thus it was a political decision—an example of domestic constitutional reason of State—decided by a narrowly divided political Court. Consider, furthermore, the oft-quoted words of Justice David Davis in *Ex parte Milligan*:

> The Constitution of the United States is a law for rulers and people, equally in war and in peace, and covers with the shield of its protection all classes of men, at all times, and under all circumstances. No doctrine, involving more pernicious consequences, was ever invented by the wit of man than that any of

---

74. For discussions of this necessary distinction, see W. REISMAN, FOLDED LIES (1979); R. NEELY, *supra* note 14; A. MILLER, *supra* note 12. This distinction is seldom if ever mentioned in the standard literature (casebooks, textbooks, law journal articles) on the Constitution and the Supreme Court. *See also* Reisman & Simson, *Interstate Agreements in the American Federal System,* 27 RUTGERS L. REV. 70, 71-75 (1973).

75. *See* A. MILLER, THE SUPREME COURT: MYTH AND REALITY (1978).

76. Home Bldg. & Loan Ass'n v. Blaisdell, 290 U.S. 398, 425 (1934).

its provisions can be suspended during any of the great exigencies of government. Such a doctrine leads directly to anarchy or despotism, but the theory upon which it is based is false; for the government, within the Constitution, has all the powers granted to it, which are necessary to preserve its existence . . . .[77]

Again, this is an evident piece of judicial hypocrisy. The Constitution, considered as one of limitations on government, simply does not cover "all classes of men, at all times, and under all circumstances."[78] Its provisions, moreover, can be and are suspended during crisis times. Davis gave the game away in the second half of the last quoted sentence: government does indeed have "all the powers . . . which are necessary to preserve its existence," but they are not enumerated. They exist and are called into action when political reality so demands. Preservation of the existence of government, *pace* Justice Davis, is another way of articulating the principle of reason of State. The Davis statement thus should be read for what it is: a political assertion by a political judge (formerly Lincoln's campaign manager) for a political tribunal. *Dames & Moore* fits into a long line of analogous decisions.

Finally: Dames & Moore suggests but does not answer the question of who is "the" United States in such situations. When Justice Sutherland set forth in *Curtiss-Wright* the proposition that when the Constitution was formed (by some occult means unexplained by him) *the* United States received all the foreign relations powers any sovereign has, he did not suggest where in the triad making up the federal government ultimate authority lay. Of course, he did maintain that the President is the sole organ for the conduct of foreign relations. But is the authority derivative from Congress or inherent in the presidency? That Sutherland did not answer. So, too, with Justice Rehnquist: he implies but does not actually say that control of the assets at issue was shared by President and Congress, but ultimately resided in Congress. Consider this language:

> Although we have declined to conclude that the IEEPA or the Hostage Act directly authorizes the President's suspension of claims for the reasons [*sic*] noted, we cannot ignore the general tenor of Congress' legislation in this area in trying to determine whether the President is acting alone or at least with the acceptance of Congress. As we have noted, *Congress cannot anticipate and legislate with regard to every possible action the Pres-*

---

77. *Ex parte* Milligan, 71 U.S. (4 Wall.) 2, 120-21 (1866).

78. Historically, American Indians were not shielded by the Constitution, and today refugees from Cuba and Haiti find themselves incarcerated while bureaucrats in Washington try to determine what to do with them. There are numerous other examples evidencing the invalidity of the Davis assertion. *See* A. MILLER, *supra* note 4.

ident may find it necessary to take or every possible situation in which he might act.[79]

What this seems to say is that Congress has the ultimate power; but being busy and finding it impossible to legislate foreign policy in detail, legislators issue an implied invitation to the President to act in foreign affairs matters. That "invitation" may be called a tacit delegation of power. Since, however, the federal power over foreign relations is, per Justice Sutherland, inherent, there was no need to concede such an invitation unless Rehnquist believes that Congress is the ultimate authority.

If this correctly interprets Rehnquist's language, in analogous situations the opinion could have portentous consequences for the nature of the division of powers between Congress and the President. I do not speak here of the source of Congress' power; that, as suggested above, is a silence of the Constitution, never really examined, yet accepted as a matter of constitutional faith. Consider, however, *Chadha v. Immigration & Naturalization Service,*[80] an attack on the validity of a one-House congressional veto now awaiting Supreme Court decision. Chadha had been granted permanent residency in the United States by the Immigration and Naturalization Service, only to have that decision summarily "overruled" by the House of Representatives.[81] Chadha immediately filed suit in the Ninth Circuit, challenging the validity of that veto. The Court of Appeals wrestled with the case for almost two years, but finally decided in December, 1980 that the veto was constitutionally invalid. The case presents at least two important questions. The first is whether the veto was valid, the argument being that the President's executive power was improperly invaded. The second question is simply this: who is the client of the Department of Justice in separation of powers litigation?[82] Even though the Department of Justice is charged with the duty of representing "the United States" in litigation, it has agreed with Chadha that the veto is unconstitutional. In so doing, the Depart-

---

79. Dames & Moore v. Regan, 453 U.S. at 678 (emphasis added).

80. 634 F.2d 408 (9th Cir. 1980), *appeal filed*. The Chadha case was argued before the Supreme Court in February 1982. *See* 50 U.S.L.W. 3687 (U.S. Mar. 2, 1982). In January 1982, the D.C. Circuit struck down another legislative veto, 3-0. *See* Consumer Energy Council v. Federal Energy Regulatory Comm'n, 673 F.2d 425 (D.C. Cir. 1982).

81. Chadha, a native of Kenya, lawfully entered the United States in 1966; his student visa expired in 1972. The INS held a deportation hearing pursuant to 8 U.S.C. § 1252(b) (1976), and suspended deportation of Chadha pending congressional action. The INS determined, however, that the deportation proceedings would be reconvened if Congress took some adverse action. On Dec. 16, 1975, the House of Representatives passed a resolution, pursuant to 8 U.S.C. § 1254(c) (1976), disapproving the suspension of Chadha's deportation. This disapproval had the effect of overriding the INS' decision. 634 F.2d at 411.

82. 28 U.S.C. § 2403 (Supp. IV 1980).

ment in effect equated *the* United States with the Executive Branch, necessitating employment of lawyers by Congress.

There is no need at this time to enter the political thicket of the legislative veto. Commentators have thoroughly discussed the subject elsewhere.[83] Whether Mr. Chadha will eventually prevail in the Supreme Court cannot easily be forecast. What can be said, however, is that the Court's decision will be on the basis of political accommodation rather than "principle"—for no one can believe that answers to such problems can logically be deduced from the spare language and silences of the Constitution. To think otherwise is fantasy. Perhaps, however, the Justices will heed Professor Jesse Choper's recommendation,[84] and avoid ruling on the merits (possibly on the grounds of mootness or because the issue falls within the doughy contours of the political question doctrine). If so, that would leave the *Chadha*-type veto and its many counterparts to be resolved in the political arena. The result would be a type of Hobbesian state of nature between Congress and the President, by no means, as Lloyd Cutler intimates, a desirable state of affairs. Mr. Chadha's fate then will have been decided by the murky workings of the House of Representatives, and the legislative veto as a means of congressional oversight of specific Executive decisions will continue.[85]

The greater significance of the case is the question of whether the Attorney General, as the chief legal officer of the government, can with constitutional propriety take sides in a tussle between Congress and President. A colleague and I have discussed this question elsewhere,[86] so there is no need for extensive analysis here. It is sufficient to say that 28 U.S.C. § 2403[87] is ambiguous and further that the theoretical question of who—President or Congress—is *the* United States in separation of powers litigation has never been seriously posed before the Supreme Court, let alone answered.

This is no mere academic question. Dozens of statutes con-

---

83. *See generally* Bruff & Gelhorn, *Congressional Control of Administrative Regulation: A Study of Legislative Vetoes,* 90 HARV. L. REV. 1369 (1977); Watson, *Congress Steps Out: A Look at Congressional Control of the Executive,* 63 CALIF. L. REV. 983 (1975).

84. J. CHOPER, JUDICIAL REVIEW AND THE NATIONAL POLITICAL PROCESS 260-379 (1980).

85. Chadha does not argue, it should be noted, that the House veto deprived him of liberty—to remain in the United States—without due process of law, even though as an abstract proposition surely it can be said that Congress, when acting in a quasi-judicial capacity as in *Chadha,* is also bound by the fifth amendment's procedural due process prescription.

86. *See* Miller & Bowman, *Presidential Attacks on the Constitutionality of Federal Statutes: A New Separation of Powers Problem,* 40 OHIO ST. L.J. 51 (1979).

87. (Supp. IV 1980).

tain some sort of legislative veto provision, and Attorney General William French Smith has stated publicly:

> In the case of laws that are clearly and indefensibly unconstitutional, the executive can refuse to enforce them and urge invalidation by the courts. When reasonable defenses are available, we will defend a statute that does not intrude upon the powers of the executive branch. That is our responsibility under the Constitution irrespective of our views on substantive policy.[88]

Apparently, the Executive will make its own determination of the constitutionality of federal statutes and enforce those which it considers to be constitutional; anything that intrudes, in the Department's opinion, on the power of the Executive will not be defended. Further, such statutes will be attacked in the courts.

If that is Smith's meaning, then we will truly have a "Protestant" rather than a "Papalist" interpretation of the Constitution.[89] Of course the Attorney General acknowledges the ultimate power of the courts to determine constitutionality, which would appear to concede a "Papalist" view of interpretation; but in context his statement urges increased self-restraint by federal judges. The impact of *Chadha* on separation of powers doctrine is unpredictable; but does the language quoted above from Justice Rehnquist's opinion in *Dames & Moore* signal a concept of legislative supremacy? Certainly it can be read that way. This is not, of course, to say that Rehnquist and colleagues will accept such an argument, even though the forgotten part of article I, section 8, clause 18 of the United States Constitution surely provides, as Professor William Van Alstyne has said, constitutional warrant for such a position.[90] But it is to say that loose language from the *Dames & Moore* opinion could be used by analogy in other situations.

In any event, the question of who is *the* United States in separation of powers litigation must eventually be answered. The spirit and some of the language of *Dames & Moore* may well be employed against the Executive—which began the process. Although Solicitor General Wade McCree argued in the government's brief that the President's authority to suspend the pending litigation was derived from both the Constitution and statutes,

---

88. Smith's statement is reproduced in the N.Y. Times, Oct. 30, 1981, at A22, col. 1.

89. I borrow the classification from Levinson, *"The Constitution" in American Civil Religion,* 1979 SUP. CT. REV. 123.

90. *See* Van Alstyne, *The Role of Congress in Determining Incidental Powers of the President and of the Federal Courts: A Comment on the Horizontal Effect of The "Sweeping Clause,"* 36 OHIO ST. L.J. 788 (1975). Professor Van Alstyne's argument was rejected by Judge Wilkey in Consumer Energy Council v. Federal Energy Regulatory Comm'n, 673 F.2d 425 (D.C. Cir. 1982).

Rehnquist did not acknowledge that. His precise language is important:

> In light of all of the foregoing—the inferences to be drawn from the character of the legislation Congress has enacted in the area, such as the IEEPA and the Hostage Act, and from the history of acquiescence in executive claims settlement—we conclude that the President was authorized to suspend pending claims. . . . As Justice Frankfurter pointed out, . . . "a systematic, unbroken executive practice, long pursued to the knowledge of Congress and never before questioned . . . may be treated as a gloss on 'Executive Power' vested in the President by § 1 of Art. II." Past practice does not, by itself, create power, but "long-continued practice, known to and acquiesced in by Congress, would raise a presumption that the [action] has been [taken] in pursuance of its consent. . . ." Such practice is present here and such a presumption is also appropriate. *In light of the fact that Congress may be considered to have consented to the President's action in suspending claims, we cannot say that action exceeded the President's powers.* (citations omitted).[91]

Whether in analogous situations, such as the congressional veto, that statement of ultimate power in Congress would mean that the Executive was "hoist with his own petard"[92] is not at all certain. As discussed above, results in separation of powers litigation are matters of political accommodation rather than logical derivations from the constitutional text or analogies to dissimilar cases.

IV.   By Way of Conclusion

What *Dames & Moore* portends for the future of presidential power is rather obvious: whatever exigencies Americans face, particularly those externally generated, will be dealt with by whatever means the political officers consider necessary at the time. Necessity is the mother of constitutional law. As in the past, interdictory law, even a written fundamental law, will not prevent actions deemed expedient in the circumstances. The principle of constitutional relativism will continue.

This may not fit neatly with the theories and beliefs of our constitutional antiquarians or of those who adhere to the ideology of "legalism."[93] But it cannot be gainsaid. It is the necessary conclusion from de Tocqueville's famous comment that in the United States many political questions are cast before the courts for reso-

---

91.   Dames & Moore v. Regan, 453 U.S. at 686 (emphasis added).

92.   W. Shakespeare, Hamlet, act III, scene iv.

93.   *See* J. Shklar, Legalism (1964). Constitutional antiquarians are numerous. *See, e.g.,* R. Berger, Government by Judiciary (1977)—a preposterous argument that the fourteenth amendment should be limited to Berger's reading of the intentions of the 39th Congress.

lution.[94] Why, if that is as accurate as it is widely accepted, any-one can still believe that courts would or should act in the classical Blackstone model of judicial behavior is completely mysterious. Numerous commentators still insist, nonetheless, that courts should be apolitical and that judges should make only those decisions that can be rationalized on "principle."[95] No one quite knows what a principled decision is.[96] That, however, does not

---

94. *Cf.* A. DE TOCQUEVILLE, DEMOCRACY IN AMERICA 330 (H. Reeve trans. 1974) ("Scarcely any question arises in the United States which does not become . . . a subject of judicial debate . . . .").

95. *See, e.g.,* J. ELY, DEMOCRACY AND DISTRUST 41 (1980): "If a principled approach to judicial enforcement of the Constitution's open-ended provisions cannot be developed . . . responsible commentators must consider seriously the possibility that courts simply should stay away from them." Professor Saphire, *supra* note 61, at 343 n.40, asserts that "the notion that a judicial decision must be 'principled'—that is, based upon nonarbitrary distinctions between the case at hand and others similarly situated—has been universally endorsed." Well, maybe. And maybe not. *Cf.* Karst, *Foreword: Equal Citizenship Under the Fourteenth Amendment,* 91 HARV. L. REV. 1, 3-4 (1977):

> It is curious, after all these years, that so much of the discussion of equal protection doctrine has continued to proceed in a substantive void. *The predominant concern, both of the Burger Court and of a strikingly large proportion of modern equal protection commentary, has been with issues of judicial role and methodology, rather than the substantive content of the equal protection clause.* Indeed, the search for a "central guiding principle" seems to have been inhibited by a widely shared assumption that the equal protection clause lacks substantive content. That assumption is mistaken. (emphasis added).

Concentration on process rather than substance of course permits commentators to avoid being labeled as "result oriented." Why that term should be one of opprobrium is completely mysterious. As the late Judge Braxton Craven maintained, all judges are result oriented. *See* Craven, *Paean to Pragmatism,* 50 N.C.L. REV. 977 (1972). Avoidance of substantive issues allows commentators to appear to be scientific and value-free (objective); that is pure fantasy. *See* Miller, *The Myth of Objectivity in Legal Research and Writing,* 18 Cath. U.L. Rev. 290 (1969); Schubert, *Academic Ideology and the Study of Adjudication,* 61 AM. POL. SCI. REV. 106 (1967); Miller, *Judicial Activism and American Constitutionalism: Some Notes and Reflections,* in CONSTITUTIONALISM: NOMOS XX 333, 352 (J. Pennock & J. Chapman eds. 1979).

96. *Compare* these statements:

> Even law professors who are in the business of making sense out of what courts do and are responsible for showing why courts act according to "legal principles," and not according to what the judges had for breakfast, have to twist themselves out of shape to reconcile . . . constant ideological shifts with any notion of a written constitution which is being "interpreted." In fact, *almost every theory defending or defaming courts has developed backward from the result sought by the commentator to some rule which dictates that result. This is not reasoning from principles, however, but mere apologizing for or criticizing the exercise of raw power.* (emphasis added).

R. NEELY, *supra* note 14, at 9. Justice Neely's views were anticipated by a leading constitutional historian, Professor Leonard Levy: "Much of the literature on the Supreme Court reflects the principle of the gored ox. Attitudes toward the Court quite often depend on whether its decisions are agreeable." Levy, *Judicial Review, History, and Democracy: An Introduction,* in JUDICIAL REVIEW AND THE SUPREME COURT 1 (L. Levy ed. 1967).

deter those who maintain that the overriding need is for principled decision-making by the Supreme Court, for decisions made in accordance with "neutral" principles. No one should—indeed, no one really can—any longer believe that constitutional decisions are babies brought by judicial storks flying in from the Great Beyond where the corpus of neutral principles reposes. Although it may be true that with "a numinous document like the Constitution or the Bible, the principles and methods of correct interpretation are as important as they are problematical,"[97] few are willing to face the ineluctable logic of such decisions as *Dames & Moore.*

This case is proof positive that the predominant decisional criterion is a conception of the national interest articulated by the President and confirmed by the Supreme Court. The Court, thus, is part of the governmental apparatus, the core principle of which is cooperation. Any sociologist of law knows that the State and the legal system are closely intertwined; *Dames & Moore* is merely one additional bit of evidence indicating that interlock. If one can say with the poet that "whatever is, is right" then the principle of "correct interpretation" in matters of perceived national interest is for the Supreme Court to go along with the President's interpretation of his powers. The Solicitor General advised the Court that "the President's primary motivation in blocking Iranian assets, entering into the Agreement with Iran, and issuing the Executive Orders implementing the Agreement was the protection of the national security and foreign policy of the United States";[98] the Court agreed.

In other words, the Constitution was in effect, although not expressly stated and not widely recognized even today, a delegation of power to later generations of Americans to write their own fundamental laws. If that conception leaves lawyers and Americans without a compass to steer by—as Macaulay said, "[y]our Constitution, sir, is all sail and no anchor"[99]—that is a fact with which we will have to live. It can be considered a tragedy only by those who look upon the Constitution as some sort of sacred document (the basic instrument of America's civil religion) or by those who view it as a strictly legal document (to be construed and inter-

---

97. E. HIRSCH, THE AIMS OF INTERPRETATION 20 (1976).

98. Brief for the Respondent at 13, Dames & Moore v. Regan, 453 U.S. 654 (1981).

99. Letter to H.S. Randall (May 23, 1857) (quoted in L. HENKIN, *supra* note 51, at 271 (1972)). The point here is that in litigated cases, as well as in many other situations, Americans are in fact adrift without a compass. Decisions are made to fit the circumstances, in accordance with conceptions of the national interest. *See* C. BEARD, *supra* note 32. Although Beard wrote mainly about foreign affairs, the point is accurate as well—at least in any case that receives Supreme Court attention on the merits—to domestic matters. The point is explored in A. MILLER, *supra* note 12.

preted as any other written instrument with which lawyers deal
such as contracts, wills, and conveyances). Judge J. Skelly Wright
was simply wrong in 1971 when he asserted that "[c]onstitutional
choices are in fact different from ordinary decisions. . . . [T]he
most important value choices have already been made by the
framers of the Constitution."[100] A legal system tolerating the
principle of *cy pres*; incorporating the principle of *rebus sic stan-
tibus* into the interpretation of treaties; allowing and perhaps even
encouraging the overt overruling of precedent by the Supreme
Court; functioning with a Court that openly uses a "balancing
test" for decisions without saying how or why divergent interests
are identified or weighed, permitting no absolutes even when the
Constitution speaks in absolute terms, and governing more by the
living or operative than by the formal Constitution, cannot be said
to be a prisoner (or beneficiary—take your choice) of "important
value choices" made in 1787, 1791, and 1868. We live under a
Constitution, but it is more than what the judges say it is; the Constitution also mirrors the various exigencies confronted by succeeding generations of Americans.

I do not suggest that the Constitution, as written, is irrelevant
in cases such as *Dames & Moore*. Of course it has pertinence, but
only as a point of departure for political decisions politically
made. The trappings of legalism remain, but the steely essence of
such cases is politics pure and simple. The Justices, to be sure, are
"lawmakers—a coordinate branch of *government*,"[101] as Justice
William Brennan has candidly acknowledged:

> The interpretation and application of constitutional and
> statutory law, while not legislation, is lawmaking, albeit of a
> kind that is subject to special constraints and informed by
> unique considerations. Guided and confined by the Constitu-
> tion and pertinent statutes, judges are obliged to be discerning,
> to exercise judgment, and to prescribe rules. Indeed, at times

---

100. Wright, *Professor Bickel, the Scholarly Tradition, and the Supreme Court,* 84
HARV. L. REV. 769, 784 (1971).

In calling Judge Wright's statement wrong, I do not mean to say that his article is
not a valuable antidote to the "principle" and "reason" commentators, *supra* notes
60-61, many of whom seem to be neo-Burkeans (neo-conservatives)—as was Alexander Bickel. *See* A. BICKEL, THE MORALITY OF CONSENT, *supra* note 11; A. BICKEL,
THE SUPREME COURT AND THE IDEA OF PROGRESS (1970). Judge Wright's article is a
thoroughgoing refutation of the Bickel position; it should be required reading for
every student of constitutional law. *See* Parker, *The Past of Constitutional Theory—
And Its Future,* 42 OHIO ST. L.J. 223 (1981), maintaining that constitutional theory is
at a crossroads and that new theory must be developed: "If we strike out in that
direction, however, we shall have to do so without clear maps. Scholarship in other
fields will be helpful. But, for the most part, past constitutional law scholarship will
not." There is "blindness and bias . . . built into its structure." *Id.* at 258.

101. Richmond Newspapers, Inc. v. Virginia, 448 U.S. 555, 595 (1980) (Brennan,
J., concurring) (emphasis in original).

judges wield considerable authority to formulate legal policy in designated areas.[102]

Brennan's point was anticipated a half-century ago by Judge Learned Hand when he wrote that litigated constitutional provisions are but "empty vessels"[103] into which a judge can pour nearly anything he wishes, and stated by Chief Justice Earl Warren in 1969 when he said that the Justices are guided only by the Constitution and "our own consciences."[104]

Does that leave the Justices free to roam at will? I suggest not. The Rule of Law may, as suggested above, often be the Rule of Barter Economics and even, as Warren intimated, also the Rule of Personal Conscience, but the Justices are also part of the governing process. Their decisions, speaking generally, reflect the realities of politics, foreign and domestic, and thus the Justices are part of the governing coalition. Only on rare occasions have the Justices ruled contrary to the wishes and expectations of that coalition—in decisions that Charles Evans Hughes once termed the "self-inflicted wounds" of the Court.[105] "To the extent that courts make law," Professor Martin Shapiro contends, "judges will be incorporated into the governing coalition, the ruling elite, the responsible representatives of the people, or however else the political regime may be expressed."[106] If that be so, and I think it is, then judicial independence (from that coalition) is part of the "myth system" of the United States. We have known—at least, we should have known—since Holmes wrote in 1873 that the law is not neutral.[107] *Dames & Moore* is an additional bit of evidence from which we can infer that when matters of important State policy are concerned the Supreme Court acts as an arm of the State. That, I maintain, is the important lesson of the strange case of the Iranian hostages.

---

102. *Id.* at 595 n.20.

103. The Spirit of Liberty, Papers and Addresses of Learned Hand 81 (I. Dilliard ed. 1952).

104. 395 U.S. *xi* (1968 remarks of the Chief Justice upon his retirement).

105. C. Hughes, The Supreme Court of the United States 50-54 (1928) (mentioning the Dred Scott, Legal Tender, and Income Tax cases as such "wounds"). See F. Graham, The Self-Inflicted Wound (1970), who assers that Miranda v. Arizona, 384 U.S. 436 (1966) (and other criminal law decisions) are another such wound. In my judgment, Hughes was correct, but Graham was not.

106. M. Shapiro, *supra* note 3, at 34.

107. *See* Holmes' Comment, *The Gas-Stokers' Strike*, 7 Am. L. Rev. 582 (1873). For discussion, see Tushnet, *The Logic of Experience: Oliver Wendell Holmes on the Supreme Judicial Court*, 63 Va. L. Rev. 975, 1029-31 (1977); Tushnet, *Truth, Justice, and the American Way: An Interpretation of Public Law Scholarship in the Seventies*, 57 Tex. L. Rev. 1307 (1979); Lerner, *Constitution and Court as Symbols*, 46 Yale L.J. 1290, 1316 n.71 (1937); Miller, Book Review, 34 Vand. L. Rev. 1463, 1465-68 (1981).

CHAPTER 8

Politics, Democracy, and the First Amendment

When in 1886 the Supreme Court determined that the business corporation was a person within the meaning of the Fourteenth Amendment, and therefore protected by that amendment's due process of law clause, the legal basis was provided for the exponential growth of corporate enterprise in the ensuing decades. Judicial protection of corporations took another large leap in the 1970s when the Court decided that corporations had other constitutional protections, such as freedom of expression. Chapter 8 discusses the most important of those decisions, a 1978 ruling that in sum equated the free speech of corporations (with their enormous assets) with that of natural persons.

The Justices simply refused to concede the immense disparity in wealth, and thus in political power, of corporations and individuals. Speech is speech is speech, said Justice Lewis Powell for the Court majority, and its worthiness depends on its content rather than its origin. On the surface, that is an appealing idea, but one, as this chapter shows, that will not withstand rigorous analysis. It is far too simplistic.

The case evidences once again that the Supreme Court in practical effect is an arm of the moneyed and the propertied; its function is to help stabilize society and protect it from attempts to change it. Continuation of the status quo becomes the principal goal of the Justices. Even when the Court makes civil rights/civil liberties decisions, the latent beneficiaries still remain the "rich and the well-born." (Compare the discussion in Chapter 5.) In Chapter 8, the Court goes even further and openly makes the latent beneficiaries of its rulings also the manifest—just as it did in the period of 1886-1937 when it systematically struck down socioeconomic legislation. The First Amendment, in the conventional legal wisdom, supposedly protects a robust "marketplace of ideas." The significance of the Court's 1978 decision is that the marketplace can be and is dominated by those with money, in much the same way that the commercial market is dominated by the giant corporations. This is a social revolution of the first magnitude.

The large private corporation fits oddly into democratic theory. Indeed, it does not fit.
—Charles E. Lindblom*

I. Introduction

"The legal machinery," Morris R. Cohen once observed, "never operates apart from human beings, judges, juries, police officials, etc. The imperfect knowledge or intelligence of these human beings is bound to assert itself. It is therefore vain to expect that the legal machinery will work with a perfection that no other human institution does."[1] Since Professor Cohen's observation surely is accurate, we should not expect perfection from the Supreme Court of the United States. Nevertheless, are we not entitled to expect that the Justices be cognizant of the economic and political facts of life, and that they give them full and due consideration? In answering this question, this article will analyze the Supreme Court's opinion in *First National Bank v. Bellotti*,[2] cast against an evaluation of the role of the Court in Professor Jesse Choper's *Judicial Review and the National Political Process*.[3] My theme may be simply stated: Neither *Bellotti* nor Choper adequately consider the brute facts of the political economy of American constitutionalism.

Bellotti arguably is the most important first amendment decision in recent memory. In that case, the First National Bank challenged a Massachusetts statute forbidding certain expenditures by banks and business corporations for the purpose of influencing the vote on referenda. Despite the fact that the referendum in question had nothing directly to do with the plaintiff-bank's business,[4] the Supreme Court invalidated the

---

* C. Lindblom, Politics and Markets 356 (1977).

[1] Cohen, *Positivism and Idealism in the Law*, 27 Colum. L. Rev. 237, 248 (1927).

[2] 435 U.S. 765 (1978).

[3] J. Choper, Judicial Review and the National Political Process (1980) [hereinafter cited as Choper].

[4] The referendum at issue dealt with a proposed constitutional amendment to allow collection of a graduated income tax on individuals. 435 U.S. at 769.

This chapter was originally published under the title of "On Politics, Democracy, and the First Amendment: A Comment on *First National Bank v. Bellotti* " in 38 Washington & Lee Law Review 21 (1981).

statute.[5] In an opinion authored by Justice Lewis Powell, the Court reasoned that the corporation is a constitutional person and, accordingly, it is to be treated as any other person (*i.e.*, a natural person) when first amendment issues are raised.[6] "The inherent worth of the speech in terms of its capacity for informing the public does not depend upon the identity of its source, whether corporation, association, union, or individual."[7] That is a nice sentiment, and if one accepts the premise that corporations are always to be equated with natural persons under the Constitution,[8] then the decision inexorably flows as a matter of simple logic. The problem, however, is in the nature of the premise. If it is faulty, as I believe it is, then Powell's conclusion is invalid.[9] Professor Choper deals with the *Bellotti* decision by ignoring it, as does Professor John Hart Ely in his recent book on the theory and practice of judicial review.[10]

The implications of *Bellotti* are abundantly clear. The assets of corporations may be used for all types of political (public) expression, without regard to whether the content of that expression materially affects the firms. And that is so even though some corporate behemoths, such as AT&T or General Motors, have assets that not only dwarf those of any natural person but also are larger than most nation-states of the world. To pretend that a corporation is a person is a person is a person—to paraphrase Gertrude Stein—and then proceed to suggest that AT&T, for example, is the same as a natural person for purposes of the first amendment is to be wilfully blind. Since we must assume that judges do not divest themselves of their preferences and predilections when they put on the black robes of judicial office,[11] the myopia of the Court is understandable, although indefensible. For Choper and Ely to ignore the portents of *Bellotti* is more puzzling, particularly since Ely

---

[5] Id. at 795. The *Bellotti* doctrine was solidified in June, 1980 when the Court held that a public utility could not be prevented from inserting propaganda in its monthly bills. Consolidated Edison Co. v. Public Service Comm'n, 100 S. Ct. 2326, 2336-37 (1980). *See also* Central Hudson Gas & Elec. Co. v. Public Service Comm'n, 100 S. Ct. 2343, 2354 (1980) (holding unconstitutional order prohibiting electric utility's promotion of electricity use).

[6] 435 U.S. at 776.

[7] *Id.* at 777.

[8] *See* Santa Clara County v. Southern Pac. Ry., 118 U.S. 394, 395-96 (1886); text accompanying notes 24-30.

[9] *See* Miller, *On the Choice of Major Premises*, in A. MILLER, THE SUPREME COURT: MYTH AND REALITY 105-31 (1978) [hereinafter cited as MILLER].

[10] J. ELY, DEMOCRACY AND DISTRUST (1980) [hereinafter cited as ELY]; *see also* Miller, *Book Review*, 39 U. FLA. L. REV. 369 (1980) (reviewing ELY).

[11] It is vain to contend with judges who have been at the bar the advocates for forty years of railroad companies, and all the forms of associated capital, when they are called upon to decide cases where such interests are in contest. All their training, all their feelings are from the start in favor of those who need no such influence.
Statement of Justice Samuel F. Miller, *quoted in* C. FAIRMAN, MR. JUSTICE MILLER AND THE SUPREME COURT 374 (1939). *See* Miller & Howell, *The Myth of Neutrality in Constitutional Adjudication*, in MILLER, *supra* note 9, at 51-87.
For a candid revelation of Justice Powell's pro-business philosophy, uttered just before

advocates a "representation-reinforcing" theory of judicial review,[12] and Choper is most interested in the protection of individual rights.[13] I do not suggest that the Court or Choper or Ely are not fully aware of the immense disparity in wealth between the disembodied entities called corporations and natural persons. Nor do I say that they are unaware of the disproportionate strength in the electoral and political processes between the two. What they do is blithely to disdain, save in a few conclusory statements in *Bellotti*,[14] discussing the question.

If the first amendment is more than the private preserve of the media—which surely it is[15]—then the full significance of *Bellotti* becomes apparent. Those with money, provided they are collectivities called corporations, now have constitutional *carte blanche* to try to manipulate the political process. The hidden underbelly of American politics is now constitutional doctrine. That makes corporations more equal, as Orwell might have said,[16] than natural persons, who by federal statute are limited in their electoral contributions. Although limitations on campaign contributions are valid,[17] *personal* campaign expenditures are limited only by the wealth of the person.[18] Corporations, to be sure, also are limited in what they can contribute to a candidate. After *Belloti*, however, they are presumably free to espouse the same views of a given candidate, and perhaps even the candidate himself,[19] because they have no direct connection with that candidate. The meaning is clear beyond

---

he went on the Court, see Powell, *Attack on American Free Enterprise System*, a memorandum dated August 23, 1971 and submitted to the U.S. Chamber of Commerce (available from that organization). Among other things, Powell said: "Business must learn the lesson, long ago learned by labor and other self-interest groups. This is the lesson that political power is necessary; that such power must be assiduously cultivated; and that when necessary, it must be used aggressively and with determination—without embarrassment and without the reluctance which has been so characteristic of American business." That statement, and the entire memorandum, clearly reveals the philosophical predicate for Justice Powell's *Bellotti* opinion. (It is worth at least passing mention that Powell's conception of American economic history is faulty at best. Businessmen have always known that "political power is necessary," and, indeed, the history of government-business relations in the United States can be and has been written around that theme). Given Powell's 1971 views, should anyone be surprised at this 1978 opinion in *Bellotti*?

[12] ELY, *supra* note 10, at 77-88.

[13] CHOPER, *supra* note 3, at 60-128. Professor Ely would limit judicial review to those issues that promote representation in government, while Professor Choper would keep the Supreme Court out of federalism and separation of powers questions. Both are interested in developing a viable theory to justify judicial review that promotes the rights of natural persons.

[14] 435 U.S. at 785 n.22, 788-92.

[15] *See* 435 U.S. at 798-99 (Burger, C.J., concurring).

[16] *See* G. ORWELL, ANIMAL FARM 112 (1946).

[17] Buckley v. Valeo, 424 U.S. 1, 29 (1976) (per curiam).

[18] Limitations on personal campaign expenditures violate the first amendment. *Id.* at 54.

[19] *See* Democratic Nat'l Comm. v. Independent Comm. for Reagan, ___ F.E.C. ___ (1980) (independent committees may expend money on behalf of candidate so long as no contact exists between candidate and committee).

doubt: In the words of the old frontier maxim, "them as has, gits." As Justice White's *Bellotti* dissent observed, money talks in the political process.[20] That, of course, is a hoary social truism, but it has been elevated into constitutional law. Nowhere in Powell's opinion is there recognition of the overwhelming political power of the economic enterprise. Nor does Choper acknowledge it, even though his book is said to be a "functional" analysis. Surely the time has come to recognize corporations for what they are — private governments — and to treat them as such under the Constitution.[21] Surely, too, Professor Choper, who advocates that the Supreme Court not decide questions of federalism,[22] should consider the giant corporations to be units of a system of "functional" federalism that is probably as important — perhaps more important — than the system of "formal" federalism.[23] As such, those firms should be held to constitutional standards — they should have *duties* as well as *rights* under the fundamental law.

II. The Function of the Court

Only by the most transparent fiction can the corporation be called a person. During the first century of our republic, this view was both generally known and widely accepted — even by the Supreme Court.[24] In 1886, however, the Court, under Chief Justice Morrison Waite, had a blinding flash of revelation: they concluded through an intuition known only to them that the corporation was a constitutional person. In *Santa Clara County v. Southern Pacific Railway*[25] the Court casually, and without even hearing argument on the point, determined that enormously important matter[26] — thereby neatly "amending" the fourteenth amendment.[27]

The significance of *Santa Clara County* cannot be over-estimated. By being able to invoke the due process clauses of the Constitution,[28] corporations have been able to wax large and strong. Those entities are unique in human history; nothing quite like them has even been seen prior to the last ninety or so years. I do not suggest that *Santa Clara*

---

[20] 435 U.S. at 812 (White, J., dissenting).

[21] *See generally* Miller, *A Modest Proposal for Helping to Tame the Corporate Beast*, 8 HOFSTRA L. REV. 79 (1979).

[22] CHOPER, *supra* note 3, at 171-259.

[23] *See* Miller, *The Constitutional Law of the "Security State,"* in A. MILLER, SOCIAL CHANGE AND FUNDAMENTAL LAW: AMERICA'S EVOLVING CONSTITUTION 43-95 (1979).

[24] *See, e.g.*, Munn v. Illinois, 94 U.S. 113, 134-35 (1877).

[25] 118 U.S. 394 (1886).

[26] *Id.* at 395-96.

[27] It is interesting to note that those who lambaste the Supreme Court for some of its fourteenth amendment decisions, *see, e.g.*, Baker v. Carr, 369 U.S. 186 (1962) (legislative apportionment); Brown v. Board of Education, 347 U.S. 483 (1954) (school desegregation), are strangely silent about *Santa Clara County. See, e.g.*, R. BERGER, GOVERNMENT BY JUDICIARY (1977) [hereinafter cited as BERGER].

[28] U.S. CONST. amend. V, § 3; U.S. CONST. amend. XIV, § 2.

County was the principal cause of that development. Surely "technological imperatives" had more to do with it.[29] Nonetheless, the favorable legal climate in which corporations operated, in both public and private law,[30] permitted those imperatives to influence the creation and growth of the modern giant business corporation. These firms are at once economic entities, sociological communities, and political orders. They are collectivities: to accord them the speech rights of natural persons, as the Supreme Court does, is myopic at best.

Neither political scientists nor economists have as yet produced a satisfactory theory of conscious economic cooperation and its effect on the constitutional order.[31] Lawyers, with invincible parochialism, still refuse to recognize the corporation for what it is, and that is so even though the giant corporation is, as Arthur Bentley said in 1908, "government through and through."[32] It is economic government, exercising sovereignty over large segments of society. Although, as Bentley went on to say, it does not ordinarily use certain "technical methods," such as hanging, "that is a detail."[33] (The State still has a monopoly on the exercise of the *legitimate* use of force.) Corporate governance is a problem for the constitutional lawyer. By allowing corporate free speech in matters that do not materially affect the enterprise, the Supreme Court has accorded the corporation rights without concomitant constitutional duties—thus giving some credence to the view that the Justices have legitimated "economic intervention" and accompanied it with an "illusion of equality, justice and freedom."[34] The Court is now, and in fact always has been, the "ultimate guardian of corporate privilege."[35]

This proposition, I realize, does not concur with the popular wisdom about the modern Supreme Court as guardian of civil rights and liberties. While the Court does have that function, as Professor Choper cogently shows,[36] it also has a greater role. My point is to pose this question: Who are the ultimate beneficiaries of those decisions of the Warren and Burger Courts? Are they about the same as those who have always benefited—those with money and property? There can be little doubt that the answer to that question is "yes." To demonstrate the validity of this proposition requires brief discussion of the function of the Court in modern America. Some reference, of course, must be made to history, but principally as a backdrop against which the drama of modern constitutional litigation is played.

---

[29] *See* J. GALBRAITH, THE NEW INDUSTRIAL STATE 11-22 (1967).

[30] *See* A. MILLER, THE MODERN CORPORATE STATE: PRIVATE GOVERNMENTS AND THE AMERICAN CONSTITUTION 37-49 (1976) [hereinafter cited as THE MODERN CORPORATE STATE].

[31] *See* THE ECONOMY AS A SYSTEM OF POWER (W. Samuels ed. 1979).

[32] A. BENTLEY, THE PROCESS OF GOVERNMENT 268 (1908).

[33] *Id.*

[34] Roelofs, *The Warren Court and Corporate Capitalism*, TELOS, No. 39, at 94 (1979).

[35] *See* THE MODERN CORPORATE STATE, *supra* note 30, at 93.

[36] *See* CHOPER, *supra* note 3, *passim.*

Any institution has both a *manifest* and *latent* function.[37] My main conclusion in what follows is similar to, but broader than, that of Professor Alan Westin: "In matters directly affecting business, as in labor relations, antitrust and tax issues, the Warren Court [was] simply an enunciator of the social capitalist status quo in American politics."[38] This observation, it seems to me, can be expanded to cover all, or at the least most, of the areas of Supreme Court adjudication. When we ask about both the manifest and latent functions of Court decisions, then it may readily be seen that "the social capitalist status quo" is furthered by many decisions which have the manifest function of protecting individual rights and liberties.

"The fundamental function of the law," McGeorge Bundy once asserted, "is to prevent the natural unfairness of society from becoming intolerable."[39] Evidence for that observation may be found in the series of Supreme Court decisions rendered during the past forty years that outwardly (and actually) protect human rights, but which also serve as symbolic victories to certain segments of society.[40] Those decisions are a means of stifling social discontent by permitting liberties which the State considers relatively unimportant to flourish in what appears to be, but often actually is not, a permissive society.[41] The basic question that must be asked and answered is: *Cui bono?* Who in fact benefits from the Court's civil rights/civil liberties decisions? To answer that question requires, first of all, a recognition that the Court's decisions are a part of a continuum of governmental actions taken during the past several decades to ameliorate the brutalities of industrialism. In the main, these involve social services—in brief, the "Welfare State"—which, as C.B. MacPherson has said, came because of "the sheer need of governments to allay working-class discontents that were dangerous to the stability of the state. It was Bismarck, the conservative Chancellor of Imperial Germany, and no great democrat, who pioneered the welfare state in the 1880s, for just this purpose."[42] And it is the Supreme Court made up of lawyer-judges who come from a conservative profession which has helped to allay some popular discontents in America.

Analysis of the beneficiaries of these decisions must proceed on two levels. First is the *ostensible* beneficiary, who often as a person is the *actual* beneficiary. But second, and of greater long-range significance, are the *hidden* winners—those who profit most from the stability of the constitutional order. During the 1930s and '40s, the Supreme Court revolutionized constitutional jurisprudence by legitimizing the growing

---

[37] *See* R. MERTON, SOCIAL THEORY AND SOCIAL STRUCTURE 115-122 (rev. ed. 1968).

[38] A. WESTIN, THE SUPREME COURT UNDER EARL WARREN 56 (1972).

[39] Statement of McGeorge Bundy, *quoted in* M. MAYER, THE LAWYERS 516 (1967).

[40] *See, e.g.*, Baker v. Carr, 369 U.S. 186 (1962) (urban voters); Brown v. Board of Education, 347 U.S. 483 (1954) (black Americans).

[41] *Compare* C. LASCH, THE CULTURE OF NARCISSISM (1978) *with* F. DONNER, THE AGE OF SURVEILLANCE (1980).

[42] C. MACPHERSON, THE REAL WORLD OF DEMOCRACY 11 (1966).

benevolent role of government in the lives of its citizens (*i.e.*, the Positive State). In the process of that reorientation, the Justices changed their principal role from being "the first authoritative faculty of political economy in the world's history"[43] to guardian of human rights and liberties. Those actions, particularly the validation of the Positive State,[44] were taken in conjunction with the political branches of government. The Court cooperated with Congress and the President in the establishment and furtherance of welfare programs. Cooperation, indeed, is the forgotten part of separation of powers, as Woodrow Wilson observed in 1908.[45] It would be odd if the Justices were so ambivalent as, on the one hand, to cooperate fully with the politicians, both federal and state, in socio-economic matters, and, on the other hand, to refuse cooperation when civil rights or liberties are involved. Cooperation took place there as well, but on the submerged or latent level. As Professor J. A. G. Griffith concluded in *The Politics of the Judiciary*,[46] "The judiciary in any modern industrial society, under whatever economic system, is an essential part of the system of government and . . . its function may be described as underpinning the stability of that system and as protecting that system from attack by resisting attempts to change it."[47]

The past forty to fifty years are unique in American history. For the first time, and then only slowly at first, the rights of "discrete and insular minorities"[48] began to receive at least some protection from the High Bench. Ethnic groups and others have begun to get at least the appearance of rights purportedly guaranteed since the beginnings of the republic. Two important questions are posed by this development, which by no means is over even though recent "conservative" appointments have slowed it in some areas.[49] The questions are: Why did the development come so late in American history?; and, What is the sociological function of increased protection of personal liberties? While each question merits attention, our main focus will be on the latter.

The Bill of Rights has been a part of the Constitution since 1791 and the fourteenth amendment since 1868. Yet it is accurate to say that the rights protected by the first eight amendments were submerged until

---

[43] J. COMMONS, LEGAL FOUNDATIONS OF CAPITALISM 7 (1924).

[44] For a discussion of the concept of the Positive State, see THE MODERN CORPORATE STATE, *supra* note 30, at 86-87; A. MILLER, THE SUPREME COURT AND AMERICAN CAPITALISM 72-132 (1968).

[45] W. WILSON, CONSTITUTIONAL GOVERNMENT IN THE UNITED STATES 166 (1908) [hereinafter cited as WILSON].

[46] J. GRIFFITH, THE POLITICS OF THE JUDICIARY (1977).

[47] *Id.* at 213. Professor Griffith's conclusion is the basis for my theme in this essay.

[48] The phrase, "discrete and insular minorities," is taken from the famous footnote in United States v. Carolene Products Co., 304 U.S. 144, 152 n.4 (1938). Full discussion of the implications of that footnote may be found in ELY, *supra* note 10, at 145-70.

[49] The "conservative" appointees are Chief Justice Burger and Justices Powell, Rehnquist, and Blackmun. For an early discussion of these appointees, see L. LEVY, AGAINST THE LAW 12-54 (1974).

well into the twentieth century.[50] Why? Additionally, why are those amendments now fully enforced, insofar as courts can? The same may be said for the fourteenth amendment: only in very recent years has the equal protection clause been fully—at least, almost fully—enforced. Again, why now?

The questions ask much. Only summary treatment can be given here. For most of our country's history, the Supreme Court read the Bill of Rights literally, not applying them to the states.[51] Only in 1925 did the first breakthrough come.[52] Equally significant is the fact that the first important freedom of expression case was not decided until 1919,[53] and then the State prevailed. Even the notorious Alien and Sedition Act of 1798[54] never got to the Supreme Court, despite harshly repressive measures. The nineteenth century, the myth to the contrary notwithstanding, was not one of widespread freedom for the mass of the people. Those who invoked the Constitution were, speaking very generally, the businessmen who wished to fend off adverse state or federal regulation. They usually prevailed, either on interstate commerce or obligation of contracts grounds before the Civil War[55] or through the Court's invention of substantive due process after that conflict.[56]

— Government in this century is not more repressive than in the past. If anything, it is less so for the people in general. Life for most people during most of American history was, as Thoreau said, one of "quiet desperation." People in the nineteenth century did not think in terms of rights—most people, that is—but in how to wrest a living from a continent which, although fabulously wealthy in natural resources, daunted all but the most courageous and tenacious. One has only to read the social histories of America,[57] as well as novels by Sinclair Lewis, Upton Sinclair, Theodore Dreiser, Hamlin Garland, and others, to realize that until well into the twentieth century life for many Americans was not only desperate but, in the well-known words of Thomas Hobbes, "poor, nasty, brutish and short." In this century, however, the productivity of labor vastly increased. Mass production was born and suddenly the

---

[50] *See generally* P. MURPHY, WORLD WAR I AND THE ORIGIN OF CIVIL LIBERTIES IN THE UNITED STATES (1979).

[51] *See, e.g.*, Barron v. Baltimore, 32 U.S. (7 Pet.) 243, 250-51 (1833) (fifth amendment intended solely as limitation on federal government and does not limit power of state governments).

[52] *See* Gitlow v. New York, 268 U.S. 652, 666 (1925) (freedom of speech and press are among fundamental liberties protected by due process clause of fourteenth amendment).

[53] *See* Schenck v. United States, 249 U.S. 47 (1919).

[54] 1 Stat. 596 (1789). *See generally* L. LEVY, LEGACY OF SUPPRESSION: FREEDOM OF SPEECH AND PRESS IN EARLY AMERICAN HISTORY (1960); J. SMITH, FREEDOM'S FETTERS—THE ALIEN AND SEDITION LAWS AND AMERICAN CIVIL LIBERTIES (1956). Not until 1964 did the Court squarely address the Act, and then only in dicta. *See* New York Times Co. v. Sullivan, 376 U.S. 254, 273-76 (1964).

[55] *See, e.g.*, Gibbons v. Ogden, 22 U.S. (5 Wheat) 1, 239-40 (1824).

[56] *See, e.g.*, New State Ice Co. v. Liebman, 285 U.S. 262, 278 (1932).

[57] *See, e.g.*, P. CARROLL & D. NOBLE, THE FREE AND THE UNFREE (1977); *but see* R. NIEBUHR, MORAL MAN AND IMMORAL SOCIETY (1932).

economy produced goods in plenty. Since necessitous men cannot be free men, the ability of more and more people to sup at the groaning tables of opulence meant that they were—at long last—able to demand and enjoy more freedom. I am aware, of course, of the characterization of Americans as a "people of plenty"[58] and the role that seemingly unlimited "free" land had to play in shaping the American experience. Nevertheless, it is only with the marriage of technology to entrepreneurship that the cornucopia of consumer goods became so large.

Surely the coming of an economy of abundance is one of the reasons for the civil rights/civil liberties explosion in constitutional law. The two phenomena—one economic and the other legal—came at roughly the same time in history. That burst of judicial activism coincided, as previously noted,[59] with political activism aimed at helping some of the disadvantaged in society—some of those left behind in the struggle for greater wealth and status. It would be quite wrong to attribute the explosion to a newly-discovered altruism in American elites, or to a special prescience of Supreme Court Justices. Principally, this change in judicial thinking was the result of an industrial economy in which brutal necessity no longer stared people down. Business required customers as well as workers. In sum, recognition of long-submerged constitutional rights coincided in time with the Golden Age in the United States—the period of roughly 1945 to 1970 when all seemed possible. The dollar was king, American military might was supreme, and for the first time both bread *and* freedom became possible.[60]

Another reason exists for the latter-day recognition of personal rights. Groups previously deeply submerged in society began to surface and demand more. The trade union movement flowered, receiving constitutional protection in 1937.[61] Black Americans, long under the thumb of a rigid caste system, became more insistent that they, too, were persons under the Constitution and entitled to its protections. Add the expansion of the franchise, coupled with incessant propaganda[62] about democracy, and another factor may be seen. Then, too, the United States fought World War II with conscripts, many—perhaps most—of whom came from the working class. A tacit perception that those who fought and won a war would not remain quiescent in the fact of either economic deprivation or denial of democratic rights may, as in Great Britain, have

---

[58] The term, "people of plenty," comes from D. POTTER, PEOPLE OF PLENTY: ECONOMIC ABUNDANCE AND THE AMERICAN CHARACTER (1954).

[59] *See* text accompanying notes 39-47 *supra.*

[60] That the post-1970 period portends a reversion of the status quo ante seems obvious. In the coming "age of frugality," which is hard upon us, the necessity of gathering sufficient supplies to live will again outweigh freedom and the enjoyment of it. *See generally* A. MILLER, DEMOCRATIC DICTATORSHIP: THE EMERGENT CONSTITUTION OF CONTROL (to be published in 1981).

[61] *See* NLRB v. Jones & Laughlin Steel Corp., 301 U.S. 1, 30 (1937) (upholding National Labor Relations Act).

[62] For an insightful discussion of propaganda as a tool of all governments, see generally J. ELLUL, PROPAGANDA (1965) [hereinafter cited as ELLUL].

been significant in the enhancement of personal rights. These rights and the government's response to them were economic, as addressed by the Employment Act of 1946,[63] and human, as reflected in the series of decisions that furthered the cause of human decency for black Americans.

I do not suggest that these reasons, which overlap and coincide, exhaust all possible explanations of a major historical phenomenon. There is, Ernest Nagel has told us, no simple and at the same time complete explanation of any social phenomenon.[64] But I do suggest that the reasons outlined above did play a considerable part in what became Supreme Court decisions, presidential actions, and congressional statutes. The *zeitgeist* has changed. Today Americans enjoy more freedom than ever before in their history. The "why" is important; but so, too, is the social function that is served.

All political or social phenomena have functions. In *The Pathology of Politics*,[65] Professor Carl J. Friedrich argued that such disfunctional—some would say aberrational—matters as violence, betrayal, corruption, secrecy, and propaganda all serve definite, identifiable functions, "notably that of facilitating the adaptation of a system or regime to changing conditions occurring either in the system or in the social structure, or in the outside environment."[66] The point is not argued here, except to say that if such socially objectionable behavior can be functional, then surely a series of Supreme Court decisions can be similarly analyzed.

Judicial decisions are political epiphenomena,[67] and the Supreme Court is an instrument of politics, both in its lawmaking proclivities and in the fact that it is a target of interest groups.[68] The Court's function is to produce decisions that are not only system-maintaining but also system-developing. "A political function," says Friedrich, "is the correspondence between a political process or institution and the needs or requirements of a political order."[69] Any political order requires not only stability but also a process of orderly change. The great and continuing task of the Justices is to facilitate both elements. Through their decisions they buttress the constitutional order—the "system"—and by progressive interpretations they enable change to occur within rather severely constricted boundaries. The need is for a constantly shifting equilibrium.

As previously suggested, one must distinguish between *manifest* and *latent* functions of societal institutions.[70] Simply put, manifest func-

---

[63] 15 U.S.C. §§ 1021-1025 (1976 & Supp. I 1979).

[64] E. NAGEL, THE STRUCTURE OF SCIENCE 447-546 (1961).

[65] C. FRIEDRICH, THE PATHOLOGY OF POLITICS (1972) [hereinafter cited as FREIDRICH].

[66] *Id.* at 224.

[67] *See generally* M. SHAPIRO, LAW AND POLITICS IN THE SUPREME COURT (1964); A. MILLER, ORACLE IN THE MARBLE PALACE: POLITICS AND THE SUPREME COURT (in process).

[68] For a discussion of how the Supreme Court was the target of the NAACP in the cases that culminated in Brown v. Board of Education, 347 U.S. 483 (1954), see generally R. KLUGER, SIMPLE JUSTICE (1976).

[69] FRIEDRICH, *supra* note 65, at 5.

[70] *See* text accompanying notes 37 & 38 *supra*.

tions are the outward or obvious ones. They are important in themselves but must be considered in conjunction with latent functions—those that do not immediately meet the eye, but which may be of far greater significance. Using that distinction, what may be said about the Supreme Court and its egalitarian decisions of the past few decades? The manifest function, quite obviously, is to bring discrete and insular minorities (and the other disadvantaged) into the mainstream of American life, to protect the individual in his personhood against arbitrary governmental acts. These goals are reflected in the range of decisions involving the status of blacks,[71] women,[72] urban voters,[73] workers,[74] and consumers.[75]

The latent function is to protect the system of those who profit most from it. Hydraulic pressures of social discontent are siphoned off in judicial decisions that protect some individuals and appear to protect many more. Ultimately, however, the beneficiaries are those who have throughout American history profited from the workings of the constitutional order—the moneyed and propertied, "the social capitalist" class. Social change is facilitated by Supreme Court rulings, at the least possible cost to those who control and rule.[76] The Justices know that in a period of extraordinarily rapid social change[77] it is more important to accommodate new demands without excessive social cost than to preserve the status quo.

I do not contend that the latent function of the Court, as I have described it, is the result of a dark and conspiratorial maneuver by a hidden power elite. The process is much more subtle than that. But I do say that human liberties receive constitutional protection only to the extent that the vital interests of the State are not jeopardized—which means the vital interests of those who profit most from the State.[78] The system, latent though it is, simply exists. It has a major prophet in Professor B. F. Skinner and a patron saint in Pavlov, the Russian scientist who discovered the conditioned reflex.

---

[71] *See, e.g.,* Brown v. Board of Education, 347 U.S. 483 (1954).

[72] *See, e.g.,* Reed v. Reed, 404 U.S. 71 (1971).

[73] *See, e.g.,* Baker v. Carr, 369 U.S. 186 (1962).

[74] *See, e.g.,* NLRB v. Jones & Laughlin Steel Corp. 301 U.S. 1 (1937).

[75] *See, e.g.,* Goldfarb v. Virginia State Bar, 421 U.S. 773 (1975).

[76] For a discussion of the "ruling class" in the United States, see G. DOMHOFF, THE HIGHER CIRCLES: THE GOVERNING CLASS IN AMERICA (1970); *see also* Miller, *Reason of State and the Emergent Constitution of Control,* 64 MINN. L. REV. 585, 589 (1980) [hereinafter cited as *Reason of State*] (discussing Principle of Economy of Means).

[77] It is truistic to note the rapid pace of social change in the twentieth century, the greatest in human history. For discussion of one aspect of this change, see Branscomb, *Information: The Ultimate Frontier,* 203 SCIENCE 143 (1979) (forecast of technological trends over next 100 years). The law must be stable, yet it cannot stand still. Legal theorists, however, have not yet been able to reconcile the notion of law (which connotes a static system) with rapid social change. Perhaps this is attributable to the fact that our legal institutions grew out of feudalism, which is a static order, and have, as Woodrow Wilson said, a Newtonian cosmology behind them. *See* WILSON, *supra* note 45, at 54-56.

[78] *See* note 76 *supra.*

In *Beyond Freedom and Dignity*[79] Professor Skinner stated that "[w]hat is being abolished is autonomous man—the inner man, the homunculus, the possessing demon, the man defended by the literatures of freedom and dignity. His abolition is long overdue. . . . A scientific view of man offers exciting possibilities. We have not yet seen what man can make of man."[80] Skinner is neither joking nor speaking in hyperbole. As an individual, he may be harmless, and no doubt he thinks that his work is beneficiently furthering the cause of humankind. Others, however, can and will seize his ideas and apply them. "Gobineau was a harmless intellectual crank, but out of his harmless theory of the intellectual superiority of the Aryan race came National Socialism. As Keynes noted: 'The political fanatic who is hearing voices in the air has distilled his frenzy from the work of some academic scribbler of a few years back.'"[81] The need perceived today is for mind manipulation and, through it, control over the human being. Aldous Huxley recognized this, stating:

> We have had religious revolutions, we have had political, industrial, economic, and nationalistic revolutions. All of them, as our descendants will discover, were but ripples in an ocean of conservatism—trivial by comparison with the psychological revolution toward which we are so rapidly moving. *That* will really be a revolution. When it is over, the human race will give no more trouble.[82]

Huxley's revolution has already begun. Man is increasingly seen as an object, and manipulable as such. Mass communications provide the technological means of accomplishing that end. National advertising promotes it. A pervasive system of propaganda—propaganda, as Jacques Ellul has said,[83] being characteristic of all governments—helps it along. During the twentieth century, the rise of the State of preeminence means that an increasing number of controls are placed upon human activity—by both public and private government, for the two interact into one overarching whole.[84] At the same time, a subtle "trade-off" accompanies the rise in social controls and mass manipulation. It is in this area that the Supreme Court has had and continues to have an important role to play. Sometimes, the Court's participation in this process is conscious, as it was in *Brown v. Board of Education*,[85] when surely the Justices knew that rising discontent among black Americans would sooner or later boil over in racial turmoil.[86]

[79] B. SKINNER, BEYOND FREEDOM AND DIGNITY (1971).

[80] *Id.* at 200, 215.

[81] W. THOMPSON, EVIL AND WORLD ORDER 24 (1976).

[82] Statement of Aldous Huxley, *quoted in* A. SCHEFLIN & E. OPTON, THE MIND MANIPULATORS 10 (1978).

[83] *See* ELLUL, *supra* note 62, at ix, x.

[84] *See* THE MODERN CORPORATE STATE, *supra* note 30, *passim*.

[85] 347 U.S. 483 (1954).

[86] Possible racial turmoil is precisely where the United States stands today. The pro-

The Supreme Court has sought to lance the boil of social discontent by constitutionalizing better conditions for the disadvantaged and a permissive society generally. In this endeavor, the Court, of course, does not act alone.[87] The Court, as an essential part of the system of government, cooperates with the other branches. The net result, not all of which is attributable to the Court, is that life styles are changing; marijuana and other drugs are widely used; alcohol consumption is escalating; abortion has been legalized; tranquilizers are a way of life for millions of Americans; the press and motion pictures have been freed from restrictions on even blatant obscenity and pornography; there is more freedom of speech and of the press today than ever before; and rights long denied to blacks and women receive at least some protection. All these, and more, have the latent function of keeping the population relatively quiescent, particularly when they are coupled with social welfare (income distribution) programs. Innocuous activities are encouraged, at times not subtly, by the mass media (*e.g.*, spectator sports). A price for increasing controls by the State is permissiveness in noneconomic areas. Aldous Huxley brilliantly forecast this development in *Brave New World*, although he thought it would be 500 years away.[88] His timing was off, as he later admitted.[89]

The Justices have been active participants in this development. Their decisions in racial segregation cases helped stifle discontent by giving blacks the hope, at least for a time, of becoming part of the mainstream of American life. That is perhaps the most obvious of the decisional areas. Other areas may be discerned as well: decisions permitting printing and showing of material that only a few years ago would have been considered obscene and punishable;[90] occasional recognitions that women have been treated unfairly and are also entitled to equal protection of the laws;[91] permitting a young man to go unpunished even though he paraded through a public building with a slogan "Fuck the Draft" emblazoned on his leather jacket;[92] and recognizing that the "rotton boroughs" of the nation violated the equal protection clause.[93] In these areas—no doubt there are others—the Court helped build the permissive society, the "culture of narcissism," the "Me Generation."[94] The

---

mise of *Brown* has not been fulfilled, and the dashed expectations of millions of blacks can easily erupt into violence. *See* G. GILL, MEANNESS MANIA: THE CHANGED MOOD (1980) [hereinafter cited as GILL].

[87] *See, e.g.*, United Steelworkers v. Weber, 443 U.S. 193, 208 (1979) (upholding voluntary affirmative action plan).

[88] A. HUXLEY, BRAVE NEW WORLD (1932).

[89] A. HUXLEY, BRAVE NEW WORLD REVISITED 4 (1958).

[90] *See, e.g.*, Roth v. United States, 354 U.S. 476 (1957).

[91] *See, e.g.*, Reed v. Reed, 404 U.S. 71 (1971). It is worth noting that the Court could have "enacted" the Equal Rights Amendment into constitutional law in the *Reed* case, but chose not to do so.

[92] Cohen v. California, 403 U.S. 15 (1971).

[93] Baker v. Carr, 369 U.S. 186 (1962).

[94] *See* C. LASCH, THE CULTURE OF NARCISSISM (1979).

pattern is not uniform, of course, for when it was perceived that the vital interests of the State were at stake the Justices upheld the power of government.[95]

Of course, the Justices are not alone in furthering the subtle controls being placed on individuals. Other government agencies participate, as do the major social groups of the nation. Furthermore, they do not outwardly assert that they are interested in fulfilling Huxley's prediction. On occasion the Court does overtly state that its decision effects a connection with the fundamental needs of "society."[96] The net result of this process has been graphically described by Solzhenitsyn:

> "[A]s every man goes through life he fills in a number of forms for the record. . . . There are hundreds of little threads radiating from every man, millions of threads in all. If all these threads were suddenly to become visible the whole sky would look like a spider's web and if they materialized as rubber bands, buses, trams and people would lose the ability to move."[97]

With the tremendous improvements in computer technology and the coming of micro-processing, the technology is now available and in place for manipulation of those threads. To Solzhenitsyn, the cobweb symbolizes strangulation and suffocation by bureaucracy in an authoritarian society. There can be no question that the United States has become "the bureaucratic state"[98] with the bureaucracies being both public and private and cooperating with each other.[99]

In summary, the Supreme Court's work prior to 1937 dealt largely with the rise of finance capitalism. Since then, however, civil rights and liberties received judicial protection for the first time in American history. While some individuals have benefited from these judicial decisions, the ultimate — the latent — beneficiary is "the ruling class" — those with money and property who have always been in control.

That conclusion makes nonsense out of the neo-conservatives' splenetic complaints that the Court acted unconstitutionally in some of its more liberal decisions.[100] The very decisions most criticized — those

---

[95] *See, e.g.*, Wyman v. James, 400 U.S. 309 (1971) (home visitation by welfare workers without warrant does not violate fourth amendment); United States v. O'Brien, 391 U.S. 367 (1968) (statute proscribing knowing destruction of draft card does not violate first amendment).

[96] *See, e.g.*, Barenblatt v. United States, 360 U.S. 109, 128 (1959) (questioning by House Committee on UnAmerican Activities necessary to ensure "national security"); Dennis v. United States, 341 U.S. 494, 501-02 (1951) (Smith Act prohibition against advocacy of violent overthrow of government does not violate first amendment because of "national security"). Both decisions are a form of "thought control." *See Reason of State, supra* note 76, 605-07.

[97] A. SOLZHENITSYN, CANCER WARD (1968).

[98] *See generally* Wilson, *The Rise of the Bureaucratic State*, 41 PUB. INT. 77 (1975).

[99] Galbraith describes the cooperative relationship between public and private bureaucracies as "bureaucratic symbiosis." J. GALBRAITH, ECONOMICS AND THE PUBLIC PURPOSE 143 (1973) [hereinafter cites as GALBRAITH].

[100] *See, e.g.*, BERGER, *supra* note 27.

dealing with racial segregation, abortion, and legislative apportionment—have the actual function of damping the fires of social discontent and of helping to achieve stability through peaceful change—the very values that neo-conservatives cherish. Were they to see beneath the surface, those critics would applaud rather than complain. Of course, the judicial decisions are mere stop-gaps, and since the Supreme Court has no enforcement power of its own, the Justices must depend upon the good will and good sense of officers in the political branches of government for compliance. Although the record on that score is spotty at best, the decisions do give the politicians time to grapple with some of the pent-up demands of long-submerged groups.

The changes wrought by the Court in recent decades are, despite the widespread publicity, minuscule. Some groups have made largely symbolic gains—for example, urban voters. Even for black Americans, the gains have been more apparent than real.[101] The system of corporate capitalism remains and flourishes, and no doubt will continue to do so if the *Bellotti* decision is any indication. The Progressive movement of the early twentieth century, the New Deal, and the constitutional revolution of the 1930s and '40s were, in final analysis, a means to perpetuate a working partnership between business and government. In the post-1937 period when the Court read Keynesian economics into the Constitution and overtly abandoned laissez-faire, it did not cease to serve the interests of the business class. The Justices merely took a more sophisticated viewpoint, in accord with the long-range interests of the dominant corporate interests. Socialism for the poor (but not for the rich) was staved off, in part by the Supreme Court's giving legal expression to some of the sources of discontent. Professor Griffith is correct: the judiciary, as an essential part of the government, protects the stability of the system of corporate capitalism and resists attempts to change it.[102]

III.   The Significance of *Bellotti*

Bellotti, in essence, is an anti-democratic decision, part of a backlash against the spread of the franchise and other aspects of mass democracy. Professor Samuel P. Huntington, in a well-known essay,[103] complains about the "democratic distemper" and the "decline in the governability of democracy"—simply, it seems, because "democracy" has been successful. Democracy is vulnerable, says Huntington, because of "the internal dynamics of democracy itself in a highly educated, mobilized, and participant society."[104] That viewpoint must be taken seriously, for Huntington spoke for a highly influential group.[105]

---

[101] *See* GILL, *supra* note 86; Miller, *Brown's 25th: A Silver Lining Tarnished With Time*, 3 DISTRICT LAWYER 22 (1979).

[102] *See* text accompanying notes 46 & 47 *supra*.

[103] Huntington, *The United States*, in M. CROZIER, S. HUNTINGTON & J. WATANUKI, THE CRISIS OF DEMOCRACY 59 (1975).

[104] *Id.* at 115.

[105] Huntington spoke for the Trilateral Commission, a small group of well-placed

The *Bellotti* decision, then, should be seen as part of a Burkean[106] counter-revolution against what are considered to be the excesses of democracy. By glossing over the enormous disparities in wealth (and thus in political power) between natural persons and corporations, Justice Powell's opinion served the interests of the dominant economic form in America—the giant corporations—by helping them to stave off the "excesses" of "a highly educated, mobilized, and participant society." Since corporate assets may now be used to further the interests of corporations by allowing them to "speak" even if the issues do not materially affect their businesses, the corporate enterprise as a political actor will, simply because of its vastly superior assets, dominate the "democratic" process of elections and direct voting by referenda or initiatives. We have come a long, long way since Chief Justice Marshall opined in 1819 that a corporation, as a mere creature of the law, possesses "only those properties which the charter of its creation confers upon it, either expressly, or as incidental to its very existence."[107] A disembodied economic entity now can speak.

The incongruity of such a conclusion suggests that the myopia of the *Bellotti* majority was willful, not accidental, and that the decision was reached with full cognizance of its portents. It was deliberately aimed at enhancing corporate power, and with the obvious secondary consequence of diminishing the power of the individual *qua* natural person. This result is achieved, even though the corporation is "a *persona ficta*, a 'legal fiction' with no pants to kick or soul to damn. What is meant is that while we can point to the corporation's steel and glass factory, or its tangible chairman of the board, or to its offices in Rockefeller Plaza, there is no physical entity *the corporation* that we can point to — or that can, of itself, adulterate foods or pollute rivers. The corporation *itself*, it is said 'does no act, speaks no word, thinks no thoughts.' "[108] It is obvious that by giving freedom of expression beyond its material needs to *the* corporation, the Court was in fact permitting those who *control*, but do not necessarily *own*, the firm to have more than a running start in the political arena. To paraphrase Chief Justice Taft in a far different decision: "All others can see and understand this. How can [the *Bellotti* majority] properly shut [their] minds to it?"[109]

---

businessmen, lawyers, and government officials in the United States, Western Europe, and Japan. *See generally* TRILATERALISM (H. Sklar ed. 1980).

[106] The reference is to Edmund Burke. The late Alexander Bickel was an avowed Burkean. *See* A. BICKEL, THE MORALITY OF CONSENT (1975). For a discussion of Burke, see F. O'GORMAN, EDMUND BURKE: HIS POLITICAL PHILOSOPHY (1973). Burke, of course, was *the* defender of the *ancien regime* after the French Revolution. *See generally* E. BURKE, REFLECTIONS ON THE REVOLUTION (1790); E. BURKE, APPEAL FROM THE NEW TO THE OLD WHIGS (1791), *reprinted in* EDMUND BURKE: ON GOVERNMENT, POLITICS AND SOCIETY (B. Hill ed.) (1976).

[107] Dartmouth College v. Woodward, 17 U.S. (4 Wheat.) 518, 636 (1819).

[108] C. STONE, WHERE THE LAW ENDS 3 (1975) (emphasis added).

[109] Bailey v. Drexel Furniture Co., 259 U.S. 20, 37 (1922).

Indeed, how can they? And, indeed, how can such a sagacious commentator as Professor Choper fail to perceive that the *Bellotti* decision will have immense long-range effects on the political order — and thus on the constitutional order? Choper maintains that he is most interested in judicial review as a means of furthering *individual* rights — an orientation precisely 180 degrees away from Powell's opinion. If man is a machine, and manipulable as such, as Skinner and others maintain,[110] then the use of corporate assets to dominate the entire political process is sure to eventuate. Corporations and other groups in our corporate society are currently able, through being parts of the "subgovernments" or "iron triangles" of American government,[111] to pursue narrow goals and to influence greatly, and probably actually control, narrow segments of the decision-making processes within much of the national government. *Bellotti* gives them a leg up on direct "democracy," including referenda and initiatives as well as elections to public office.

Of course, corporations *as such* cannot speak. Identifiable human beings, and only those beings, can. They are the corporate officers, those who control but, except in family-held firms, do not own. When they speak, their voices are not merely the voices of disparate individuals, but the stentorian utterances of the wellnigh bottomless barrels of corporate assets. Those assets give those officers an advantage no other natural person can hope to have. It is not, as Justice Powell suggested, merely a matter of giving an even break to the business enterprise (or of looking at the communication only). The *Bellotti* Court loaded the political dice in favor of corporations, by relying on the argument that the primary function of the first amendment is to inform the public, and that the people are capable of assessing the relative merits of communications received. True, informing the public is basic to the first amendment, but the informing function is based on the assumption that those who speak or would speak are roughly equal in lung power. That assumption is, as Professor Jerome Barron has shown, wholly inaccurate.[112]

The editors of the *Harvard Law Review* have advanced the odd argument that there is an even stronger rationale for the decision in *Bellotti*: "Corporate political expression should be protected as the speech and associational activity of the individual owners."[113] That astonishing position completely ignores the facts of business life in large,

---

[110] Many humanists share Skinner's view that man is a manipulable machine. *But see* D. EHRENFELD, THE ARROGANCE OF HUMANISM 236-49 (1978).

[111] For a discussion of subgovernments see D. CATER. POWER IN WASHINGTON (1964). For an analysis of iron triangles, see Heclo, *Issue Networks and the Executive Establishment*, in THE NEW AMERICAN POLITICAL SYSTEM 87 (A. King ed. 1978). The terms refer to informal but enduring accommodations linking executive bureaus, Congressional committees, and interest groups with a stake in particular programs. *See* G. MCCONNELL. PRIVATE POWER AND AMERICAN DEMOCRACY *passim* (1966).

[112] *See* J. BARRON. FREEDOM OF THE PRESS FOR WHOM? 3-7 (1973) (access to modern media is subject to approval of media managers).

[113] *The Supreme Court, 1977 Term*, 92 HARV. L. REV. 1, 165 (1978).

publicly-held firms. For those editors to maintain that "[c]orporate political expression is simply shareholder speech or the product of shareholder associational activity" is to confuse the entity with its shareholders—a relationship which simply does not exist. While a family-held corporation, such as Cargill or even the Washington Post Company does reflect its shareholders,[114] General Motors or AT&T do not.[115]

If the Supreme Court's basic theory of the first amendment—that there should be robust debate in a marketplace of ideas—is valid, then an unfair advantage, which in time will amount to domination of the process, will be the result of *Bellotti*. It is no answer to say, as did Chief Justice Burger in his concurring opinion, that a "disquieting aspect of Massachusetts' position is that it may carry the risk of impinging on the First Amendment rights of those who employ the corporate form . . . to carry on the business of mass communications. . . ."[116] To maintain that a state may regulate the non-business related expression of a corporation by no means suggests that the state could similarly regulate, say, the New York Times; for after all, expression *is* the *raison d'etre* of the Times. Chief Justice Burger should decide that wholly fanciful hypothetical case when it arises, not in a gratuitous dictum uttered in a dissimilar case. The answer to Burger is the same as Holmes gave to John Marshall's assertion in *McCulloch v. Maryland*[117] that the power to tax involves the power to destroy: "Not," Holmes said, "while this Court sits."

IV. Conclusion

This essay has been directed toward pointing out some of the implications of Justice Powell's majority opinion in *First National Bank v. Bellotti*. When coupled with the decisions in *Buckley v. Valeo*[118] and *Consolidated Edison Co. v. Public Service Commission*,[119] the conclusion is inescapable: a majority of the Justices perceive much of their job to be that of protecting the class from whence they came—its property, its status, its position of political power. They have no apparent interest in

---

[114] Cargill is a family-held corporation, see D. MORGAN, THE MERCHANTS OF GRAIN 183 (1979). Even though the Washington Post is now a publicly-held firm, the Graham family owns more than 50% of the voting stock.

[115] *See* GALBRAITH, *supra* note 99, at 218.

[116] 435 U.S. at 796 (Burger, C.J., concurring).

[117] 17 U.S. (4 Wheat.) 316 (1819).

[118] 424 U.S. 1 (1976).

[119] 100 S. Ct. 2326 (1980). In *Consolidated Edison*, Justice Powell held that the first amendment protected the utility's placement of written material advocating nuclear power in its billing envelopes. *Id.* at 2311. On the same day, Powell delivered the opinion in Central Hudson Gas & Elec. Corp. v. Public Serv. Comm'n, 100 S. Ct. 2343 (1980), which struck down a ban on an electric utility's promotion of the use of electricity. *Id.* at 2354. *Central Hudson*, however, deals with "commercial speech" rather than the non-business related speech involved in *Bellotti*. *Id.* at 2351-52. For a discussion of commercial speech, see J. BARRON & C. DIENES, HANDBOOK OF FREE SPEECH AND FREE PRESS §§ 4.1-4.10 (1979).

approving any type of wealth distribution scheme, such as was involved in *San Antonio Independent School District v. Rodriguez.*[120] That, to be sure, was an equal protection decision, but the Court's opinion (written by Justice Powell) permitted the rich, in Professor Laurence Tribe's words, "to create their own secure haven of privilege and exclusion."[121] Justice Powell also authored the Court's opinion in *Bakke,*[122] which might be thought to strike a different note. It does not, for the dispute there was between "have-nots," not a "have-not" against the "haves" — as in *Rodriguez.*

The United States has travelled a long road since the constitutional convention of 1787 produced the sacred document which is the main object of worship in our secular religion of Americanism (or nationalism or patriotism).[123] Of major, perhaps greatest, importance in that journey has been the expansion of the franchise to metes far beyond those of 1789, when the Constitution went into effect. Then only those with money and property could vote. Today all but a minute number of wealth limitations have been eliminated,[124] women can vote, the voting age has been lowered to eighteen and even those who cannot speak or read English can vote.[125] That has created a new situation — mass "democracy" —

---

[120] 411 U.S. 1 (1973). In *Rodriquez,* the Supreme Court upheld a system of local property taxes imposed to supplement school budgets. *Id.* at 55. The plaintiffs in *Rodriquez* unsuccessfully contended that an educational system that depends on local property taxes is unconstitutional because it operates to the disadvantage of the poor; some school districts received more funds than others.

[121] L. TRIBE, AMERICAN CONSTITUTIONAL LAW § 16-56, at 1133 (1978).

[122] 438 U.S. 265 (1978). *See* LaRue, *The Rhetoric of Powell's* Bakke, 38 WASH. & LEE. L. REV. 43 (1981). Professor LaRue states that Justice Powell's argument "seems to be that corrective justice is permissible, but distributive justice is not," and finds that to be "an astonishing proposition." *Id.* at 52. If I understand the terms, "corrective" and "distributive" justice, correctly, I do not find Powell's position (as defined by Professor LaRue) at all astonishing. As I have tried to show in this comment, Powell, like other members of the Court, has no interest in distributive justice as such. Insightful analysis of the problems of distributive justice may be found in L. THUROW, THE ZERO-SUM SOCIETY (1980).

[123] Brest, *The Misconceived Quest for the Original Understanding,* 60 B. U. L. REV. 204, 234 (1980); *see generally* Levinson, *"The Constitution" in American Civil Religion,* 1979 SUP. CT. REV. 123; Lerner, *Constitution and Court as Symbols,* 46 YALE L. J. 1290 (1937). It is worth mentioning that although there is a constitutional separation of *church* and State in the United States pursuant to the first amendment, by no means are *religion* and the State separated. *See* Zorach v. Clauson, 343 U.S. 306, 313 (1952) ("We are a religious people whose institutions presuppose a Supreme Being"). For discussion of the two moralities in American public policy — the pagan and the Judeo-Christian — see *Reason of State, supra* note 76, at 588-613. For further discussion of civil or secular religion in the United States, see M. NOVAK, CHOOSING OUR KING (1974).

[124] One wealth limitation on voting that remains is restriction of eligibility to vote for the board of directors of water districts to landowners. *See* Salyer Land Co. v. Tulare Lake Basin Water Storage Dist., 410 U.S. 719, 730 (1973). *Salyer,* however, may be an aberration. The Court is usually hostile to any type of overt voting restriction. *See, e.g.,* Hill v. Stone, 421 U.S. 289, 300-01 (1975) (striking statute which limited right to vote in bond elections to those who paid property taxes that year).

[125] *See* Katzenbach v. Morgan, 384 U.S. 641, 656 (1966).

which, when coupled with the rise of new pluralistic groups to positions of power, means that democracy (and pluralism) are considered by some to be faulty simply because they have been successful.

Politics today is a matter of moving the masses, as congregated in groups. Groups dominate the political order.[126] At the same time, however, a counter-movement has arisen, one designed to retain (or regain) control by those with money and property through those elected to public office. We are witnessing, as Galbraith recently said, "the revolt of the rich against the poor."[127] The Supreme Court's opinions in *Bellotti* and elsewhere are part of that revolt.

A final note: I realize that some of what is said in this essay cuts against the grain of much of the popular wisdom or conventional writing about the Supreme Court. Many commentators, it seems, like to parse Court opinions to determine whether "neutral principles" were invoked,[128] or they assume that the Justices do not bring their heredity and biography with them when they join the High Bench. So much nonsense has been written about "neutral principles" and "reasoned elaboration" and similar unattainable goals that generations of students go through law school believing that judges so act, or, if they do not, that they should.[129] That they do not and, indeed, cannot has long been known, but also has been the subject of a conspiracy of silence among most who comment on the judicial process.

Judges are not fungible, as Justice William O. Douglas once said.[130] They bring their "can't-helps" to the bench with them. Try as they might to achieve a complete disinterestedness, the human mind is not up to that and myopia is the result. All judges, the late Judge Braxton Craven maintained, are "result-oriented" — the only difference between them be-

---

[126] *See* R. DAHL, PLURALIST DEMOCRACY IN THE UNITED STATES (1967); T. LOWI, THE END OF LIBERALISM 55-101 (2d ed. 1979); L. THUROW, THE ZERO-SUM SOCIETY (1980).

[127] Galbraith, *How to Get Ahead*, N.Y. REV. OF BOOKS (July 19, 1979).

[128] The seminal essay on the "neutral principles" approach is Wechsler, *Toward Neutral Principles of Constitutional Law*, 73 HARV. L. REV. 1 (1959) [hereinafter cited as Wechsler], *criticized in* A. MILLER, THE SUPREME COURT: MYTH AND REALITY, 51-87 (1978).

[129] For a celebration of Wechsler, *supra* note 128, see Greenawalt, *The Enduring Significance of Neutral Principles*, 78 COLUM. L. REV. 982 (1978) [hereinafter cited as Greenawalt]. Although both Wechsler and Greenawalt, and diverse others, promote the indispensability of a search for an identification of neutral principles of constitutional adjudication, it is odd but true that none of them has ever educated us as to when the Supreme Court has so acted. Are we not entitled to consider it a bootless quest? The same may be said for those who believe in "reasoned elaboration." See H. HART & A. SACKS, THE LEGAL PROCESS §§ 161-70 (10th ed. 1958); White, *The Evolution of Reasoned Elaboration: Jurisprudential Criticism and Social Change* 59 VA. L. REV. 279 (1973).

[130] Chandler v. Judicial Council, 398 U.S. 74, 137 (1970) (Douglas, J., dissenting). Everyone knows that judges are not fungible, or at least they should know it, yet it is odd but true that not one of the coursebooks in constitutional law published for use in law schools makes reference to that fact of legal life. Those who plump for neutral principles or reasoned elaboration analysis, *see* note 129 *supra*, simply ignore the limits of the human mind.

ing that some know it and some do not.[131] This essay opened with a quotation from Morris R. Cohen about the "imperfect knowledge or intelligence" of those in the legal machinery. It is not so much that as the evaluation placed by judges upon the data brought to them and upon information that should be known to all. Intelligence the Justices have, of that there can be no doubt, although some on the present Court surely rank intellectually higher than others. Again, however, it is how a Justice uses his intelligence that is important — to what ends, for what purposes, for whose benefit. For the *Bellotti* Court to speak of "democracy" as if it meant something precise, which emphatically it does not,[132] and to equate the political powers of the natural person with that of corporate enterprise is, as Justice Robert H. Jackson said in another context, to extend "a promise to the ear to be broken in the hope, a teasing illusion like a munificent bequest in a pauper's will."[133]

[131] Craven, *Paean to Pragmatism*, 50 N. Car. L. Rev. 977, 977 (1972). The term "result-orientation" has become fashionable in recent years as one of opprobrium for judges and commentators, who are enjoined by some deep-thinkers to eschew who wins — the results — and look to the reasons. See, *e.g.*, Greenawalt, *supra* note 129, at 1021; Griswold, *Of Time and Attitudes—Professor Hart and Judge Arnold*, 74 Harv. L. Rev. 81, 93-94 (1961); Wechsler, *supra* note 128, at 18. *See also* R. Funston, Constitutional Counter-revolution? 29 (1977): ("Opinions based upon reasoned principle . . . are necessary to the very self-preservation of the Supreme Court. Assuming that the institution is worth preserving, Justices must sometimes sacrifice what they conceive to be a desirable result, if they cannot logically justify that result.") Professor Funston's statement is consummate nonsense. Judge Craven, of course, was correct. One does not have to agree with the results reached to argue that judges (and others) are result-oriented. It is one of the failures of legal (and other) scholarship for commentators to assume that they, too, are neutral or objective. *See generally* Miller, *The Myth of Objectivity in Legal Research and Writing*, 18 Cath. U. L. Rev. 290 (1969).

[132] There are at least 200 definitions of the term "democracy." *See* M. Rejai, Democracy: The Contemporary Theories 23-48 (1967); E. Schattschneider, The Semisovereign People 130-31 (1960) ("The great deficiency of American democracy is intellectual, the lack of a good, usable definition."); *see also* Crick, *Introduction* to N. Machiavelli, The Discourses 27 (B. Crick ed. 1970) ("to call government 'democratic' is always a misleading piece of propaganda. . . . It confuses doctrine with theory; we may want the democratic element in government to grow greater, but it is still only an element while it is government at all."); H. Arendt, On Revolution 117 (1963).

[133] Edwards v. California, 314 U.S. 160, 186 (1941) (Jackson , J., concurring). *See* M. Carnoy & D. Shearer, Economic Democracy 131 (1980) ("The principle of one person/one vote in the political arena . . . confronts the reality of unequal economic rights and an unequal distribution of economic power. The two cannot be separated. The 'free speech' of a General Motors is obviously greater than that of any individual."). *See also* Hart & Shore, *Corporate Spending on State and Local Referendums:* First National Bank of Boston v. Bellotti, 28 Case West. Res. L. Rev. 808, 829 (1979).

CHAPTER **9**

Taming the Corporate Beast

*This brief chapter adumbrates the basic idea that corporations are private govern-
ments and, as such, should be brought within the purview of constitutional norms.
Americans, it is argued, are ruled as much or more by so-called private groups,
mainly the giant corporations, than by public governance. The corporate behemoths
are creatures of the last 100 years, and could not have remotely been in the minds of
those who drafted the Constitution.*

*Were the Constitution to be rewritten today, what would be—what should
be—said about the corporations and their place in the social order? This essay
probes that question. It suggests that the time is long past for constitutional
limitations to be placed on certain corporate behavior—to recognize, that is, their
large capacity for governance. A corporation is a government internally, in the
relationships among those who make up the corporate "community," and
externally, particularly in how it affects and influences public governmental
decisions. Application of the due process principle to corporate actions would help
alleviate problems welling up internally. Externally, however, some more creative
constitutional lawmaking would be necessary. In the main, these new principles
would seek to impose certain constitutional duties upon corporate giants—for
example, to consider the common good when making major decisions.*

*Concededly, neither development has taken place. The argument is that they
should occur, if democracy in theory and practice is to prevail.*

A corporation is government through and through. . . . Certain technical methods which political government uses, as, for instance, hanging, are not used by corporations, generally speaking, but that is a detail.

—Arthur Bentley[1]

Arthur Bentley wrote in 1908. Yet his insights lay fallow until Professor David Truman rediscovered them in 1951.[2] Since then the group basis of politics has been the accepted wisdom among students of the political process. Not so, however, with lawyers, who with invincible parochialism still insist that the corporation is a person because the Supreme Court said so in 1886,[3] and who consequently refuse to recognize that the corporation is a collectivity—a political organization—and should be dealt with as such.[4] Economists, too, have not produced a theory of conscious economic cooperation. Irrespective of each discipline's degree of oblivion to the realities of the world, questions of politics, law, and economics eventually or ultimately become questions of constitutional theory. The need to constitutionalize the corporation is the theme of this essay. Corporate governance, in brief, is a problem for the constitutional lawyer. Not solely, for the corpus of corporate law (including administrative law) merits continuing attention, but ulti-

---

1. A. BENTLEY, THE PROCESS OF GOVERNMENT 268 (1908).

2. *See* D. TRUMAN, THE GOVERNMENTAL PROCESS (1951). Seventeen years earlier, Karl Llewellyn made a passing reference to Bentley's ideas. Llewellyn, *The Constitution as an Institution*, 34 COLUM. L. REV. 1, 1 n.1 (1934).

3. Santa Clara County v. Southern Pac. R.R., 118 U.S. 394, 396 (1886). *See* B. TWISS, LAWYERS AND THE CONSTITUTION 94 (1942). Corporate personality is, of course, a legal fiction, but it is an enduring one that has had significant consequences. *See* C. STONE, WHERE THE LAW ENDS 2 (1975).

4. Few have done so. One who did early on was the late Alexander Pekelis. *See* A. PEKELIS, LAW AND SOCIAL ACTION 91-127 (M. Konvitz ed. 1950). For a more recent treatment, see A. MILLER, THE MODERN CORPORATE STATE 188-244 (1976).

This chapter was originally published under the title of "A Modest Proposal for Helping to Tame the Corporate Beast in 8 Hofstra Law Review 79 (1979), and is reprinted with the permission of the Hofstra Law Review.

mately the problem of the corporation and its place in the social order is one of the political economy of American constitutionalism.

As used in this essay, "constitutionalize" has two meanings. Although written one hundred and ninety years ago, the words of the Constitution must find definition and legitimacy in the contemporary world. Constitutional law has largely been concerned with adapting the Constitution to changing social, political, and economic realities and to our changing notions of justice. The changing *zeitgeist* is frequently reflected in the actions of the majoritarian branches of government. When the Supreme Court sanctions congressional and executive actions, the spirit of those governmental actions is constitutionalized, and it infuses the words of the Constitution with new life. The term is also used to signify imposing these evolving constitutional norms on organizations that have become de facto governments—the giant corporation being the principal, but by no means only, exemplar. This second meaning is the principal focus of this essay.

DEFINING THE CORPORATION

The Corporation as Person

Americans are ambivalent about corporations. They want the material benefits of corporate enterprises, but they have an inchoate fear of big business. This is one of the "biformities" of what Professor Michael Kammen calls our "contrapuntal civilization."[5] The biformity has produced a number of incongruities. First, the charade of the antitrust laws is permitted, laws whose control of business enterprise is more ostensible than real.[6] Next, business can call itself private, even though it has been known for decades that there is nothing except share ownership, but not control, that is truly private about the giant corporation. Third, the law defines corporations as constitutional persons,[7] which has meant that companies get the benefits of the Constitution without the concomitant duties. Finally, corporations are concentrations of economic power that are permitted to wield an inordinate amount of political

---

5. M. KAMMEN, PEOPLE OF PARADOX 116 (1972).

6. For an early discussion of this point, see T. ARNOLD, THE FOLKLORE OF CAPITALISM (1937). Nothing that has happened since Arnold wrote dilutes his incisive observations. The antitrust laws are more hortatory than interdictory. The current federal antitrust action against IBM is illustrative. United States v. International Business Machine, Inc., No. Civ. 69-200 (S.D.N.Y., filed Jan. 17, 1969).

7. *See* Santa Clara County v. Southern Pac. R.R., 118 U.S. 394, 396 (1886).

power internally within the corporate community and externally upon society at large.[8]

Chief Justice Marshall's well-known definition of a corporation provides a useful starting place for discussing the constitutional problems of corporate governance.

> A corporation is an artificial being, invisible, intangible, and existing only in contemplation of law. Being the mere creature of law, it possesses only those properties which the charter of its creation confers upon it, either expressly, or as incidental to its very existence. These are such as are supposed best calculated to effect the object for which it was created. Among the most important are immortality, and . . . individuality; properties, by which a perpetual succession of many persons are considered as the same, and may act as a single individual. They enable a corporation to manage its own affairs, and to hold property, without the perplexing intricacies . . . of perpetual conveyances for the purpose of transmitting it from hand to hand. It is chiefly for the purpose of clothing bodies of men, in succession, with these qualities and capacities, that corporations were invented, and are in use. By these means, a perpetual succession of individuals are capable of acting for the promotion of the particular object, like one immortal being.[9]

When Chief Justice Marshall described that "mere creature of law" in 1819, the corporation was by modern standards a tiny, localized company. Relatively few corporations existed, and, as Chief Justice Marshall said, they did so to promote a "particular object." Sixteen decades later, corporations are the characteristic form of doing business. We live in a corporate society[10] where corporations have not only waxed so large and strong that they straddle

---

8.   The question of whether to call a corporation a constitutional person goes to the legitimacy of the corporate enterprise in a polity that calls itself democratic. Corporations are legitimate in the strictly legal sense, simply because the Supreme Court has accorded them that status. But there are other dimensions to legitimacy, as Professor Douglas Sturm has observed:

> Legitimation is first of all a strictly legal process; but more profoundly it is a political process of ascertaining the acceptance, criticism and direction of the people; and finally it is a religious and philosophical process of subjecting the economic association to the tests of some vision of the nature and destiny of man within the context of reality as a whole.

Sturm, *Corporations, Constitutions and Covenants*, 41 J. AM. ACADEMY RELIGION 331, 353 (1973).

9.   Dartmouth College v. Woodward, 17 U.S. (4 Wheat.) 518, 636 (1819).

10.   Gossett, *Corporate Citizenship*, in 2 THE RANDOLPH TUCKER LECTURES 159, 177 (1957).

the globe, but with the death of the ultra vires doctrine,[11] they no longer are confined to particular objects. A new constitutional world has been created;[12] and the puerility of allowing the corporation to be a constitutional person without accompanying duties should be obvious even to lawyers.

Efforts to make the corporation a person, and therefore capable of triggering the due process and equal protection clauses of the fourteenth amendment, began within a few years of the amendment's ratification. Those first efforts were still-born,[13] but the Supreme Court suddenly reversed itself in *Santa Clara County v. Southern Pacific Railroad*[14] when it casually and without hearing argument held that a corporation was indeed a person within the terms of the first section of the fourteenth amendment.[15]

While the corporation has been a person under the Constitution for less than a century, personhood has meant much to that disembodied entity. Witness the 1978 decision of the Supreme Court in *First National Bank v. Bellotti*,[16] where the Court held that a corporation has a first amendment right to speak even if the issues do not materially affect its business.[17] This means that the enormous assets of corporations[18] can be employed anywhere in the political process on any issue, irrespective of the issue's relevance to the company's business. Thus, the limitations set out by Chief Justice Marshall in 1819 are no longer the law. To be sure, as Chief Justice Burger's concurrence in *Bellotti* points out, this merely gives all corporations the same first amendment rights as the media;[19] but it leaves unanswered, save in some conclusory assertions by Justice Powell,[20] the question of how to balance the enormous economic power of an artificial person with the comparatively meager resources of a natural person.[21] Even Justice

---

11. *See* D. VAGTS, BASIC CORPORATION LAW 169-70 (1973).

12. *See* A. MILLER, *supra* note 4, at 86-112.

13. *See* Munn v. Illinois, 94 U.S. 113 (1877); Slaughter-House Cases, 83 U.S. 36 (1873).

14. 118 U.S. 394 (1886).

15. *Id.* at 396. The Supreme Court moves in wondrous ways its miracles to perform. One of the most important decisions in its history was made outside the parameters of the adversary system.

16. 435 U.S. 765 (1978).

17. *Id.* at 783-84.

18. In 1979, AT&T had $100 billion in assets.

19. 435 U.S. at 796-802 (Burger, C.J., concurring).

20. *Id.* at 788-92.

21. Justice Powell, writing for the Court, pointed out that "corporate advertising may influence the outcome of [a] vote; this would be its purpose. But the fact

Rehnquist, not known for his aversion to business, could not stomach the majority's conclusions.[22] In his dissent he echoed[23] Justices Black[24] and Douglas,[25] who on separate occasions maintained that the 1886 bit of judicial lawmaking should be reexamined and overruled.

Such aberrant views are not likely to be followed, however, and the corporation will probably remain a constitutional person.[26] Therefore, while depersonalizing the corporation may be desirable, the law must move in other directions if it is going to deal in a meaningful way with the problems posed by large corporations. If the corporation is a person, then it must shoulder burdens analogous to those borne by natural persons. The ultimate duty the State can impose upon a natural person is to make him defend and fight, and perhaps die, for the corporate entity called the nation.[27] But there is more. Despite the seeming absolutes of the thirteenth amendment and the due process clauses, a natural person can not only be drafted into military service,[28] he or she can also be required to work on public roads without compensation[29] and forced to serve on juries.[30] In addition, contracts of seamen, which fall under the scope of "services which have from time immemorial been treated as exceptional," may be enforced even though they require the surrender of a certain amount of personal liberty.[31] These duties reached their zenith—or rather their nadir—when Justice Black held in *Korematsu v. United States*[32] that citizenship involved duties as well as rights.[33] Therefore, native-born Ameri-

---

that advocacy may persuade the electorate is hardly a reason to suppress it . . . ." *Id.* at 790. Justice Powell believed that a corporation's ability to influence a vote is offset by the electorate's ability to judge a viewpoint by identifying its source and weighing its credibility. *Id.* at 791-92.

22.   *Id.* at 828 (Rehnquist, J., dissenting).

23.   435 U.S. at 822 (Rehnquist, J., dissenting). The Court is exploring business' right to free speech this term. *See* Central Hudson Gas & Elec. Corp. v. New York Pub. Serv. Comm'n, No. 79-565 (U.S., filed Oct. 5, 1979); Consolidated Edison Co. v. New York Pub. Serv. Comm'n, No. 79-134 (U.S., filed July 27, 1979).

24.   Connecticut Gen'l Life Ins. Co. v. Johnson, 303 U.S. 77, 87 (1937) (Black, J., dissenting).

25.   Wheeling Steel Corp. v. Glander, 337 U.S. 562, 576-81 (1949) (Douglas, J., dissenting).

26.   But not a citizen, except in diversity cases.

27.   *See generally* United States v. O'Brien, 391 U.S. 367 (1968).

28.   *See* Selective Draft Law Cases, 245 U.S. 366, 390 (1918).

29.   *See* Butler v. Perry, 240 U.S. 328, 332-33 (1916).

30.   *See* 28 U.S.C. § 1861 (1976).

31.   *See* Robertson v. Baldwin, 165 U.S. 275, 282 (1897).

32.   323 U.S. 214 (1944).

33.   *Id.* at 219.

can citizens of Japanese descent were not protected from government efforts to place them in concentration camps, even though their only "crime" was having Japanese ancestors.

Since the Constitution does not impose any such duties on corporations, the artificial person, as Orwell might have said,[34] is more equal than the natural person. Whatever limitations corporations suffer come from statutes and the regulatory process. Moreover, despite plaintive cries from the business community and its minions in academia, even these limitations are more ostensible than real. The enormous influence and control that corporations have over the political process is one of the truisms of the day, and it has debilitated the pluralism of our political order.[35] How can a nominally democratic political system tolerate an obviously despotic economic system? Corporations are incompatible with "democratic theory and vision":[36] They are not private phenomena, and it can no longer be argued that they do not have a decisive impact on the entire nation. Corporations, therefore, pose constitutional problems of the first magnitude.

The Corporation as Community

Far from being a "thing" or an "it," the corporation is more nearly a method or process. It is a type of private collectivism, a congery of disparate groups cooperatively banded together.[37] At times, the cooperation is antagonistic, at least outwardly so, as when union officers confront corporate managers at the bargaining table. But cooperation it is; and it is, accordingly, fruitful to discuss at least giant firms, if not all companies, as communities. They are, as Peter Drucker maintained in 1953, the local self-governments of modern society; "the logical successor to manor, village and town."[38] Corporations are a new form of social order; loyalties and rewards, the very stuff of citizenship, derive as much from the enterprise as from the nation-state. Law and other disciplines have all but ignored these phenomena, but as corporations grow larger there can be little doubt that they will indeed take over more of the sovereign's role. A major transfer of power is occurring similar

---

34. *See* G. ORWELL, ANIMAL FARM 112 (1946).

35. *See, e.g.*, H. KARIEL, THE DECLINE OF AMERICAN PLURALISM 30-31 (1961); T. LOWI, THE END OF LIBERALISM 55 (1969).

36. C. LINDBLOM, POLITICS AND MARKETS 356 (1977).

37. *See* A. MILLER, *supra* note 4, at 154-61.

38. Drucker, *The Meaning of Mass Production*, 57 COMMONWEAL 547, 549 (1953).

to the rise of the nation-state itself out of the ruins of feudalism. A new feudalism has arisen consisting of the "supercorporations." The feudal barons are not the owners of the corporations, since ownership was separated from control long ago,[39] but the corporate managers. Government, including the Federal Government, does not really control the corporate manager; rather, governmental officers cooperate with them. The two groups—corporate manager and governmental officer—are in a symbiotic relationship, a condition of syzygy. The name for this is the "corporate State, American style."[40]

Only inferentially does American constitutional law recognize this development. Although it is true that a native form of corporatism was enacted in the National Industrial Recovery Act of 1933,[41] it was soon invalidated by a Supreme Court that found no warrant for it in the Constitution.[42] Soon thereafter, however, first Congress[43] and then the Court, by sanctioning the legislative action, constitutionalized private collectivism and in effect incorporated it into the governing structure. The key case is *NLRB v. Jones & Laughlin Steel Corp.*,[44] which rewrote the commerce clause to accommodate the National Labor Relations Act of 1935.[45] In political-economy terms, the meaning is clear: A system of political pluralism was read into the Constitution, and labor unions could operate as a countervailing force to the power of the corporations. The assumption was that the bargains between unions and corporations would inure to the public good, a type of Adam Smith's "invisible hand" theory writ large. As is now becoming evident, this assumption is valid only during periods of sustained economic growth—precisely what occurred in the post-1937 period and, equally precisely, what is *not* happening today.

What does, or what should, the Constitution say about corporations and other so-called private groups within the nation, such as labor unions? My proposal, labelled "modest" because it could

---

39. *See generally* A. BERLE & G. MEANS, THE MODERN CORPORATION AND PRIVATE PROPERTY (1932).

40. *See* A. MILLER, *supra* note 4, *passim*.

41. National Industrial Recovery Act of 1933, Pub. L. No. 73-67, 48 Stat. 195.

42. Not because it established a corporate state, but (delegation of powers grounds. *See* Schechter Poultry Corp. v. United States, 295 U.S. 495, 539 (1935); Panama Refining Co. v. Ryan, 293 U.S. 388, 414-15 (1935).

43. National Labor Relations Act of 1935, Pub. L. No. 74-198, 49 Stat. 449 (codified at 29 U.S.C. §§ 151-169 (1976)).

44. 301 U.S. 1 (1937).

45. Pub. L. No. 74-198, 49 Stat. 449 (codified at 29 U.S.C. §§ 151-169 (1976)).

go much further, is to make the corporation amenable to the constitutional commands of legally concretized decency that are the essence of the due process and equal protection clauses.

INTERNAL GOVERNANCE

Turning first to the problem of the internal governance of the corporate community, the question is how the enormous power of corporate concentrates can be made more tolerable and decent insofar as it touches small satellite corporations and natural persons affected by its behavior.

The threshold problem, in orthodox constitutional terms, is how to bring the corporation within the ambit of state action under the fourteenth amendment. Since the *Civil Rights Cases*[46] it has been popular wisdom that the terms of that amendment run against governments only. But what is a government? The Supreme Court has included within the concept of state action those private organizations that have a "symbiotic relationship" with government as well as those that have assumed governmental functions. In the *White Primary Cases*,[47] the Court held that the Democratic Party is sufficiently like a government to have the Constitution brought to bear against it.[48] In *Burton v. Wilmington Parking Authority*,[49] the Court established the "symbiotic relationship" test in holding that a private restaurant's refusal to serve a black man was state action since the restaurant was located in a state facility.[50] While some of the "sit-in" cases[51] came close to eliminating the state action requirement entirely, all of those cases should be read in light of the special civil rights circumstances in which they arose.

Holodnak v. AVCO Corp.[52] is an extreme example of the growing interrelationship between "private" industry and government. Holodnak was fired from his job because he published an article critical of labor-management relations at AVCO.[53] The case first went to arbitration, where the arbitrator found just cause for the discharge.[54] Holodnak then brought suit in federal court,

---

46.   109 U.S. 3 (1883).
47.   Smith v. Allwright, 321 U.S. 649 (1944).
48.   *Id*. at 664-65.
49.   365 U.S. 715 (1961).
50.   *Id*. at 724.
51.   *E.g.*, Bell v. Maryland, 378 U.S. 226 (1964).
52.   514 F.2d 285 (2d Cir. 1975).
53.   381 F. Supp. 191, 195 (D. Conn. 1974), *aff'd*, 514 F.2d 285 (2d Cir. 1975).
54.   *Id*. at 197.

alleging that the discharge violated his first and fourteenth amendment rights of free speech and due process. He won in both the district court[55] and the court of appeals.[56] The Second Circuit based its finding of state action on the existence of a symbiotic relationship between AVCO and the federal government. The federal government owned the company's land, buildings, and machinery; and AVCO was not required to pay any rent. Moreover, "by far the large proportion of the work done at the plant at the time of Holodnak's discharge was performed under contract to the Department of Defense."[57] The federal government, therefore, had gone beyond "mere regulation of private conduct" and had become "in effect a partner or joint venturer in the enterprise."[58]

Increasingly, groups have found it useful to merge their power with the state's in an interlocking series of relationships that allow groups not only to retain their economic sovereignty, but also to call upon the political sovereign for aid and assistance when needed.[59] The corporation and the state work in harmony in more instances than they conflict. Each needs and uses the other.[60] Thus a growing symbiotic relationship is emerging between private organizations and government, and it takes only a small jump for a court to move from *Burton* and *Holodnak* to the supercorporations and other pluralistic social groups of our corporate society. As Chief Justice Vinson remarked in *American Communication Association v. Douds*,[61] "[P]ower is never without responsibility. And when authority derives in part from Government's thumb on the scales, the exercise of that power by private persons becomes *closely akin, in some respects, to its exercise by Government itself.*"[62]

---

55.   *Id.* at 207.

56.   514 F.2d at 293.

57.   *Id.* at 289.

58.   *Id.* at 288 (distinguishing Jackson v. Metropolitan Edison Co., 419 U.S. 345 (1974)).

59.   A. MILLER, *supra* note 4, at 160. Witness the Chrysler Corporation's recent success in securing federal financial assistance. Chrysler Corporation Loan Guarantee Act of 1979, Pub. L. No. 96-185, 93 Stat. 1324 (to be codified in 15 U.S.C. §§ 1861-1901).

60.   A. MILLER, *supra* note 4, at 161.

61.   339 U.S. 382 (1950).

62.   Id. at 401 (emphasis added). Although the Court has recently restricted the public-function test, *see, e.g.*, Hudgens v. NLRB, 424 U.S. 507 (1976); Jackson v. Metropolitan Edison Co., 419 U.S. 345, 352-54 (1974); Lloyd Corp. v. Tanner, 407 U.S. 551 (1972), there are no solid reasons for not making the supercorporations accountable to the Constitution.

The problem is one of accountability, of having to answer in another place and to give reasons for one's actions.[63] People who work for corporations and those who deal with them as either suppliers or dealers—in sum, all members of the "corporate community"[64]—should be able to trigger the Constitution and make the internal political order of the corporation as accountable as the political order of public government. Once the actual governing power of corporations is acknowledged, the jump can be made without difficulty.

When that development is made, or, more accurately if made, it will subject corporations to a type of private regulation. This has definite benefits. First, it can be accomplished by using present-day judicial machinery. No new bureaucracy would have to be established, as would be necessary should federal chartering become a reality. Second, because judges have life tenure they are far less likely than administrative agencies to become captives of the regulated, even though these judges are almost invariably drawn from the establishment. Third, the true nature of our constitutional order—that of a corporate State—could have its basic theory worked out in a series of decisions. Since the Supreme Court acts as an authoritative faculty of political theory, particularly in its constitutional decisions, it is—barring an unlikely constitutional convention—the only official body that can through time develop the politico-legal theory of corporatism.[65] And finally, as Professor Leicester Webb has pointed out,

> [s]ince there is as yet no comprehensive and accepted theory of group-State relationships to guide legislators and since the association, individual and State are in constantly changing equilibrium, it may be that the harmonizing of these three elements, which Acton regards as "the true aim of politics," is best carried out through the flexible processes of a widely-competent judiciary; and it is partly for this reason that the pluralistic character of the State appears more securely established in America than in any other country.[66]

In sum, a major segment of corporate governance involves the application of constitutional norms to business. In suggesting this I recognize that political government itself is far from pristine insofar

---

63. *See generally* M. MINTZ & J. COHEN, AMERICA, INC. (1971).
64. *See* A. MILLER, *supra* note 4, at 27-29. *See also* Gossett, *supra* note 10.
65. My book now in progress, tentatively entitled "Oracle in the Marble Palace: Politics and the Supreme Court," develops this idea in detail.
66. L. WEBB, LEGAL PERSONALITY AND POLITICAL PLURALISM 194 (1958).

as arbitrariness is concerned. The recent civil rights explosion in constitutional litigation is impressive testimony that the Augean Stables of governmental indecency are far from clean. That long overdue movement should be neither slowed nor halted. My proposal is that it should be expanded to private government, the other and equally important segment of the social order.

EXTERNAL MATTERS

The powerlessness of the individual in the age of public and private bureaucracy requires no documentation. It is a theme that runs through both scholarly literature[67] and contemporary fiction.[68] Leicester Webb's suggestion that a widely competent judiciary could harmonize the relationships between individual, group, and State[69] has thus far only managed to harmonize the relationship of group to State. The individual remains submerged in a congery of groups. It was suggested above that one way to alleviate this rapidly worsening situation would be to make the corporation subject to constitutional norms. That is not a panacea, however; it is merely one step among many that could be taken.

When one moves to questions about a corporation's relations with those outside the corporate community, the corporate governance problems are vastly greater. In the final analysis, the corporation's external affairs are a problem in political, and therefore constitutional, theory: How can the pluralistic social groups once extolled as a highly desirable counter to the rise of the State be controlled so that they take the public or national interest into consideration when making important decisions? The hope of pluralism has been well expressed by Professor Frank Tannenbaum:

> The true well-being of a society . . . lies in diversity rather than in identity of interests. The greater the variety of groups, the richer is the community and the more certain of continuous harmony. The harmony best suited to a society is one which comes from many-sided inner tensions, strains, conflicts, and disagreements. Where disagreement is universal, men can agree only on particulars, and where men can really quarrel only about particulars they have too many things in common to tear the community apart. Divergence of interests within the community . . . is the condition of healthy controversy and social peace.[70]

---

67. *E.g.*, Gramm, *Industrial Capitalism and the Breakdown of the Liberal Rule of Law*, 7 J. ECON. ISSUES 577 (1973).
68. *E.g.*, J. HELLER, CATCH-22 (1955); F. KAFKA, DER PROZESS (1937).
69. *See* text accompanying note 66 *supra*.
70. F. TANNENBAUM, THE BALANCE OF POWER IN SOCIETY 25 (1969).

Well and good, except that the hope has not been realized in practice. Groups abound and there are conflicts, but what emerges out of those tussles in the political arena tend to be either the dominance of one group[71] or watered-down compromises that represent the common denominator among affected interest groups. Public policy—statutes, administrative rules, and some court decisions —generally tends to reflect those compromises. In net: "Groups become virtuous; they must be accommodated, not regulated."[72] The essential problem is not the consensus of compromise, but the failure of those who control pluralistic social groups, including corporations, to take into account the overarching public or national interest. Pluralism fails precisely because the oligarchs of the groups do not do this.[73]

Is there a way out? Surely it is not by the nation-state ceding authority and power to the corporation, as Tannenbaum,[74] Berle,[75] and others have suggested. Those who control corporations work for the good of the enterprise and have little interest in or regard for the general good. The same may be said for other ostensibly "private" groups, as Professor Grant McConnell has shown.[76] Not even the President can do much more than bargain with interest groups and their surrogates in Congress and the bureaucracy, even though as the sole officer elected by all of the people he theoretically has the power to transcend the lowest common denominator. Those bargains work tolerably well during periods of sustained economic growth or all-out national emergency. Those social conditions, however, do not now exist. The bargains the President strikes only fortuitously coincide with an overarching public interest.[77] It is only by equating the public interest with a procedural concept, and saying that whatever government does is by definition in the public interest, can it be maintained that pluralism works.[78]

Obviously, something more is needed if what Sir Henry

---

71. One example is the "seven sisters" that dominate the oil industry. *See* A. SAMPSON, THE SEVEN SISTERS (1975).

72. T. LOWI, *supra* note 35, at 48.

73. All groups are eventually run by oligarchs, falling prey to Robert Michels' "iron law of oligarchy." *See* R. MICHELS, POLITICAL PARTIES 342 (1st ed. 1911).

74. F. TANNENBAUM, *supra* note 70, at 63.

75. A. BERLE, THE 20TH CENTURY CAPITALIST REVOLUTION 175 (1954).

76. G. McCONNELL, PRIVATE POWER AND AMERICAN DEMOCRACY (1966).

77. *See generally* T. CRONIN, THE STATE OF THE PRESIDENCY (1975). *But see* R. PIOUS, THE AMERICAN PRESIDENCY (1979).

78. *See* A. MILLER, SOCIAL CHANGE AND FUNDAMENTAL LAW 90-95, 92 & n.161 (1979).

Maine called "the necessary and natural duties" of government are to be accomplished in any reasonably adequate manner.[79] How can those hard decisions that cut against the interests of important interest groups be made? How can divergent parochial interests be translated into the national interest? Would further constitutionalization of the corporation aid in that preeminent goal?

In answering these questions some recent proposals by Professor Christopher Stone merit serious attention.[80] Writing in 1976, he summarily—and rightly in my judgment—dismissed the notion of federal incorporation as little more than substituting a bureaucrat in Washington for one in Wilmington.[81] Stone's sweeping proposals are aimed at locating "the critical points of organizational breakdown" and reaching "into the company's inner world to demand the necessary changes directly."[82] Included are:[83] Establishment of minimum qualifications for holding corporate office, creation of new corporate offices, definition of role functions, creation of "limited public directors," imposition of "socially desirable configurations" of information flow within the organization, and requirements that companies "make and publish 'findings' prior to action that may have a significant impact on the environment, worker safety, or public health." Stone maintains that these can be done by innovative judges within the existing corpus of corporation law.[84]

Of particular importance is his final suggestion about the need for "findings." For me, this is a call for corporate managers to publish social impact statements before important decisions are made. Environmental impact statements are already mandated by federal law.[85] Stone is saying that the EIS should become the SIS. Indeed it should. And indeed it could be, given the necessary push by lawyers and a concomitant wisdom by judges.

One way to do that would be to constitutionalize the corporation. It is possible to find an emerging notion of constitutional duty in recent constitutional law decisions.[86] If this nascent develop-

---

79. H. MAINE, POPULAR GOVERNMENT 60-61 (1885).

80. Stone, *Stalking the Wild Corporation*, WORKING PAPERS FOR A NEW SOCIETY, Spring 1976, at 17.

81. *Id.* at 20.

82. *Id.* at 87.

83. *Id.* at 87-89.

84. *Id.* at 92.

85. National Environmental Policy Act of 1969, § 102, 42 U.S.C. § 4332 (1976).

86. *See* A. MILLER, *supra* note 78, at 95-178. The latest manifestation of this development came on July 2, 1979, when the Supreme Court upheld mandatory

ment is expanded to include private governments, one can easily see how judges could at times not only say what corporations can or cannot do, but also what they *must* do. If Stone is correct, as I think he is, then the requirement of published findings prior to significant corporate action could well move the corporation and other social groups toward taking the public or national interest into account.

As Eugen Ehrlich has asserted, the view of any statutory construction or rule of law as a closed book "never was anything but purely theoretical pedantry. Juristic science has never been able to offer prolonged resistance to great and justifiable social or economic needs . . . ."[87] So it is with constitutions and the development of constitutional law: Law is an open-ended process, not a closed body of logically consistent concepts. The development of American constitutional law must keep abreast of fast-moving socio-economic changes. One of those changes is the rise of the corporation. Constitutional law has not yet developed to meet the needs created by this new condition. When it does so, as it must, it will constitutionalize the corporation—both in its internal order and its external importance.

In Brief Summation

The problem of governance is two-fold: The urgent tasks of government must be performed, but at the least possible social cost. A generation ago Professor Howard Bowen called for social audits of business enterprise[88]—a call that has thus far gone unheeded. My point in this brief essay is to suggest that such an audit could be the product of a case-by-case application of constitutional norms to the business enterprise. We may then achieve the goal Alfred North Whitehead once called for: "A great society is a society in which its men of business think greatly of their functions."[89] The United States is a business-oriented society—a corporate society. The time has come for the Supreme Court to help businessmen "think greatly of their functions."

---

busing to achieve racial integration in public schools. *See* Dayton Bd. of Educ. v. Brinkman, 99 S. Ct. 2971 (1979); Columbus Bd. of Educ. v. Penick, 99 S. Ct. 2941 (1979).

87. E. Ehrlich, Fundamental Principles of the Sociology of Law 430 (Moll trans. 1936).

88. H. Bowen, Social Responsibilities of the Businessman 155 (1953).

89. Whitehead, *Introduction* to W. Donham, Business Adrift at xxvii (1931).

CHAPTER 10

Toward Recognition of a Constitutional Right to a Job

The United States—indeed, the entire world—is in the midst of a profound social transformation: the coming of an automated, information-oriented society. Computers and robotics not only are changing the social structure generally, but are working massive alterations in the workplace specifically. We are witnessing the loss of work itself for increasing numbers of people who are ready and able to work. This may be seen in Great Britain, for example, where unemployment remains at a high level, and in the United States, where a seven to eight percent unemployment rate is now considered to be desirable. This means that in America alone, at least ten to fifteen million workers are permanently out of work, with no hope of getting any.

To counteract this development, some trade unions are beginning to demand that serious attention be paid to the need for working opportunities to be provided to all who wish to have them. Among the more important proposals is that of the International Association of Machinists, who recently put forth "A New Technology Bill of Rights." Chapter 10 discusses the constitutionality of the proposal and goes even further: It suggests that serious consideration be paid to the need for a constitutional right to a job to be created. This, of course, would take a major restructuring of the political economy. The essay maintains that the time has come to do precisely that.

There is a war on, but only one side is armed: this is the essence of the technology question today. On the one side is private capital, scientized and subsidized, mobile and global, and now heavily armed with military-spawned command, control, and communication technologies. Empowered by the second Industrial Revolution, capital is moving decisively now to enlarge and consolidate the social dominance it secured in the first. . . .

On the other side, those under assault hastily abandon the field for lack of an agenda, an arsenal or an army. Their own comprehension and critical abilities confounded by the cultural barrage, they take refuge in alternating strategies of appeasement and accommodation, denial and delusion, and reel in desperate disarray before this seemingly inexorable onslaught—which is known in polite circles as "technological change."

—David F. Noble[1]

I.

Unemployment is something we can all grasp and understand—and fear, too, for *Homo sapiens* has always been *Homo faber* as well. People are significant in the eyes of others not so much for what they *are* but for what they *do*. Meet someone for the first time at almost any cocktail party and the inevitable question soon pops out: "Where do you work?" or perhaps "What do you do?" In an ostensibly classless society, one's occupation or vocation solidifies his status in so-

---

1. Noble, *Present Tense Technology*, 3 DEMOCRACY No. 2, at 8 (1983).

This chapter was originally published under the title of "Were the Luddites Necessarily Wrong? A Note on the Constitutionality of the 'New Technology Bill of Rights' " in 8 Nova Law Journal 515 (1984) (a part of a symposium on the proposed "Bill of Rights").

ciety. Work is the central factor of Western nations. Those who do not work, unless they have been favored by fortune with inherited wealth, are often scorned: They are called "welfare cheaters" or "bums." As Dr. Ralf Dahrendorf, Director of the London School of Economics, has observed: "Labor at the center of society means that every aspect of life must accommodate it—education, vacations, and retirement. In the labor society education conforms to the discipline and demands of work. Vacations serve as recovery periods, time to renew energies to return to work refreshed. For progressive labor societies, at least, retirement is a 'well earned rest after a lifetime of hard work.' "[2] It is beyond question that the United States has always been a "labor society."

The essential question posed by the International Association of Machinists (IAM's) "New Technology Bill of Rights" is how Americans should adapt to the sudden end of such a society and its transmutation into a society in which human labor has been largely eliminated. The IAM believes that adaptation should not be left to chance or to the vagaries of the "market." Theirs is a suggestion that affirmative governmental action be taken to deal with a new situation in the human condition. I will leave to others the question of the wisdom of the IAM proposal. In this brief commentary I pose and seek to answer the question of whether constitutional impediments exist that would bar the Bill of Rights of the IAM from going into effect.

The short answer to that question is "no"—there is nothing in the Constitution, as a document or as construed, that would invalidate what the IAM proposes. Let me explain. I begin with several assumptions. *First*, the new technologies of microprocessing and computers pose a clear and present danger to *Homo faber*. Mass man has become obsolete, superfluous to the needs of the emergent politico-economic order. Too many people are chasing too few jobs, a diminishing number of jobs. No one quite knows what to do with surplus people, although Professor Richard Rubenstein has developed some grim scenarios about what might happen.[3] *Second*, it is, as Jacques Ellul has maintained,

---

2. Dahrendorf, *The End of the Labor Society,* WORLD PRESS REVIEW, March 1983, at 28. Dahrendorf also says, "There is no cure for today's unemployment." *Id.*

3. R. RUBENSTEIN, THE AGE OF TRIAGE (1983); Rubenstein, *The Elect and the Preterite*, 59 SOUNDINGS 357 (1976) (discussing "the rise of a mammoth, world-wide superfluous population that can no longer emigrate to underpopulated regions of the globe"). Rubenstein further comments:

[A]lthough Americans tend to regard technology as a means of solving problems, the problem of surplus people in contemporary America is as

"impossible to trust the spontaneous employment which men will make of the available technical means."[4] The meaning is clear: positive action should be taken to ameliorate the adverse consequences of new technologies. *Third*, corrective action, should it come (which by no means is certain), can derive only from government—the federal government. That is so because a holistic approach is indispensable, one that encompasses the entire spectrum of man's position in nature and his relationships with his fellow humans. No other societal institution is capable even of considering, let alone undertaking, a program of comprehensive adaptation to what the scientists and technologists have wrought.

I do not propose to prove those assumptions. They are self-evident, and stated as givens in order to set the pattern for the ensuing brief discussion of validity of one of the consequences of technological change—the terminal sense of the loss of work itself by increasing numbers of Americans (and others throughout the world). My net conclusion is that the advent of the new technologies requires a thorough re-examination and reorganization of the political economy of the nation—indeed, of the world. The New Technology Bill of Rights is a proper step in that direction.

II.

The time has come for serious consideration to be given to the idea that constitutions should be directed toward the reasonable satisfaction of human needs and deserts, as well as merely establishing frameworks of government and setting forth a set of negative limitations on what government officers can do.[5] What follows is in many respects a variation on a theme struck by Leon Duguit many years ago:[6] "Any system of public law can be vital only so far as it is based on a given sanction to the following rules: First, the holders of power cannot do certain things; second, there are certain things they must do." In recent de-

---

much the 'product' of technological rationality as are the automobile, the computer and the nuclear bomb. . . .The threat of permanent economic superfluity now confronts millions of American workers."
Id. at 358-59.
    4.   J. ELLUL, *The Technological Order*, in THE TECHNOLOGICAL ORDER: PROCEEDINGS OF ENCYCLOPEDIA BRITANNICA CONFERENCE 10, 25 (C. Stover ed. 1963).
    5.   This is the thesis of my book in progress, *supra* note *.
    6.   L. DUGUIT, LAW IN THE MODERN STATE 26 (H. Laski translation 1919).

cades, all three branches of the national government have risen in some degree to confront Duguit's challenge. Congress has enacted numerous statutes, the sum of which is to institutionalize the American version of the welfare state. The Executive has cooperated, in greater or lesser degree, by putting those legislative commands into operational reality. And the Supreme Court has constitutionalized those efforts to meet the "must do" part of Duguit's formulation. The requirement now it to face up to the challenge posed by the IAM.

Since enactment of the IAM proposal would constitute a structural change in government, a basic alteration in what I have elsewhere called the Political and the Economic Constitutions,[7] purists might argue that if it is to come it should be by constitutional amendment. That, however, is not necessary. Amendment at best is a ponderous blunderbuss ill-suited to the requirements of a rapidly changing nation. That, it be noted, has been true since at least 1791, when the Bill of Rights was added to the Document drafted in 1787. Only the fourteenth amendment may be said to be of supreme importance. The other fifteen vary in significance from the repealed eighteenth to the nineteenth (voting rights for females); those of any consequence could have been put into law by innovative congressional action pursuant to section V of the fourteenth amendment.

We have become accustomed to and by and large agree with the notion of judicial exegesis of the Constitution. However much some may disagree with specific constitutional decisions by the Supreme Court, there can be no question that the Justices do sit as a continuous constitutional convention. They progressively update the fundamental law. Each generation of Americans writes its own constitution, having received a tacit delegation of powers from the framers to do so. (The Supreme Court also received a tacit delegation of powers from those who drafted the Document of 1787.) And the Constitution has always been relative to circumstances.[8] It could scarcely be otherwise. Government and law are more reflective of social conditions than determinants of those conditions—at least historically. Law, including constitutional law, is less *a priori* than *a posteriori*.

The new technology poses constitutional problems. Can they be

---

7. Miller, *Toward a Definition of "The" Constitution*, 8 U. DAYTON L. REV. 633 (1983).

8. *See* A. MILLER, DEMOCRATIC DICTATORSHIP: THE EMERGING CONSTITUTION OF CONTROL *passim* (1981); A. MILLER, TOWARD INCREASED JUDICIAL ACTIVISM: THE POLITICAL ROLE OF THE SUPREME COURT (1982).

met by means other than amendment? The answer can only be "yes," once it is perceived that the interpretation and development of the Constitution is emphatically not a judicial monopoly. The myth system is to the contrary: Under it, amendment or judicial exegesis are the only legitimate ways to alter the fundamental law. But under the operational code of the American constitutional order the Constitution is constantly in a state of becoming, altered not only by judicial decrees but by certain legislative and executive acts.

A number of statutes can be viewed as "quasi-constitutional in nature"; they sought to "clarify and define certain basic relationships among the branches of government."[9] At least the following statutes fall into that category (although I see no reason to soften the label with a "quasi"): the Judiciary Act of 1789, the Sherman Antitrust Act, the statute establishing the Federal Reserve Board, the Budget and Accounting Act of 1921, the National Labor Relations Act of 1935, the Employment Act of 1946, the Civil Rights Act of 1964, the National Environmental Policy Act of 1969, the War Powers Resolution of 1973, and the Budget and Impoundment Control Act of 1974. There may be others, notably the National Security Act of 1947 and the National Emergencies Act, but that listing clearly demonstrates that Congress does indeed make constitutive decisions. Each of the statutes effected something of a structural change in the nature of American government; they delineate "structures and processes"[10] rather than setting forth substantive policies.

As with Congress, so with the President: some of the Chief Executive's decisions or actions merit consideration as alteration of the Constitution. The ready example is the warmaking power. Expressly vested in Congress by Article I, and thus under the myth system solely a legislative power, that notion was dealt a body blow by President Lincoln at the beginning of the Civil War.[11] Bit by bit since then—and even before then—the White House has become the center of effective control over the use of violence. That is so even though Congress has sought to retrieve some of its lost powers by the War Powers Resolution. Events since 1973 increasingly indicate that the Resolution is a

---

9. G. GUNTHER, CASES AND MATERIALS ON CONSTITUTIONAL LAW 398 (10th ed. 1980).

10. *Id.* at 397.

11. For discussion, see C. ROSSITER, CONSTITUTIONAL DICTATORSHIP: CRISIS GOVERNMENT IN THE MODERN DEMOCRACIES (1948); Miller, *Reason of State and the Emergent Constitution of Control*, 64 MINN. L. REV. 585, 595-97 (1980).

"paper tiger."[12] A constitutional shift of major proportions has taken place.

By no means are Congress and the President always at loggerheads. Many presidential actions, taken without express authority, get at least tacit congressional approval through appropriations and other means. Despite the conventional wisdom to the contrary, the norm between the branches is cooperation rather than conflict. Witness the manner in which Congress routinely appropriated funds for waging a presidential war in Vietnam. Witness also the establishment of the National Security Agency by a still secret executive order. In both instances, Congress did not dissent from presidential incursions on the legislative turf. There is a further lesson: In general, the Supreme Court goes along with congressional and executive constitutive decision-making. Examples are easily found: the *Prize Cases*, the *Jones & Laughlin* decision sustaining the National Labor Relations Act, and the brace of decisions upholding the Civil Rights Act.[13] The Justices, as Professor Martin Shapiro has commented, are part of the governing coalition of the nation; and judicial independence exists more in the myth system than in the operational code.[14]

Enactment, therefore, of the IAM's proposed "New Technology Bill of Rights" would embed into the law a statute that would approach the dimension of a constitutional amendment. It would basically change the relationship of the workers to the "private" governments of the nation, principally the supercorporations. There is nothing in the proposal that would, under present doctrine, fail to pass constitutional muster. A series of Supreme Court decisions beginning with the *Gold Clause Cases*, passing through *Jones & Laughlin* and *Katzenbach v. McClung*, and extending to *United States v. Perez*[15] is proof positive that existing law would validate what on first glance seems to be a revolutionary proposal by the IAM. Given the requisite political will to enact the proposal, it is wholly safe to forecast that the Supreme Court

---

12. For brief but insightful discussion, see Halperin, *Declaring War*, 9 First Principles, Sept.-Oct. 1983, at 12.

13. Prize Cases, 2 Black 635 (1863); National Labor Relations Board v. Jones and Laughlin Steel Corp., 301 U.S. 1 (1937); Heart of Atlanta Motel v. United States, 379 U.S. 241 (1964); Katzenbach v. McClung, 379 U.S. 294 (1964).

14. M. Shapiro, Courts: A Comparative and Political Analysis 34 (1981).

15. Perez v. United States, 402 U.S. 146 (1971); *Katzenbach*, 379 U.S. at 294; *Jones & Laughlin*, 301 U.S. at 1; Norman v. Baltimore & Ohio R. Co., 294 U.S. 240 (1935).

would not invalidate it. The persistent and unresolved problem, of course, is how to generate that political will.

No one expects either House of Congress to rush forward in full or even partial acceptance of the proposal. That it merits full consideration, and soon, should go without saying. Call it Luddism if one wishes, but the point is not that, but of determining who should bear, if indeed anyone should, the dreadful costs of adapting to a new economy. It cuts against the grain of the constitutional commitment to "equal justice under law" to say that displaced workers should alone shoulder the brunt of the loss of work itself.

III.

If it is assumed, as it should be, that Congress is far from likely to enact anything remotely similar to the IAM's proposal, does that end the matter? Not necessarily. But it would be enormously difficult to get something substantial done. Again, let me explain.

I set aside the notion that any one or even a combination of the several states could do the necessary. A company can play off one state against another and choose the one that maximizes the firm's interests. Furthermore, since under *Wickard v. Filburn* and *Katzenbach v. Mc-Clung*[16] there is very little of economic importance that does not fall within the ambit of the federal government's power to govern commerce, the constitutional hurdle of unduly burdening interstate commerce would have to be surmounted. There is little reason to expect that the present-day Supreme Court, dominated as it is by corporation lawyers, would validate, say, an attempt by the state of Ohio to prevent runaway plants or to ensure that corporations, once established in the state, stay there. Profit maximization is the primary, if not the sole, goal of corporate management. An effort by any one state to enact the IAM proposal for companies doing business within that state would certainly engender hostile opposition from the entire business community. That hostility, in turn, is not likely to allow the state to prevail before the Supreme Court when lawsuits are brought, as surely they would. The pro-business attitude of today's Court is illustrated in, to cite only one decision, *First National Bank v. Bellotti.*[17]

---

16. *Katzenbach*, 379 U.S. at 294; Wickard v. Filburn, 317 U.S. 111 (1942).

17. 435 U.S. 765 (1978). *See* Miller, *On Politics, Democracy, and the First Amendment*, 38 WASH. & LEE L. REV. 21 (1981); Wright, *Money and the Pollution*

The ultimate need, if anything is going to be done, is for a great national debate about the pros and cons of the new technology to take place. How can it be started—and continued? "If there's ever gonna be change in America, it's gonna be cause every community in America's ready for it and—boom! There's gonna be a big tidal wave, and it's just gonna crash down on Washington, and the people are finally gonna be heard."[18] That "tidal wave" could create the necessary political will in Congress. How can it be done? I venture, very tentatively and with full cognizance of the inherent difficulties in the proposition, that the Supreme Court could, at least in theory, provide the catalyst for stimulating such a debate.

I have argued elsewhere that the Supreme Court should strive to make decisions that maximize human dignity.[19] Just as in *Brown v. Board of Education* the Warren Court struck a blow for the decent treatment of black Americans and in *Roe v. Wade* the Burger Court carried on that theme (holding that women should have the right to control their own bodies),[20] so it is here: The Court arguably can help in achieving a smoother transition to the new society that is fast becoming the norm. It, of course, would not be easy. But since both *Brown* and *Roe* can be read as official statements that precipitated great national debates (on race and abortion), it would not be a novel proposition for the Supreme Court to do something similar about the societal impact of technology. Two ways theoretically exist: first, the Court could attempt to impose affirmative duties on Congress and the President to take appropriate action concerning technology; and second, the corporation could be constitutionalized by updating the "state action" doctrine, followed by finding that workers—those willing and able—had a constitutional right to a job (in general, but not a specific job). I shall discuss each in turn, repeating at the outset the admonition that the ideas are proffered only tentatively.

---

of Politics: Is the First Amendment an Obstacle to Political Equality?, 82 COLUM. L. REV. 609 (1982).

18. S. TERKEL, AMERICAN DREAMS LOST AND FOUND 312 (1981) (quoting a community organizer). *See generally* S. BOWLES, D. GORDON, & T. WEISSKOPF, BEYOND THE WASTE LAND: A DEMOCRATIC ALTERNATIVE TO ECONOMIC DECLINE *passim* (1983).

19. MILLER, TOWARD INCREASED JUDICIAL ACTIVISM: THE POLITICAL ROLE OF THE SUPREME COURT ch. 11 (1982).

20. Roe v. Wade, 410 U.S. 113 (1973); Brown v. Bd. of Educ., 347 U.S. 483 (1954).

A.   Affirmative Duties on Government

I begin by acknowledging that for the Supreme Court to try to impose affirmative duties on Congress and the President to deal properly and effectively with the impact of new technologies is not a particularly promising avenue to take. But it is worth exploring, even though what immediately follows may be categorized as utopian thinking. There is a value in such thinking,[21] if only to encourage people to elevate the level of their responses to new social conditions. The Supreme Court has long acted as what Judge J. Skelly Wright once termed "the conscience of a sovereign people." In recent decades—at least since *Brown v. Board of Education*—the courts have become targets of pressure groups, especially when the avowedly political branches of government refuse or fail to act and deal with what are perceived by segments of the citizenry as justified grievances.

Judicial interpretation (and enforcement) of affirmative duties of government is by no means novel. In race relations, legislative reapportionment, administration of the criminal law, and perhaps elsewhere,[22] obligations have been placed on governmental officers to do something positive (as distinguished from refraining from not doing something—the time-honored ideal of constitutions as limitations on government). Add the fact that since *Cooper v. Aaron*,[23] and perhaps before, it is widely accepted that the logically impossible has been by some means known only to the Justices transmogrified into the possible—that a *general* principle can be inferred from *one* particular—and it is apparent that the Court has indeed become a *de facto* third (and perhaps highest) legislative chamber.

The argument, telescoped here,[24] derives from (perhaps antedates, although I know of no prior judicial statement) Chief Justice Charles

---

21. *See* W. GALSTON, JUSTICE AND THE HUMAN GOOD ch. 2 (198). Professor Galston maintains that utopian thought "performs three related political functions. First, it guides our deliberation. . . . Second, it justifies our actions. . . .Third, it serves as the basis for the evaluation of existing institutions and practices. . . .I am convinced that no political theory that seeks to be practical can dispense with it." *Id.* at 14-15.

22. *See* Miller, *Toward a Concept of Constitutional Duty*, 1968 SUP. CT. REV., *reprinted in* A. MILLER, SOCIAL CHANGE AND FUNDAMENTAL LAW: AMERICA'S EVOLVING CONSTITUTION ch. 5 (1979).

23. 358 U.S. 1 (1958); *see* Miller, *Constitutional Decisions as De Facto Class Actions: A Comment on the Implications of Cooper v. Aaron*, 58 U. DET. J. URB. L. 573 (1981).

24. For further discussion see A. MILLER, *supra* note 22, at chapters 4-5.

Evans Hughes' opinion in *West Coast Hotel v. Parrish*.[25] There, Hughes, dealing with the validity of a state's minimum wage legislation, said in part:

> The principle which must control our decision is not in doubt. The constitutional provision invoked is the due process clause of the Fourteenth Amendment, governing the states, as the due process clause invoked in the Adkins case governed Congress. In each case the violation alleged by those attacking minimum wage legislation is deprivation of freedom of contract. What is this freedom? The Constitution does not speak of freedom of contract. It speaks of liberty and prohibits the deprivation of liberty without due process of law. In prohibiting that deprivation, the Constitution does not recognize an absolute and uncontrollable liberty. Liberty in each of its phases has its history and connotation. But the liberty safeguarded is liberty in a social organization which requires the protection of law against the evils which menace the health, safety, morals and welfare of the people. Liberty under the Constitution is thus necessarily subject to the restraints of due process, and regulation which is reasonable in relation to its subject and is adopted in the interests of the community is due process.

With that language, particularly the concluding two sentences, Hughes changed the nature of liberty under the Constitution. "From being a limitation on legislative power," Professor Edward S. Corwin explained, "the due process clause became an actual instigation to legislation of a leveling character."[26] In effect, Hughes adopted without acknowledgment Thomas Hill Green's concept of positive freedom and of collective well-being. To Green, freedom meant "a positive power or capacity of doing or enjoying something worth doing or enjoying. . .in common with others." Freedom thus depends on the "help and security" given by others, and which a person helps to secure for others.[27] As Chief Justice Hughes put it, the liberty protected by due process is in a "social organization" that *requires* the protection of law against social evils.

Do the deleterious second-order consequences of new technolo-

---

25. 300 U.S. 391 (1937).

26. E. CORWIN, LIBERTY AGAINST GOVERNMENT 161 (1948).

27. T. GREEN, *Lecture on Liberal Legislation and Freedom of Contract*, in 3 WORKS OF THOMAS HILL GREEN 365, 371 (R. Nettleship ed. 1900). *See* M. PHILLIPS, THE DILEMMAS OF INDIVIDUALISM: STATUS, LIBERTY, AND AMERICAN CONSTITUTIONAL LAW *passim* (1983).

gies—mainly unemployment—require "the protection of law?" The answer can only be "yes." What can the Supreme Court contribute to the fulfillment of that requirement? As all know, the Justices have identified new rights outside of the constitutional text, both historically (as in liberty of contract),[28] and contemporaneously. Privacy is the ready example here; but there are others.[29] Can a similar right be created in the economic sphere? As we have seen, there is already an explicit governmental commitment to maximize employment and to further the economic well-being of Americans, seen, for example, in the Employment Act of 1946 and the Humphrey-Hawkins Act of 1978.

For the Supreme Court to do the necessary—to, that is, require political action "reasonable in relation to its subject"—would necessitate judicial innovation of a high level. The orthodox doctrine of judicial power under the Constitution requires that there be a justiciable controversy before courts can act. Some person, preferably someone out of work and wanting a job, would seek a court decree mandating that serious attention be accorded to employment security, followed by action which would affirm "every worker's right to be employed with decent wages at some job or another—but not necessarily always at the same job."[30] Or, in the plaintive language of a retired policeman and former marine, "I don't think our system is all bad. . . .What I object to is, there's no planning, I don't care how much money it takes. They should put every guy that wants to work, to work."[31] The implication, of course, is that there should be a constitutional right to a job.

Merely stating such an idea does violence to the accepted norms of judicial behavior under the Constitution. But is the notion really so extreme? I think not, although I readily concede that there is little authority, as lawyers understand authority, to buttress it. To my knowledge, the only Justice of the Supreme Court who ever suggested as much is the late Justice William O. Douglas, who in 1955 asserted in a Supreme Court conference: "There is a constitutional right in this country for a citizen to have a job. There is a constitutional right to be a policeman or a lawyer."[32] (The second sentence was an attempted

---

28. Lochnar v. New York, 198 U.S. 45 (1905) is the *locus classicus*.

29. *See* M. PERRY, THE CONSTITUTION, THE COURTS AND HUMAN RIGHTS (1982).

30. S. BOWLES, D. GORDON, & T. WEISSKOPF, *supra* note 18, at 275.

31. *Quoted in* S. TERKEL, AMERICAN DREAMS LOST AND FOUND 232 (1981).

32. *Quoted in* B. SCHWARTZ, SUPER CHIEF: EARL WARREN AND HIS SUPREME COURT—A JUDICIAL BIOGRAPHY 184 (1983).

refutation of the Holmes dictum, followed by his disciple Justice Frankfurter, that "there was no constitutional right to be a police-man.")[33] The basic principle that would have to be established (in-vented) is that the liberty protected by due process includes a right to a job; or perhaps more concretely, that the citizenry have property rights in jobs. Recognition of such a due process right, when viewed ab-stractly, is certainly no more extreme or revolutionary than the Su-preme Court's unexplained flash of revelation in 1886 that a corpora-tion—a disembodied economic entity—was a person within the meaning of the fourteenth amendment; or, for that matter, the 1973 similar revelation that a woman could have an abortion by invoking a right of privacy (which, incidentally, meant that the Justices refused to recognize that a fetus is a constitutional person). This is said, be it noted, not to take sides on either question, but simply to mention the obvious: that the Justices have found rights lurking somewhere in the interstices of the Constitution that could not possibly have been in the minds of those who wrote and those who ratified the Document and its amendments. The Bill of Rights and the Civil War amendments are statements of legally-concretized decency aimed at government and designed to canalize its relationships with the populace. Or as Justice Frankfurter observed in 1949: "It is of the very nature of a free society to advance in its standards of what is deemed reasonable and right. Representing as it does a living principle, due process is not confined within a permanent catalogue of what may at a given time be deemed the limits or the essentials of fundamental rights."[34] So, I suggest it is here. Judicial exegesis, and expansion, of the Constitution is routine, as Justice Byron White stated in 1966 and Justice William Brennan in 1980.

Consider, for example, such cases as *Wesberry v. Sanders, Powell v. McCormack*, and *Buckley v. Valeo*,[35] each of which dealt with Con-gress as either actual or tacit defendant. Consider, too, the spate of recent decisions—the landmark case in *United States v. Nixon*[36]—which are judicial interventions into the area of presidential power and discretion. Taken in their entirety, they evidence a growing

---

33. *Id.* The Holmes assertion may be found in McAuliffe v. Mayor of New Bed-ford, 155 Mass. 216, 220 (1892).

34. Wolf v. Colorado, 338 U.S. 25, 27 (1949).

35. Buckley v. Valeo, 424 U.S. 1 (1976); Powell v. McCormack, 395 U.S. 486 (1969); Wesberry v. Sanders, 376 U.S. 1 (1964).

36. 418 U.S. 683 (1974).

willingness of the Supreme Court to intervene in both the national legislative and the executive processes. *Wesberry*, for example, told the House of Representatives (via the state governments) how Representatives had to be elected; and *Nixon* was an order to a sitting President to act as an ordinary citizen in criminal law matters. Add to *Nixon* the *Steel Seizure Case*,[37] which was really directed toward President Truman, and it can readily be seen that the Justices consider themselves to be a constituent part of government, equal in title and equal in dignity to the other branches. Judicial legislation has become a commonplace.

The sticking points in present context are, of course, the questions of justiciability and of enforcement. As for the former, the Court would have to take a mental leap and make what Frankfurter once called a "logically arbitrary but sociologically nonarbitrary" decision to find a constitutional case or controversy. Not that the method would be anything novel: Justiciability has long been characterized by judicial fiat. As in *Perkins v. Lukens Steel Co.*,[38] the "reasoning," such as it is, to justify finding or not finding justiciability (standing, etc.) usually is circular. That is accepted, with little opposition, as proper judicial behavior. If, then, the National Treasury Employees Union could succeed in a suit against President Nixon to enforce a statutory responsibility,[39] it would take no major extension of that principle for courts to find justiciable controversies in present context. The point, to be sure, is debatable and also controversial. After all, if the Court in the *Weber* case could determine the "spirit" of the relevant statute,[40] why could it not further determine that the spirit of the Employment and Humphrey-Hawkins Acts gave someone the requisite status to have their provisions carried into effect?

Enforcement is quite another matter. There is no present way that the Justices can do more than try to precipitate a great national debate that would, sooner or later, end in political action. The Justices, however, have long been America's first faculty of political economy, a vital national seminar in which the nation's values are often first debated and articulated. Could that "seminar" discussion be raised to the level

---

37. Youngstown Sheet & Tube Co. v. Sawyer, 343 U.S. 579 (1952).

38. 310 U.S. 113 (1940).

39. National Treasury Employees Union v. Nixon, 492 F.2d 587 (D.C. Cir. 1974).

40. United Steelworkers of America v. Weber, 443 U.S. 193, 202-06 (1979) (upholding affirmative action plan, despite statutory language prohibiting basing employment decisions on race).

of serious consideration of a constitutional right to a job? A tribunal that rose to the challenge of rectifying long-standing practices of racial discrimination, that created a constitutional right to an abortion, that eliminated the "rotten boroughs" of the nation, that stared down a sitting President, and that revamped the administration of the criminal law, surely is capable of dealing with the problem of how the economic rights of workers are to be determined under the Constitution.[41]

That, of course, is constitutional heresy. I do not expect ready agreement (in any degree) with such a proposal. But the Court has always been deeply immersed in politics. To Judge Spencer Roane of Virginia the decision of the Supreme Court in *Cohens v. Virginia*[42] was heretical: "It can only be accounted for by that love of power which history informs us infects and corrupts all who possess it, and from which even the upright and eminent judges are not exempt." To Roane, the *Cohens* decision was "most monstrous and unexampled."[43] It was heresy when I was in law school to assert that judicial action could be state action within the meaning of the fourteenth amendment, but the Court took the plunge in *Shelley v. Kraemer* and *Barrows v. Jackson.*[44] In like manner, Justice Hugo Black outraged Justice Felix Frankfurter when he maintained in *Adamson v. California* that the fourteenth amendment incorporated the Bill of Rights as a limitation on the states as well as the federal government.[45] As all know, Black's heresy has now become the conventional wisdom. Consider, furthermore, the firestorm of disapproval that erupted when the Court held in 1954 that black Americans were entitled to decent treatment in the public schools. *Roe v. Wade* received a similar reaction. The point is that the Supreme Court may have decided some issues that turned out to be "self-inflicted wounds";[46] but even so, it has emerged from the fray

---

41. *See generally* A. MILLER, TOWARD INCREASED JUDICIAL ACTIVISM: THE POLITICAL ROLE OF THE SUPREME COURT (1982). A contrary view may be found in Abraham, Book Review, 51 GEO. WASH. L. REV. 477 (1983); Rabkin, *The Charismatic Constitution,* THE PUBLIC INTEREST, Fall, 1983, at 142.

42. 19 U.S. (6 Wheat.) 264 (1821).

43. *See* C. WARREN, 1 THE SUPREME COURT IN UNITED STATES HISTORY 555 (1926).

44. Shelley v. Kraemer, 334 U.S. 1 (1948); Barrows v. Jackson, 346 U.S. 249 (1953).

45. 332 U.S. 46 (1947).

46. The term comes from C. HUGHES, THE SUPREME COURT OF THE UNITED STATES 50 (1928). Hughes listed the Dred Scott decision, Dred Scott v. Sanford 60 U.S. (19 How.) 393 (1857), the legal tender cases, Knox v. Lee, 79 U.S. (12 Wall.)

seemingly stronger than ever. (None of the cases listed immediately above falls into a category of a self-inflicted wound. *Dred Scott's Case*[47] is perhaps the chief example of such judicial behavior.)

The need, as has been suggested, is to generate a national debate on what should be done about the adverse second-order consequences of new technologies. My thought in this subsection is that the Supreme Court (courts generally) could play an important role in stimulating that debate. That, however, does not mean that the Justices could not act in another direction also. The focus of the next subsection concerns judicial recognition of the fact that corporations are "private" governments, the important actors of the Economic Constitution, and as such should have duties placed upon them.

B.   Constitutionalizing the Corporations

That the United States is a corporate society is one of the commonplaces of the day. It has long been recognized that "voluntary private associations" play an important role in social affairs. I should like at this time to single out the business corporation—and of the corporations, the giant firms—for particular scrutiny. These companies dominate the private sector of the nation. Economically, that sector is a triad, consisting of the corporate economy (the giants), the small-business economy (much of which is also incorporated), and the nonprofits. Each part meshes with the others, but the giants—the supercorporations—are paramount, even though they are numerically much smaller. Those gigantic companies not only straddle the nation but usually operate throughout the world. They set the tone for and greatly influence the entire economy, government itself, and, indeed, all of society.

My thesis is that supercorporations are both economic entities and sociopolitical organizations that exist midway between natural persons and the state; as such, they should be perceived as "private" governments and held answerable to constitutional norms. They wield significant social and political power, but their constitutional legitimacy—their right or title to govern—has only a tenuous base. Rather

---

457 (1871), and the income tax case, Pollock v. Farmers' Loan & Trust Co., 158 U.S. 601 (1895) as "three notable instances [in which] the Court has suffered severely from self inflicted wounds." F. GRAHAM, THE SELF-INFLICTED WOUND (1970) claims that Miranda v. Arizona, 384 U.S. 436 (1966) was another such wound. He, contrary to Hughes, is not persuasive.

47.   60 U.S. (19 How.) 393 (1857).

like the way that Copernican astronomy superseded Ptolemaic cosmology, supercorporations have so eroded the premises of both classical economics and its political counterpart, liberal democracy, that new theories must be devised. Economists have yet to explain or to justify such massive conscious economic cooperation. So, too, with lawyers and political scientists: the corporation's place in the constitutional system is far from settled. A new political economy has emerged in the United States in this century, but ancient and outmoded ideas of politics and economics still abide. "We are living in tomorrow's world today, still using yesterday's ideas."[48]

The preponderant social invention of the past century, supercorporations today occupy a place in society comparable in importance and influence to the Holy Roman Church in medieval Europe. With enormous assets, often running into tens of billions of dollars, they are concentrations of non-statist economic, and therefore of political, power not before known in human history. Corporate giants cannot avoid influencing human lives the world over on a scale similar to, and at times even dwarfing, public governments. Accordingly, Dr. Willis Harman maintains, "they face a demand that has historically been made only of government—that they assume responsibility for the welfare of those over whom they wield power."[49] The question in present context is whether that demand for corporate responsibility can be fulfilled through judicial action. Corporations have rights under the Constitution. Do they have concomitant duties? Corporations are constitutional persons. As such, do they have duties analogous to but not the same as those that natural persons have?

I answer those questions affirmatively. More specifically, I suggest that the Supreme Court could not only constitutionalize the corporation but could, following Chief Justice Hughes in the *Parrish* case, require that the giant firms develop policies that would include the welfare of the workers (as well as that of the stockholders). Again, I do not expect the present Court to leap to the challenge (save to shoot it down); but certainly the time has come to recognize the true nature of the supercorporations and do what is reasonably necessary about their undoubted power.

To bring the supercorporations within the ambit of the state action concept requires no major leap of doctrine. Indeed, the Supreme Court some years ago moved tentatively in that direction. But that movement

---

48.   H. Cleveland, The Management of Sustainable Growth 15 (1979).

49.   Harman, *The Coming Transformation,* The Futurist, Fall 1977, at ___.

was halted with the appointment of the Nixonites to the High Bench, so that today it surely is accurate to say, with Charles Black, that state action is a "conceptual disaster area"; and with Christopher Stone that it is "now, more than ever, a shambles."[50] The reason for such conceptual disarray is not difficult to locate: the Constitution was drafted on the assumption that only two important juridical entities existed—government and the natural person—but during recent years the United States has moved into what James Q. Wilson has called "the bureaucratic state."[51] Few judges know quite how to deal with the admitted economic power of disembodied economic entities. The state action concept may have made some sense during the nineteenth century, when society's groups were small and decentralized; the public-private distinction, Morton Horwitz asserts, was "a rough approximation of reality" in the last century.[52] Today's world is different.

Marsh v. Alabama[53] is still in the United States Reports. It exists as a time bomb ticking away awaiting a time when lawyers and judges can perceive the obvious: that the corporations, as the principal exemplars of the Economic Constitution, are indeed private governments. There is no need to labor the point. The rise of the group and the emergence of a corporate, an organizational society, is plain beyond doubt. Constitutions, thus, should consider all—whether public or nominally private—who exercise significant power in the socio-political arena.

Over that hurdle, then the application of constitutional norms to purported private entities follows as a matter of course. The very concept of constitutionalism arose a few centuries ago as a means of combatting the overweening power of the political sovereign. Today we have both political *and* economic sovereigns, which are ever increasingly joined together in a form of corporatism, and the same type of thinking that contributed to the growth of constitutionalism should be applied to all organizations that wield significant social power. Profes-

---

50.   Black, *"State Action," Equal Protection, and California's Proposition* 14, 81 HARV. L. REV. 69, 95 (1967). Stone, *Corporate Vices and Corporate Virtues: Do Public/Private Distinctions Matter?* 130 U. PA. L. REV. 1441, 1484 n.156 (1982). *See generally* Phillips, *The Inevitable Incoherence of Modern State Action Doctrine (1984) (forthcoming in a legal periodical).*

51.   Wilson, *The Rise of the Bureaucratic State,* THE PUBLIC INTEREST, Fall 1975, at 77.

52.   Horwitz, *The History of the Public/Private Distinction,* 130 U. PA. L. REV. 1423, 1428 (1982).

53.   326 U.S. 501 (1946).

sor David Ewing of the Harvard Business School observed in 1977:[54]

> During the first two centuries of United States history, the trend was unmistakably to broaden the reach of the Constitution. Universal male suffrage, the abolition of slavery, bargaining rights for unions, female suffrage, the many extensions of due process to people under arrest or surveillance—these and many other events marked the ever-widening application of the Constitution. But the Constitution does not yet penetrate the organizational sector, the still-dark ghetto of American rights.

Ewing advocates that corporations (organizations, generally) be subjected to the limitations of an organizational bill of rights. He maintains that during America's third century, one of the hallmarks of constitutionalism "should be concern for the rights of employees."[55]

What, however, are those rights? Professor Ewing's call is basically one of bringing due process—*procedural* due process—to the workplace. He makes a persuasive case. The question posed in this essay is whether that conception can be carried a step further—into the realm of *substantive* due process. A generation ago the Vice-President and General Counsel of the Ford Motor Company, William T. Gossett, maintained that corporate management "no longer represents exclusively the interests of stockholders. With the passage of time, it must develop a variety of devices and procedures to assure that its dealings with other groups are fair and just."[56] The other groups Gossett had in mind were employees, suppliers, dealers, customers and plant communities, "each of which has a separate claim on the corporation."[57]

What, then, is "fair and just"? And how can corporate management be stimulated to do more than pursue the single-minded goal of profit? Gossett tells us that there are conflicts of interest among the various groups in the corporate community; and then goes on to make this relevant statement:[58]

> One of the most dramatic conflicts of interest revolves about

---

54. D. Ewing, Freedom Inside the Organization: Bringing Civil Liberties to the Workplace 217-18 (1977).

55. *Id.* at 218. *See* Miller, *A Modest Proposal for Helping to Tame the Corporate Beast,* 8 Hofstra L. Rev. 79 (1979).

56. W. Gossett, Corporate Citizenship 178 (1957) (reprint from the John Randolph Tucker Lectures, 1953-1956, Washington & Lee University).

57. *Id.*

58. *Id.* at 187.

the decision of a large enterprise to move into a given community, or out of it—particularly the latter. There have been numerous instances where a single plant is the sole or major source of income for an entire community, and a callous attitude toward the effects of moving out could mean destruction for that community. The narrow interests of efficiency and profit-making for the stockholder might require such a move be made without delay. Yet the interests of local employees and the community might be so severely prejudiced that the corporation could not in good conscience move out without making every reasonable effort to mitigate the consequence of its going.

The problem, thus, is that of catching the conscience of the economic sovereigns—those who head the supercorporations. Courts are well suited to take on that task. The principle involved can be easily stated: Thou shalt not unreasonably harm members of the corporate community. Or put in affirmative terms: corporate management's decisions must take into consideration all segments of the corporate community, not merely one (the stockholders).

Here, of course, is a legal no-man's land. But the moral principle is clear, and can be translated into law by judicial decree. Consider, in this respect, what the well-known corporate lawyer, Adolf A. Berle, said in 1954:[59]

> Power to deal at will with other men's property and occupation, however absolute it may be as a matter of technical contract law, is subject to certain limitations. They still lie in the field of inchoate law: we are not yet able to cite explicit case and statute law clearly stating those limitations. We can only say that in this field a matrix of equity jurisdiction is beginning to appear.

I do not wish at this time to do more than call attention to Berle's idea of "inchoate law"; and then go on to suggest that in a few recent cases the Supreme Court has, for the public sector at least, rendered a series of decisions that evidence an emergent tendency—in Berle's language, an "inchoate" tendency—toward finding a right to a job. In *Elrod v. Burns*,[60] for example, the Court held that a newly elected Democratic sheriff could not fire some Republican employees simply because they

---

59. A. BERLE, THE TWENTIETH-CENTURY CAPITALIST REVOLUTION 82 (1954).
60. 427 U.S. 347 (1976).

were members of another political party. And in *Branti v. Finkel*,[61] the Justices expanded the immunity of non-civil services employees from patronage dismissals. Said Justice John Paul Stevens: "it is manifest that the continued employment of an assistant public defender cannot properly be conditioned upon his allegiance to the political party in control of the county government." In *Perry v. Sindermann*,[62] a non-tenured college professor alleged an interest in continued employment, "though not secured by a formal contractual or tenure provision, was secured by a no less binding understanding fostered by the college administration."[63] Sindermann asserted that the "college had a de facto tenure program, and that he had tenure under that program," and offered to prove that he had "no less a 'property' interest in continued employment than a formally tenured teacher" at colleges with a tenure system.[64] Sindermann prevailed.[65]

Are those decisions harbingers of things to come? That, of course, is possible but not probable. Other recent decisions, such as *Board of Regents v. Roth* and *Bishop v. Wood*,[66] point in a contrary direction. The most that can be said is that the issue has not really been settled. It is in flux. My position is that of Justice William Brennan in the *Bishop* case: "There is certainly a federal dimension to the definition of 'property' in the Federal Constitution,"[67] a sentiment that Justice Stevens, writing for the majority, called "remarkably innovative." Brennan believed that state discharges implicated a constitutionally protected liberty interest.

I believe that there is much to be said for the Brennan position. That it has not yet commanded a majority, save in such decisions as *Elrod*, *Branti*, and *Sindermann*, means that the Court is still searching for a doctrine (or doctrines) that would control public employment situations. If the *Elrod* principle is carried over into the private governments of the nation, then something approximating a constitutional right to a job would be in the making. Or if not a right to a job, at least a right that, once hired, a person must not be treated arbitrarily.

---

61.   445 U.S. 507 (1980).*Id.* at 519.

62.   408 U.S. 593 (1972).

63.   *Id.* at 599.

64.   *Id.* at 600.

65.   *Id.* at 601.

66.   Board of Regents v. Roth, 408 U.S. 564 (1972); Bishop v. Wood, 426 U.S. 341 (1976). *See generally* Van Alstyne, *Cracks in "The New Property: Adjudicative Due Process in the Administrative State*, 62 CORNELL L. REV. 445 (1977).

67.   *Bishop*, 426 U.S. at 343.

IV.

A brief word by way of conclusion: The IAM proposal presents critical questions about the nature of the American political economy. I believe that Robert A. Dahl was correct when he recently observed that "the commitment to corporate capitalism needs to be reconsidered. Earlier, when the framers had discussed their fears about majorities that might invade the rights of minorities, more often than not they mentioned rights to property. Their reasoned justification of a right to property, if they held one, would no doubt have been Lockean. Yet the Lockean justification makes no sense. . .when it is applied to the large modern business corporation."[68] Historical capitalism is dying; of that there can be little doubt. What will replace it is by no means certain at this time. Capitalism today is ever increasingly collectivist in nature, which means that its economic decisions are made politically. It is not a stable system, as the IAM proposal evidences. For that reason, and perhaps for others, many nations today are moving toward nationalization. State-owned companies are on the rise. Professors Monsen and Walters tell us, throughout Western Europe.[69] "European governments," they show, "now have a direct ownership stake in over half of Europe's largest companies." Those firms, plus the more market-oriented enterprises in the East, pose a direct challenge to American industry. How United States firms will react is one of the crucial politico-economic—that is, constitutional—questions of the day. The rise of the new economies will have to be met, in some form or another, by the United States. I believe that the consequence will be a growing form of an indigenous type of corporatism.[70] If so, then the public-private distinction is on its way out. And it becomes all the more important that proposals such as the "New Technology Bill of Rights" be given comprehensive and respectful attention by those who wield effective power in America.

Finally: I do not wish to be placed in the position of using constitu-

---

68. Dahl, *On Removing Certain Impediments to Democracy in the United Statese*, in BEYOND THE WELFARE STATE, 71, 90 (I. Howe ed. 1982).

69. R. MONSEN & K. WALTERS, NATIONALIZED COMPANIES: A THREAT TO AMERICAN BUSINESS (1983).

70. *See* A. MILLER, THE MODERN CORPORATE STATE: PRIVATE GOVERNMENTS AND THE AMERICAN CONSTITUTION *passim* (1976); Miller, *Toward a Definition of "The" Constitution*, 8 U. DAYTON L. REV. 633, 691-700 (1983).

tional arguments as a form of "desperate legal acrobatics."[71] Surely, however, the relationship of the populace—in present context, that of the workers—to the public *and* private governments of the nation is an important constitutional question. (Can someone name another that is more important?) If the IAM proposal necessitates the complete re-examination of the political economy of the nation, then such a scrutiny is long overdue. Furthermore, as Chief Justice Charles Evans Hughes once observed, "Behind the words of the constitutional provisions are postulates which limit and control."[72] One such postulate, I suggest, is a surpassingly important human need: the need to be needed. If the Constitution should, as has been suggested above, evolve into one that fulfills human needs and human deserts within environmental constraints, then the requirements of *Homo faber* should be recognized and realized. Government, I maintain, has no other purpose than to make every reasonable effort to see that human needs and deserts are in fact satisfied. More specifically, if "our constitutional system rests on a particular moral theory, that men have moral rights against the state,"[73] I maintain that high among those "moral rights" is that of a constitutional right to a job.

---

71. Levinson, Book Review, 57 TEX. L. REV. 847, 858 (1979).
72. Principality of Monaco v. Mississippi, 292 U.S. 313, 322 (1943).
73. R. DWORKIN, TAKING RIGHTS SERIOUSLY 147 (1977).

CHAPTER 11

Crisis Government
Becomes the Norm

In previous chapters, particularly the third, it has been argued that the Constitution has always been relative to circumstances. This chapter extends that analysis into the future. The United States is unquestionably moving—has moved—into a novel social milieu in which constitutional mechanisms devised two centuries ago must operate. That they do so badly is the gist that is suggested here. For a variety of reasons, including the Cold War, planetary interdependence, growing scarcities of natural resources, and the slowing down of economic growth, it is becoming increasingly apparent that the political order established in 1789, even as updated by later interpretations, will have to deal with unprecedented problems—so much so that a grave question exists as to its adequacy.

Since law is more a reflection than a molder of events, it seems wholly clear that constitutional law in the future wil have to confront a condition of continuing crises. Emergency government, in sum, has become and will continue to be the norm in the United States (and elsewhere). This means that sooner or later more and more authoritarian controls will be placed on human behavior. The chapter thus complements much of what was said in previous chapters, and points directly to the need for hard thinking about constitutional changes.

There can be little doubt that humanity is on the verge of a profound social transformation, at the edge of a new social frontier.[1]

I. INTRODUCTION

Any forecast of the direction American constitutional law will take must perforce be based on a view of the type of society, national and planetary, in which the Document of 1787 and its 26 amendments will operate as this nation's fundamental law. Both predictions—of law and of society—are risky, but necessary. The time is past when lawyers can fly backwards to see what has happened. Law must be avowedly instrumental, for America has assumed the task not only of saying what the law is, but what it ought to be. The themes of this essay are multiple: (a) law, including constitutional law, reflects society; it is, in brief, the *zeitgeist* rather than "the law" that guides constitutional change;[2] (b) change will remain a constant in the social order, as the scientific-technological revolution continues its dizzy, uncharted pace; and (c) the United States has entered a time when crisis will become the norm. In what follows, those themes will be developed in the context of several constitutional relationships: (a) changes within the separation of powers in the national government; (b) alterations in federalism; (c) adaptation of the Constitution to life on Spaceship Earth; (d) recognition of the dimension of private governance; and (e) the desuetude of the individual as the basic unit of American society.

Those are indeed large matters; each can be dealt with only summarily in this brief essay. Much has had to be left out, not only in analysis of the five categories just mentioned, but also with regard to specific doctrines.[3] It is difficult, and no doubt rash, to peer into the future. At best, the future is a shore dimly seen; at worst, it can, because of developments not now known or foreseeable, be wholly different from what one envisages.[4] Even so, there seems to be a growing realization, not yet a consensus, that

---

1. L. BROWN, THE TWENTY-NINTH DAY 324 (1978).

2. *See* A. MILLER, THE SUPREME COURT: MYTH AND REALITY 3-9 (1978).

3. By and large, this essay is one in which I say what is likely to be, not what should be. Specific doctrines may be inferred from the five trends discussed.

4. *See* D. PRICE, THE SCIENTIFIC ESTATE (1965).

This chapter was originally published under the title of "Constitutional Law: Crisis Government Becomes the Norm" in 39 Ohio State Law Journal 736 (1978), and is reproduced here with the permission of the Ohio State Law Journal.

Homo sapiens is in for a continuing time of troubles.[5]   Lord Ashby of Brandon believes that we are not merely in a crisis but a "climacteric."[6]   If so, that is something new under the constitutional sun.   I agree with him, but do not welcome what seems sure to come. We have, however, to accept life and the world as they are, not as we wish them to be.   Only harm will come from refusing to confront and attempt to deal with the coalescing troubles—the "vulnerabilities"[7]—of man kind.   My main thesis, then, is that crisis government will soon become the norm, not only in the United States but also worldwide; and that will place unprecedented strains on the American constitutional order.   Whether it will survive in anything like its present form—the Constitution's original texts, plus almost two centuries of gloss—is not at all likely.   It is probable, as Arnold Toynbee has said, that increasingly despotic governments will develop as economic growth slows and population expands. "In all developed countries," he said in 1975, "a new way of life—a severely regimented way—will have to be imposed by a ruthless authoritarian government."[8]

In 1974, Senators Frank Church and Charles Mathias asserted that "emergency government has become the norm."[9]   There is no way to prove such a contrafactual proposition. Only time will give the answer.   One believes it or one does not; to me the overwhelming weight of thoughtful opinion and the likelihood of being correct is on the side of the Toynbees[10] and Browns[11] and Commoners[12] of the nation, rather than the Kahns.[13]

---

5.   *See* E. CORNISH, THE STUDY OF THE FUTURE (1977) for an outline of the thinking of those who have given serious attention to studying the future.

6.   Lord Ashby, A Second Look at Doom, The 21st Fawley Lecture delivered at Southampton University (Dec. 11, 1975) (photocopy of typed text). *See* E. ASHBY, RECONCILING MAN WITH THE ENVIRONMENT (1978); M. SHANKS, WHAT'S WRONG WITH THE MODERN WORLD? AGENDA FOR A NEW SOCIETY (1978). *See also* W. HARMAN, AN INCOMPLETE GUIDE TO THE FUTURE xi (1976):
> The world is headed for a climacteric which may well be one of the most fateful in the history
> of civilizations.   This convulsion is now not far off and most people sense something of it—
> although interpretations vary widely, like the well-known interpretations of the elephant by
> blindfolded people who feel different parts of the animal.

7.   The term comes from H. BROWN, THE HUMAN FUTURE REVISITED 179-218 (1978).   He lists thermonuclear war, energy shortages, dependence on nonfuel minerals, food, social disruption, terrorism, and economic disruptions (such as inflation) as the vulnerabilities of an industrial nation. In sum: "Industrial man now lives in a complex and largely synthetic ecological system, new in the human experience and inadequately understood." *Id.* at 227.

8.   Quoted in Takaski Oka, *A Crowded World: Can Mankind Survive in Freedom?*, Christ. Sci. Mon., Feb. 10, 1975, at 5, col. 1 [herinafter cited as Toynbee].

9.   CHURCH & MATHIAS, FOREWORD TO A BRIEF HISTORY OF EMERGENCY POWERS IN THE UNITED STATES, A WORKING PAPER PREPARED FOR THE SPECIAL COMMITTEE ON NATIONAL EMERGENCIES AND DELEGATED EMERGENCY POWERS UNITED STATES SENATE, 93d Cong. 2d Sess. at v (1974).

10.   Toynbee, *supra* note 8.

11.   L. BROWN, *supra* note 1; H. BROWN, *supra* note 7.

12.   B. COMMONER, THE POVERTY OF POWER (1975).

13.   Herman Kahn is perhaps the leading exponent of the view that the future will be rosy. *See, e.g.*, H. KAHN, W. BROWN & L. MARTEL, THE NEXT 200 YEARS: A SCENARIO FOR AMERICA AND THE WORLD (1976). *See also* R. MILES, AWAKENING FROM THE AMERICAN DREAM—THE SOCIAL AND POLITICAL LIMITS TO GROWTH (1976).   A useful selected bibliography of future-oriented books may be found in E. CORNISH, *supra* note 5, at 259-82.

Even if the proposition is not accurate in detail, it surely is in general terms. That is as much as one can essay at this time.

The Constitution is predicated on the assumption that crisis is aberrational. No provision is expressly made for emergency government;[14] but since the beginnings of the Republic, actions have been taken to deal with emergencies, actual or perceived.[15] In all that time, the theory was that the Constitution remained the same. Conditions could change, as Chief Justice Hughes said in the *Blaisdell* case,[16] which would enable extraordinary actions to be taken. But the Supreme Court has always adhered, without overt deviation, to the principles announced by Justice Davis in *Ex parte Milligan*:[17] "The Constitution is a law for rulers and people, equally in war and in peace, and covers with its shield of its protection all classes of men, at all times, and under all circumstances." That is a nice sentiment, were it true; but it is not—not only in the past, but also in the present and surely in the future.

II. TRENDS OF CONSTITUTIONAL DEVELOPMENT

Law school study of constitutional law employs, speaking generally, the case method, with the case being defined as a Supreme Court opinion. Scholarship tends to be patient analyses of the intricacies of the reasoning, or lack of it, in given opinions. Well and good, so far as it goes; the trouble is that it does not go nearly far enough. Required is attention accorded to the Constitution "in operation" as well as the Constitution "of the books";[18] and further, to the trends of structural development in the government brought into being by the Document of 1787. The present essay is concerned with several structural trends, rather than with specific constitutional doctrines.

A. *Separation of Powers*

That power in the American constitutional order has always flowed, albeit at times discontinuously, toward the Executive is a truism. That it will continue to do so may be predicted with confidence. However much Congress, in the wake of Watergate and the resignation of Richard Nixon, is trying to retrieve ceded powers or gain new ones, by no means can it do so. In 1967, a perceptive French observer dismissed the power of modern legislatures as an "illusion," maintaining that "the organs of representative

---

14.   Save, perhaps, in the habeas corpus and declaration of war clauses. Some nations, notably France, with written constititutions do make express provision for emergencies. *See* M. VOISSET, L'ARTICLE 16 DE LA CONSTITUTION DU 4 OCTOBRE 1958 (1969). To date, Article 16 has been employed once, by President Charles de Gaulle, in the Algerian crisis in 1961. *Id.* at 414-15.

15.   *See* A. SOFAER, WAR, FOREIGN AFFAIRS AND CONSTITUTIONAL POWER: THE ORIGINS (1976); A. MILLER, PRESIDENTIAL POWER IN A NUTSHELL (1977).

16.   Home Bldg. & Loan Ass'n v. Blaisdell, 290 U.S. 398 (1934).

17.   71 U.S. (4 Wall.) 2, 120-1 (1866).

18.   W. WILSON, CONGRESSIONAL GOVERNMENT ¶10 (1885).

democracy no longer have any other purpose than to endorse decisions prepared by experts and pressure groups."[19]   The problems of governance are too many and too complex for two committees, one of 100 persons and the other of 435, to do much more than that. Efforts now being made to impose "Congressional vetoes" on specific actions of the public administration are by no means sure to survive constitutional challenge.[20] Members of Congress participate in the many "subgovernments"[21] of Washington, but usually as individuals not as a collectivity.

Woodrow Wilson could write in 1885 that the chairmen of the standing committees of Congress were the most powerful governmental officials;[22] but by 1908 he had changed his mind and clearly saw the rise of executive hegemony in government.[23]   That trend has accelerated since then.   Wars and rumors of wars, economic depressions, deep and irreversible immersion of the nation in world affairs, a monopoly of expertise in the Executive Branch—all these, and more, are forces that militate toward an even stronger President and bureaucracy.   The President is not merely *primus inter pares* in the tripartite division of powers; he is *primus*. Period. Whoever lives in the White House, of whatever party, will continue to be the focal point of attention—and of actual governing power. The troubles of President Carter, so obvious in 1978, should not be taken as the norm.

Presidents will, to be sure, have to negotiate with Congress and with the bureaucracy, which is a force in its own right.   But there can be no doubt that, in terms of formal authority as well as effective control, the reins of government are in the hands of the man living at 1600 Pennsylvania Avenue, not in the hands of those who work on Capitol Hill. No government of any consequence in the world is run otherwise.   The spare generalities of Article II do not begin to demonstrate the range and nature of presidential power. Executive power, of course, has come without amendment; it has both been seized by the Executive and delegated to the public administration, including the President, by a Congress only too willing to forego scrutiny of the myriad details of routine problems of governance.

In recent years, the bureaucracy in Congress has greatly increased in size and influence. Little doubt exists about the actual legislative powers of the "third branch" of Congress—the oft-times nameless and faceless individuals who serve on committee or Congressional staffs. It is literally impossible for any one member of Congress to be privy to the details of the

19.   J. ELLUL, THE POLITICAL ILLUSION (1967).

20.   *See, e.g.,* Atkins v. United States, 556 F.2d 1028 (Ct. Cl. 1977), *cert. denied,* 434 U.S. 1009 (1978); Miller & Knapp, *The Congressional Veto: Preserving the Constitutional Framework,* 52 IND. L. J. 367 (1977), and works cited therein.

21.   *See* D. CATER, POWER IN WASHINGTON (1964).

22.   W. WILSON, *supra* note 18.

23.   W. WILSON, CONSTITUTIONAL GOVERNMENT IN THE UNITED STATES (1908).

many programs of government or even of the bills on which he votes. So reliance is placed either on the leadership or, more likely, on staff members. Nevertheless, as compared with the nearly three million Executive Branch bureaucrats, Congress has no real chance to do more than to play catch-up on a few details of government. Public policy matters, large and small, ever more are settled with only perfunctory legislative cognizance and participation. The most that Congress can hope to do, and then not very often, is to make those in the Executive Branch think twice before acting. The future, to repeat, belongs to the Executive.

As with Congress, so too with the courts. Despite a flurry of activism in the past three decades, government by judiciary (the title of a remarkably silly book published in 1977)[24] is mere fantasy. Judges simply do not have the time or the power to do much more than erect standards toward which they can hope the people and the politicians will aspire. Judicial review of administrative action, for example, is noteworthy for its rarity; when it does take place, the administrator is usually sustained. Of the untold millions of administrative decisions made annually, what the administrator decides is usually final in fact, though not in theory. So, too, with the Supreme Court, which in fits of hyperbole has been described as an extraordinarily powerful political actor.[25] That simply is not true, given the range and nature of decisions important to Americans, whether as individuals or as members of groups. Lawyers and others like to think otherwise, to be sure; but it is clear that the power of the Supreme Court specifically, and of courts generally, is greatly overrated today, and that it will be even more attenuated in the future.[26] That is so despite *United States v. Nixon*[27] and the *Steel Seizure Case*.[28] We should, furthermore, always remember that constitutional interpretation is distinctly not a judicial monopoly.

---

24.   R. BERGER, GOVERNMENT BY JUDICIARY (1977).

25.   *E.g.*, A. BERLE, POWER 342 (1969): "[A] revolution has taken place and is in progress" and "the revolutionary committee is the Supreme Court of the United States"; Hutchins, *The Case for Constitutional Change*, 3 CENTER REP. NO. 5 (Dec. 1970) cited in Book Review, 71 COLUM. L. REV. 502 n.4 (1971): "The Court has become 'the highest legislative body in the land.' "

I do not say that the Court has no power; of course it has some. My point is that it is far less than that attributed to it by the conventional wisdom. *See* A. MILLER, THE SUPREME COURT: MYTH AND REALITY (1978).

26.   "[I]t is not possible to avoid the conclusion that something quite fundamental has begun to go wrong with Western civilisation." E. MISHAN, THE ECONOMIC GROWTH DEBATE: AN ASSESSMENT 265 (1977). If that be so, and I think it is, I am unable to perceive how lawyer-judges sitting on courts will be of much use in trying to extricate *Homo sapiens* from the predicament the species is in. The law schools have not yet come to grips with that situation; study of law, including constitutional law, tends to be based on concepts long since dead or moribund.

27.   418 U.S. 683 (1974).

28.   Youngstown Sheet and Tube Co. v. Sawyer, 343 U.S. 579 (1952). The limitations on the Executive are political rather than judicial. It is only by an intellectually indefensible fiction that the powers of the President can be deduced from the spare generalities and the silences of Article II. *See* A. MILLER, *supra* note 2.

In the past, during times of all-out emergency, such as declared war, judges and legislators deferred to the Executive. So it will be in the future—perhaps in the remainder of this century and surely in the 21st. The coalescing problems of the climacteric of mankind will not permit the stately ritual of judicial decision-making or the pulls and tugs of the legislative process. Events will move too fast for that. This is not to say that the Executive will be efficient, merely that that branch will be dominant.

B. *Federalism*

Federalism was the price paid for the Constitution of 1787, which established, in Corwin's terminology, a system of "dual federalism."[29] That system has long been moribund: The allegedly sovereign states are more a source of Senators and of presidential candidates than they are repositories of actual governing power. Problems are *national* or *planetary*, and have been since at least the promulgation of the sixteenth amendment. A nation with a central income tax cannot be truly federal, in the sense of dual powers between central and local governments. Economic planning, furthermore, is the scourge of original federalism; splintered, autonomous decision-making cannot be brooked, whether under planning by the "first economy" of the giant corporations or by public government itself.[30] Not that planning by government has gone very far; it has not. There can be little doubt, however, that it will quickly develop.

This means that some type of incomes policy and the imposition of wage and price controls are probable—in the near, rather than the far distant, future. At the very least. A consensus is now being formed in the United States that can only lead to economic planning on a grand scale. When it occurs, as it will, the Constitution will be able to tolerate it. There is enough room in the interstices of the affirmative powers in Article I to make that certain. The courts will not impose any barriers. States, then, will ever more become administrative districts for centrally promulgated policies. These policies, be it noted, are established today both by the private governments of the giant corporations and in the rapidly increasing programs of the federal government.[31]

A further meaning is clear, but not likely to get any serious attention: there is no need whatsoever for fifty-one political districts (the states plus the District of Columbia); that decentralized political order makes no sense when laid against the realities of power in the present and emergent constitutional order. One example will suffice to evidence the point: when

---

29. Corwin, *The Passing of Dual Federalism*, 36 Va. L. Rev. 1 (1950).

30. *See* A. Miller, The Modern Corporate State: Private Governments and the American Constitution (1976).

31. *Id.*

in recent years New York City got into financial straits, it did not try to solve its own problems and did not even seriously try to get the state government in Albany to extricate it from near bankruptcy. Quite the contrary: the eyes of New York, city and state, swung covetously toward Uncle Deep Pockets in Washington. What useful purpose, in such a circumstance, is served by the cost of running a state government in New York? Examples could be multiplied, but, heeding William of Occam, will not be. The lesson is clear: traditional federalism is dying or may already be dead. The problems of economics and the imperatives of technology are simply too much for, say, Rhode Island or South Dakota, let alone larger and wealthier states. They are even too much, as will be discussed below, for the United States to act alone.

As population increases, as economic growth declines, as the nation becomes even more deeply intertwined with others, that trend will accelerate. Nothing in the Constitution will stop it. Nothing the Supreme Court might do will stop it. We are superstitious and venerate the written word of the fundamental law; but that is constitutional fetishism. Some also venerate the past and the saints—the Founding Fathers—in America's hagiology. The first amendment protects such beliefs and the expression of them. There is nothing unconstitutional about being an antiquarian. It merely does not comport with reality, contemporaneous or futurist. Neither the present nor the future are mere extensions of the past.

C. *Planetary Interdependence*

"It has seldom been more important," *The Economist* said in April 1978, " to gear national policies to fit international goals, rather than the other way round."[32] Precisely. The problem for American constitutionalism is the further adaptation of an essentially domestic fundamental law to the realities of life on a shrinking planet. Science and technology have diminished time and distance. The United States has an interest in happenings anywhere in the world—and, indeed, far into outer space. This, again, is something new under the constitutional sun.

Can those necesssary accommodations, which are sure to come— have already come—be made without amendment? Professor Paul Freund, peering into the future in 1956, maintained that "any really thoroughgoing commitment to supranational authority would be brought about by constitutional amendment, necessarily so if the measures of the world union were to be established as the supreme law of the land secured against change brought about by subsequent national legislation."[33] No doubt that is true if, but only if, the change is a "thoroughgoing commitment to supranational authority"; by no means is it likely that such

---

32. *Moving the World Uphill*, The Economist (London), April 29, 1978, at 89, col. 1.
33. Freund, *Law and the Future: Constitutional Law*, 51 Nw. L. Rev. 187, 194-95 (1956).

a revolutionary event will occur. Rather, barring catastrophe, changes will come as they usually have come in the development of the Constitution—incrementally.[34] American adherence to supranationalism will be built bit by bit, rather like the slow growth of a coral reef instead of a mighty volcanic explosion. If so, then the Constitution as now written can accommodate the accretive commitment to larger than national resolutions of public policy problems.[35] Sooner or later, those accretions will become in fact a "thoroughgoing commitment."

That development has already begun, and surely—absent a catastrophe such as a nuclear war—will continue. The little known but greatly important International Monetary Fund is one example. NATO is another. International commodity agreements others. The list is not long, but it is significant: There is a slow but steady trend toward less than a planetary but more than a national confrontation and resolution of common problems. No constitutional problems of any importance are posed by that trend. Bit by bit sovereignty—that ostensibly indissoluble attribute of nation-states—is being chipped away; slowly, the coral reef of multinationalism grows.

The political development parallels, of course, the actions of businessmen. No American corporation of any consequence is purely domestic in its operations.[36] The multinational corporation has become a familiar participant in the world arena. With the businessman goes the lawyer; many American law firms now have branches in other countries, sometimes many branches. The late Stephen Hymer said:

> [W]e seem to be in the midst of a major revolution in international relationships as modern science establishes the technological basis for a major advance in the conquest of the material world and the beginnings of truly cosmopolitan production. Multinational corporations are in the vanguard of this revolution, because of their great financial and administrative strength and their close contact with the new technology.[37]

Corporations often can shape the environment in which the problems of American external relations grow and can also define the axiomatic in public policy. An axiomatic decision is one that is almost automatic—actions by government which are rarely accompanied by debate and do not require any means-end calculation. It is axiomatic, for example, to protect American property abroad. Where economics goes, politics follows—and the Constitution is not far behind. The question is not

34.   *See* C. LINDBLOM, THE POLICY-MAKING PROCESS (1968).

35.   *Cf. A Law for Europe*, The Economist (London), June 17, 1978, at 17, col. 1, suggesting that it is "possible for the European court [of the Common market] to play the sort of role the Supreme Court of the United States plays, pioneering political advances by the way it chooses to interpret the Rome treaty."

36.   *See* R. BARNET & R. MULLER, GLOBAL REACH (1974).

37.   Hymer, *The Multinational Corporation and the Law of Uneven Development*, in ECONOMICS AND WORLD ORDER: FROM THE 1970s TO THE 1990s (Bhagwati ed. 1972).

whether the Constitution follows the flag, as some have said, but whether the decisions by governmental officers, indubitably valid under the Constitution, serve to chip away at the foundations of American sovereignty. The answer can only be yes—today and even more so in the future.

No discussion of foreign affairs should avoid mention of the most perilous of all crises: nuclear war and the proliferation of nuclear capability. Of that, space permits only two statements. First, the possibility—nay, probability—of nuclear war has "amended" the Constitution by making the power to enter into war a presidential, not a congressional, decision. Presidents—for example, Lyndon Johnson and Richard Nixon—publicly assert a power in the President to use lesser violence without regard to Congress.[38] The Vietnam conflict is the classic instance of that position. But there are others. Second, nuclear war will mean that for the first time, save perhaps for the Civil War, violence will have been "socialized" for Americans. All of us, particularly those in metropolitan areas, are vulnerable, either to attack from another nation or from some terrorist who succeeds in constructing a nuclear device.

In all of this the Constitution is irrelevant. Emergency is the problem, and survival is the goal. Law of any type will not stand in the way of attempted fulfillment of that most fundamental of all the aims of any society. "The possibility of all-out thermonuclear war," Dr. Harrison Brown says, "is the most serious danger confronting industrial civilization today."[39] Nothing in the Constitution or any other law will inhibit those who govern us from trying to prevent that catastrophe; or if it happens, doing what is necessary to cope with it.

D. *Private Governance*

More than thirty years ago Alexander Pekelis predicted that the next generation of constitutional lawyers would be concerned with the problems of private governments, by which he meant mainly the giant corporations.[40] He was echoed by Adolf Berle, among others.[41] They

---

38. President Johnson's views on his powers in Vietnam are quoted in G. GUNTHER, CASES AND MATERIALS ON CONSTITUTIONAL LAW 442 (1975); for President Nixon's views, see Select Committee to Study Governmental Operations with Respect to Intelligence Activities, United States Senate, Final Report, Book IV at 157-58 (1976) (Nixon's answer to an interrogatory). President Ford held similar views, as in the Mayaguez incident. *See* A. MILLER, *supra* note 15, at 192-94. Historically a similar pattern is visible. *See* L. FISHER, THE CONSTITUTION BETWEEN FRIENDS (1978); J. RANDALL, CONSTITUTIONAL PROBLEMS UNDER LINCOLN (rev. ed. 1951).

39. H. BROWN, *supra* note 7, at 180.

40. Pekelis, *Private Governments and the Federal Constitution*, in LAW AND SOCIAL ACTION 91 (M. Knovitz ed. 1950).

41. The relevant citations may be found in Miller, *The Corporation as a Private Government in the World Community*, 46 VA. L. REV. 1539 (1960).

were only partially correct. The Supreme Court, which broke new ground in *Marsh v. Alabama*,[42] extended that decision in 1968;[43] but with the advent of the Nixon Court, that movement was aborted. *Tanner*[44] and *Hudgens*[45] make it clear that the present Court is quite unwilling to equate private power with public governance—and thus to extend the state action principle to cover some of the pluralistic social groups of the nation. Whether that doctrine of the Nixon Court will endure is the question. Despite evidence to the contrary, the answer, in my judgment, is negative.

The time has come—indeed, it is long past—for the giant corporation to be "constitutionalized."[46] That this will be done—that Pekelis' forecast will come true—seems reasonably sure. First, in such statutes as the Civil Rights Act of 1964, Congress in effect made private enterprises subject to something akin to constitutional restraints. Equal opportunity became a statutory right, upheld by the Supreme Court. There was less need, then, to apply the fourteenth amendment to private corporations, for they had come under the aegis of a congressional command. Second, the Court in at least two 1978 decisions gave corporations the protections of the first and fourth amendments.[47] Those who receive such protection will ultimately have to pay the price of an obligation to obey the Constitution themselves. Finally, more and more people—for example, Professor David Ewing of the Harvard Business School[48]—are coming to perceive the immense power of corporations and to argue that there should be an employee's bill of rights. The giant corporation simply does not fit the realities of orthodox constitutional theory and interpretation. "Constitutionalizing" it is, therefore, an idea whose time has come. Despite the present composition of the Supreme Court, the questions of arbitrary treatment by private groups will not be easily quelled. The corporation is a constitutional person (for diversity cases, it is a citizen) and should be held to the view, as Justice Black put it in the *Korematsu* case,[49] that citizenship—personhood—has its duties as well as its rights.

One could argue, as Justices Black[50] and Douglas[51] did, that the corporation should be "depersonified." After all, it was not until 1886, and then casually without hearing argument, that the Supreme Court

---

42. Marsh v. Alabama, 326 U.S. 501 (1946).

43. Food Employees Union, Local 590 v. Logan Valley Plaza, Inc. 391 U.S. 308 (1968).

44. Lloyd Corp. v. Tanner, 407 U.S. 551 (1972).

45. Hudgens v. NLRB, 424 U.S. 507 (1976).

46. *See* A. MILLER, *supra* note 30; Miller, *Toward "Constitutionalizing" the Corporation: A Speculative Essay*, 80 W. VA. L. REV. 187 (1978).

47. First Nat'l Bank of Boston v. Bellotti, 435 U.S. 765 (1978); Marshall v. Barlow's, Inc., 436 U.S. 307 (1978).

48. D. EWING, FREEDOM INSIDE THE ORGANIZATION (1977).

49. Korematsu v. United States, 323 U.S. 214 (1944) (upholding military curfew of persons of Japanese ancestry even though many were native-born American citizens).

50. Connecticut Life Ins. Co. v. Johnson, 303 U.S. 77, 85 (1938) (Black, J., dissenting).

51. Wheeling Steel Corp. v. Glander, 337 U.S. 562, 579 (1949) (Douglas, J., dissenting).

endowed the corporation with the status of a constitutional person.[52] What the Court has wrought it can take away; but in this instance it is not likely to do so. Far more probable is the recognition of the dimension of private governments, a development for which I have argued elsewhere.[53] This, after all, is truly an age of collective action. But if private governance is recognized and indeed occurs, and the giant corporation is brought under the ambit of the state-action concept, no one should think that individual freedoms will suddenly take a jump. Some freedoms, yes, but for others the answer is no.

E. *The Individual in the Bureaucratic State*

We live, as Professor James Wilson has argued, in the age of administration,[54] at a time when the bureaucratic state has risen to a position of great prominence and influence. That development has crucial significance for the relationship of the individual *qua* individual vis-a-vis the state. The natural person confronts bureaucracies wherever he turns. With some exceptions, of course, he works in groups, socializes in groups, and does almost everything except die (and sometimes even then) as a member of a group.

That, too, is a fairly recent development, at least to the extent to which it exists today. Yesteryear was different, but only in degree. The net result is starkly clear: The individual spends his life as a member of groups and is significant only as a member of groups. Whatever may have been the original theory behind the Constitution, the United States is not composed of atomistic individuals operating as such. As long go as 1927, John Dewey maintained that

> the human being whom we fasten upon as individual *par excellence* is moved and regulated by his association with others; what he does and what the consequences of his behavior are, what his experience consists of, cannot even be described, much less accounted for, in isolation.[55]

Political scientists since Arthur Bentley, writing in 1908,[56] have viewed the political process as the clash of conflicting groups. So, too, with economists; Peter Drucker is an example: it is "the organization rather than the individual which is productive in an industrial system."[57] Lawyers have lagged behind, although the Supreme Court in recent years has found a constitutional right of association in the delphic pronounce-

---

52. Santa Clara County v. Southern Pac. R. Co., 118 U.S. 394 (1886); *see* Justice Rehnquist's dissenting opinion in First Nat'l Bank of Boston v. Bellotti, 435 U.S. 765, 822 (1978) (Rehnquist, J., dissenting).

53. A. MILLER, *supra* note 30.

54. Wilson, *The Rise of the Bureaucratic State*, 41 THE PUB. INTEREST 77 (Fall 1975).

55. J. DEWEY, THE PUBLIC AND ITS PROBLEMS 188 (1927).

56. A. BENTLEY, THE PROCESS OF GOVERNMENT (1908).

57. P. DRUCKER, THE NEW SOCIETY 6 (1950).

ments of the first amendment.[58]   The "organizational revolution"—
Kenneth Boulding's term[59]—is slowly finding its way into constitutional
law.

This has large consequences.   First, freedom under the Constitution
is ever increasingly becoming merely freedom of which group to join. Even
then, some groups limit membership.   I have elsewhere argued that the
Supreme Court, albeit unwittingly, is putting Thomas Hill Green's view of
freedom in a social organization into the notion of individual liberty.[60] The
key case—the turning point—was *West Coast Hotel Co. v. Parrish.*[61]
When the Court legitimized congressional encouragement of group action
in the *Jones & Laughlin* case,[62] the pattern became clear. *NAACP v.
Alabama ex rel. Patterson*[63] merely capped a previous development.

Individual liberty, in the second place, is subject to the constraints,
often arbitrary, of the group—rather, groups—in which the natural person
operates.   This is best seen, perhaps, in the business corporation, where, as
noted above, the problem of individual rights in the working place is now
getting more attention.   But it also appears, *inter alia,* in labor unions and
in private clubs.   The individual is submerged into the overall well-being
of the group, as determined by those—usually an oligarchy—who control
it.[64]

Third, an inability to join a group may result in severe deprivations.
For example, when a "whistle blower" is fired by a company (or
government agency), he finds it difficult to locate other employment.
Polygraph tests, imperfect though they are to determine a person's
integrity, are nonetheless widely used.   With the increasing use of
computers and data processing, a person's record follows him wherever he
goes; and all too often he finds doors barred to him for reasons about
which he knows nothing.

Finally, the individual is powerless, or almost so, in trying to alter
group behavior, whether in a public or a private bureaucracy.   Not always,
to be sure.   On occasion the lone person can and does make a difference,[65]
but only if he can use another group—*e.g.,* Congress, the judiciary, or an

---

58.   NAACP v. Alabama *ex rel.* Patterson, 357 U.S. 449 (1958).   *See* D. FELLMAN, THE
CONSTITUTIONAL RIGHT OF ASSOCIATION (1963).

59.   K. BOULDING, THE ORGANIZATIONAL REVOLUTION (1953).

60.   Miller, *Toward A Concept of Constitutional Duty,* 1968 SUP. CT. REV. 199 (1968).

61.   300 U.S. 379 (1937).

62.   NLRB v. Jones & Laughlin Steel Co., 301 U.S. 1 (1937).

63.   357 U.S. 449 (1958). The deeper meaning is that concept of "status" may now be seen, at least
in an emergent state, in constitutional law.   The rights and liberties of some Americans, that is, depend
on the group to which they belong.   The obvious example is military personnel; but many others exist.
Constitutional law scholarship has done little or nothing to note this important development.   *But see*
R. HORN, GROUPS AND THE CONSTITUTION (1956); Phillips, *Thomas Hill Green, Positive Freedom and
the United States Supreme Court,* 25 EMORY L. J. 63 (1976).

64.   The reference here is to Michels' "iron law of oligarchy." *See* R. MICHELS, POLITICAL
PARTIES (1911).

65.   Ralph Nader is perhaps the best example.

economic power group, such as a union—to help him in disputes with, say, a private corporation or a governmental agency. The pattern, however, is otherwise.

That the movement toward bureaucracy will both continue and intensify cannot be seriously doubted. As population grows, as technology continues its dizzy pace, as cities expand, as corporations grow, as government becomes even larger, as emergencies occur, as they will, the natural person will find that he faces a congeries of groups too powerful to battle. The Constitution will not bar that continuing development.

Paradoxically, at the very time that the nature of freedom has changed (in the four decades since *Parrish*), there are more individual freedoms of a certain type than ever before. Right now—1979—the individual is more protected by the Constitution and judicial (and other) interpretation than at any previous time in American history. This is the Golden Age of individual rights (of a certain type). The reasons for this seeming paradox are not hard to locate. One is economic: Human freedoms are more fully protected today because of the high growth rate in the economy since the late 1930s. This means that the economic pie was for about thirty-five years getting larger and that more people could get a slice of it than ever before. Since necessitous men cannot be free men, that means that the gross national product had a definite relationship to the recent expansion of freedoms. However, economic growth has slowed and may be stopping. If that continues, as I think it will, then more and more people will be contesting for a relatively smaller pie. People will be willing to forego other freedoms in order to obtain an adequate income. In other words, the social basis of the recent expansion of freedoms appears to be vanishing. (Even more portentous is the high probability of social turmoil.) In the unlikely event that zero population growth is attained, it will not be until far in the future; the number of Americans will total at least 300 million in the 21st century—a 50 percent increase over today.[66]

Of more importance, however, is the fact that individual freedoms are permitted or tolerated by the state only when important interests of the state are not jeopardized. *Cohen v. California*[67] is an example; whether Cohen would have prevailed at, say, the time that *United States v. O'Brien*[68] was decided is far from self-evident. Why someone should be able publicly to flaunt a "Fuck the Draft" slogan on his jacket while another who burned his draft card in protest against Vietnam went to jail is explainable, in my view, only because in *Cohen* the interests of the state *at that time* were not jeopardized. In *O'Brien*, the interests of the state were held to be significant because public opposition to Vietnam had not yet hardened.

---

66. *See* 6 INTERCOM 3 (1978).

67. 403 U.S. 15 (1971).

68. 391 U.S. 367 (1968).

This can, and should, be put in a different way; as Professor J. A. G. Griffith said in his recent important book, *The Politics of the Judiciary:* "[T]he judiciary in any modern industrial society, however composed, under whatever economic system, is an essential part of the system of government and . . . its function may be described as underpinning the stability of that system from attack by resisting attempts to change it."[69] The three years between *O'Brien* (1968) and *Cohen* (1971) should be viewed as years in which the *zeitgeist* noticeably turned against the Vietnam conflict. So Cohen got off; O'Brien deserved at least the same, and probably more.

There is a larger, deeper meaning to what has been said. As more and more economic controls are placed on the individual, by both public and private governments, a subtle tradeoff is occurring. Freedom in personal lifestyles is being permitted, but only when the stability of the system is not threatened. That, it seems to me, is the probable reason for permitting today what would once have been called obscene, for the decision in *Stanley v. Georgia*,[70] for permissiveness in cohabitation, for the probable legalization of marijuana, for the widespread use of other narcotics without punishment, for acceptance of other behavior patterns (*e.g.*, nude bathing). In none of these situations is the stability of the system placed in even minimal jeopardy. Should any one of them do so, it may be said with complete confidence that a crackdown will immediately take place—and will be constitutionally valid.

The "tradeoff" may be likened to Aldous Huxley's soma pills.[71] The people are kept quiescent by individual freedoms that mean something only to the persons, not to "society"[72] at large or to the state. I am not suggesting that this is a deliberate maneuver, conducted in a dark and conspiratorial way. But, when coupled with the economic factor mentioned above, it does seem to be the most likely explanation of the present-day expansion in individual liberties. Those liberties will continue to grow until such time as they collide with the interests of the state. In economic matters, that collision has already occurred; that will intensify in the future. More "soma pills" will be permitted, as more controls are applied. Whether those "pills" will suffice cannot be answered at this time.

In this connection, it is well to distinguish between authoritarian and totalitarian governments. Under the former—Franco Spain is an example—a considerable amount of personal freedoms (not important to the state) are possible; but under totalitarianism—China, Albania, the U.S.S.R.—total control is the rule. I think the United States will become

---

69.   J. Griffith, The Politics of the Judiciary 213 (1977).

70.   394 U.S. 557 (1969).

71.   A. Huxley, Brave New World (1932). *See* A. Huxley, Brave New World Revisited (1958).

72.   The concept of society is one of the neglected areas of constitutional scholarship. Judges

authoritarian in the future, but will be able to stave off totalitarianism for some time.

III. CONCLUSION

We have come a long way, at a far too rapid and oversimplified pace. Limitations of time and space did not permit more than conclusory statements. Much has been left out—necessarily so.[73] What has been said, furthermore, is controversial. Many, perhaps most, people do not like to think in "gloom and doom" terms. Neither do I. But the facts are there, for those who are able and willing to see them. Dr. Harrison Brown asserts:

> Today we are children, but finally after a million or so years our childhood is about to end. With the end of childhood three things can happen: we can exterminate ourselves; we can go back to the ways of life of our ancestors; we can make a quantum jump upward to a new level of civilization, undreamed of by the philosophers of the past.[74]

If he is correct, as I think he is, the final question is whether our governmental institutions—our constitutional order—have the capacity to cope quickly and effectively with the manifold problems of the last part of the twentieth century.

The jury is really not still out on that question. Our obvious inability to deal with both inflation and unemployment, with energy and nuclear proliferation, to mention only a few current problems, does not give much basis for hope. Some constitutional changes could be suggested—but that's another essay. The editors of this *Journal* wisely asked the authors of the symposium to limit themselves to approximately 5000 words. What can be said is that there is enough play in the constitutional joints to enable the political leaders of the nation to take almost any action they wish. Whether they will do so is an entirely different question. That political power is constitutionally permissible does not mean that it will be used. I am not optimistic that the necessary adjustments in public policy will be made. The American system of pluralism is not working.[75] A nation of avowed pragmatists, who tend to pursue rather narrow, hedonistic goals, is not going to change its ways by rational argument. What will change

and commentators often use the word, but without defining it; or in interest-balancing situations, revealing how societal interests are identified and weighed. Legal writers, including judges, would rather chop logic with appellate judges than think deeply about such matters.

73. One of the more important areas for scholarly consideration is the reconciliation of the concepts of liberty and equality in constitutional interpretation. *See* R. DWORKIN, TAKING RIGHTS SERIOUSLY (1977). *See also* J. RAWLS, A THEORY OF JUSTICE (1971) *and* R. NOZICK, ANARCHY, THE STATE AND UTOPIA (1974). I have paid little attention to the economic crisis. On this, see F. ALLVINE & F. TARPLEY, JR., THE NEW STATE OF THE ECONOMY (1977). Many other areas need study.

74. H. BROWN, *supra*, note 7, at 249.

75. It does not give enough efficiency in government and it is not protecting individual liberties sufficiently. *See* T. LOWI, THE END OF LIBERALISM (1969). Pluralism works only when there is common, albeit tacit, agreement on the ends of society. *See* Y. SIMON, PHILOSOPHY OF DEMOCRATIC GOVERNMENT (1951). That is precisely the opposite of what is occurring today. *See* R. MOSS, THE COLLAPSE OF DEMOCRACY (1977).

those ways is disaster, actual or imminent; predictions of disaster, including this one, are not enough.

The United States has survived and prospered thus far, not because of the Constitution but in spite of it. Only by extra-constitutional adjustments to the original conception has government operated at all effectively. The crucial problem now is how to make governmental power that is necessary as tolerable and decent as possible. I have suggested elsewhere,[76] and repeat now, that this at the very least requires rethinking of the concept of separation of powers. The urgent tasks of government must be accomplished, but that power must also be accountable. As matters now stand, we have little efficiency in government and not much accountability. That, in sum, is the pressing constitutional problem of the present and of the coming years.[77]

I return, finally, to Dr. Lester Brown's statement in the headnote to this paper. The "profound social transformation" of which he speaks is already occurring. One has to be at least a glandular optimist to believe that better conditions will come from that transformation. Uncontrolled change is the enemy. We are aboard a train running down the rails out of control; there is no one in the engine cab and there may be demons at the switches; most people, including almost all lawyers, are in the caboose looking backwards.[78] In such circumstances, to be an optimist one has to be a pessimist. Not a cynic. Not sunk in despair. Merely fully aware of the nature of the problem, with a determination to do something about it.[79] The challenge is obvious: Will it be met?

---

76.   A. MILLER, PRESIDENTIAL POWER IN A NUTSHELL (1977); Miller, *Separation of Powers—Does It Still Work?*, 48 POL. Q. 77 (1977).

77.   *See* Moynihan, *Imperial Government*, 65 COMMENTARY 25 (June 1978).

78.   *See* R. LAPP, THE NEW PRIESTHOOD: THE SCIENTIFIC ELITE AND THE USES OF POWER (1965).

79.   *Compare* H. BROWN, *supra* note 7, *with* E. MISHAN, *supra* note 26. Mishan concludes at 265:

> In the circumstances, only an extension of state power and a diminution of personal freedoms will prevent a disintegration into social chaos. And this process . . . is under way. The growing fears today of violence, terrorism and urban disruption, the public's apprehension of the grave threats posed by the new technology, and the intensification of group conflicts within our "pluralistic" societies—all of these untoward features, traceable . . . to the technological revolution of the past century, have weakened popular resistance to the assumption of wider powers of control by modern governments. An instinct for survival is impelling the Western democracies along the road to the totalitarian state.

Dr. Brown is not so despairing:

> I am by no means without hope—if I were, "I would not have written this book. . . . In short, I believe that although the dangers which confront us are immense, we nevertheless have it in our power to create a new level of civilization—an abundant, just, and peaceful world in which people can not only develope to their fullest terrestrial potential—they can reach out to the stars as well.

H. BROWN, *supra* note 7, at 10-11.

Bibliographic Essay

Much, perhaps most, scholarship about American constitutionalism tends to be legalistic. There is little of any consequence that seeks to project the shape of things to come into even the near future. This essay collects some of the better books and articles, each of which contains extensive bibliographic data (as do the works cited in the footnotes to the present volume).

Perhaps the foremost student of the politics of the judiciary, and thus of constitutionalism, is Professor Martin Shapiro. His *Law and Politics in the Supreme Court* (New York: Free Press, 1964) is still useful, albeit somewhat dated, and his *The Courts: A Comparative and Political Analysis* (Chicago: University of Chicago Press, 1981) is a provocative assessment of the judiciaries in several different cultures. A political analysis of the British judiciary may be found in J.A.G. Griffith, *The Politics of the Judiciary* (Manchester: Manchester University Press, 1977); it is in turn analyzed in Arthur S. Miller, "The Politics of the American Judiciary," 49 Political Quarterly 200 (1978). John R. Schmidhauser, *Constitutional Law in American Politics* (Monterey, CA: Brooks/Cole, 1984) is a recent addition; designed as a teaching tool, it is a careful study of the interaction of law and politics in American constitutional history. The emphasis in all of these is upon the courts and, of them, the Supreme Court of the United States.

The legitimacy of Supreme Court lawmaking is discussed in Raoul Berger, *Government by Judiciary: The Transformation of the Fourteenth Amendment* (Cambridge, MA: Harvard University Press, 1977); John R. Commons, *Legal Foundations of Capitalism* (New York: Macmillan, 1924); Herbert Wechsler, *Principles, Politics and Fundamental Law* (Cambridge, MA: Harvard University Press, 1961); Louis Lusky, *By What Right? A Commentary on the Supreme Court's Power to Revise the Constitution* (Charlottesville, VA: Michie Co., 1975); and Philip B. Kurland, *Politics, the Constitution and the Warren Court* (Chicago: University of Chicago Press, 1970). A slashing attack on the Supreme Court is Lino Graglia, *Disaster by Decree* (Ithaca, NY: Cornell University Press, 1976).

Additional works seeking to justify Supreme Court lawmaking include John Hart Ely, *Democracy and Distrust* (Cambridge, MA: Harvard University Press, 1980); Jesse Choper, *Judicial Review and the National Political Process* (Chicago: University of Chicago Press, 1980); Arthur Selwyn Miller, *Toward Increased Judicial Activism: The Political Role of the Supreme Court* (Westport, CT: Greenwood Press, 1982); and Ronald Dworkin, *Taking Rights Seriously* (Cambridge, MA: Harvard University Press, 1977).

Perhaps the best collection of essays on the theory and practice of American constitutionalism is J. Roland Pennock and John W. Chapman (eds.), *Constitutionalism* (New York: New York University Press, 1979); see particularly Thomas C. Grey, "Constitutionalism: An Analytic Framework" (p. 189) and Richard B. Parker, "The Jurisprudential Uses of John Rawls" (p. 269). See also Michael J. Perry, *The Constitution, the Courts, and Human Rights* (New Haven, CT: Yale University Press, 1982); "Symposium: Judicial Review Versus Democracy," 42 Ohio State Law Journal 1 (1981); Don K. Price, *America's Unwritten Constitution: Science, Religion, and Political Responsibility* (Baton Rouge: Louisiana State University Press, 1983); and Laurence Tribe, *American Constitutional Law* (Mineola, NY: Foundation Press, 1978).

On the matter discussed in Chapter One, see Arthur Selwyn Miller, *The Supreme Court: Myth and Reality* (Westport, CT: Greenwood Press, 1978) and *Social Change and Fundamental Law: America's Evolving Constitution* (Westport, CT: Greenwood Press, 1979); Gerhard Casper, "Constitutional Constraints on the Conduct of Foreign and Defense Policy," 43 University of Chicago Law Review 463 (1976); Kenneth Dam, "The American Fiscal Constitution," 44 University of Chicago Law Review 271 (1977); Thomas C. Grey, "Do We Have an Unwritten Constitution?" 27 Stanford Law Review 703 (1975); Karl Llewellyn, "The Constitution as an Institution," 34 Columbia Law Review 1 (1934); Sanford Levinson, " 'The Constitution' in American Civil Religion," 1980 Supreme Court Review 123; Louis Fisher, *The Politics of Shared Power: Congress and the Executive* (Washington, D.C.: Congressional Quarterly Press, 1981); Richard B. Saphire, "Constitutional Theory in Perspective," 78 Northwestern University Law Review 1435 (1984); and Stephen R. Munzer and James W. Nickel, "Does the Constitution Mean What It Always Meant?" 77 Columbia Law Review 1029 (1977).

On constitutional reason of state, see Arthur Selwyn Miller, *Democratic Dictatorship: The Emergent Constitution of Control* (Westport, CT: Greenwood Press, 1981); Friedrich Meinecke, *Machiavellism: The Doctrine of Raison d'Etat and Its Place in Modern History* (New Haven, CT: Yale University Press, 1957); Paul L. Murphy, *The Constitution in Crisis Times* (New York: Harper & Row, 1972); Franz Neumann, *The Democratic and the Authoritarian State* (Glencoe, IL: Free Press, 1957); Carl J. Friedrich, *Constitutional Reason of State* (Providence, RI: Brown University Press, 1957); Clinton Rossiter, *Constitutional Dictatorship: Crisis Government in the Modern Democracies* (Princeton, NJ: Princeton University Press, 1948); Hannah Arendt, *The Origins of Totalitarianism* (Cleveland: World Publishing Co., 1958); Noam Chomsky. *For Reasons of State* (London: Fontana, 1973); Otto Kirchheimer, *Political Justice: The Use of Legal Procedure for Political Ends* (Princeton, NJ: Princeton University Press, 1961); J. L. Talmon, *The Origins of Totalitarian Democracy* (London: Secker & Warburg, 1955); Alan Wolfe, *The Seamy Side of Democracy: Repression in America* (New York: David McKay, 1973); and Howard Zinn, *A People's History of the United States* (New York: Harper & Row, 1979).

On equal protection and the concept of equality, see J. R. Pole, *The Pursuit of Equality in American History* (Berkeley: University of California Press, 1978); John Rawls, *A Theory of Justice* (Cambridge, MA: Harvard University Press, 1971); Robert Nozick, *Anarchy, State, and Utopia* (New York: Basic Books, 1974); Michael Parenti, *Democracy for the Few* (New York: St. Martin's Press, 3d ed., 1980);

Robert A. Goldwin and William A. Schambra (eds.), *How Democratic Is the Constitution?* (Washington, D.C.: American Enterprise Institute, 1980); and Philip Green, *The Pursuit of Inequality* (New York: Random House, 1981). See also J. Skelly Wright, "Judicial Review and Equal Protection Clause," 15 Harvard Civil Rights-Civil Liberties Law Review 1 (1980), reprinted in Arthur Selwyn Miller (ed.), *On Courts and Democracy: Selected Nonjudicial Writings of J. Skelly Wright* (Westport, CT: Greenwood Press, 1984).

David Miller, *Social Justice* (New York: Oxford University Press, 1976) is an insightful discussion of the concept. See also Richard Brandt (ed.), *Social Justice* (Englewood Cliffs, NJ: Prentice-Hall, 1962); William A. Galston, *Justice and the Human Good* (Chicago: University of Chicago Press, 1980); and Ross Fitzgerald (ed.), *Human Needs and Politics* (Rushcutters Bay, Australia: Pergamon Press, 1977).

The legality of nuclear weaponry is thoroughly analyzed in Arthur Selwyn Miller and Martin Feinrider (eds.), *Nuclear Weapons and Law* (Westport, CT: Greenwood Press, 1984). Burns H. Weston (ed.), *Toward Nuclear Disarmament and Global Security: A Search for Alternatives* (Boulder, CO: Westview Press, 1984) is a valuable collection of articles. Dick Ringler, *Nuclear War: A Teaching Guide* (Bulletin of the Atomic Scientists, December 1984) is a first-rate introduction into the intricacies of nuclear weaponry; it lists books, journals, organizations, and educational materials on the subject.

The best discussion of the First Amendment may be found in Thomas I. Emerson, *Toward a General Theory of the First Amendment* (New York: Viking Press, 1966). Also of importance are Jerome A. Barron, *Freedom of the Press for Whom?* (Bloomington: Indiana University Press, 1973) and Robert Bork, "Neutral Principles and Some First Amendment Problems," 47 Indiana Law Journal 1 (1971). See also David Kairys, "Freedom of Speech," in David Kairys (ed.), *The Politics of Law: A Progressive Critique* (New York: Pantheon Books, 1982), and in the same collection, Mark Tushnet, "Corporations and Free Speech"; Also J. Skelly Wright, "Money and the Pollution of Politics: Is the First Amendment an Obstacle to Political Equality?" 82 Columbia Law Review 609 (1982).

On corporations and the Constitution, see Arthur Selwyn Miller, *The Modern Corporate State: Private Governments and the Constitution* (Westport, CT: Greenwood Press, 1976); John Kenneth Galbraith, *The New Industrial State* (Boston: Houghton Mifflin, 1967); Arthur S. Miller, "The Corporation as a Private Government in the World Community," 46 Virginia Law Review 1539 (1960); Morton Mintz and Jerry Cohen, *America, Inc.* (New York: Dial Press, 1971); and R. Jeffrey Lustig, *Corporate Liberalism: The Origins of Modern American Political Theory, 1890-1920* (Berkeley: University of California Press, 1982). See also Warren J. Samuels (ed.), *The Economy as a System of Power* (New Brunswick, NJ: Transaction, Inc., 1979).

On the question of recognition of a right to a job, see Lester Thurow, *The Zero-Sum Society* (New York: Basic Books, 1980); Robert Kuttner, *The Economic Illusion: False Choices Between Prosperity and Social Justice* (Boston: Houghton Mifflin, 1984); David F. Noble, *Forces of Production: A Social History of Industrial Automation* (New York: Alfred A. Knopf, 1984); George C. Lodge, *The American Disease* (New York: Alfred A. Knopf, 1984); and Samuel Bowles, David M. Gordon, and Thomas E. Weisskopf, *Beyond the Waste Land: A Democratic*

Alternative to Economic Decline (Garden City, NY: Anchor Press/Doubleday, 1983). For a provocative analysis of the question of overpopulation, see Richard L. Rubenstein, *The Age of Triage: Fear and Hope in an Over-crowded World* (Boston: Beacon Press, 1983).

Finally, the following books bear to some degree on the themes addressed in this volume. Andrew Bard Schmookler, *The Parable of the Tribes: The Problem of Power in Social Evolution* (Berkeley: University of California Press, 1984) is an important analysis of the hypothesis of the destructive logic of human systems. Robert Samuel Summers, *Instrumentalism and American Legal Theory* (Ithaca, NY: Cornell University Press, 1982) discusses the tendency of law, including constitutional law, to be instrumental. Michael Novak and John W. Cooper (eds.), *The Corporation: A Theological Inquiry* (Washington, D.C.: American Enterprise Institute, 1981) contains some interesting essays on the role of the corporation in American society. On the same theme, see Richard J. Barber, *The American Corporation: Its Power, Its Money, Its Politics* (New York: E. P. Dutton, 1970). Robert Hessen, *In Defense of the Corporation* (Stanford, CA: Hoover Institution Press, 1979) is a brief but interesting analysis, well described in its title. R. Gordon Hoxie (ed.), *The Presidency and National Security Policy* (New York: Center for the Study of the Presidency, 1984) contains a collection of essays by leading students of foreign affairs. Martin Carnoy, Derek Shearer, and Russell Rumberger, *A New Social Contract* (New York: Harper & Row, 1983) is an argument for an extended role of government in ordering economic affairs. A more theoretical version is Martin Carnoy, *The State and Political Theory* (Princeton, NJ: Princeton University Press, 1984). Joel I. Nelson, *Economic Inequality: Conflict Without Change* (New York: Columbia University Press, 1982) is an important study of the idea that economic equality goes hand-in-hand with economic gain. Michael J. Sandel, *Liberalism and the Limits of Justice* (Cambridge, England: Cambridge University Press, 1982) is a penetrating critique of modern liberalism. For a sustained analysis of modern legal education, including its failure to address important present-day social problems, see the 674-page symposium in 36 Stanford Law Review 1 (1984); this is a comprehensive discussion of the so-called Critical Legal Studies movement in some of the law schools.

Index

DATE DUE

NOV 19			
JUN 1 1992			
MAY 08 1992			
APR 1 7 1999			
GAYLORD			PRINTED IN U.S.A.